Rational Commitment and Social Justice

Essays for Gregory Kavka

Gregory S. Kavka (1947–1994) was a prominent and influential figure in contemporary moral and political philosophy. The new essays in this volume are concerned with fundamental issues of rational commitment and social justice to which Kavka devoted his work as a philosopher. The essays take Kavka's work as a point of departure and seek to advance the respective debates. The topics include the relationship between intention and moral action (as part of which Kavka's famous "toxin puzzle" is a focus of discussion), the nature of deterrence, the rationality of morals, contractarian ethics, and the contemporary relevance of Hobbes' political thought.

Incorporating important new philosophical statements of problems and fresh contributions to the ongoing debate about rational intention, this volume will interest not only philosophers but also political scientists and economists.

Contributors: Christopher W. Morris, Tyler Burge, Brian Skyrms, Daniel M. Farrell, David Gauthier, Michael E. Bratman, Gilbert Harman, Edwin Curley, S. A. Lloyd, Jean Hampton, Gary Watson, Jeff McMahan.

Gregory S. Kavka (Photo courtesy of Terence Parsons.)

Rational Commitment and Social Justice

Essays for Gregory Kavka

Edited by

JULES L. COLEMAN

CHRISTOPHER W. MORRIS

CAMBRIDGE
UNIVERSITY PRESS

PUBLISHED BY THE PRESS SYNDICATE OF THE UNIVERSITY OF CAMBRIDGE
The Pitt Building, Trumpington Street, Cambridge CB2 1RP, United Kingdom

CAMBRIDGE UNIVERSITY PRESS
The Edinburgh Building, Cambridge CB2 2RU, UK   http://www.cup.cam.ac.uk
40 West 20th Street, New York, NY 10011-4211, USA   http://www.cup.org
10 Stamford Road, Oakleigh, Melbourne 3166, Australia

First published 1998

Printed in the United States of America

Typeface Times Roman 10/12 pt.   *System* Quark XPress™   [AG]

*A catalog record for this book is available from
the British Library.*

Library of Congress Cataloging in Publication Data
Rational commitment and social justice : essays for Gregory Kavka /
edited by Jules L. Coleman, Christopher W. Morris.
p.   cm.
ISBN 0-521-63179-3 (hardbound)
1. Social justice.   2. Commitment (Psychology)   I. Coleman, Jules L.
II. Morris, Christopher W.   III. Kavka, Gregory S., 1947–1994.
JC578.R365   1998
303.3'72–dc 21   98-20681
CIP

ISBN 0 521 63179 3 hardback

Contents

Acknowledgments   *page* vii
List of Contributors   viii

Introduction: The Moral and Political Philosophy of Gregory Kavka   1
CHRISTOPHER W. MORRIS

Some Personal Memories   9
TYLER BURGE

The Shadow of the Future   12
BRIAN SKYRMS

A New Paradox of Deterrence   22
DANIEL M. FARRELL

Rethinking the Toxin Puzzle   47
DAVID GAUTHIER

Toxin, Temptation, and the Stability of Intention   59
MICHAEL E. BRATMAN

The Toxin Puzzle   84
GILBERT HARMAN

Religion and Morality in Hobbes   90
EDWIN CURLEY

Contemporary Uses of Hobbes's Political Philosophy   122
S. A. LLOYD

The Knavish Humean   150
JEAN HAMPTON

Some Considerations in Favor of Contractualism   168
GARY WATSON

Justice, Reasons, and Moral Standing   186
CHRISTOPHER W. MORRIS

Wrongful Life: Paradoxes in the Morality of Causing People to Exist   208
JEFF McMAHAN

Gregory S. Kavka's Writings   249

Acknowledgments

We are grateful to our editor at Cambridge University Press, Terence Moore, for his support in making this collection of essays commemorating our colleague and friend Gregory Kavka possible and to several anonymous referees for the Press for useful comments and suggestions. We also wish to thank our contributors for their advice, especially the late Jean Hampton, who was particularly helpful, and our thanks to Gary Watson for bringing us together for a conference held in Greg's honor ("Rationality, Commitment, and Community") at the University of California at Irvine, February 10–12, 1995, where seven of the essays published here were first presented.

Contributors

Michael E. Bratman, Howard H. and Jessie T. Watkins University Professor of Philosophy, Stanford University

Tyler Burge, Professor of Philosophy, University of California, Los Angeles

Jules L. Coleman, John A. Garver Professor of Jurisprudence and Philosophy, Yale Law School

Edwin Curley, Professor of Philosophy, University of Michigan, Ann Arbor

Daniel M. Farrell, Professor of Philosophy, Ohio State University

David Gauthier, Distinguished Service Professor of Philosophy, University of Pittsburgh

Jean Hampton, late Professor of Philosophy, University of Arizona

Gilbert Harman, Professor of Philosophy, Princeton University

S. A. Lloyd, Associate Professor of Philosophy, University of Southern California

Jeff McMahan, Associate Professor of Philosophy, University of Illinois, Urbana–Champaign

Christopher W. Morris, Professor of Philosophy, Bowling Green State University

Brian Skyrms, Distinguished Professor of Philosophy, University of California, Irvine

Gary Watson, Professor of Philosophy, University of California, Irvine

Introduction: The Moral and Political Philosophy of Gregory Kavka

CHRISTOPHER W. MORRIS

Gregory Kavka was a remarkable philosopher, certainly, to have written so many distinguished essays and books in his short life, for he was only forty-six when he died on February 16, 1994. Even greater testimony to his exceptional nature as a thinker may be his influence on contemporary moral and political philosophy. His contributions to several areas of practical philosophy are significant. His work falls into four overlapping areas: (1) the ethics of war – in particular, the ethics and rationality of nuclear policy; (2) the general theory of rational choice; (3) Hobbes studies; and (4) various topics in moral theory, applied ethics, and policy. In each of these areas his contributions have been striking and have opened new areas of thought.

Kavka wrote extensively about the ethics of war and of defense, especially nuclear conflict and its deterrence. His writings kindled contemporary interest in the philosophical and ethical issues concerning nuclear war. Most importantly, they showed how wider lessons are to be found in seemingly narrow issues about aspects of nuclear deterrence and policy. In a well-known and widely reprinted essay, "Some Paradoxes of Deterrence" (1978),[1] Kavka showed how certain sorts of deterrent situations give rise to moral difficulties with which our standard accounts are ill equipped to deal. These situations are those in which an agent must intend (conditionally) to harm innocent people in order to forestall some great harm and injustice. Deterring an adversary by means of threatened nuclear retaliation is often thought of as a "special deterrent situation" of the sort Kavka has in mind. An enemy state is deterred from attacking by its belief that we would retaliate massively. Central to the moral problem is the fact that retaliation of the sort envisaged, and intended, would target a large number of innocent civilians and would be morally wrong – a point conceded about nuclear deterrence by virtually everyone. Rather than conclude, as some moralists have, that nuclear deterrence (or sincerely threatening nuclear retaliation) is forbidden, Kavka points to the significant moral value of successful deterrence: "evil" intentions, he notes, "may pave the road to heaven, by preventing serious offenses and by doing so without actually harming anyone." He argues that a variety of principles that "bridge" our moral evaluations of acts and of agents are shown to be problematic in such situations. In particular, the influential "wrongful intentions principle," stating that it is wrong to intend to do what one knows to be wrong, he argues, should not be applied to deterrent intentions like the ones in question. Other problematic rules are "the right–good principle" – doing something is right if and only if a morally good person would do the same thing in the given situation – and "the virtue preservation principle" – it is wrong deliberately to lose or debase one's moral virtue.

In addition to initiating and framing the philosophical discussions of these issues, Kavka contributed to virtually every debate about the ethics of nuclear policy in the seventies and eighties. He challenged the popular philosophical defenses of unilateral nuclear disarmament as well as the moral case influential in defense policy circles for "space defense." Most of his writings on these topics are reprinted, with revisions, in his *Moral Paradoxes of Nuclear Deterrence* (1987).

Some of Kavka's contributions to the theory of practical rationality, or rational choice, emerged from his reflections on deterrence and conflict. He was skeptical of orthodox accounts of rational choice in contexts such as special deterrent situations in which the outcome of conflict can be disastrous. In cases such as these – choices made under uncertainty, with several potentially disastrous outcomes – he thought that the influential principles of expected utility maximization (using subjective probabilities) or of maximin (which would have one minimize maximum losses or maximize minimum gain) are not satisfactory methods of making choices. He proposed instead a "disaster avoidance principle," which would have agents in such situations choose the options for which the probability of disaster is smallest.[2]

Kavka may be best known in the field of rational-choice theory for a "puzzle" he announced in a few pages published in *Analysis* (1983). A millionaire presents you with a vial of toxin, which, if imbibed, will make you very ill for a day but with no lasting or life-threatening effects. The wealthy eccentric offers you $1 million if tonight you (genuinely) *intend* to drink the toxin tomorrow. The money will be paid to you soon after you form the intention, independently of your carrying it out; you need not drink the toxin to receive the money. A number of important questions about reasons and intentions are raised by this seemingly innocent tale, and it has been the subject of considerable discussion since the time of its presentation. There is, first of all, the question of whether a rational person could, while remaining rational, intend now to do something later that he or she believes to be irrational. So, if one thinks that one would lack sufficient reason to drink the toxin tomorrow, one could not rationally form the requisite intention today. There is also the question of what sorts of reasons are provided by intentions (or plans) and whether these could be sufficient to have one (rationally) do something one would not otherwise have reason to do. One might rationally, though Kavka thought not, *decide* to drink the toxin and act on the intention thus formed, enriching oneself as a consequence.

As will be seen by the three essays in this volume touching directly on this puzzle (the chapters by Gauthier, Bratman, and Harman), the issues are very difficult and go to the heart of many debates about practical reason. Kavka's little essay and his subsequent discussions have initiated a debate that has proven strikingly interesting and fruitful, not unlike the upshot of Robert Nozick's essay several decades ago on the Newcomb problem.[3]

In Hobbes studies Kavka's influence is unassailable: his *Hobbesian Moral and Political Theory* (1986), along with Jean Hampton's *Hobbes and the Social Contract Tradition,* published the same year, revived Hobbes scholarship and placed Hobbesian theory at the center of discussions in political philosophy. Kavka's secondary aim was to interpret Hobbes' thought; his principal ambition was to offer a "Hobbesian" theory that reconstructed Hobbes' own account in ways that make it especially relevant and plausible to contemporary thinkers. The theory that emerges is one that offers some justification for liberal welfare states but not for the master's favored absolutist state. Kavka argues as well that Hobbes' account of the relations of morality to self-interest is more promising than most have thought, even if it fails to capture large aspects of morality.

The project that Kavka left uncompleted at his death was entitled *Governing Angels: Human Imperfections and the Need for Government.* A preliminary statement may be found in his posthumous essay, "Why Morally Perfect People Would Need Government" (1995).[4] It was to focus on the same objects as the Hobbes work, namely conflict and the need for government, and it would generalize the idea, found in both the Hobbes work and that on nuclear deterrence, that much conflict is due to structural features of human interaction, not to moral failings of the agents. In this work Kavka was to challenge the view of government expressed in James Madison's famous words in *Federalist Paper* 51, "If men were angels, no government would be necessary." To the contrary, he thought, even morally perfect individuals would find themselves in conflicted situations that government might justly remedy.

In addition to topics in the ethics of war, rational-choice theory, and Hobbesian political theory, Kavka wrote extensively on a number of issues in moral philosophy, applied ethics, and public policy. He was one of a handful of thinkers to initiate philosophical reflection on the problems of future generations that are so topical in contemporary ethics.[5] His article on "Disability and the Right to Work" (1992) has attracted some attention in policy fields, and the author consequently seems to be highly esteemed among activists for the disabled. His essay "The Reconciliation Project" (1984) is one of the best statements of the ambitions and difficulties of neo-Hobbists like David Gauthier to link morality with individual rationality.[6]

The particular theses and arguments that Kavka put forward continue, in several areas of philosophy, to foster debate. It is possible, however, that a greater measure of his intellectual significance is provided by an appreciation of the fields that he initiated or influenced. Their number is striking, especially for one who died so young.

The present volume of essays commemorates Gregory Kavka's work in several ways. Tyler Burge's essay pays tribute to his person, and many of the essays discuss some particular idea or thesis of his. All pay him the greater compliment of developing themes associated with him. The first set of five essays focuses on topics about rational choice, intention, and deterrence that are the focus of much of Kavka's work. Brian Skyrms brings to bear recent game-theoretic work on rational interaction in repeated situations to the problem posed by Hobbes' infamous Foole, who questions whether reason always demands compliance with one's covenants. Hobbes, as well as Hume, may be read as grounding cooperation in long-term interest where "the shadow of the future" comes into play. Skyrms suggests that the manner in which the shadow of the future supports cooperation in our world has more to do with incomplete information than with infinite time horizons. After a careful account of Kavka's views about the paradoxes of deterrence, Daniel Farrell develops a new such paradox in his essay. Accepting that a rational and fully decent person could not intend (conditionally) to harm a number of innocent people as part of a deterrent strategy to protect another group of innocents from wrongful harm, Farrell argues that it would nevertheless be possible for such an individual to activate an "automated retaliation device." This is paradoxical, or at least puzzling. Farrell's case implies, significantly, that a complex deterrent account of punishment such as that developed by the late Warren Quinn cannot be right.[7]

In the first of three essays focusing on the toxin puzzle, David Gauthier argues, against Kavka and others, that although it is true that one can intend rationally to do only what one expects to have reason to do, it is not the case that what *acts* one has reason to perform can be determined independently of an evaluation of the consequences of *intentions* to perform those acts. One cannot, he thinks, assume that one has no reason to drink the toxin given that there is no gain from drinking it. Even if there is no gain from drinking the toxin – the $1 million is already in one's bank account – it does not follow that there is no reason to drink it. For consuming the poison may be part of the best *plan* or *course of action* available to one the day before, when presented with the eccentric millionaire's offer – what Edward McClennen dubs "resolute choice." As part of a rational plan, the intention to drink the toxin is a reason for drinking it. Gauthier urges, in conclusion, good deliberators to drink up! Michael Bratman, however, is loath to imbibe. His sophisticated account of intention and practical rationality lead him to be sympathetic with Gauthier's concern that deliberations settle future action, but he thinks as well that rational agents retain some control over their future actions. "Following through with one's plan," he claims, "is not . . . like following through with one's tennis swing." Bratman, like Gauthier, thinks that ideal rationality is not mere "sophisticated" planning, that is, limiting one's plans to those courses of action one will want to carry out at the time of action. He thinks that the "resolute" approach favored by Gauthier, McClennen, and others fails to recognize the temporal and causal location of our agency: what is in our control is (choice from) the set of alternatives we face now, at the moment of choice. Introducing a condition barring regret in the carrying out of plans, Bratman develops an alternative account that, though different from the resolute approach, does not collapse into a form of sophisticated choice. Gilbert Harman's approach to the toxin puzzle is different from that of many. He argues that one has an "intrinsic" desire for something to the extent that one does not desire it as a means to something else one may want. If we have instrumental reasons to form an intrinsic desire for something, the reasons provided by the latter, once it exists, are not exhausted by the original, instrumental concerns; one can retain the desire long after the original reasons for forming it have been satisfied. When faced with the toxin choice, Harman suggests that one can form a stable and enduring intrinsic desire to drink the toxin, enabling one to expect to drink when the time comes, and thus making possible the forming of an intention to do so. He thinks that the account proposed a type of sophisticated choice but expresses skepticism about the sophisticated–resolute distinction. It is possible, however, that Harman has developed a response to the toxin problem that falls in between these alternatives as they are usually characterized.

The problem posed by Hobbes' Foole, discussed by Skyrms (and often not far from the surface of Gauthier's text), raises questions about the rationality of commitment. The Foole, of course, who says in his heart "that there is no such thing as justice," has also said "in his heart that there is no God."[8] Although philosophers today usually read Hobbes as developing an essentially secular moral and political theory, many, if not most, attribute to him some sort of theism, however unconventional. Edwin Curley wishes to challenge this implicit assumption of contemporary philosophical readers. He seeks to show that Hobbes was most likely an atheist, or at least deeply skeptical about theism, and that this is crucial to an understanding of *Leviathan*. He sees Hobbes as "one member of an underground movement, which also included Spinoza and Hume, whose purpose was to subvert the dominant religion of their culture, and to free people from the authority of the priests and their sacred texts." Hobbes' secular morality may offer lessons for our world and answers to our Fooles. By contrast, Sharon Lloyd challenges the suggestion that Hobbes' lengthy and detailed discussions of religious doctrine are a cover for his atheism and questions the standard reading of his theory – accepted, broadly speaking, by Gauthier, Kavka, and most contemporary political philosophers – as based on mechanistic materialism and as concluding that human beings are self-interested creatures who take the appetites to be the proper measure of good and evil. In contrast to Kavka, who professed to be less interested in interpreting Hobbes correctly than in offering an account that was interesting, relevant, and plausible, Curley and Lloyd are historians, whose first aim is to understand past thinkers correctly. Both, however, are also interested in the contemporary relevance of Hobbes' doctrine, rightly interpreted. The matter of Hobbes' theistic beliefs, for Curley, is important to an evaluation of the success of his sort of political theory in addressing the political divisiveness of religious disagreement and containing the seditious tendencies of religious dissidents. This is Lloyd's concern as well; she thinks Hobbes' theory is ideally suited for the pluralistic societies characteristic of our world. In her view, Hobbes offers a political solution to the problem of social disorder caused by "transcendent" interests, one that differs from and may be superior to both Gauthier's "morals by agreement" and Rawls's "political liberalism."

The counterpart to Hobbes' Foole, in David Hume's writing, is the "sensible knave" who may prefer vice to virtue, in the case of justice. The knave reasons: "That *honesty is the best policy,* may be a good general rule, but is liable to many exceptions; and he, it may perhaps be thought, conducts himself with most wisdom, who observes the general rule, and takes advantage of all the exceptions."[9] The problem he poses is, on most readings, similar to that of the Foole. But Hume's response and the resources thought to be available to him are different from Hobbes'. Hume suggests that the heart of most will "rebel against such pernicious maxims"; they will be reluctant "to the thoughts of villainy or baseness," will have a strong "antipathy to treachery and roguery"; and "Inward peace of mind, consciousness of integrity, a satisfactory review of our own conduct" will be cherished by most. Jean Hampton calls these sentiments "exploitation-blocking," because they are what prevents us, on this account, from taking advantage of others where it might pay to do so. She wants to challenge this sort of reply to the knave (or Foole) and argues that, in fact, sentimental models cannot make sense of aspects of moral behavior.[10]

Hobbes' political theory is contractarian, and his account of morality is thought to be so as well. Hume's account of justice and of property has been interpreted by many as conventionalist or contractarian, and there are obvious contractarian elements in the political thought of Rousseau and Kant. In contemporary philosophy, John Rawls and David Gauthier are the two most prominent contractarian moralists. In his contribution to this volume, Gary Watson argues that contractualist moral theory is better able to articulate the ways in which moral rights and responsibilities serve our interests by constraining them, a feature of morality that has seemed perplexing to some. Watson argues that utilitarian and consequentialist theories have sought to accommodate it in ways less satisfactory than contractualism. Without making the right derivative in some manner from the good (or resorting to a two-tier structure), contractualism is able to show that moral rights are linked pervasively to human good and that the reasons the former yield do not reduce to beneficence. Additionally, the conditions under which moral requirements may be infringed or overridden are determined in the same manner as the content and nature of the rights themselves, namely, by the basic agreement. Watson thinks contractualism's comparative advantages are possessed by Hobbesian as well as by Kantian versions. But his own sympathies lie more with the latter, as he conjectures that the Hobbesian version will yield, at best, "a seriously revisionist conception of moral practice." Worries about this feature of Hobbesian contractarian moral theory are the motivation for my other contribution to the volume. In "Justice, Reasons, and Moral Standing," I acknowledge that such contractarian theories face what Kavka has called "the problem of group egoism": although cooperation is generally advantageous, not everyone need the cooperation of all others – for instance, of the weak and the unproductive. This problem compounds a worry I have long had about such theories, namely, that they tend to restrict the scope of justice so that it excludes many we would ordinarily think possess moral standing (or that it includes them only insofar as others care for them). I argue that, in the end, the problem is due to an "internalist" assumption that moral requirements always provide reasons for action – no reason, then no duty or obligation. Relaxing this assumption, even if it is central to the tradition, may be necessary to salvage the general account.

Jeff McMahan's essay, "Wrongful Life: Paradoxes in the Morality of Causing People to Exist," addresses certain ethical issues "at the margins of life" somewhat different from those discussed in my contribution. He considers a variety of hypothetical cases in which, owing to the negligence of a physician, a severely mentally handicapped child is born. In one case the negligent act took place prior to conception, in the other after conception (I simplify). In the first case the timing of the negligent act is such that in its absence a different child would have been born, an instance of Derek Parfit's "non-identity problem." These and other cases of the non-identity problem may be thought to threaten commonsense moral beliefs. (In the first case, just mentioned, it is not clear that the physician has a debt to the child.) McMahan considers a number of reactions to these sorts of cases, one of them invoking Parfit's "Impersonal Comparative Principle," which would have us evaluate outcomes (involving the same number of people) solely in terms of quality of life, whoever exists. McMahan offers several reasons for objecting to these reactions, especially the principle just mentioned, and conjectures that impersonal accounts will fail to support a number of our convictions. Impersonal accounts reject the intuitive idea that sometimes, at least, the explanation of why a person's death is worse than the failure to bring a person into existence has to do with the fact that the former is worse for someone whereas the latter is not. McMahan defends an "Encompassing Account," which accords weight to person-affecting as well as impersonal considerations, but which considers them distinct and nonaddictive.

Notes

1. Full references for my Kavka citations are given in "Gregory Kavka's Writings" at the end of this volume.
2. See "Deterrence, Utility, and Rational Choice" (1980).
3. See Kavka's "What Is Newcomb's Problem About?" (1980). His other essays on topics in rational-choice theory include "Some Social Benefits of Uncertainty" (1990), "Is Individual Choice Less Problematic than Collective Choice?" (1991), and "Rational Maximizing in Economic Theories of Politics" (1991).
4. Several chapters of the book project exist in draft form.
5. See "The Futurity Problem" (1978), "The Paradox of Future Individuals" (1982), and "Political Representation for Future Generations" (1983).
6. See his essay "The Problem of Group Egoism" (1993), as well as several essays in this volume (especially Hampton, Morris, and Watson), for some of the difficulties with this project.
7. Warren Quinn, "The Right to Threaten and the Right to Punish," *Philosophy and Public Affairs* 14 (1985), 327–73.
8. Thomas Hobbes, *Leviathan,* ed. Edwin Curley ([1651/1688]; Indianapolis: Hackett, 1994), xv, p. 90.
9. David Hume, *An Enquiry Concerning the Principles of Morals,* ed., L. A. Selby-Bigge, rev. P. H. Nidditch ([1751]; Oxford: Clarendon Press, 1975), ix, ii, pp. 282–3.
10. The essay from which I quote, which Jean Hampton was not able to revise before her death, may be seen as part of a larger skeptical treatment of neo-Humean and neo-Hobbesian practical philosophy. Her account of this tradition's views of normativity and practical rationality are to be found in her posthumous book, *The Authority of Reason* (Cambridge University Press, 1998).

Some Personal Memories

TYLER BURGE

This book commemorates the intellectual contributions of Greg Kavka. I wanted to say something to celebrate his person. He lived a life full of character, courage, strength, love, caring, and even satisfaction. And he did so despite enduring an astonishing series of misfortunes.

I met Greg twenty-six years ago, when he first came to UCLA. It was not love at first sight. I thought I wouldn't like him. He seemed boyish and old-fashioned. I saw my mistake within a week of knowing him. I had mistaken the boyishness for lack of awareness or sophistication. What drew us together was an impatience with pretension and an enjoyment of UCLA basketball. Gradually, weekends between our families became a regular matter. We developed a four-way friendship. It was just a matter of spending time together in simple pursuits. It was Greg's way. He was aggressively unpretentious in his tastes – Pepsi instead of wine, pizza rather than salmon, *Sports Illustrated* before the *New Yorker,* loafers not Guccis, basketball over Proust.

We went through some hard times. One misty winter's night in Pacific Palisades, I had to tell him that his tenure case was in trouble. He was not given tenure because a few senior philosophers saw the boyishness as I first did and failed to recognize his intellectual power and persistence. Most of his adversaries have since acknowledged their mistake. He took the news with an objectivity and dispassionateness that characterized all his responses to adversity. Discussing it, planning how to fight it, and working through the consequences made us closer. I thought him admirable throughout. An emotional bond formed and remained between us to the end. He was my closest male friend. His loyalty and depth of caring remained even through periods when life became hellish for him.

When he went to the University of California at Irvine, we saw less of each other but still kept up regular contact – on the phone and through visits. His career bloomed. He won prestigious awards from the National Endowment for the Humanities and from the Ford Foundation. He published over fifty articles and two books on philosophy. He wrote a widely admired book on Hobbes and created a series of brilliant articles on nuclear deterrence that opened a new area of practical philosophy. He made significant contributions to the ethics of biotechnology. When he died, he was working on a new book on the charming but naïve dictum of President James Madison – that if men were angels they would not need government. Greg argued that even angels would need organization, cooperation, and constraint to live together. It was typical of his work – on Hobbes, on nuclear deterrence, on government – that he looked the weaknesses of people and the hardness of life full in the face and reasoned about how to salvage something that was worthwhile. He was well known throughout the profession as a creative thinker who had done his work despite exceptional misfortune.

When he first learned that he had cancer, he did not withdraw into a shell; he called for help. My wife Dorli and I spent a long day with him and Virginia, talking through the grim prospects. He expressed his fear and discouragement. But he remained objective, practical, and strong. We reenacted this horrible disaster-confronting scene twice more – once when he had to make a terrible choice between disfiguring operations and radiation, and once, weeks before he died when he faced the depressing prospect of another round with cancer. I saw him many times in between, suffering through the daily oppressive consequences of his disease-fighting decisions. He was always himself – human and expressive, yet objective, dispassionate, good-humored, and courageous. He and Virginia showed superhuman strength through the worst and most prolonged physical troubles of anyone I have known.

He did not think that just any life was worth living. Some pain would be too nasty, too brutish. But he was willing to face an incredible amount of pain, disfigurement, and daily aggravation to salvage the goods from life.

The meaning of his life lay in those goods: they were his relations, his work, and his simple pleasures. He loved Virginia and his daughter Amber. He told me that leaving them would be hardest. He loved his parents and his sister and her family. I felt I knew them through him. He loved his friends. Even when he was experiencing the greatest physical hardship, he maintained interest in his friends. Even in the deepest trouble, he remembered to ask about the lives of others. He had a knack for holding friends, once friendships were made. He kept up and cared.

He continued to work to the end. He kept planning and thinking. He had written a stylish book about his bouts with cancer. It was one of his ways of understanding, mastering, and sharing with others the good in his experience. He intended to expand it by interspersing chapters on philosophical problems among the chapters on his life. The book would have been unique. He was working on that and on the book on Madison's dictum when he died.

He knew how to have fun. My last time with him combined the most serious discussion of his life prospects with immersion in a professional football game on television. Neither of us cared much who won, but he threw himself into the game in an infectious way that was characteristic of him.

He lived life at all levels. He thought hard about abstract problems. He was an original philosopher who made genuine contributions known all over the world. He faced the greatest pain, felt the deepest emotions, gave of himself to others steadily and profoundly, carried on long-term relations in the fullest, most loyal way. He understood people – their goodness and badness, their strengths and weaknesses, their conscious and unconscious. He took pleasure in little things – high school memories, soft drinks, sports, gentle (or even not so gentle) gossip, children. He gave pleasure to others. He became a favorite uncle to my older son and thought up joint gifts for us to give him. He hung on and fought for his life so persistently because he loved life, found it interesting and rewarding, and knew how to enjoy it. He knew how to enjoy it, even though he experienced its worst horrors – its unfairness and cruelties.

We who knew him can celebrate a life of depth, character, and love. We can be happy that he lived life well, salvaged its goods, and gave them to others. We can be happy that he was spared a last hopeless round of pain and agony. He leaves a daughter who will remember in her bones that he loved her. He leaves all of us a piece of his mind and spirit.

The Shadow of the Future

BRIAN SKYRMS

I. The Foole

The Foole of Thomas Hobbes' *Leviathan* argues that reason does not require commitment,

> seriously alleging, that every man's conservation and contentment, being committed to his own care, there could be no reason, why every man might not do what he thought conduced thereunto: and therefore also to make, or not make; keep or not keep Covenants, was not against Reason, when it conduced to one's benefit.[1]

Hobbes is particularly interested in the possibility of viable agreements in the state of nature. For simplicity, consider an agreement between two people. Hobbes is addressing the question as to whether someone who has promised to do his part is required *by reason,* when the other member has already done her part at some cost, to do his part. The Foole thinks not. According to the Foole, honoring the agreement may be *against reason* if the required action is costly and the benefit of the other's act has already been gained. Hobbes disagrees: "But where either one of the parties has performed already; or where there is a Power to make him performe; there is a question whether it be against reason, that is, against the benefit of the other to perform, or not. And I say it is not against reason."[2]

The Foole analyzes the situation as an extensive form game: First A plays, then B. Each either performs his part of the agreement or not. Performance is costly to the performer but beneficial to the other; mutual performance is better for each person than mutual nonperformance. An example is given in Figure 1. The question that Hobbes asks is this: "What is the rational act for B if A has performed and B knows it?" The Foole reasons that if A has already chosen to perform (or will be compelled to do so by some power), then B is faced with a very simple subgame in which he has the only move and the choice is a choice between a payoff of 4 and a payoff of 3.

Hobbes's Foole does not comment on the dictates of reason for player A in

It is a privilege to be able to participate in this volume honoring Gregory Kavka, colleague and friend. This essay bears the marks of many discussions with him.

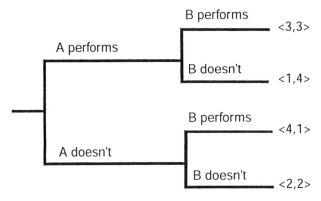

Figure 1. Hobbes' game.

this game, but David Hume – who has considerable sympathy with the Foole – does. After pointing out that many aspects of human commerce, including barter of goods and exchange of services and actions, can give rise to situations with the basic structure displayed in Figure 1, Hume analyzes an example:

Your corn is ripe to-day; mine will be so to-morrow. 'Tis profitable for us both, that I should labour with you to-day and that you should aid me to-morrow. I have no kindness for you, and know you have as little for me. I will not, therefore, take any pains upon your account; and should I labor with you upon my own account, in expectation of a return, I know I shou'd be disappointed, and that I shou'd in vain depend upon your gratitude. Here I leave you to labour alone: You treat me in the same manner. The seasons change; and both of us lose our harvests for want of mutual confidence and security.[3]

Hume agrees with the Foole that if B is rational and self-interested and has the payoffs we have specified,[4] B will not perform. He adds that if A knows these relevant facts about B, A should be able to deduce that B will not perform. Consequent to this deduction, A is, in effect, left with a choice between unreciprocated performance and no performance. Then if A – like B – is rational, self-interested, and has the payoffs specified, A will not perform.

Hume has analyzed the problem by a technique that Ernst Zermelo later used to show that every extensive form game of perfect information has a solution, the technique that game theorists call "backward induction." One goes to the final decisions in the game tree and assumes the optimal choice at each choice point. (This works for games where the optimal choice is always unique.) This procedure eliminates the final choice as a choice. Now one goes to the previous choice, and one repeats the procedure until the optimal act at the first choice is decided. It is remarkable that Hume not only grasps the technique but also appreciates its presuppositions concerning A's knowledge of B's rationality and payoffs.

II. Hobbes' Response to the Foole

Unlike David Gauthier[5] and Edward McClennen,[6] Hobbes does not believe that the Foole has made a mistake concerning the nature of rational decision. Rather, he accuses the Foole of a myopic mis-specification of the relevant game: "He therefore that breaketh his Covenant, and consequently declareth that he thinks he may with reason do so, cannot be received into any Society that unite themselves for Peace and Defence, but by the error of them that receive him."[7] According to Hobbes, the Foole's mistake is to ignore the future. His present acts generate a reputation that conditions others' actions toward him, and this affects his future payoffs. The relevant game-theory model must therefore be much more complicated than that shown in Figure 1. In the situations of prime interest in Hobbes' discussion – defensive coalitions in the state of nature – a member of a coalition who does not perform when his partner(s) have already come to his aid will not be aided in the future and will perish. Hobbes believes that for a rational, self-interested decision maker who takes the long view, "the shadow of the future" leads to the keeping of covenants in the present.

Hume gives a more circumspect version of this thesis. In favorable circumstances, the shadow of the future may allow self-interest to support cooperation:

Hence I learn to do a service to another, without bearing any real kindness; because I foresee, that he will return my service, in expectation of another of the same kind, and in order to maintain the same correspondence of good offices with me and with others. And accordingly, after I have serv'd him, and he is in possession of the advantage arising from my action, he is induc'd to perform his part, as foreseeing the consequences of his refusal.[8]

The most that moralists can do is to teach us that this is so – "that we can better satisfy our appetites in an oblique and artificial manner, than by their headlong and impetuous motion."[9]

What are those favorable circumstances under which the shadow of the future can exert its beneficial effect?

III. A Shadow of the Future

In 1957 Duncan Luce and Howard Raiffa proposed a model in which the shadow of the future allows rational agents to cooperate in repeated prisoner's dilemma games. The prisoner's dilemma game is like the strategic situation discussed by Hobbes and Hume, except that it lacks the sequential structure. Both players simultaneously and independently decide whether to perform or not. You might think of them keeping their end of a bargain by simultaneously acting at different locations. Since each actor prefers to free-ride if the other performs and prefers not to perform if the other doesn't, neither performs in an isolated single play of the game.

Luce and Raiffa suggest that we consider an indefinitely repeated prisoner's dilemma game. The same players play the game again and again. The number of repetitions will be finite, but the number of repetitions is governed by chance. Suppose, for instance, that at the first play the probability of a second play is 99 percent, and that the probability of a third play conditional on there having been a second play is 99 percent, and so forth. After any number of plays, if the players update their beliefs by conditioning, prospects for play continuing in the future look the same. The constant probability of at least one more play, here 99 percent, is called the "discount rate" of the repeated game. A discount rate of less than 100 percent allows expected payoffs for the game to be well defined.

In this repeated-game setting, cooperative play can be sustained as an equilibrium. Suppose that each player adopts the "grim trigger" strategy: Perform on the first play, but perform on subsequent plays if and only if each player has performed on all previous plays. Then both players always perform. Furthermore, neither can profit by unilaterally changing her strategy. A different strategy, which always called for performance against the stated strategy, would do equally well but no better. A strategy that called for some nonperformance at some time would elicit nonperformance thenceforth from the other, and this punishment would carry a cost to the nonperformer greater than the gain gotten by the single free ride (of nonperforming while his partner performed). Essentially the same reasoning works for the repeated form of the sequential game considered by Hobbes and Hume.

The shadow of the future can have just the effect that Hobbes said it should have in the repeated-game setting. And it is worth noting that the discount rate is a measure of the magnitude of the shadow cast by future events. If the discount rate is low, new encounters are unlikely, and the future is not important. If the discount rate is low enough, the only equilibria have both players never performing. If the discount rate is high, the future is important, and cooperation can be supported. The severity of the punishment required to sustain cooperation can depend on the discount rate.

What if, rather than having the same two players repeat their game, the players are members of a large community and continue to pair with new players on each repetition? Whether the shadow of the future can support cooperative behavior in this setting depends on the flow of information within the community. If information about past plays is shared and the discount factor is sufficiently high, then the shadow of the future can operate in much the same way as when the game is repeated between the same two partners; where information is not shared, the only possible equilibrium outcomes yield noncooperative behavior where no player ever performs. In such a setting, sharing information generates value for all concerned. One might expect institutions for sharing information to evolve and players to be willing to bear the costs of these institutions. This in fact happened in the case of medieval private commercial judges prior to the rise of the state. The story is juxtaposed with relevant repeated-game models in a fascinating essay by P. R. Milgrom, D. C. North, and B. R. Weingast.[10]

There are many types of strategic interaction other than that modeled by the prisoner's dilemma game. In the prisoner's dilemma, punishing a player who has failed to cooperate is not costly to the punisher. This may not be true in other games. It is not immediately obvious, then, that the effect of the shadow of the future in the prisoner's dilemma game generalizes to repetitions of other games. That it indeed does, however, is the message of a series of so-called folk theorems of repeated-game theory. They are called "folk theorems" because the general message of the theorems – that repetition allows the shadow of the future to sustain mutually beneficial play as an equilibrium – was widely believed by game theorists before the precise theorems were proved. A folk theorem for the kind of indefinitely repeated game we have been considering has been proved by D. Fudenberg and E. Maskin.[11]

As in the case of the repeated prisoner's dilemma game, we can generalize to the case where agents are members of a large community and partners are changed after every play. With enough shared information, there is an equilibrium in strategies that call for me to punish someone who defects against you. M. Kandori[12] proves the relevant theorem for this kind of "community enforcement" in repeated games.

Repeated games thus give us quite a rich framework within which the shadow of the future can be effective in sustaining socially optimal behavior by rational, self-interested agents. That is not to say that this framework forces the solution to be socially beneficial. Nasty behavior can also be sustained as an equilibrium in repeated games. If both players play the strategy "Never perform" in the repeated version of the Hobbes–Hume game with which we started, they are at an equilibrium of the game (for any discount). It is even possible to have an equilibrium, in a repeated game, that is worse for all players than any equilibrium of the one-round game being played.[13] Thus we should not slip from this thesis – "The shadow of the future allows cooperative behavior to be consistent with rational self-interest" – to a different thesis – "The shadow of the future shows that rational self-interest requires cooperative behavior" – as Hobbes appears to do in his discussion of the Foole. Rather, the repeated-game framework greatly expands the range of possible behaviors that may be supported by strategies in equilibrium. This expansion of possibilities may not be all that social philosophers have dreamed of, but how can its importance be denied?

IV. The Foole's Rejoinder

Life is short, says the Foole. Certainly it is finite. If the number of encounters is finite, the argument from reputation unravels by an extension of Hume's reasoning. Suppose, to start with, that the strategic situation of Figure 1 is repeated twice. At the end of the second repetition, B is called upon to move. There is no shadow of the future here, since it is the last move. If B is rational and self-interested at this point, B will not perform. Suppose that A knows this and knows that B will indeed be rational and self-interested at this point. Then A knows that B will not perform on the last move, and thus there is no shadow of the future for A on the next-to-last move. Then if A is rational and self-interested at this point, A will not perform. Suppose that at the previous move, B knows that A will be rational and self-interested at the time of the next move, and that A will at that time know that B will be rational and self-interested on the subsequent move. Then if B is rational and self-interested at this point, B will not perform. If A knows all this, and knows that rational self-interest and knowledge of it, and knowledge of knowledge of it, will hold up at subsequent times, then there *is* no initial shadow of the future for A. Backward induction shows that the only solution to the game is the one in which no one performs.

The story is no different for one hundred repetitions, or for one thousand, except for the cumbersome elaboration of the knowledge assumptions. For an assumption strong enough to cover any finite *n,* we could assume continuing *common knowledge*[14] of rational self-interest.[15]

Hobbes might reply that although life is finite, we do not know precisely how long our lives will be or how many repeated plays of a strategic interaction we will have in that life. But Gregory Kavka supplied the Foole with a devastating answer.[16] All that is necessary for the backward-induction argument to work here is that an upper bound to the number of plays be common knowledge among the players. Then, at the last possible play, if reached, there is no shadow of the future; so, at the next-to-last possible play, if reached, there is no shadow of the future, and so forth. If our uncertainty about the number of plays has this character instead of the structure posited by the theory of indefinitely repeated games, the shadow of the future is ineffective.

The theory of repeated games, however, has another card to play. If individuals have lifetimes of approximately fixed length, a mutually desirable equilibrium can be sustained by *overlapping generations*. Binmore introduces the idea with an example of mothers and daughters.[17] For simplicity, assume that only one mother and her daughter are alive at any one time. Young daughters produce bread; old mothers are unproductive. Mothers and daughters are assumed to be completely selfish. Nevertheless there can be an equilibrium at which everyone adheres to the norm: if young, give your mother half the bread, unless she herself has violated this norm when she was young. Someone who unilaterally deviates from this norm will starve in her old age. How widely is the overlapping-generations model applicable? M. Kandori proves the folk theorem for overlapping generations.[18] The overlapping-generations model can deliver everything that one can get from the repeated-game models previously discussed. An upper bound on individual lifetimes is consistent with the effective operation of the shadow of the future.

Despite the impressive power and scope of these results, the Foole is intransigent: an individual with no bounds to her lifetime has been replaced by a society with no bounds to its lifetime. Will the sun not eventually expire? Is there not some indisputable upper bound to the number of generations? If so, the overlapping-generations model will unravel by backward induction just as the repeated-games model did. The shadow of the future is without effect.

V. Another Shadow of the Future

The Foole's rejoinder claims that the shadow of the future is effective only in highly idealized models where the upper bound on some sort of repetition is infinite, whereas we live in a finite world. But, as Kavka[19] points out, the Foole's rejoinder also rests on an idealization – the assumption that sufficient common knowledge exists to carry out the backward induction. In the real world it is hardly a truism that everyone is perfectly rational and self-interested, let alone that everyone knows this, and that everyone knows that everyone knows this – and so on, *ad infinitum.*

But in the absence of this common knowledge, the operation of the shadow of the future is quite possible, and even consistent with the hypothesis that everyone is, in fact, rational and self-interested. Consider the finitely iterated prisoner's dilemma game. Just to make things difficult, we suppose that there is a fixed, commonly known number of trials. But the game is a game of incomplete information – players are not sure what their opponents are like. For all they know, their opponents may not be rational, in the sense of maximizing expected payoff. Or their opponents may be maximizing expected payoffs for a different game – which behaviorally can come to the same thing.[20]

Suppose both players are rational and self-interested, but each suspects that the other may be a *grim trigger* player. Then, if the number of repetitions is large enough relative to the magnitude of this suspicion, each may initially cooperate, in the hope of inducing reciprocal cooperation. Cooperation will break down at the end as each tries to exploit the other, but if the series of trials is long, cooperation will be the usual observed behavior.

Now, suppose that both players are rational and self-interested, and furthermore that each knows that the other is, but each suspects that the other does not know that she is and suspects that the other may be a grim trigger player. Then again, if the number of repetitions is large enough relative to the magnitude of the suspicion, each may initially cooperate, hoping to fool the other into thinking that she is a grim trigger player and thus inducing the other to initially cooperate, as in the previous case. In fact, an uncertainty at any level of the belief hierarchy can lead to predominantly cooperative behavior in the finitely repeated prisoner's dilemma game, provided that the number of plays is large enough. The details of the story are told in an article by Kreps, Milgrom, Roberts, and Wilson.[21]

In situations characterized by incomplete information, the backward-induction argument does not work, and the shadow of the future can operate in finitely repeated games. In the foregoing examples it carries the Hobbesian moral that in repeated games selfish strategies may support cooperative behavior. How generally can the shadow of the future operate in this context?

Fudenberg and Maskin[22] show that the effect of the shadow of the future can be as strong for finitely repeated games with incomplete information as it was for indefinitely repeated games with complete information. They prove a folk theorem of the former case that is the counterpart of the folk theorem for the latter case. For a long enough series of repetitions, the payoffs of any optimal[23] outcome of the one-trial game can be approximated arbitrarily closely by an equilibrium in the finitely repeated game of incomplete information. Of course we must always remember that nonoptimal equilibrium outcomes are also possible.

We should, however, keep in mind a difference between the theory of the indefinitely repeated game and the theory of the finitely repeated game under incomplete information. In the latter case, there is an endgame, and cooperative behavior may unravel in the endgame. This phenomenon, if fact, has been observed in experimental studies.[24] That fact can only reinforce the plausible assumption that the shadow of the future that we find operating in the real world has more to do with imperfect information than with infinite time horizons.

The moral for Hobbesian political theory is that a great deal rests on a distinction that Hobbes himself did not make – and that Hume perhaps only glimpsed. That is the distinction between a society composed of rational, self-interested agents and one where the rational self-interest of all agents is continuing common knowledge. For the latter case, the Foole gives a compelling analysis. In the former case, the Hobbesian shadow of the future can operate. How it operates depends on the nature of the uncertainty of the members of society.

The theory of finitely repeated games of incomplete information opens up a great variety of possible solutions. One is that described by Hobbes in his reply to the Foole, but another is the Foole's solution. If players are convinced that others will not perform, then they may well conclude that they would be fools to do so. In between are all sorts of other possible equilibria. Which one results from rational play depends on the degrees of belief of the players over types of possible opponents. Questions of the dynamics of the formation and transformation of belief must lie at the center of Hobbesian political theory.

Notes

1. Thomas Hobbes, *Leviathan,* ed. C. B. Macpherson ([1651]; London: Penguin, 1985), xv, 4, p. 203.

2. Ibid., par. 5, p. 204.
3. David Hume, *A Treatise of Human Nature*, ed. L. A. Selby-Bigge ([1739]; Oxford: Oxford University Press, 1967), pp. 520–1.
4. There is no extra unspecified component to the payoffs due to kindness or sympathy.
5. David Gauthier, *Morals by Agreement* (Oxford: Clarendon Press, 1986).
6. Edward McClennen, *Rationality and Dynamic Choice: Foundational Explorations* (Cambridge: Cambridge University Press, 1990).
7. Hobbes, *Leviathan*, xv, 5, p. 205.
8. Hume, *Treatise*, p. 521.
9. Ibid., p. 521.
10. Paul R. Milgrom, Douglas C. North, and Barry R. Weingast, "The Role of Institutions in the Revival of Trade: The Law Merchant, Private Judges, and the Champagne Fairs," *Economics and Politics* 2 (1990), 1–23.
11. Drew Fudenberg and Eric Maskin, "The Folk Theorem in Repeated Games with Discounting or with Incomplete Information," *Econometrica* 54 (1986), 533–54.
12. Michihiro Kandori, "Social Norms and Community Enforcement," *Review of Economic Studies* 59 (1992), 63–80.
13. See Roger B. Myerson, *Game Theory: Analysis of Conflict* (Cambridge, MA: Harvard University Press, 1991), p. 331, for an example.
14. See David Lewis, *Convention* (Cambridge, MA: Harvard University Press, 1969).
15. Articulation of the common-knowledge assumptions behind backward induction is a surprisingly delicate task. If one can make a move that will cause another player to lose her rationality or her knowledge of the game, or cause her to think that you have lost your rationality or your knowledge of the game, etc., then backward induction can break down. My use of the phrase "continuing common knowledge" is a gesture in the direction of these considerations, which I will address more fully in another essay.

   The interested reader might consult Robert J. Aumann, "Backward Induction and Common Knowledge of Rationality," *Games and Economic Behavior* 8 (1995), 6–19; Cristina Bicchieri, "Strategic Behavior and Counterfactuals," *Synthese* 76 (1988), 135–69; Ken Binmore, "Modeling Rational Players," pts. 1–2, *Economics and Philosophy* 3–4 (1987–8), 179–214, 9–55; Philip Reny, "Rationality in Extensive Form Games," *Journal of Economic Theory* 59 (1993), 627–49; Robert C. Stalnaker, "Knowledge, Belief and Counterfactual Reasoning in Games," in *The Logic of Strategy*, ed. Cristina Bicchieri, Richard Jeffrey, and Brian Skyrms (Oxford University Press, in press).
16. Gregory Kavka, "Hobbes's War of All against All," *Ethics* 93 (1983), 291–310. See also J. Carroll, "Indefinite Terminating Points and the Iterated Prisoner's Dilemma," *Theory and Decision* 22 (1987), 247–56, and "Iterated *n*-Player Prisoner's Dilemma Games," *Philosophical Studies* 53 (1988), 411–15.
17. Ken Binmore, *Playing Fair*, vol. 1 of his *Game Theory and the Social Contract* (Cambridge, MA: MIT, 1994), pp. 73–4.
18. Michihiro Kandori, "Repeated Plays Played by Overlapping Generations of Players," *Review of Economic Studies* 59 (1992), 81–92.
19. Gregory S. Kavka, *Hobbesian Moral and Political Theory* (Princeton: Princeton University Press, 1986).
20. See John Harsanyi, "Games with Incomplete Information Played by 'Bayesian' Players," *Management Science* 14 (1967–8), 159–82, 320–34, 486–502.
21. See David Kreps, Paul Milgrom, John Roberts, and Robert Wilson, "Rational Cooperation in the Finitely Repeated Prisoner's Dilemma," *Journal of Economic Theory*

27 (1982), 245–52, and also David Kreps and Robert Wilson, "Reputation and Incomplete Information," *Journal of Economic Theory* 27 (1982), 273–89, and Paul Milgrom and John Roberts, "Predation, Reputation and Entry Deterrence," *Journal of Economic Theory* 27 (1982), 280–312.

22. Fudenberg and Maskin, "Folk Theorem."

23. That is to say, Pareto-optimal outcome. Outcome 1 Pareto dominates outcome 2 if some player does better in outcome 1 and no player does worse. An outcome is Pareto optimal if it is not Pareto dominated.

24. For experimental results and discussion, see Reinhard Selten and Rolf Stoecker, "End Behavior in Sequence of Finite Prisoner's Dilemma Supergames: A Learning Theory Approach," *Journal of Economic Behavior and Organization* 7 (1986), 47–70, and James Andreoni and John H. Miller, "Rational Cooperation in the Finitely Repeated Prisoner's Dilemma: Experimental Evidence," *Economic Journal* 103 (1993), 570–85.

A New Paradox of Deterrence

DANIEL M. FARRELL

Some years ago, in what has since become a widely known and highly regarded essay, Gregory Kavka articulated what he called three "paradoxes of
deterrence."[1] In brief, he claimed to have identified three quite plausible and
eminently defensible moral claims, each of which, he argued, was logically
inconsistent with some other very appealing moral claim; and he maintained,
further, that what was to be learned from his reflections was that the latter three
claims, though widely accepted by both philosophers and ordinary people,
were not strictly (i.e., universally) true. Showing this was particularly important, Kavka felt, because the claims whose truth he wanted to call into question actually functioned, in many moral systems, as critically important
"bridge principles" that were supposed to enable us to understand the connection, in a given system, between principles for morally assessing human
actions and principles for morally assessing human agents and their psychological states.[2]

   I have discussed this famous essay at length elsewhere, trying to show in what
respects I think Kavka was right in what he argued there and in what respects
he may be wrong.[3] In addition, I have tried to show, in a number of other essays, the implications, both for moral theory and for certain other areas of philosophy, of those parts of Kavka's doctrine that seem to me to be true.[4]

   In the present essay I want to do something quite different: after reviewing
Kavka's original efforts in this area and indicating what is and is not genuinely
paradoxical about the matters with which he was concerned, I want to try to articulate a new paradox of my own – one that is in the spirit of Kavka's original
paradoxes but that is, at the same time, not one that Kavka himself identified.
Having identified this new paradox, I will go on to show why it seems to me

I have been helped by a great many people over the past ten years or so as I have worried over and
written about the many problems Kavka's work raises for our consideration. I have thanked these
parties individually in the several essays of mine cited in the notes, and I hope they will forgive me
if I do not thank all of them again by name here. I do wish to say here, though, one last time, how
deeply indebted all of my work in this area is to both the work and the personal encouragement of
Gregory Kavka himself. As anyone who knew him knows, he was a philosopher's philosopher, as
well as an extraordinarily gifted philosopher, and an incredibly decent and inspiring human being.

not only interesting and important in its own right, but also for what it suggests about the resolution of other, seemingly unrelated philosophical problems.

I

We need to begin by noting two oddities in Kavka's use of the term "paradox." Typically, we think of a paradox as constituted by a set of two logically inconsistent propositions, each of which can be supported by what appears to be a completely compelling argument. Kavka, though, does not use the term in this (formal) sense. Rather, he uses it to refer to what those who accept the formal definition would say is simply one member of the pair of propositions that together constitute the paradox he is examining. Thus, Kavka calls proposition P_1 (in my next section) his first "paradox" of deterrence, despite the fact that, strictly speaking, the whole paradox he has in mind cannot be stated without also stating the principle known as the "wrongful intentions principle." Of course, because Kavka does identify, in each case, what someone who insists on using the term "paradox" in the standard way would say is the missing member of the relevant pair, no real harm comes of his somewhat idiosyncratic usage. Still, we need to bear in mind that what Kavka calls "the paradoxes of deterrence" are, in each case, actually just single statements that Kavka thinks are clearly true and that he thinks are clearly inconsistent with certain other statements that he supposes most of us, at any rate, will be likely to think are also true.

A second sense in which Kavka's usage is somewhat odd, though, arises from the fact that he does not, of course, think the paradoxes he has identified are genuine paradoxes. He does not, that is to say, really believe that there are equally plausible and seemingly quite compelling arguments for each member of the allegedly inconsistent pairs of propositions he thinks he has identified. On the contrary; as we have already noted, one of Kavka's central aims in elaborating his paradoxes is to convince us that certain moral principles most of us are inclined to think are obviously true cannot be true, given the truth of certain other principles (or claims) that are logically inconsistent with the former and that Kavka thinks clearly *are* true. Thus, whereas ordinarily the proponent of a new paradox argues that it is not at all clear which of the apparently true propositions in question is not in fact true, Kavka is anxious to convince us that, given his arguments for one member of each pair, it is quite clear that the other member is, despite appearances, not true.

I remark on this second oddity in Kavka's usage partly because doing so seems necessary if one is to understand what he is about, and partly to call attention to a fairly obvious feature of his usage that will be important later in this essay when I articulate the new "paradox" I want to defend. What Kavka really believed, it seems to me, is not that he had discovered anything remotely like a set of formal paradoxes, even apparent ones, but rather that he had uncovered some moral truths that were not only important truths but also rather puzzling truths, given certain other things that (as he believed) most of us are inclined to take for granted. And it is in this sense, it seems to me, in which something is "paradoxical" inasmuch as it is rather deeply puzzling, that Kavka can indeed be said to have identified at least one genuine paradox of deterrence and to have provided, at the same time, the basis for another, which will be articulated in due course. First, though, we need to remind ourselves of what Kavka claimed he had achieved, and we need as well to ask how much of what he claimed can still plausibly be said to hold up.

II

We can begin this task by recalling what Kavka had in mind when he discussed "special deterrence situations" (SDSs). A person is in an SDS, Kavka said, when the following conditions apply to him:

First, it is likely he must intend (conditionally) to apply a harmful sanction to innocent people, if an extremely harmful and unjust offense is to be prevented. Second, such an intention would very likely deter the offense. Third, the amounts of harm involved in the offense and the threatened sanction are very large ... {and the relevant probabilities and amounts of harm are such that a rational utilitarian evaluation would substantially favor having the intention}. Finally, he would have conclusive moral reasons not to apply the sanction if the offense were to occur.[5]

An example of such a situation, Kavka went on to say, would be the situation of a head of state who correctly believes that unless he sincerely threatens massive, and clearly immoral, nuclear retaliation, his nation's principal international antagonist will very likely attempt a massive, and equally immoral, first strike, and who has reason to believe as well that by sincerely making such a threat he will very likely be able to deter his antagonist from making the first strike.[6]

Kavka believed that in at least some situations of this sort, it would be morally right (and possibly even morally obligatory) to adopt the intention one has to have if the wrongful attack is to be deterred. And it is this, of course, that he thought gave rise to the first of his three paradoxes. For he was also inclined to believe, as he thought most philosophers and ordinary people were inclined to believe, that it is clearly wrong to intend to do what one grants it would be wrong to do. And to Kavka, at least, it seemed clear that these beliefs could not both be true.

I have argued elsewhere that Kavka was mistaken to suppose that these beliefs cannot both be true.[7] In a moment I shall return to this issue, since it bears on the principal new points I wish to make. First, though, it will be helpful to state, explicitly, this and the other two paradoxes that Kavka claimed to have identified in his early essay "Some Paradoxes of Deterrence." This, of course, means listing what Kavka called "the paradoxes" and listing, as well, the three "bridge principles" that are needed to generate the alleged inconsistency in each case.

Apart from one or two very small (stylistic) changes, Kavka's statement of his paradoxes, which I shall call P_1, P_2, and P_3, is the same in both his famous article and the slightly revised version that appeared as a chapter in his book *Moral Paradoxes of Nuclear Deterrence:*

> P_1: There are cases in which, although it would be wrong for an agent to perform a certain act in a certain situation, it would nonetheless be right for . . . {that agent}, knowing this, to form the intention to perform that act in that situation.[8]

> P_2: There are situations (namely SDSs) in which it would be right for agents {if they could} to perform certain actions (namely, forming the intention to apply the sanction) and in which it is possible for some agents to perform such actions, but impossible for rational and morally good agents to perform them.[9]

> P_3: In certain situations, it would be morally right for a rational and morally good agent to deliberately (attempt to) corrupt himself.[10]

The paradoxicality of P_1 is made manifest, Kavka says, if we compare it with the wrongful intentions principle (WIP). In his famous article, this principle is stated as follows:

> WIP: To intend to do what one knows to be wrong is itself wrong.[11]

The paradoxicality of P_2, Kavka continues, is made evident by comparing it with what he calls the "right–good principle" (RGP):

> RGP: Doing something is right if and only if a morally good . . . {person} would do the same thing in the given situation.[12]

Finally, the paradoxicality of P_3, Kavka says, is clear when we compare it with what he calls the "virtue preservation principle" (VPP):

> VPP: It is wrong to deliberately lose (or reduce the degree of) one's moral virtue.[13]

Our (current) question, of course, is this: what reason is there to believe that each of these propositions is arguably true, much less that the truth of each of the first three propositions is inconsistent with the truth of the correlative bridge principle to which Kavka has drawn our attention?

III

We can begin with P_1 and the so-called wrongful intentions principle.[14] Kavka thought P_1 was true because it is supported by a moral principle that he accepted and that he thought virtually no one would be willing to deny – the principle that when one is in a choice situation with just two options and the difference in expected utilities associated with those options is extremely large, amounting, for example, to the difference between almost certain death for a large number of innocent people, on the one hand, and a very small risk of death for an equal number of other (innocent) people, on the other hand, one should choose the option with the dramatically higher utility, since in such situations "other moral considerations are overridden by utilitarian considerations."[15] It would be easy, of course, to think of deontological objections to this principle, though it is perhaps worth remarking that, suitably formulated, the principle does in fact appear to be accepted by a surprisingly large number of people, theorists and nontheorists alike. Here, though, I want to grant this principle for the sake of argument, since I believe there is another, much more difficult problem with Kavka's view.

To see this, let us also grant, just for a moment, the truth of WIP (noting, though, that there are obvious problems of interpretation that remain to be discussed in this connection, and noting as well that Kavka is almost certainly mistaken in supposing that most ordinary people accept some version of this principle). Even granting all this, it seems to me to be quite clear that Kavka has a problem here. For he holds that P_1 (or, if one prefers, the assumption of the truth of P_1) is *paradoxical* because P_1 is "the direct denial" of WIP.[16] And this is simply not so. P_1, after all, is a claim about the propriety of *forming* or *adopting* a certain kind of intention. Suppose, with Kavka, that under certain circumstances it would be morally permissible to adopt an intention of the relevant sort. It is quite consistent with granting this, it seems to me, to hold as well that such an intention would be a "wrongful" or "immoral" intention in the following sense: to *have* such an intention, or to so intend, is *eo ipso* to be liable to a certain amount of moral opprobrium and to be so liable precisely *because* one so intends.

My argument here assumes, of course, that it is possible for a person to be justified in *adopting* an intention that she will nonetheless be liable to moral opprobrium for *having* once she has adopted it. This assumption, which Kavka himself is certainly in no position to reject, will be defended shortly. My argument also assumes, however, that WIP, properly understood, is a principle that has to do, not with the propriety of adopting the relevant sorts of intentions, but rather with the moral standing of those who have those intentions once they have been adopted. And this assumption might well be thought to be mistaken. Indeed, Kavka himself implicitly rejects it in his book. For there, in what is otherwise a virtually unrevised version of his original essay, he reformulates WIP as follows:

> WIP*:   To form the intention to do what one knows to be wrong is itself wrong.[17]

Obviously, if Kavka can show that this interpretation of the relevant principle is sound, he can claim that in fact he has indeed shown that WIP is inconsistent with P_1.

There are two problems, though, with Kavka's reinterpretation of WIP. For one thing, his own arguments for the *prima facie* plausibility of this principle, which are identical in the article and in the book, are arguments for a principle like the one suggested by my own remarks in the second paragraph of this section, rather than for a principle such as WIP*.[18] His arguments tend to support a principle, that is to say, that focuses on the objectionability of *having* the relevant intentions rather than on the objectionability of *forming* or *adopting* such intentions in the first place. (Very briefly, these arguments amount to an attempt to show that someone who intends to do wrong in a certain way is someone who is in an important sense already just as reprehensible as someone who has done wrong in that way.) Thus, insofar as the principle that interests him is best identified by looking at his own arguments for that principle, Kavka is better advised to stick with his original choice (WIP) than with his later choice (WIP*).

More importantly, though, Kavka's move to WIP* is undermined by additional, independent considerations as well. For suppose we ask, not how Kavka's arguments for the relevant principle suggest that the principle is to be understood, but how the best arguments available, whether his or some others, suggest that it is to be understood. Here too, it seems to me, we are driven to the same conclusion: the real insight behind the relevant principle is an insight about the moral ramifications of someone's *having* the relevant sort of intention, not about the justifiability of someone's forming or adopting that sort of intention.

To see this, we need to ask why someone might initially be sympathetic to some such principle, whether it is stated as Kavka originally states it or as he states it in revised form in his book. One answer, of course – which, as we have just seen, is in fact suggested by Kavka, as well as by a number of other authors – is this: Most of us tend to regard a person who fully intends to perform a wrongful act and is prevented from doing so solely by external circumstances as being "just as bad as the person who . . . [actually succeeds in performing] a like wrongful act."[19] Whether it is reasonable to react to such a person in this manner is, of course, a difficult question. The point to be emphasized here is simply that, as an argument for some sort of wrongful intentions principle, this is an argument not for WIP* but rather for something like WIP.

Another account of the attractiveness of some such principle, however – the best account, I believe – is an account that begins from an analysis of what a future-directed intention *is*. Very briefly, this account holds that to intend, at one point in time, to do something at some later point in time is to be *committed* to doing it at that later date. Suppose this is true. It then follows that to intend to do wrong, either conditionally or unconditionally, is to be committed to doing wrong. And how could one be committed to doing wrong, even when one's being so committed is for the best, without its following that one is *ipso facto* just as liable to moral opprobrium as one who has actually done the sort of wrong that one currently intends to do?[20]

There are plenty of objections to this line of thought that we would need to consider if we were currently engaged in the project of defending the version of WIP that is suggested in the argument just sketched. This is not our current project, though. Rather, we have merely been attempting to determine why someone might be tempted by some version or other of such a principle and to determine, as well, exactly what version the best arguments for such a principle support. And the answer to this question, it seems to me, is quite clear: the best arguments for WIP, and in fact the most common, are arguments that focus not on the act of adopting the relevant sorts of intentions but that focus, instead, on the moral status of the individual who has those intentions once they have been adopted.[21]

I have been suggesting that Kavka was closer to the truth when he articulated the wrongful intentions principle as WIP than when he articulated it as WIP*. I now want to suggest, however, that an even better version of the principle can be provided. To see this, notice first that, from the standpoint of what we have just been saying, there is something very odd about WIP: in alleging that to intend to do wrong is itself wrong, WIP might plausibly be thought to suggest that a future-directed intention is itself a kind of action. After all, it is actions that are most appropriately called "right" or "wrong." Thus, in alleging that certain future-directed intentions (or "intendings") are themselves wrong, WIP might be taken to be suggesting, at least obliquely, that intending, or having certain intentions, is itself a way of acting.

Now, for a variety of reasons – not the least of which is simple accuracy – I think it is important to block the suggestion, in our statement of the relevant principle, that to intend to do something is to perform an action of some sort. I suggest, therefore, that a more perspicuous version of this principle would be the following:

> WIP**:   Someone who intends to do wrong in a certain way (either conditionally or unconditionally) is *eo ipso* liable, regardless of how desirable it is that he or she so intends, to whatever moral opprobrium it would be appropriate to

direct at someone who had actually done wrong in that way.

What is attractive about this version of the principle, it seems to me, its prolixity notwithstanding, is that it shares the intuitive plausibility of WIP, on the one hand, without, on the other hand, suggesting that future-directed intentions are actions, and hence things that can coherently be called either right or wrong.

Suppose I am correct and WIP** is indeed the most accurate expression of the intuition that lies behind WIP. It then follows, it seems to me, that my original claim has been made good: there is no apparent conflict between P_1 and the wrongful intentions principle, regardless of whether we state the latter – somewhat carelessly, in my view – as Kavka himself originally states it, or as WIP**. For, clearly, one might applaud a person for *adopting* an intention, or otherwise bringing it about that she *has* an intention, which one nonetheless believes she will be liable to a certain amount of moral opprobrium for *having* once she has brought it about that it is hers.

Or so it appears. At this point we need to consider the following objection. Suppose it is true that someone who intends to do wrong is *eo ipso* someone who is liable to whatever opprobrium would be appropriate for someone who has actually *done* wrong in that way. Then, in bringing it about that she intends to do wrong – either by simply adopting the relevant intention or by achieving this state in some other, more roundabout way – a person would be corrupting herself in an obvious way. And surely this sort of moral self-corruption is wrong, someone might say, and is wrong regardless of the good that will likely be achieved as a result of one's having corrupted oneself in this manner. Thus, according to this objection, at any rate, my concluding statement in the preceding paragraph is clearly mistaken: one could not, coherently, applaud a person for bringing it about that she has an intention that one is prepared to condemn her for *having* once she has brought it about that she has it.

Here, of course, we are implicitly addressing Kavka's third paradox, which tells us that it can sometimes be right for a person to corrupt herself in certain ways, despite the fact that we are ordinarily inclined to think that self-corruption is always wrong. Notice, though, that if there is a paradox here, it will be the only (apparent) paradox Kavka has so far given us. For his first paradox, as we have seen, turns out not to be even apparently paradoxical, when inspected carefully (when we compare P_1 with either WIP or WIP**, that is to say). Thus, even if we become convinced that the introduction of the prohibition against self-corruption generates at least an apparent paradox, this will not be another (apparent) paradox but rather the first (apparent) paradox Kavka has stated.

Clearly, though, there will not be even an apparent paradox here unless we suppose that it is at least arguable that self-corruption of the relevant sort is always wrong. Is this, then, a defensible moral view? Kavka himself suggests no reason whatsoever for supposing that it is. His aim, of course, is to show that, although superficially plausible, the view that self-corruption is always wrong must ultimately be called into question, inasmuch as, when conjoined to P_3, it leads to paradox. He never in fact indicates, however, why he thinks the principle known as the "virtue preservation principle" (VPP) is even superficially plausible, and a moment's reflection, it seems to me, shows that it is not. For one thing, of course, a *consequentialist* need not hold that self-corruption is even "bad," or a moral evil, much less that every act that produces such an evil is *ipso facto* morally wrong. What about a deontologist, then, whom Kavka can be presumed to have in mind? It is, to be sure, open to the deontologist to hold that self-corruption is always wrong, on balance and regardless of the consequences of engaging in it, and some deontologists may actually believe this. I can think of no argument for believing it, however, on deontological grounds, nor can I think of any prominent deontologist, Kant included, who defends it.[22]

IV

Thus far I have argued that two of Kavka's three paradoxes are not, upon reflection, really paradoxical, or puzzling, in the sense I believe he had in mind. His argument for the paradoxicality of P_1 fails, I have argued, because the proposition with which P_1 is supposed to be inconsistent is, while arguably true, not a proposition with which P_1 is actually inconsistent. His argument for the paradoxicality of P_3 fails, on the other hand, because, while P_3 is indeed inconsistent with the companion proposition that Kavka calls to our attention, the latter is not arguably true.

We are left, then, with Kavka's second paradox, which, as he states it, consists of the claim that there are circumstances in which "it would be right for an agent to perform [a] certain [action] (namely, forming the intention to . . . [perform an immoral action]), and in which it is possible for some agents to perform such [an action], but impossible for rational and morally good agents to perform [it]."[23] Kavka thinks this constitutes a paradox, of course, because he believes it is inconsistent with the following claim, which he also thinks is arguably true: "Doing something is right if and only if a morally good person would do the same thing in the given situation."[24]

One problem with Kavka's suggestion here is this: it is not clear why the so-called right–good principle cannot be reformulated so that it is perfectly consistent with P_2. If we formulate the former as follows, for example, the inconsistency that Kavka's version establishes is eliminated and is eliminated by means of a straightforward and seemingly quite plausible move:

> RGP*:   Doing something is right if and only if a morally good person would do the same thing in the given situation *if she*

could (i.e., if it were both physically and logically possible for her to do it).

I shall not pursue this objection here, however. For regardless of whether or not Kavka can identify a pair of statements that constitute an apparent paradox in this connection, it is certainly true that P_2 would be both interesting and rather puzzling if it could be shown to be true. This, of course, is because it would be odd if there really were things that it would be morally desirable for one to do but that one would be able to do only if one were to some degree deficient in either one's moral virtue or one's overall rationality.

Why, though, should we suppose that P_2 is true? Both in his original essay and in his book, Kavka argues for P_2 as follows:

An agent in an SDS recognizes that there would be conclusive moral reasons not to apply the sanction if the offense were committed. If he does not regard these admittedly conclusive moral reasons as conclusive reasons for him not to apply the sanction, then he is not moral. Suppose, on the other hand, that he does regard himself as having conclusive reasons not to apply the sanction if the offense is committed. If, nonetheless, he is disposed to apply it, because the reasons for applying it motivate him more strongly than do the conclusive reasons not to apply it, then he is irrational.[25]

Ignoring for now the fact that Kavka uses the notion of an agent's "dispositions" here, when he ought, I think, to be referring to the agent's *commitments* or *intentions,* we can state his argument formally as follows:

(1) A morally good agent regards conclusive moral reasons for or against a given course of conduct as conclusive reasons for or against that course of conduct.

(2) In circumstances of the sort that interest us, therefore, such an agent will regard himself as having conclusive reasons not to perform the relevant action (i.e., the action we are supposing it would be morally right for him to adopt an intention to perform, supposing he could in fact adopt such an intention).

(3) A rational agent cannot (logically) intend to do something that he recognizes he will have conclusive reasons not to do.

(4) In circumstances of the sort that interest us, therefore, a rational and morally good agent could not (logically) intend to perform the relevant action, despite the fact that it would be morally right for him to adopt an intention to perform it if he could.

One problem with this argument is that even if we suppose it is sound, it does not prove what Kavka wants to prove – namely, that a rational and morally good agent would not be able to adopt a future-directed intention to act immorally, even if it would be right for her to do so if she could. This, of course, is because, at best, the argument shows only that such an agent would not be able to *have* such an intention consistent with her assumed rationality and goodness. Further argument is required to show that intentions a rational and morally good agent cannot have are intentions she also cannot adopt.

We shall return to this problem in a moment. First, though, it will be useful to ask why Kavka thinks the argument he presents is sound.

Kavka suggests no defense for premise (1), apparently considering it obvious that the concept of a morally good agent includes the concept of an agent who regards conclusive moral reasons for action as conclusive reasons for action. Suppose we grant this for now. Since premise (2) simply articulates, for circumstances of the sort that interest us, the implications of premise (1), and since premise (4) follows validly from premises (2) and (3), the crucial question concerns the plausibility of premise (3).

Kavka's defense of premise (3) is rather sketchy. He says in the passage just quoted that an agent would be "irrational" if she were disposed to act in a way she grants she has conclusive reasons *not* to act, and he goes on to say, in the following paragraph, that this is so "because, as recent writers on intentions have suggested, it is part of the concept of rationally intending to do something that the disposition to do the intended act be caused (or justified) in an appropriate way by the agent's view of the reasons for doing the act."[26] This is surely rather obscure, however, and, in any case, much too facile. What exactly is the relation that needs to hold, on this view, between an agent's view of the reasons there are (or will be) for performing an act, on the one hand, and her disposition or intention to perform it, on the other hand, if she is to count as "rational" and *therefore* "not irrational"? And why should we suppose that it *is* in fact "part of the concept of rationally intending to do something" that this relation holds?

Kavka does not answer these questions. Nonetheless, I think we ought to grant him premise (3). For, as I have tried to show elsewhere, in a rather different context, there are in fact good reasons for accepting the view that (3) asserts.[27] At bottom, these are reasons that have to do with what a future-directed intention is and with how the notion of the rationality or irrationality of a person is best made out. Here, however, it will have to suffice to recall an argument that I sketched earlier in defense of WIP**, our final formulation of the so-called wrongful intentions principle. We noted there that one reason for supposing a fully virtuous person could not, consistent with her virtue, intend to do what she grants it will be immoral for her to do, is this: Exactly that feature which would make her liable to moral opprobrium for actually performing an immoral act – namely, her willingness to do what she knew to be wrong – would be a feature that already applied to her when she merely (but quite sincerely) intended to perform that act. Let us continue to suppose this argument is sound. An exactly analogous argument can then be used in defense of Kavka's premise (3). For the same feature that would make us say that someone who had actually performed an admittedly irrational act was thereby exhibiting that she was less than fully rational – namely, her willingness to do what she knew to be irrational – would also be present and enable us to say the same of someone who merely intended to do what she knew would be irrational.

Suppose we grant (3), then, and therefore (4). Clearly, Kavka needs more than this, as we have already seen, if he is to establish P_2. He needs to show that an intention that a fully rational person could not have is an intention a fully rational person could not adopt.

Unfortunately, Kavka does not attempt to show this, either in his early article or in his book. All he says is that once we grant that a rational agent could not *intend* to do what she grants it will be irrational for her to do, we have to grant as well that she could not *form* or *adopt* such an intention, since this would entail having that intention, something that is by hypothesis incompatible with full rationality. And this will not do. For why should we not suppose that it is possible for a rational agent to "corrupt" herself, when circumstances require this, by adopting an intention that she knows will entail that she is less rational once she has it? Kavka, at any rate, gives us no reason to suppose that self-corruption of this sort is impossible for a rational individual.

Our situation, then, is this. We want to know whether the following claim can be made good:

> (5) If it is impossible for a rational agent to have a certain intention, because of the implications of having it [or: because she would be irrational if she had it], then it will be impossible for a rational agent to adopt that intention in the first place, and it will be impossible for her to do this even if it is by hypothesis morally desirable for her to have it.

From this, of course, and premise (4), we could infer premise (6), which, with premise (4), articulates the paradox that currently interests us (i.e., Kavka's P_2):

> (6) In cases of the sort that interest us, a rational and morally good agent will be unable to adopt the relevant intentions, despite the fact that they are intentions that it would be morally right for her to adopt if she could in fact adopt them.

The problem is to find an argument for premise (5).

To see that such an argument is possible, we shall need to make a number of assumptions about what a "future-directed intention" is and about what "adopting" a future-directed intention involves. Suppose first, then, as we did earlier, that to intend, either conditionally or unconditionally, at one point in time, to do something at some later point in time is to be *committed* to doing it at that later time. And suppose as well that a person is thus committed to future action just in case (a) she is inclined to reason in certain ways as time goes by (e.g., to exclude from consideration, on the one hand, actions that would make it impossible for her to perform the intended action, and to have a careful regard, on the other hand, for doing those things that must be done if she is eventually to be able to perform that action); (b) her overall dispositional "set" is such as to ensure that she would in fact perform the intended action were that set to persist more or less unchanged until the time for action arrives; and (c) she is disposed not to reopen, in the absence of significant changes of a certain sort, the question of whether or not she will perform that action when the time arrives.[28] Finally, suppose that to adopt an intention to act in some way in the future is simply to come to be thus committed to doing it as a result of reflection, either conscious or not, on one's current beliefs and desires (including, of course, one's current beliefs about one's likely future beliefs and desires). Then, so far as premise (5) is concerned, our question is why we should suppose that a fully rational individual could not come to be committed, in the sense and in the manner just described, to performing an action that she grants it will be irrational for her to perform.

Recall, first, as we attempt to answer this question, that we are assuming that a person who intends to perform an action she grants it will be irrational to perform is *eo ipso* less than an ideally rational individual. This follows from the "rationality" analogue of WIP that we agreed earlier to accept for the sake of argument. Hence, our question here is in effect a question about the possibility, for an ideally rational agent, of a certain kind of self-corruption – namely, that which would be involved in bringing it about that she is less than ideally rational, as a result of bringing it about – by forming or *adopting* the relevant intention – that she intends to do what she grants it will be irrational for her to do when the time comes to do it. Our question, therefore, is this: Why should we suppose, with premise (5), that self-corruption of this sort would be impossible for an ideally rational individual?

Now, one answer to this question – not the best answer, I believe, but the only one I am prepared to defend at present – is this: a commitment to act as one believes it will be irrational to act is a commitment that would necessarily be unstable, in the case of an otherwise rational individual, and that would be unstable in a way that would be inconsistent with its being the sort of commitment we are supposing is necessary for a future-directed intention to exist. To see why this is so, let us suppose that a fully rational individual *could* adopt, at least momentarily, a commitment to act irrationally (in the future) of just the sort that would, if it persisted, clearly constitute an intention, conditional or otherwise, to perform the relevant action. Could such a commitment be maintained, for more than a moment, by an otherwise rational individual (i.e., by an individual who would by hypothesis be fully rational, except for the fact that he is currently, at least momentarily, committed to the performance of what he admits will be an irrational action)? It seems to me it could not. For suppose it could – that is, suppose that reflection on the fact that it was a commitment to act irrationally would not necessarily undermine it. It would then be possible for an otherwise rational individual to make such a commitment and for that commitment to persist, undiminished, up to the time at which the intended action is supposed to be performed. But, then, the action will, at that time, be performed, supposing no other changes have occurred, since we are supposing that the commitment in question is such that, were it present at the time of action, the action will be performed. This, however, is absurd, since we cannot suppose that a basically rational individual could, consistent with her rationality, knowingly perform an action that she grants it is irrational for her to perform.

We must suppose, therefore, that reflection on the irrationality of what one intends to do will inevitably undermine one's intention, at least if one is otherwise a basically rational individual, since its not being undermined would show one to be even more deeply irrational than one's supposed intention already shows one to be. And this means that one's commitment is not, after all, a commitment of the sort that is required for the existence of a genuine intention to perform the relevant action. For such an intention, we have supposed, can be constituted only by a commitment with the dispositional and reasoning-centered components sketched earlier. And how can it be said of someone whose commitment to action is unstable, in the sense just sketched, that she is disposed not to think about whether or not to perform that action when the time comes to perform or not perform it?[29]

V

If the argument of the preceding section is sound, Kavka's P_2 has been made good. As I have indicated earlier, because I believe there are problems with Kavka's version of RGP, I do not believe we can say, even here, that Kavka has identified a genuine apparent paradox. However, as I have also indicated, I do not find this to be especially damaging to the point I take Kavka to have wanted to prove. For I certainly do believe that there is indeed something "paradoxical," in the broad, colloquial sense I think Kavka had in mind – that there is indeed something deeply puzzling, in other words – about the proposition our argument for P_2 establishes. This, of course, is because, as I have noted, it surely does seem odd to suppose that there are things that it would be morally desirable for one to do but that one would be able to do only if one were to some degree deficient in either one's moral virtue or one's overall rationality. And yet our argument suggests that there are such things, at least in theory, and I believe our argument is sound.

I have discussed elsewhere what I think are the most important practical and theoretical consequences of this conclusion.[30] One of the most interesting consequences, if I am right, is that Kavka was mistaken, in his brief discussion of his own famous Toxin Puzzle, to write as though, in the circumstances he had imagined, it would be unclear what a rational agent would do.[31] For if the principle embodied in premise (5) is true, it follows immediately that, barring the sort of special-effects technologies Kavka explicitly rules out in the Toxin Puzzle, an ideally rational agent simply would not be able to adopt the intention she has to have in order to get the $1 million.[32]

Another consequence of the assumption that our argument is sound, of course, has to do with what would be possible, for an ideally rational and virtuous head of state, in an SDS like the one that Kavka describes in his discussion of P_2 – a situation in which the relevant individual has good reason to believe that only by sincerely threatening massive and clearly immoral nuclear retaliation can he hope to deter a massive and clearly immoral first strike, and where he has good reason to believe, as well, that by sincerely making such a threat he will likely avert the first strike. Obviously, if P_2 is true, an ideally moral and fully rational head of state would be unable to threaten, sincerely, what we supposed she would have to threaten, and mean to do, if the probability of the imagined first strike were to be suitably diminished, whereas someone less than ideally good, or less than ideally rational, might well be able to do what her fully moral and rational counterpart would not be able to do. This, of course, is because a sincere threat requires a concomitant intention to actually do what one is threatening to do, and this is an intention that, in the relevant circumstances, P_2 entails an ideally moral and rational agent could not adopt. Thus, we might suppose that, in this respect, at any rate, we would under certain circumstances be better off with leaders who were less, rather than more, rational or good. And this would be right, it seems to me, if we continue to rule out special technologies for bringing it about that one has intentions one could not, because of one's decency and rationality, adopt in the way one normally adopts the intentions one comes to have.

It is at this point, though, that I think we can begin to see the possibility for a new paradox of deterrence. For suppose that in the circumstances we are imagining, although we do not have the sort of special-effects technologies Kavka explicitly ruled out, we do have available to us at least one other means of trying to prevent our adversary from launching a first strike (one means, that is, other than the making of a sincere threat to retaliate if the first strike occurs): We can activate what I shall call an "automated retaliation device" – a device that will automatically initiate a retaliatory strike in the event of a first strike against us and that cannot be deactivated, at least for a certain period of time, once it has been activated. Obviously, if we had such a device available to us, we could consider using it, in place of an ordinary conditional threat, as a means of deterring our adversary from undertaking a first strike. For we could simply activate the device, telling our adversary, as we do so, *that* we are activating it and why (i.e., solely as a way of deterring her from launching the first strike).

There would be many obstacles, of course, in the path of a project devoted to justifying the use of such a device, particularly in circumstances of the sort we are imagining. Entering upon this project, though, is not part of my aim here. What I want to show here, rather, is that if there is indeed an argument against the justifiability of activating such a device in circumstances like those we have imagined, this argument will have to utilize some premise or set of premises over and above those used in our argument for P_2. For, interestingly enough, nothing in the latter argument precludes the possibility that a rational and wholly decent person could, consistent with her rationality and decency, activate the relevant device, in a situation of the sort we have imagined, despite the fact that, if I am right, that argument does indeed show, conclusively, that a rational and fully decent person could not adopt a *conditional intention* to retaliate as part of a threat strategy aimed at achieving exactly the same end as the automatic retaliation strategy would be aimed at achieving.[33]

This may at first seem crazy: how could it be that assumptions strong enough to make it impossible for a rational and decent individual to adopt a conditional intention to retaliate in the relevant circumstances, where this intention was part of an overall deterrent strategy of the kind just described, would not at the same time be sufficient to make it impossible for a rational and decent individual to activate a device that will ensure conditional retaliation in exactly similar circumstances (and for exactly the same purposes for which he would, if he could, be adopting the relevant intention)? To see how this could be – to see that it is in fact the case – we need to note, first, that, at bottom, what makes it impossible for a rational and decent person to adopt the requisite intention in the relevant sort of case is the fact that in adopting that intention she would be adopting an intention to do, subsequently, something that she admits it will be morally wrong, and therefore irrational, for her to do. And a basically rational person, we said, cannot, logically, adopt intentions to do things she grants it will be irrational for her to do. In the case of the automated retaliation strategy, by contrast, one is not called upon to adopt, for the sake of deterring the first strike, an intention to do, at some later point in time, what one grants it will be immoral, and therefore irrational, for one to do at that time. To be sure, one adopts and acts on a certain intention in this latter case – namely, the intention to activate the device as a means of deterring the first strike. And it may be that this intention, and the subsequent intentional action, is prohibited by sound moral principles. It is not prohibited, however, by P_2, nor by any of the principles that support P_2, since it is not, like the conditional intention in the original case, an intention to do what one grants it will be wrong to do when the time comes to do it.

Someone who believes that there is a conclusive argument against the use of an automated retaliation strategy in a case of the sort we are imagining – an argument based, say, on a prohibition against risking serious harm to one set of innocents in order to dramatically reduce the risk of serious harm to another set of innocents – might be tempted to argue that, given this argument, P_2 will then preclude the possibility of a rational and fully decent person adopting an intention to activate the device that needs to be activated for the automated retaliation strategy to work. This, however, while true, is not only consistent with my point but actually supports it. For what we have to assume in order to make P_2 relevant to the case that now interests us is that it would be wrong to activate the device – something about which P_2, and the principles that support it, are silent. P_2 precludes the possibility of a rational and decent person sincerely threatening to retaliate against a first strike, because we are assuming, for the sake of argument, that retaliating against a first strike would be morally wrong (partly, no doubt, because it would be pointless once the first strike had occurred, and partly because it would involve intentionally killing hundreds of thousands of innocent civilians). This assumption, however, does not itself entail the wrongfulness of intentionally risking the automatic occurrence of the same result that voluntary retaliation would involve; indeed, it is precisely the need for an independent argument for the wrongfulness of thus risking harm to the innocent that forces us to say that our argument for P_2 does not entail that a decent and rational individual could not, consistent with her decency and rationality, ensure, for deterrent purposes, the occurrence of exactly that eventuality that, in light of our argument, we can say she cannot sincerely threaten to bring about as part of a strategy for achieving the very same (and quite admirable) end.

Not convinced by the argument so far, and remembering that our own argument for P_2 depended on an appeal to an analogue of the so-called wrongful intentions principle, someone might be tempted to argue, at this point, as follows. Central to the argument for P_2 is the assumption that, if she intends to retaliate subsequent to a first strike, our imagined chief of state will be intending, now, to perpetrate, later, massive harms she knows (now) she will have no reason to inflict. This is part (we may suppose) of why we have been assuming, with Kavka, that her intention is an intention to do something that it will be wrong to do. But, then, the argument continues, exactly the same criticism can be made against the person who activates the automated retaliation device as a way of attempting to deter the first strike. For, in intentionally activating the device, she is intentionally bringing it about that massive harms will be caused to the innocent at a point in time when, we may suppose, no good will come from the imposition of those harms. Hence, like the ordinary threatener, the person who resorts to the automated retaliation strategy has "committed her will," as we might say, to massive needless harm to the innocent, as part of a strategy for preventing similar harms in the first place. She intends that the innocent shall suffer, in other words, should her strategy fail, and she intends this as part of the price of that very strategy.

As tempting as it is, though, this argument seems to me to be unsound. To see why, we need to note that what is objectionable about the agent's "will" in our first (ordinary threat) case is that it is committed, albeit conditionally, to the performance of an admittedly immoral action. The agent's will in the second (automated) case, by contrast, is not similarly directed – or so we must assume, at any rate, as long as we supposing that we do not yet have an argument for the wrongfulness of risking harm to one group of innocents in order to protect other innocents from harm. To be sure, the agent in the second case "accepts," we might say, the possible harm to the one group of innocents as the price of protecting the other group from harm. And it is this that makes it tempting to say that she, like the first agent, intends harm to the innocent as a way of protecting other innocents from harm. But the fact is that she does not intend *to harm* the innocent, at a point in time when harming them will be pointless, and that is the crucial difference.[34]

VI

Suppose I am right: for all our argument for P_2 tells us, an ideally rational and fully decent person could, consistent with her rationality and decency, activate a device that would ensure the destruction of the innocent, as part of a strategy to protect other innocents from wrongful harm, even though, according to us, she could not, consistent with her rationality and decency, adopt a conditional intention to impose those same harms on those same innocents as part of an exactly similar strategy to protect the other innocents from harm. Where's the paradox? As in the case of Kavka's paradoxes, I do not think the truth of this new claim is demonstrably inconsistent with the truth of some other, equally plausible moral claim. I do think this new claim is quite puzzling, though, and I am certain, from my own experience, that it is a claim that many people, philosophers and nonphilosophers alike, will be inclined to deny. For how could risking certain and quite terrible harm to the innocent be possible for a rational and decent individual, if, in exactly similar circumstances, that same individual would not be able, *qua* ideally rational and decent being, to adopt a conditional intention to do what the machine will do automatically in the analogous case?

I have tried to sketch the answer to this question, and thus "justify" this new "paradox," in the preceding section. Notice here, though, that we can say even more, at least if we take Kavka's point of view. For if we continue to assume, for the sake of argument, the truth of the moral principle briefly discussed in section III, according to which in certain circumstances utilitarian considerations override all other (nonutilitarian) considerations, it follows that in at least some circumstances of the sort we have been imagining, a rational and decent agent would not only be *able* to activate the automated retaliation device – she would be *obligated* to activate that device, and hence, *qua* rational and moral agent, she would activate it, despite the fact that, *qua* rational and decent person, she would not be able to adopt a conditional intention to retaliate, on her own, absent the device. For if conditions are such as to ensure application of Kavka's principle – and let us stipulate, for the sake of argument, that they are – and if the principle is taken to be obligation imposing as well as right conferring, as Kavka seemed inclined to say it is, then it follows that in such circumstances the agent would be obligated to act to prevent the one disaster by ensuring the conditional occurrence of the other, given that his only alternative is to do nothing, thus allowing the probability of the first strike to remain unchanged. And since we may suppose that an ideally rational and moral individual invariably does what she grants she is obligated to do, we must suppose that, given our current assumptions, this individual would in fact activate the device, rightly and rationally, despite the fact that, in an exactly analogous case, she would not, because she could not, make the corresponding threat (i.e., the sincere threat to retaliate, on her own, in the event of a first strike).[35]

So there is, I think, something deeply and interestingly puzzling, especially (but not exclusively) for someone with Kavka's views, about the fact that the permissibility of activating the relevant sort of device is independent of our (and his) argument against the possibility, in the case of an ideally rational and moral agent, of adopting the relevant sort of intention (the conditional intention to retaliate, that is to say, in the case where one is imagined using an ordinary-threat strategy to prevent the first attack rather than an automated retaliation strategy). And I think that showing this would have been important, because philosophically interesting, even if nothing followed from it as far as work in other areas of philosophy is concerned. Significantly, though, our results so far do have important implications for work in certain other areas of philosophy, and I want to conclude by showing briefly why I believe this is so.

VII

Imagine yourself stranded on a desert island with just one other person, under circumstances where it is reasonable for you to expect a rescue team to come to your aid, but unreasonable to expect them to get to you really quickly. In fact, suppose you can be fairly certain the rescuers will arrive before your provisions give out, but suppose, too, that you can count on this only because you and the other person plan to utilize those provisions very carefully. For a while, let us suppose, all goes well: you and your fellow islander stick to your rationing plan, and it looks as though your provisions will hold out until the expected arrival of your rescuers. As time goes by, though, you notice that your partner is beginning to feel the strain of too little to eat and drink. In fact, it is becoming increasingly clear to you, let us suppose, that he is thinking a lot about how nice it would be for him if he had the provisions entirely to himself. Indeed, let us suppose that, after a short time, it is quite clear that he will kill you, if he gets the chance, plausibly making it look like an accident, so that he can have all the food and drink for himself and at the same time avoid leaving any evidence of having done what it is now quite clear he plans to do.

What do you do? Obviously, if we continue to describe the case along the lines we have sketched so far, we can imagine you justifiably resisting a murderous attack quite violently – indeed, with deadly force, if necessary – in the event it occurs. We can also imagine, though, that you will want to try to prevent the initiation of such an attack, and we can imagine, as well, that it might occur to you that one way in which to try to do this would be to threaten your fellow islander with severe consequences in the event he tries to attack and fails (fails to succeed in killing you, that is to say). So let us suppose you try this latter strategy: you tell him that you will resist any unjustifiable attack against you, with extreme violence if need be, and you tell him, in addition, that if he attempts to murder you and fails, you will harm him very seriously indeed for that attempt. In fact, let us suppose that, knowing him as well as you do, you know that the only threat that's likely to significantly decrease the probability of an attack is a threat of death, and so you threaten to kill him if he attacks you, your sole motive in making this threat being the prevention of a murderous attack against yourself.

I have written elsewhere about when and why self-protective threats of this sort might be thought to be morally justifiable.[36] Here, I want to ask the reader simply to assume with me, for the sake of argument, that there are circumstances, not unlike those we have just imagined, in which some such threats might plausibly be said to be justifiable. An even more difficult issue then arises, if we imagine your partner attacking you, with intent to kill, despite your threat, and failing in his attempt. For then we face the question of whether you would be justified in carrying out your threat, and why.

This too is an issue I want mostly to ignore here, though it too is one about which I have written elsewhere.[37] Notice, though, that it is easy enough to imagine circumstances in which at least some of us, situated in your place subsequent to the latest (post-threat) attack, would feel that enforcing the threat is at best morally problematical. For suppose that, subsequent to this latest attack, it is clear that, having foiled it, you have no further reason to fear future attacks from your fellow islander: he has been so severely injured, say, as you justifiably fought to protect yourself, that there is no question of his attempting another attack before the rescue crew arrives. No doubt, some people in your situation in these circumstances would feel confident that they would be justified in enforcing the earlier threat – retributivists, for example, like Kant, who describes a case somewhat similar to ours and who insists that justice requires that your partner be executed for what he has done.[38] Retribution aside, though, many of us would feel, as I have indicated, that enforcing the earlier threat would be morally questionable in circumstances like these, especially if we add the assumption that your attacker is guaranteed never to be in a position to harm anyone at all once you are both rescued, plus the assumption that no one else will ever know that you made and then failed to enforce the relevant threat.

Now, imagine someone who feels not that it would be *doubtful* that one would be justified in enforcing the earlier threat in these circumstances, but who feels that it would clearly be *wrong* to enforce the threat in circumstances like these. And imagine this person facing a situation in which, even before he had a chance to make the relevant threat, it is clear that, if there is another attack and he survives it, his situation will be exactly as we have just imagined your situation: he will unquestionably have no forward-looking reason for enforcing the relevant threat. Suppose as well, though, that this person knows that unless he makes that threat, and makes it meaning to enforce it if it is ignored, he has no chance whatsoever of deterring his fellow islander from attempting a murderous attack. In these circumstances, it seems to me, our new protagonist is in a situation exactly analogous to one we have considered at length earlier – a situation in which P_2 entails that, insofar as we imagine him being a fully rational and morally virtuous individual, he will not be able to adopt the intention he has to adopt if he is to make the (sincere) threat he has to make to protect himself from a murderous attack. For that intention would be an intention to do what, by his lights, it would be morally wrong for him to do; and P_2 tells us that an ideally rational and fully virtuous person could not adopt an intention of this sort.

This is itself a rather interesting conclusion, it seems to me, though I shall not pursue its puzzling character here. (Its puzzling aspect is, of course, just an instance of the general puzzle that is Kavka's second paradox of deterrence.) Instead, I now want to indicate how all of this is relevant to the question of whether our new paradox has any interesting implications for work in philosophy outside of those areas in which it is most obviously based. And to do this, I want to begin by making the following observation: agreeing that the protagonist in the case just described would not, if we suppose him to be a fully rationally and ideally virtuous individual, be able to adopt the intention he needs to adopt if an ordinary threat strategy is to work (in protecting him from a[nother] murderous attack) does not entail agreeing that this person could not, consistent with his virtue and rationality, activate an automated retaliation device to protect himself in the way an ordinary threat would have protected him if he could have made an ordinary threat. This, of course, is just to repeat the lesson of our new paradox: what makes it impossible for a rational and decent person to adopt certain intentions, as part of a certain kind of deterrent strategy, does not necessarily make it impossible for such a person to undertake an automated retaliation strategy instead. There are imaginable circumstances, in other words, in which an ideally moral and rational agent would not be able to protect himself via an ordinary threat strategy but would be able, given the right assumptions, to protect himself via an automated retaliation strategy.

Suppose all this is right. It follows, I believe, that one recent, very powerful, and very promising theory of punishment cannot be correct. This, of course, is the theory according to which punishment is best thought of as a system of deterrent threats, and according to which we are justified in making and enforcing exactly those threats, in our efforts to deter crime, that we would be justified in programming an automated retaliation device to inflict instead, as part of a strategy that is aimed at achieving exactly the same end.[39] For, as the case imagined earlier makes clear, it is possible for a person to be in a situation where she would be justified in activating an automated retaliation device in an attempt to deter wrongful aggression against her, but where she would not be justified, at least by her own lights, in making and then *enforcing* an equivalent verbal threat.[40]

There are, of course, any number of objections that would have to be considered before the very brief remarks just sketched could be taken to be conclusive. So let me just assert here what I would try to show, given more time, on another occasion: there really are circumstances where, given certain not implausible assumptions, one would be justified in protecting oneself with a suitably constrained automated retaliation device, but where one would not be justified in both making and enforcing an analogous verbal threat, at least if we suppose, as we have been doing, that the decision whether or not subsequently to enforce that threat will be a free decision of the original threatener.[41]

VIII

Where are we left? I have tried to show where I think Kavka was right in his claims about the paradoxes of deterrence and where I think he was wrong. I have, in addition, suggested a new paradox, to be added to the other paradox that I think survives critical reflection on Kavka's work in this area. And, finally, I have tried to show how this new paradox, like the old one, is relevant to philosophical work in at least one area of current research other than that, or those, in which Kavka had already foreseen the application of his views. There are, I believe, other problems, outside Kavka's own areas of special interest, to which his work, and my modest contribution here, are also relevant, but limitations of time and space prevent me from pursuing these here. Suffice it to say that, in my view, the richness and wonderful implications of Kavka's work are still far from having been plumbed in anything more than an extremely preliminary way.

Notes

1. Gregory S. Kavka, "Some Paradoxes of Deterrence," *Journal of Philosophy* 75 (1978), 285–302. This essay has been widely reprinted and is currently available in

a number of different anthologies. It is reprinted in slightly revised form in Kavka's *Moral Paradoxes of Nuclear Deterrence* (Cambridge: Cambridge University Press, 1987), pp. 15–32; note, though, the one significant change in this revised version, discussed at some length in section III of the present chapter. Cited hereafter as "Paradoxes" and *Paradoxes*, respectively.

2. "Paradoxes," especially pp. 285–6.

3. Daniel M. Farrell, "On Some Alleged Paradoxes of Deterrence," *Pacific Philosophical Quarterly* 73 (1992), 114–36.

4. Daniel M. Farrell, "Strategic Planning and Moral Norms: The Case of Deterrent Nuclear Threats," *Public Affairs Quarterly* 1 (1987), 61–77; "Intention, Reason, and Action," *American Philosophical Quarterly* 26 (1989), 283–94; "Immoral Intentions," *Ethics* 102 (1992), 268–86; and "Utility-maximizing Intentions and the Theory of Rational Choice," *Philosophical Topics* 21 (1993), 53–78.

5. Kavka, "Paradoxes," p. 286; *Paradoxes*, p. 19. Words in braces, here and in the quotations that follow, are found in *Paradoxes* but not in the original essay.

6. A "sincere" threat, in this context, is a threat one means to keep – i.e., it is a threat one intends, as one makes the threat, to keep, when the time for action arrives.

7. Farrell, "On Some Alleged Paradoxes of Deterrence," pp. 117–18.

8. "Paradoxes," p. 288; *Paradoxes*, p. 19.

9. "Paradoxes," p. 294; *Paradoxes*, p. 24.

10. "Paradoxes," p. 295; *Paradoxes*, p. 25.

11. "Paradoxes," p. 289. Kavka's statement of this principle in the book is significantly different, as we shall see.

12. "Paradoxes," p. 294; *Paradoxes*, p. 24.

13. "Paradoxes," p. 298; *Paradoxes*, pp. 27–8.

14. In this section and the next, I borrow material from sections I and II of my essay "On Some Alleged Paradoxes of Deterrence," pp. 115–26.

15. "Paradoxes," pp. 286–91; *Paradoxes*, pp. 16–21.

16. "Paradoxes," p. 289; *Paradoxes*, p. 19.

17. *Paradoxes*, p. 19.

18. "Paradoxes," pp. 289–90; *Paradoxes*, pp. 19–20.

19. "Paradoxes," p. 289; *Paradoxes*, p. 19.

20. On the relevant notion of "commitment," see Farrell, "Strategic Planning and Moral Norms," pp. 62–5, and Michael E. Bratman, *Intention, Plans, and Practical Reason* (Cambridge, MA: Harvard University Press, 1987), esp. pp. 15–18 and 107–10. For a fuller development of the argument sketched here, see Farrell, "Strategic Planning and Moral Norms," pp. 62–6, and also Farrell, "Intention, Reason, and Action," pp. 283–4. Note that the point is not that one would be liable to opprobrium, according to this argument, for *bringing it about* that one has the relevant commitment but that one would be liable to opprobrium for *being* so committed once one has (perhaps justifiably) brought it about that one *is* so committed.

21. An argument very much like the argument that I have just sketched is briefly discussed by Jeff McMahan in "Deterrence and Deontology," *Ethics* 95 (1985), 522–3. Unfortunately, McMahan fails to note the difference between WIP and WIP*, much less between both of these and WIP**, defined shortly, and in fact his remarks in this otherwise extremely important essay are frequently undermined by this failure. (McMahan states the wrongful intentions principle in terms of WIP but often writes as though the principle he is discussing is WIP*.) The argument McMahan discusses is also problematical, *inter alia*, in that he supposes that what it aims to prove is that someone who intends to do wrong "but [who] is prevented by external circum-

stances from doing so" can still be "regarded as having done something wrong" (p. 523). The problem here, of course, is that what the considerations to which McMahan appeals prove is not that such a person has, in so intending, *done* wrong but, rather, that he is, in so intending, already liable to the moral opprobrium that someone who has done such a wrong can be said to bear.

22. For a fuller discussion of this issue, with explicit arguments against VPP, see my "Immoral Intentions," pp. 278–86.

23. "Paradoxes," p. 292; *Paradoxes,* p. 24. Material in brackets has been added for the sake of clarity.

24. "Paradoxes," p. 294; *Paradoxes,* p. 24.

25. "Paradoxes," p. 292; *Paradoxes,* p. 22.

26. Ibid.

27. Cf. my "Intention, Reason, and Action," pp. 283–4.

28. Cf. Bratman, *Intention, Plans, and Practical Reason,* pp. 15–18 and 107–10.

29. This is a summary of an argument that I elaborated in "Intention, Reason, and Action," pp. 287–90. Note that this argument depends on the assumption that momentarily adopting a commitment that would, if it lasted, be an intention to perform an irrational action is not the sort of thing that is likely, in and of itself, to bring it about that one is insufficiently rational to appreciate the incongruity between that commitment and the action toward which it is directed. I can think of no reason why we should suppose that this seemingly very plausible assumption is false, especially for cases where the individual in question is, apart from his momentary commitment to act irrationally, otherwise a basically rational individual, but obviously a fuller account of these matters would have to say more on this score. Notice, also, that my argument here is meant to apply only to intentions adopted in what I have elsewhere called "the normal way" (ibid.). Obviously, an agent could avoid the implications of the argument that I have just sketched if he could find a way to make himself unaware of the irrationality of his intended action or sufficiently irrational not to care about the irrationality of that action. Here I am supposing that these are not things one could do without special help – special drugs, for example, or behavioral conditioning, or something else of this sort. And notice, finally, that I am not supposing here that a rational person *could* be committed, in the relevant sense, to an irrational action, the only problem being that such a commitment must inevitably be undermined by reflection on the irrationality of the intended action. Rather, my point is that what might look like an instance, however momentary, of the relevant sort of commitment, on the part of an otherwise rational agent, could not in fact *be* the relevant kind of commitment in the case of a reflective, basically rational individual.

30. See the references in notes 3 and 4. In addition, see Farrell, "On Threats and Punishments," *Social Theory and Practice* 15 (1989), 125–54.

31. Gregory Kavka, "The Toxin Puzzle," *Analysis* 43 (1983), 33–6.

32. Cf. Farrell, "Intention, Reason, and Action," pp. 283–90, and "Utility-maximizing Intentions and the Theory of Rational Choice," pp. 53–60. (Note, incidentally, that we do not need P_2 in order to get the result I claim we can get. All we need is the principle embodied in premise (5). My argument here assumes, of course, with Kavka, that actually drinking the toxin, once one either had or did not have the $1 million, would clearly be irrational, regardless of whether or not one had managed to adopt, the day before, the intention to drink the toxin on the following day. This assumption has been challenged by a number of recent writers, though limitations of space prevent me from considering this issue here. See, in particular, David Gauthier,

"In the Neighborhood of the Newcomb-Predictor (Reflections on Rational Choice),"
Proceedings of the Aristotelian Society 89 (1988–9), 179–94, and Edward Mc-
Clennen, *Rationality and Dynamic Choice: Foundational Explorations* (Cam-
bridge: Cambridge University Press, 1990). I discuss these views critically in
"Utility-maximizing Intentions and the Theory of Rational Choice," pp. 60–77.

33. The argument that follows was first sketched, in a somewhat protean form, in my
"Strategic Planning and Moral Norms," pp. 66–73. I did not there, though, appreci-
ate the fact that my conclusion can be said to be genuinely paradoxical in the sense
I now believe Kavka to have had in mind when he used this term.

34. It is not clear to me that it is even correct to say that the agent in a case like this intends harm to the innocent in the event the device fails, but that is not an issue I can
pursue here. The point is that, even if we can say this, her situation is crucially different from the situation of someone who does intend to harm the innocent, need-
lessly, if her threat fails to deter the first strike. The latter individual is committed
to performing not just an immoral action but an irrational action, by our earlier argument, and that is what makes it impossible for a rational agent to make the commitment she has made (or to adopt the intention she has adopted). The former individual, by contrast, even if we say that she is committed to the suffering of the
innocent in the event her strategy should fail, and hence "intends" the suffering that
will ensue if her strategy fails, is not committed to performing what we can so far
say is either an immoral or an irrational act.

35. Notice that our argument for P_2 applies to utilitarians and nonutilitarians alike. The
point is that no ideally rational and moral individual could adopt the relevant intention, given that we are assuming, for whatever reason, that it is an intention to do
what that individual grants it would be morally wrong to do.

36. Farrell, "On Threats and Punishments"; "The Justification of Deterrent Violence,"
Ethics 100 (1990), 301–17; and "Deterrence and the Just Distribution of Harm,"
Philosophy and Social Policy 12 (1995), 220–40, reprinted in *The Just Society,* ed.
Ellen Frankel Paul, Fred D. Miller, Jr., and Jeffrey Paul (Cambridge: Cambridge
University Press, 1995).

37. Ibid.

38. Kant does not require that a prior threat have been made in order for retributive punishment to be appropriate. I should note that, contrary to a widespread misconcep-
tion, the theory of punishment that Kant defends in *The Metaphysics of Morals* is a
nonutilitarian deterrence-based theory, not a retributive theory in any ordinary sense
of the term. See especially *The Metaphysical Elements of Justice,* tr. John Ladd (Indianapolis: Bobbs-Merrill, 1965). For a relevant and extremely insightful analysis
of Kant's theory of punishment, see Sarah Holtman, "Toward Social Reform: Kant's
Penal Theory Reinterpreted," *Utilitas* 9 (1997), 3–21.

39. See especially Warren Quinn, "The Right to Threaten and the Right to Punish," *Philosophy and Public Affairs* 14 (1985), 327–73.

40. My argument here is, of necessity, very brief. For a much more careful treatment,
including a critical analysis of Quinn's view, see my essay "On Threats and Punishments."

41. For a defense of this claim, see, again, "On Threats and Punishments."

Rethinking the Toxin Puzzle

DAVID GAUTHIER

I

"As our beliefs are constrained by our evidence, so our intentions are constrained by our reasons for action."[1] With Gregory Kavka's conclusion to "The Toxin Puzzle" I have no quarrel. As a rational person, I can intend only what I expect to have reason to do. What follows from this? Kavka notes that "we are inclined to evaluate the rationality of the intention both in terms of its consequences and in terms of the rationality of the intended action" (p. 36). Combining his conclusion with his claim about evaluation, we should infer that an intention is rational if and only if it is directed at an action that would be rational and no alternative intention directed at an action that would be rational has more favorable consequences. And with this I have no quarrel. But we could easily be misled by the way in which I have expressed this inference. For we could suppose that whether an intended action is rational can be determined independently of and prior to considering whether the intention to perform that action has best consequences. And this I deny.

Consider the toxin puzzle. I shall be paid "one million dollars tomorrow morning if, at midnight tonight, [I] *intend* to drink" a vial of "toxin tomorrow afternoon" that "will make [me] painfully ill for a day, but will not threaten [my] life or have any lasting effects" (p. 33).[2] The only problematic feature of this account that need detain us concerns how my intention is to be established. Kavka postulates a "'mind-reading' brain scanner and computing device" that I am to believe "will correctly the presence or absence of the relevant intention" (p. 34). But since I doubt that such a machine is possible, I shall fall back on the claim that I am well acquainted with the person who must decide whether to make the payment and am convinced from both firsthand experience and the testimony of others that she is an extraordinarily astute judge of the real intentions of her fellows, so that I should be foolish indeed to think that at midnight tonight I could deceive her about whether I intend to drink the toxin.

Kavka thinks that I have good reason to intend to drink the toxin (since so intending will almost certainly gain me $1 million). He also thinks that I have no reason to drink it (since drinking it will gain me nothing and make me ill for a day). If, as he says, "our intentions are constrained by our reasons for action" (p. 36), then it seems that we must conclude that I cannot (rationally) intend to drink the toxin. Even though the intention would have best consequences, it is not directed at an action that it would be rational to perform.

But I disagree. I grant, of course, that drinking the toxin does not have best, or even good, consequences, so that I have no *outcome*-oriented reason to drink it. But drinking the toxin is part of the *best course of action* – in terms of its consequences – that I can embrace as a whole. For I do better to intend to drink the toxin, even at the cost of actually drinking it, than not to intend to drink the toxin. And although I should do better still to intend to drink the toxin but not drink it, I cannot embrace this as a single course of action.[3] To be sure, I am "perfectly free to change [my] mind after receiving the money and not drink the toxin" (p. 34). I know this at the outset. And I know that I should like to change my mind. But if I am rational, and understand my situation, this knowledge is of no use to me. Either I suppose that I shall have no reason to drink the toxin, in which case insofar as I am rational I cannot have the mind to do so, or I suppose that I shall have reason to drink it, in which case I can have the mind to do so but no good reason to change it. Changing my mind is not part of a course of action that I can embrace.

Intending to drink the toxin is part of my best course of action. And come tomorrow afternoon, I can and shall still recognize this. Tomorrow afternoon I shall have no ground for doubting that intending to drink the toxin is part of my best course of action, and so I shall not then have good reason to change my course of action. Intending to drink the toxin, I shall drink it. My reason for drinking it will be that drinking it is part of the best course of action that I could embrace as a whole – best not only prospectively, but still best at the time of drinking.

As a rational agent, I can intend only what I expect to have reason to do.[4] I can intend to drink the toxin, because I expect to have reason to drink it – not on account of its own consequences, but because it is part of the course of action with best consequences. The intention to drink the toxin is rational, because it is directed at an action that is rational and has best consequences among intentions so directed. Note in this connection that the intention not to drink the toxin is also directed at an action that is rational – since if I do not intend to drink the toxin I have no reason whatsoever to drink it. But of course, intending not to drink the toxin has consequences that are not as favorable as the consequences of intending to drink it, and so is not rational.

II

Let me spell out the crucial steps in my argument. (A) It is rational for me to form an intention if (i) were I to form it, I should expect to have adequate reason to execute it, and (ii) among alternative intentions satisfying condition (i) it has best consequences. (B) I should expect to have adequate reason to execute an intention if I should expect that, were I to execute it, I should be doing better than had I not formed it.

Consider now the intention to drink the toxin. Were I to form it, I should expect to have adequate reason to execute it, since I should expect to be doing better were I to execute it than had I not formed it. So condition (i) is satisfied. And compared with the alternatives – intending not to drink the toxin or not intending anything (either of which also satisfies condition (i)) – it has best consequences. So it is rational for me to form it.

I claim that this is the correct resolution of the toxin puzzle. On any account, the situation is puzzling – either because one supposes that I cannot form the enriching intention, or because one supposes that I have reason to perform an action that has only undesirable consequences. But the puzzle arises because intending here has consequences independent of those of the intended action but of greater overall significance. We do not easily accommodate our intuitions about what is rational to such situations. We need to reflect on the role that deliberation plays in enabling a person to realize his overall concerns, and to appeal to this role in assessing his reasons for intending and acting. Someone who took himself to have no reason at all to drink the toxin, because he had no *outcome-oriented* reason to drink it, would be deliberating ineffectively in a situation in which what mattered most to the realization of his concerns was not what he did but what he intended.

A person deliberates in order to decide on and realize his concerns. In the toxin puzzle we assume that the only relevant concerns arise from the money that may be gained and the illness that may be incurred, and that the former outweighs the latter. The considerations that weigh with a person in determining what to do in order to realize his concerns are what he takes to be his reasons for acting. But he may be mistaken. His real reasons for acting are those considerations that would weigh with him in deliberation *directed effectively* at the realization of his concerns. These of course include, but are not restricted to, outcome-oriented considerations.

To guard against misunderstanding my account of deliberation, it is essential to emphasize that deliberative reasons relate to effective direction. They are not simply whatever considerations would need to weigh with someone if he is to realize his concerns.[5] If I were subject to a being whose power enables her to control what happens to me and whose astuteness enables her to judge accurately my deliberative procedures, then I might be unable to engage in rational deliberation, directed effectively at the realization of my concerns. For she might see to it that, on the one hand, if I take her directives as reasons for acting in themselves, independently of how they relate to my concerns, then I should do well, whereas on the other hand, if I consider how best to realize my concerns, I should do badly. Deliberation *directed* at the realization of my concerns would then be ineffective, whereas the *effective* realization of my concerns would depend on deliberation that ignores them. Subjected to such a being, I should do best were I to believe that her directives in themselves afforded me reasons for acting. My belief would of course be false. Her directives would be relevant to my deliberation not in themselves, but only in virtue of her power to relate how well I do to how I deliberate. But were I to believe this, I should do badly.

The pragmatic standard for rational deliberation and reasons for acting that I embrace does not lead to the absurd view that rationality is simply a matter of what in fact pays. A being of sufficient power and astuteness could frustrate any attempt to deliberate rationally and could make a particular form of deliberation pay, even though it was bad or irrational. I shall consider presently whether such a being manifests herself in the toxin puzzle.

III

It is rational, I claim, to form the intention to drink the toxin, and to drink it. More generally, it is rational to form an intention, if one reasonably expects at the time that forming and executing it will better realize one's objectives than not forming it; and it is rational to execute an intention, if one reasonably expects at that time that one's objectives will be better realized after executing it than they would have been had one not formed it. So, if you will confer some benefit on me if you expect that I shall reciprocate, and I do better to receive the benefit and reciprocate than not to receive it, and I believe that offering a sincere assurance that I shall reciprocate is likely to be both necessary and sufficient to give you the expectation that I shall reciprocate, then it is rational for me to form the intention to reciprocate that a sincere assurance requires. And if you do confer the benefit on me, and when the time comes to reciprocate I still judge that reciprocating leaves me better off than I could have expected to be had I not sincerely assured you of my intention to reciprocate, then it is rational for me to reciprocate, even if some other action would then better realize my objectives.

There is an important difference between reciprocation, as I have characterized it, and the situation envisaged in the toxin puzzle. In a situation calling for reciprocation, your concern is not with what I intend but with what I do. Of course you must act before I act, so you cannot make what you do depend on what I do, but you take my assurance of my intention as justifying your belief about what I shall do. You have no concern with my intention as such, but only with its evidential value for my prospective action. But in the toxin puzzle, the concern of the person who offers the $1 million is strictly with my intention, and not at all with my action. As Kavka insists, I am "perfectly free to change [my] mind after receiving the money and not drink the toxin" (p. 34).

Intention plays only a secondary role in reciprocation. Indeed, in many contexts we may dispense with any reference to it. In situations in which one person will benefit another in the expectation of an appropriate return, a rational deliberator will normally take herself to have adequate reason to reciprocate where its cost to her is less than the benefit she receives. For if she characteristically deliberates in this way, then others who know her will expect an appropriate return and will not need to seek any assurance from her of her intention. And when she is asked for an assurance, she can offer it simply because she takes herself to have adequate reason to reciprocate. Rather than forming an intention to reciprocate which then gives her reason to do so, she recognizes a reason to reciprocate on which she can base her intention to do so.

Mutual benefit through reciprocation is a familiar and readily intelligible form of interaction. A person can understand the rationale of engaging in such interaction as a reliable reciprocator, even without valuing the interpersonal relationships that are based, or partially based, in reciprocation. She can see the benefit of her acts of reciprocation, even though it is not *her* benefit. The toxin puzzle does not represent any common mode of interaction. We are not typically willing to reward others for their intentions when we have no interest in or expect no benefit from the performance of the intended actions. Indeed, we may see an attempt to exercise a form of thought control in the offer of such a reward, especially for an intention to act in a way that is harmful to the agent.

But is there such an attempt? Consider an alternative puzzle, which does seem more directly to involve an attempt at thought control. Suppose that what is required of me, if I am to receive $1 million tomorrow morning, is not that at midnight tonight I intend to drink a vial of toxin tomorrow afternoon, but rather that at midnight tonight I believe that I shall have good or sufficient reason to drink a vial of toxin tomorrow afternoon. If, as I have assumed, I can intend only what I expect to have good reason to do, then this revision may seem to make no difference. For if having the belief is necessary for forming the intention, I can be rewarded for having the intention only if I also have the belief. Or rather, this holds insofar as my intention is rational. For I may simply unthinkingly intend to do something that, were I to reflect, I should recognize that I did not expect to have reason to do. But since our concern is with rational agency, we may put this qualification aside.

And now there does seem to be a problem. Considering whether to form the intention to drink the toxin, I reflect on the benefits of intending even at the cost of performing, in relation to not intending, and I make up my mind to drink – or so I claim. But considering whether to believe that I shall have good reason to drink the toxin, what do I do? Do I reflect on the benefits of so believing, even at the cost of performing, in relation to not believing? This does not lead me to adopt the belief. For believing is believing *true,* and reflecting on the benefits of believing that I have reason to drink the toxin seems quite irrelevant to determining whether the belief is true. It may seem plausible to claim that if I would benefit from forming an intention, despite the cost of executing it, then

I have reason to form and (if all turns out as I expect) carry out the intention. But it does not seem plausible to claim that if I would benefit from adopting a belief, despite the cost of acting in accordance with it, then I have reason to adopt and (if all turns out as I expect) act on the belief.

It is not valid to argue: p, because it would pay me to believe that p. Substituting "I have a reason to drink the toxin" for p does not improve the argument. I do not have a reason to drink the toxin because it would pay me to believe that I do. And no other reason to drink the toxin seems in the offing. So if what is required for me to receive $1 million is that I believe myself to have reason to drink the toxin, then it would seem that I am unable, as a rational person, to acquire the belief and gain the $1 million.[6] But this argument moves too quickly. For it ignores the possibility that I can give myself a reason to drink the toxin, and so come rationally to believe that I have such a reason. In some cases p may be such that, if it would pay me to believe that p, I can bring about p, and thereby come rationally to believe that p. Is my having a reason to drink the toxin such a case?

Can I give myself a reason to drink the toxin? It may seem that I can do so by forming the intention to drink it. Although in most situations I would form an intention by considering the outcome-oriented reasons for performing the intended act, here I recognize that the intention has consequences of its own, and so I consider the entire course of action – intention and execution. And, as in the original version of the toxin puzzle, it may seem that the best course of action that I can adopt as a whole, whether I consider the choice prospectively or at the time of performance, is to intend to drink the toxin and to drink it. But alas, this is not so. For recall that it is rational for me to intend to drink the toxin only because I expect to have adequate reason to drink it, and that I expect to have adequate reason to drink it because (and, in the circumstances, only because) I expect that I should do better were I to drink it than had I not formed the intention to drink it. The likely effect of my forming the intention is that I gain $1 million. In the revised puzzle, forming the intention does not have this effect. What would gain me $1 million would be believing that I had reason to drink the toxin.

In the situation of the original puzzle, I believe reasonably that, were I to form the intention to drink the toxin, I should have reason to drink it. And having formed the intention, I believe reasonably that I shall have reason to drink the toxin tomorrow afternoon. Forming the intention gives me reason to execute it. But it does so because forming the intention enables me to gain $1 million. My reason for executing the intention is explained by the beneficial effect of forming it. In the revised puzzle this is not so. Forming the intention has no beneficial effect, and so gives me no reason to execute it. I have no basis for believing that I have reason to drink the toxin.

So the earlier analysis is confirmed: in the revised puzzle, I cannot give myself reason to drink the toxin, and so am unable, as a rational person, to acquire the belief that I have such reason. Although neither intentions nor beliefs can be produced to order, there are significant differences in the conditions that must be met for them to be rationally formed, and these are revealed by comparing the original and revised puzzles.

The comparison should help allay the concern that there is any attempt at thought control in the original puzzle. Rewarding someone for the formation of an intention is not rewarding him for the formation of a belief. The deliberation that leads to forming – and executing – the intention does not involve the acquisition of a belief on grounds of utility rather than truth. And it has a parallel in deliberation about reciprocating benefits, even though intention plays a different and lesser role in reciprocation.

IV

But, as I have insisted, the parallel between the toxin puzzle and benefit reciprocation is by no means a complete one. And it is not only the role of intention that differs between the two. There is a deep structural difference, which emerges if we try to conceptualize the toxin puzzle as involving an exchange of benefits. For if we do this, then the benefit that I confer, in return for the $1 million, can be only the formation of the intention to drink the toxin. Drinking the toxin is explicitly dismissed as of no concern or relevance. But if formation of the intention is the "benefit," then it does not directly involve reciprocation. In a situation calling for reciprocation, you are prepared to confer a benefit on me if you expect me to return it. I am the second performer, and the problem lies in establishing my reason for benefiting you. But in the toxin puzzle, the person offering the $1 million is prepared to confer a benefit on me if I have already "benefited" her by forming the intention to drink the toxin. I am the first performer. The problem lies in the peculiar nature of my "performance" – in the fact that I can rationally perform only if I take myself to have reason to carry out a further act that is costly to me and confers no benefit on the other party.

We may contrast the toxin puzzle with a Newcomb problem. In a standard Newcomb problem, a person whose astuteness in judging her fellows makes her an excellent predictor of their choices offers me the opportunity to take only an opaque box, or an opaque box and a second transparent box containing $1,000. If she has predicted that I will take only the opaque box, she has put the familiar $1 million in it; if she has predicted that I will take both boxes, she has put nothing in the opaque box. Here the parallel with reciprocation is much closer. The person offering the choice is prepared to benefit me if she expects that I shall then "benefit" her by taking only the opaque box. Now, the problem is not usually presented in these terms. A person who thought of a Newcomb problem as involving reciprocation, and who correctly understood the rationale for being a reciprocator, would, I think, be disposed to take only the opaque box.

But of course this way of conceptualizing the problem can be undermined if the predictor makes clear that her interest in the situation is simply in the experimental study of choice behavior – that I should not think of myself as benefiting her by taking only the opaque box. (After all, if she thinks that I shall choose only the opaque box, it will cost her $1 million.) Nevertheless, the problem shares the structure of reciprocation situations. Just as it is rational for me to form the intention to make a return, so that you, recognizing my intention, will have good reason to benefit me, so it is rational for me to form the intention to take only the opaque box, so that the experimenter, recognizing my intention, will have good reason to put $1 million in it.

The toxin puzzle is not a Newcomb problem. Consider, then, a different comparison. Sometimes one person acts to benefit another with the expectation of an appropriate return, but also with the recognition that he is incurring a subsequent cost that in itself is unnecessary to the exchange of benefits. You are strapped for cash; I advance you some money, with the explicit expectation that you will make yourself available to house-sit for me sometime next summer. But in advancing you the cash, I knowingly run myself short, so that I have to pay late fees and interest charges on some of my bills. Even with these charges I consider our exchange worthwhile, but I should of course avoid them if I could. Now this situation has a structure similar to that of the toxin puzzle, except of course that when my bills come due I cannot choose but accept the fees and charges, whereas tomorrow afternoon I can choose not to drink the toxin.

Of course, if I were to find myself after all able to pay my bills on time, I would welcome the opportunity to do so. With this in mind, one may be tempted to think that the toxin puzzle provides a similarly welcome opportunity. Just as I expect to incur late fees and interest charges, so I expect to incur a day's illness from the toxin. But when the time to drink comes, I realize with relief that I can avoid the cost. Why should I not take advantage of my good fortune? Why should I not look upon drinking the toxin as an unwelcome aftereffect that, happily, I can avoid?

But there is a crucial difference between the toxin puzzle and the usual situations with unwelcome aftereffects. In our example, I make you an advance in the expectation that I shall unfortunately run myself short, but making the advance is in no way affected by whether I have such an expectation. In the toxin puzzle, I form the intention to drink the toxin in the expectation that I shall drink it, and here forming the intention requires that I have this expectation. If, realizing in advance that drinking the toxin is unnecessary to gaining the $1 million, I think that I therefore have no reason to drink, then I no longer have the expectation that I shall drink, and I cannot rationally form the intention to drink.

An unreflective person, faced with the toxin puzzle, might not think that he will actually be in a position to choose whether to drink the toxin after the decision whether to put $1 million in his bank account has been made and might, then, simply form the intention to drink because it seemed obviously advantageous to do so. Such a person might come to realize that he would have a choice, with nothing to gain by choosing to drink, only after midnight had passed, and he would have every reason then to abandon his intention and so not to drink the toxin. He would have had the intention at the time that mattered and would have no further use for it. But in forming his intention he would not have deliberated in a fully rational way about his situation. Rationally forming an intention requires looking ahead to its execution and considering whether one may expect to have reason to carry it out.[7] We need not suppose that the person who offers to reward the intention to drink the toxin limits her offers to rational deliberators. But the thought that some persons could gain the $1 million without drinking the toxin by misrepresenting the situation as one with an unwelcome aftereffect that at first seems unavoidable but later proves not to be is of no use to those whose correct understanding of the situation prevents this misrepresentation.

It may seem puzzling that someone who has considered her reasons for and against drinking the toxin, in forming the intention to drink it, will have good reason to drink it when the time comes, whereas someone who considers his reasons for and against drinking the toxin only when the time comes will have good reason not to drink it. Surely one's reasons for and against drinking the toxin do not change. And indeed, construed narrowly they do not. What does change is the context within which these reasons are weighed. The person who, in forming her intention, considers her reasons for and against drinking the toxin assesses her course of action – intention and execution – as a whole. She asks herself whether she has good reason to drink the toxin as part of her course of action, and, in concluding that she does, she recognizes that her reasons for forming the intention to drink outweigh her reasons for not drinking. And once she undertakes a course of action as a whole, she must rationally continue to assess her particular actions as part of that whole, unless she comes to have reason to abandon her course of action. On the other hand, the person who considers his reasons for and against drinking the toxin only when it comes time to decide whether or not to drink has not assessed and chosen his course of action as a whole. If he has formed the intention to drink the toxin, he has done so without deliberating about executing his intention. For him, the choice of whether or not to drink is not a choice within a course of action that he has undertaken. And so he considers only his reasons for and against drinking the toxin considered in itself, concluding, of course, that he has good reason not to drink.

V

The nature of the situation exemplified by the toxin puzzle, as it emerges from our discussion, is this: if I benefit the other party, then she will benefit me in return; the benefit I confer on her leads to an aftereffect for me that is unwelcome (though worth the benefit I receive), which I am aware of, which I know I must choose to bring about or avoid, but which, if I am to confer the benefit, I must intend to bring about. In the toxin puzzle, the benefit is of course the intention to bring about the unwelcome aftereffect, but what is essential, I propose, is only that the benefit requires that I have this intention, not that the benefit be the intention itself.

When we generalize the toxin puzzle in this way, we can use it to illustrate the role of future-directed intentions in rational deliberation. Usually, no doubt, a person adopts such an intention on the basis of what she expects to be her reasons for performing the intended act. She deliberates, as Michael Bratman says, "about what to *do* then, not what to intend now, though of course a decision about what to do later leads to an intention now so to act later."[8] But "usually" is not "always," and in situations such as that of the toxin puzzle a person may adopt an intention on the basis of her present reasons for performing an act that requires it. Now, of course she may not rationally ignore what she expects to be her reasons for – and against – performing the intended act. Nor may she simply treat her present reasons for performing the act requiring the intention as overriding those reasons. She must consider, in her deliberations, both the intention-requiring act and the intention-executing act – and it is important in treating the general case to recognize that the required intention may be conditional, so that she will have to choose whether or not to execute it only if some condition is satisfied.

Deliberating from her present standpoint, she may first suppose that she has good reason to perform the intention-requiring act if, taking for granted that she would perform the intention-executing act should the question of performing it arise, she expects to do better than if she performs any alternative act. But to deliberate in this manner is to assume that, should the question of performing the intention-executing act arise, she will have adequate reason to perform it simply because she *expected* to do better at the outset by performing the intention-requiring act. *But this expectation may have been falsified.* It may be that she expected to do better because she expected that the question of performing the intention-executing act would not arise.

Consider this variant of the toxin puzzle. Suppose that persons with an extremely rare genetic configuration would be permanently disabled by drinking the toxin. I have no reason to believe that I have this rare configuration – the odds against it are 10 million to 1 – and I think the minuscule risk of being disabled by the toxin worth running in order to gain $1 million. But tomorrow noon, before I actually decide whether to drink the toxin, a doctor will examine me to determine whether I have this configuration. If I were found to have it, then I should be stark bonkers to go ahead and drink the toxin, whether I have $1 million in my bank account or not. I should be far worse off were I to drink than if I had not formed the intention to do so. Even if it would be rational for me to drink the toxin, knowing that I had a 1 in 10 million chance of being disabled by it, it would not be rational, knowing that I was the 1 in 10 million who would be disabled by it. And realizing all this now, I cannot rationally form an intention to drink that would extend to the case in which I were found to have the adverse genetic configuration.

If the expectation that I shall do better to perform the intention-requiring act than any alternative is falsified at the time that I must decide whether to perform the intention-executing act, so that I should not only do better not to perform it, but have done better never to have performed the intention-requiring act, then it is not rational for me to perform the intention-executing act. But I can form an intention rationally only if I expect to have reason to execute it, and so I cannot form an intention rationally if I am aware that it would apply to circumstances in which I should do worse executing it than had I not adopted it. In the toxin puzzle, I can rationally intend to drink only in circumstances in which I should expect to do better to drink than had I not formed the intention to do so.

Rational deliberation concerning future-directed intentions thus must consider both the formation and the execution of the intention. At the time of formation, may one rationally expect to do better overall by performing the intention-requiring act than by performing any alternative? At the time of execution, may one rationally expect to do better by performing the intention-executing act than one would have done had one not performed the intention-requiring act? Deliberatively, the second question must be resolved prior to the first. Only intentions that one expects one would do better to execute than one would have done had one not formed them are eligible for adoption.

The toxin puzzle may still occasion unease. Is it – can it be – really rational to drink the toxin, when all that one accomplishes by drinking it is to make oneself ill for a day? Yes, indeed it can, in the quite unusual circumstances in which the question whether to drink arises. I have tried to show that deliberation about the formation of the intention to drink the toxin, and about the subsequent execution of the intention, may be accommodated in a more general account of deliberation about future-directed intentions. This more general account has a pragmatic rationale in the role that deliberation plays in directing persons to act in ways that best fulfill their overall concerns. Good deliberators should drink up!

Notes

1. Gregory S. Kavka, "The Toxin Puzzle," *Analysis* 43 (1983), 33–6, at 36. Cited hereafter in parentheses in the text, with page number.
2. I have substituted the first for the second person.
3. More precisely, I cannot do this straightforwardly. I might of course be able to arrange to be hypnotized so that I would intend to drink the toxin, and then to be released

from the hypnosis before actually drinking it. And if such hypnosis were available at a cost less than that of a day's illness, no doubt I should do well to avail myself of it. But it need not be – and for the purposes of the present argument we may assume that it is not – available.

4. I take this to express a conceptual truth about intention: an agent rationally intends to do only what she expects that it will be rational for her to do. For present purposes I must leave this as an assumption of my argument.

5. Thus, what I said in another essay – "deliberative procedures are rational if and only if the effect of employing them is maximally conducive to one's life going as well as possible" – needs emendation. As a first approximation, we might say that deliberative procedures are rational if and only if they are effectively directed to making one's life go as well as possible. David Gauthier, "Assure and Threaten," *Ethics* 104 (1994), pp. 620–721, 701.

6. Recall that I am assuming that unorthodox methods of belief acquisition, unrelated to the truth of the belief acquired, such as hypnosis, are unavailable.

7. An agent who formed her intentions without looking ahead to their execution and considering whether she might expect to have reason to carry them out would not, in general, be forming them in a way effectively directed to realize her concerns. To be sure, she would do better in the unusual circumstances of the toxin puzzle. One might, then, think that a truly rational agent would normally form her intentions while looking ahead to their execution but would refrain from doing this if faced with a situation such as the toxin puzzle. But alas, she could realize the benefits of refraining only after she had looked ahead. And, as rational, she could intend only what she would expect to have reason to do.

8. Michael E. Bratman, *Intention, Plans, and Practical Reason* (Cambridge, MA: Harvard University Press, 1987), p. 103.

Toxin, Temptation, and the Stability of Intention

MICHAEL E. BRATMAN

I. Instrumentally Rational Planning Agency

We frequently settle in advance on prior, partial plans for future action, fill them in as time goes by, and execute them when the time comes. Such planning plays a basic role in our efforts to organize our own activities over time and to coordinate our own activities with those of others. These forms of organization are central to the lives we want to live.[1]

Not all purposive agents are planning agents. Nonhuman animals who pursue their needs and desires in the light of their representations of their world may still not be planning agents. But it is important that we are planning agents. Our capacities for planning are an all-purpose means, basic to our abilities to pursue complex projects, both individual and social.

Why do we need to settle on prior plans in the pursuit of organized activity? A first answer is that there are significant limits on the time and attention we have available for reasoning.[2] Such resource limits argue against a strategy of

An earlier version of this essay was presented at the conference held in honor of Gregory Kavka ("Rationality, Commitment, and Community," Feb. 10–12, 1995, University of California, Irvine). A revised version was presented at the March 1995 Pacific Division meeting of the American Philosophical Association, and parts of that version were presented in my 1995 Potter Lecture at Washington State University. The present essay is a substantially revised version of the APA paper. A number of the ideas in this essay were also presented, and usefully criticized, in yet-earlier papers given at Yale University, the University of North Carolina at Chapel Hill, NYU, Rutgers University, Johns Hopkins University, the University of Maryland, and the University of Arizona. The paper, in very roughly its present form, was presented and usefully criticized in March 1996 at Davidson College and Duke University, and at the University of California at Berkeley School of Law Workshop on Rationality and Society in November 1996. I have greatly benefited from the comments and criticisms of many people, including Bruce Ackerman, Nomy Arpaly, Lawrence Beyer, John Broome, Daniel Farrell, Claire Finkelstein, Gerald Gaus, Olav Gjelsvik, Jean Hampton, Gilbert Harman, John Heil, Thomas Hill, Frances Kamm, Keith Lehrer, Edward McClennen, Alfred Mele, Elijah Millgram, Christopher Morris, Michael Pendlebury, John Pollock, Samuel Scheffler, Tim Schroeder, David Velleman, and Gideon Yaffe. I have learned a lot from a series of exchanges – formal and informal – with David Gauthier. Special thanks go to Geoffrey Sayre-McCord for a long and extremely helpful discussion. Final work on this essay was completed while the author was a Fellow at the Center for Advanced Study in the Behavioral Sciences. I am grateful for financial support provided by the Andrew W. Mellon Foundation.

constantly starting from scratch – they argue against a strategy of never treating prior plans as settling a practical question. A second answer is that our pursuit of organization and coordination depends on the predictability to us of our actions.[3] Coordinated, organized activity requires that we be able reliably to predict what we will do; and we need to be able to predict this despite both the complexity of the mechanisms underlying our behavior and our cognitive limitations in understanding those mechanisms. In treating prior plans as settling practical questions we make our conduct more predictable to cognitively limited agents like us by simplifying the explanatory structures underlying our actions.

Intelligent planning agents may differ in their desires, cares, commitments, and concerns. They may, in particular, endorse various noninstrumental, substantive ideals of steadfastness, of sticking to one's prior plans in the face of challenge.[4] But we can ask what "instrumental rationality" – rationality in the pursuit of one's desires, cares, commitments, and concerns – requires of planning agents, despite possible differences in those desires, cares, commitments, and concerns.[5] A theory of instrumentally rational planning agency may not exhaust all that is to be said about rational intentions and plans. But it will, if it is successful, characterize important structures of rational planning agency that are, as it is said, neutral with respect to diverging conceptions of the good.

Such a theory needs to be responsive to a fundamental tension. On the one hand, a planning agent settles in advance what to do later. On the other hand, she is an agent who, whatever her prior plans, normally retains rational control over what she does when the time comes. Following through with one's plan is not, after all, like following through with one's tennis swing. We need to do justice to both these aspects of planning agency.[6]

II. A Basic Model

A planning agent, we may suppose, has a background of values, desires, cares, and concerns.[7] These support considered rankings of various kinds of alternatives, in light of relevant beliefs. I will call such rankings *evaluative rankings*. These rankings express the agent's considered ordering at a time, an ordering she sees as a candidate for shaping relevant choices.

A planning agent is in a position to have an evaluative ranking of alternative actions available beginning at a given time. She is also in a position to have an evaluative ranking of alternative plans for acting over time, and of alternative general policies. As a planning agent she will sometimes decide on a future-directed plan or policy. This involves settling on – and so, in an important sense, being committed to – ways of acting in the future. She might, for example, settle on a detailed plan for an anticipated job interview; and she might settle in advance on a general policy about, say, alcohol consumption. In settling on such plans or policies she comes to have relevant intentions to act in specified ways in specified future circumstances.

By settling now what she will do later a planning agent puts herself in a position to plan appropriate preliminary steps and means, and to filter options that are incompatible with planned action. This will work only if her plans are to some extent stable and she is not constantly reconsidering her prior decisions – not constantly starting from scratch. A theory of instrumentally rational planning agency is in part a theory of intention and plan stability: a theory of when an instrumentally rational planning agent should or should not reconsider and abandon a prior intention.

Many important issues about the rational stability of prior intentions concern appropriate strategies, given limitations of time and attention, for responding to unanticipated information that one's prior planning did not take into account.[8] Perhaps I settled on a plan for an interview on the assumption that Jones would be the interviewer. When I get to the interview, I discover that Smith has taken her place. Should I stop to reconsider and, perhaps, replan? Here issues about our resource limits and the costs of reconsideration and replanning loom large. And here it seems natural to have a broadly pragmatic, two-tier model: we seek general habits and strategies of reconsideration that are, in the long run, effective in the pursuit of what we (rationally) desire. In a particular case we reasonably implement such pragmatically grounded general habits and strategies and, depending on the case, reconsider or refrain from reconsideration. This means that a planning agent may sometimes rationally follow through with a prior plan even though she would have rationally abandoned that plan if she had reconsidered it in light of relevant unanticipated information.

What about, in contrast, cases in which one's circumstances are, in all relevant respects, those for which one has specifically planned? Here it may seem natural simply to say that if one's plan was rational when formed, then surely it would be rational, barring relevant unanticipated information or change in basic desires or values, to execute it in those circumstances for which one specifically planned. But the issues here are complex.

III. Autonomous Benefits: Toxin

Begin with Gregory Kavka's ingenious toxin case.[9] A billionaire has access to a technology that allows her to discern other people's intentions with almost flawless accuracy. She credibly offers to give me a lot of money on Tuesday if I form the intention on Monday to drink a disgusting but nonlethal toxin on Wednesday. I would be more than willing to drink the toxin in order to get the money. However, to get the money I do not need to drink the toxin; I just need to intend on Monday to drink it. But I need to arrive at this intention in a clear-headed way and without exploiting any external mechanisms (e.g., a side bet).

I would love to form this intention, but I have a problem. The benefit of the intention is, to use Kavka's term, "autonomous":[10] It does not depend causally on my actually executing the intention. I know that when Wednesday arrives I will already either have the money or I will not. In either case it seems that on Wednesday I will have no good reason to drink the stuff, and a very good reason not to, in precisely the circumstances in which I would have planned to drink it.[11] So it is not clear that I can rationally form the intention in the first place, despite its autonomous benefits.[12]

There are two ideas in the background here. The first is a principle that links the rationality of a prior intention with the rationality of the later retention and execution of that intention. We may state this as a constraint on rational, deliberation-based intention: If, on the basis of deliberation, an agent rationally settles at t_1 on an intention to A at t_2 if (given that) C, and if she expects that under C at t_2 she will have rational control of whether or not she A's, then she will *not* suppose at t_1 that if C at t_2, then at t_2 she should, rationally, abandon her intention in favor of an intention to perform an alternative to A. Call this statement of a link between rational intention formation and supposed rational intention retention the *linking principle.*[13]

Second, there is the common idea that the instrumental rationality of an action, in the kind of no-unanticipated-information cases of interest here, depends on the agent's evaluative ranking at the time of the action of options available then. Call this the *standard view.* On Wednesday my evaluative ranking will favor nondrinking over drinking. We infer, given the standard view, that even if I had earlier decided to drink toxin, when Wednesday arrives and the money is in the bank, instrumental rationality would require nondrinking. But then, given the linking principle and given that I am aware of these features of the case, I cannot rationally form the intention to drink in the first place. So there is a problem for rationally settling in advance on an intention to drink toxin despite the attractions of the autonomous benefit, a problem traceable to the joint operation of the linking principle and the standard view.

There is a complication. We have been supposing that in my prior deliberation on Monday about whether to drink toxin on Wednesday I take into account the autonomous benefit of an intention to drink. Does this mean that in my deliberation on Monday I am deliberating directly about the plan: intend on Monday to drink toxin on Wednesday, and then on Wednesday drink toxin? The problem with this is that my deliberation on Monday seems instead to be about what to do on Wednesday, not what to intend on Monday, though I know that a decision on Monday about what to do on Wednesday would involve an intention on Monday so to act. Granted, I might deliberate directly about whether on Monday to cause myself to intend to drink on Wednesday – for example, by taking a certain pill, or engaging in self-hypnosis. But that is a different matter.

Suppose, however, that on Monday I am directly deliberating about whether to drink toxin on Wednesday. I am not deliberating directly about the intention, on Monday, to drink. But this does not by itself show that I cannot include in my reasons for deciding to drink the fact that if I do so decide I win the money, whereas if I instead decide not to drink toxin I do not win the money.[14] The barrier to winning the money in the toxin case is not a simple exclusion of the consideration of autonomous benefits in deliberation. If there is a barrier, it is, rather, the combination of the linking principle and the standard view.

IV. Autonomous Benefits: Reciprocation

Consider a second example. You and I are mutually disinterested, instrumentally rational strangers about to get off an airplane. We know we will never see each other – or, indeed, the other passengers – again. We also know that we each have a pair of suitcases, and that each of us would benefit from the help of the other in getting them down from the overhead rack. We each would much prefer mutual aid to mutual nonaid. Given our seating arrangements, however, you would need to help me first, after which I could help you. You will help me only if you are confident that I would, as a result, reciprocate. But we both see that once you help me I will have received the benefit from you that I wanted. My helping you later would, let us suppose, only be a burden for me. Of course, most of us would care about the plight of the other passenger, and/or have concerns about fairness in such a case. But let us here abstract away from such concerns, for our aim here is to determine what is required solely by instrumental rationality. Let us also suppose, again artificially, that my helping you or not would have no differential long-term effects (including reputation effects) that matter to me now. Given these special assumptions, it seems I would not have reason to reciprocate after you have helped me. Seeing that, you do not help me, so we do not gain the benefits of cooperation.[15]

In such a situation I might try to assure you I would reciprocate. But suppose I am not very good at deceit and will only be convincing to you if I really intend to reciprocate if you help me.[16] I would, then, very much like to provide a sincere assurance. Can I?

If an assurance from me issued in a moral obligation to reciprocate, then perhaps I could get a new reason to reciprocate simply by issuing such an assurance. But let us put direct appeal to such moral considerations to one side and see where the instrumental rationality of mutually disinterested agents would by itself lead. To achieve the benefits of a sincere assurance I must intend to reciprocate. But in the very special circumstances described, it seems that I will have, when the time comes, no reason to reciprocate. So it seems I cannot rationally intend to reciprocate, and so cannot gain the benefits of cooperation in such circumstances.

The point is not that there are no relevant considerations of fairness or of assurance-based obligation. The point is only that we may not get at such reasons, when, in such special cases, we confine our attention solely to instrumentally rational planning agency.

So we have two autonomous benefit cases: toxin and reciprocation. In each case I consider at t_1 whether to act in a certain manner (drink the toxin, help you if you have helped me) at t_2. I know that my so intending at t_1 would or may well have certain benefits prior to t_2 – my becoming richer; my being aided by you. But I also know that these benefits would be autonomous: they would not depend causally on my actually doing at t_2 what it is that at t_1 I would intend to do then. The execution at t_2 of the relevant intention would bring with it only the burden of being sick or of helping you.[17] In each case, however, I prefer throughout the package of autonomous benefit and burden of execution over a package of neither.

Given my considered preference for such a package, can I in such cases rationally settle at t_1 on a plan that involves (conditionally or unconditionally) so acting at t_2? The linking principle tells us that rationally to settle on such a plan I cannot suppose that at t_2 I should, rationally, abandon my intention concerning t_2 – the intention to drink, or to reciprocate. But I know that under the relevant circumstances at t_2 my ranking would favor not drinking, or not helping. The standard view, then, says that at t_2 I should not execute my prior intention. If that is right then, given the linking principle, I cannot rationally and in a clearheaded way decide on the plan in the first place. Instrumental reason is an obstacle to gaining the autonomous benefits in such cases, even though I would gladly drink the toxin, or help you, in order to achieve those benefits.[18]

Is that right?

V. Sophistication and Resolution

An agent who adjusts her prior plans to insure that what she plans to do will be, at the time of action, favored by her then-present evaluative rankings has been called a "sophisticated" planner.[19] Given the conjunction of the linking principle with what I have termed the standard view, an instrumentally rational planning agent will be sophisticated, and so will not be in a position deliberatively to form the intention needed to get the autonomous benefits in our two cases.

The intuition that, to the contrary, instrumental rationality should not always stand in the way of such autonomous benefits suggests an alternative approach, one that retains the linking principle but abandons the standard view. The basic idea is that if it was best in prospect to settle on a prior plan, and if there is no unanticipated information or change in basic values, then it is rational to follow through with that plan in those circumstances for which one specifically planned. Settling on a plan to drink toxin, or to reciprocate if helped, might well be best in prospect, given relevant autonomous benefits. So it may be rational to follow through with such a plan in planned-for circumstances, even though, at the time of follow-through, one would thereby be acting contrary to one's then-present evaluative ranking of one's then-present options. So, instrumental rationality need not stand in the way of the money or of mutual aid. Borrowing a term from Edward McClennen, we may call this a version of "resolute choice."[20] In anticipation of a later distinction I will call it, more specifically, *strong resolution*.

Call the conjunction of the linking principle and the standard view *sophistication*. Both sophistication and strong resolution accept the linking principle, and both allow one to consider autonomous benefits in deliberation about plans for the future. Where they differ is in their view of rational intention retention and execution. Sophistication accepts the standard view; strong resolution says, instead, that a prior plan settling on which was – because of autonomous benefits – best in prospect, can trump a later, conflicting evaluative ranking concerning planned-for circumstances.

To these two approaches we may add a third, a qualified form of resolution defended by Gauthier.[21] Suppose that settling on a certain prior plan at t_1 is favored by one's evaluative ranking then. Suppose that the attractions of settling on this plan include expected autonomous benefits prior to t_2; and suppose that this plan specifically calls for one to A at t_2, given circumstance C. Suppose C does obtain at t_2; and suppose there is neither unanticipated information about this circumstance nor change in basic values. Gauthier proposes that one should stick with the plan if and only if one thereby does better than one *would have* done if one had not settled on the plan in the first place, at t_1.

This view qualifies strong resolution with a further, counterfactual test on rational follow-through. There are autonomous-benefit cases in which strong resolution would call for follow-through and yet Gauthier would not. These include certain cases of failed threats.[22] In the toxin case and the reciprocation case, however, Gauthier's view matches strong resolution. In drinking toxin or reciprocating one does better than one would have done if one had initially not settled on the plan to drink or to reciprocate. So one may rationally drink the toxin, and one may rationally reciprocate. Let us call Gauthier's view *moderate resolution*.

Both strong and moderate resolution focus on the evaluation of courses of action, as individuated by the agent's intentions and plans.[23] Strong resolution treats the prior evaluation of a course of action as critical, allowing it, in certain cases, to determine the rationality of later follow-through in planned-for circumstances. Gauthier adds a further, counterfactual test on rational follow-through, a test that concerns the comparative evaluation at the time of action of the overall course of action. But both views agree that if one's intentions and plans see one's conduct at t_2 as fitting into a larger course of action that began at t_1 (perhaps only with a decision), then it is the assessment of that larger course of action, a course of action some of which is already in the past, that is crucial. Strong resolution highlights the assessment at t_1 of that course of action; at t_2 one refers back to that assessment. Gauthier adds a role for a comparison at t_2 of that course of action with its t_1 through t_2 alternatives. But both agree that it is the overall course of action that is one's concern, even at t_2. That is why, for Gauthier, one should follow through and reciprocate if one has been helped; for the course of action that began at t_1 with a sincere assurance that one would reciprocate if helped, and then includes reciprocating after having been helped, is seen at t_2 as superior to alternative courses of action available beginning at t_1.[24]

One evaluates, then, not simply alternatives from now on but courses of action, as individuated by one's intentions and plans. These courses of action can include elements already in the past, elements over which one no longer has causal control. On both views, then, intentional structure can trump temporal and causal location.

This is in tension with a basic fact about our agency. As time goes by we are located differently with respect to our plans. Along with a change in temporal location normally goes a change in the agent's causal powers. What is up to the agent is what to do from now on. So she will normally want to rank alternatives beginning from now on.

Granted, the agent may well rank her alternatives with respect to past events: she may, for example, be grateful for past benefits or want revenge for past harms. The point is not that a rational agent does not care about the past. The point concerns, rather, what is now under the control of the agent. What is now under her control are her alternatives from now on.[25] So it seems she will want to rank those alternatives. Both versions of resolution concern themselves instead with courses of action that typically include elements no longer in the agent's causal control. This seems to me not to do justice to the significance of temporal and causal location to our agency. Strong and moderate resolution, in seeking a strong role for planning in achieving the benefits of coordination over time and across agents, seem not to do justice to the basic fact that as agents we are temporally and causally located.

A reply will be that in giving such priority to intentional structure a resolute agent employs a deliberative procedure that is, in the words of Gauthier, "maximally conducive to one's life going as well as possible."[26] One who employs such a procedure will win money in toxin cases and gain benefits of cooperation. But it is difficult to see why this shows that *at the time of action* one will not reasonably consult one's ranking of options that are at that time in one's control. If one is concerned with what is "maximally conducive to one's life going as well as possible," why wouldn't one be concerned with which action, of those presently in one's control, is "maximally conducive to one's life going as well as possible"? Faced with the toxin on Wednesday, however, the action presently in one's control that is maximally conducive to that benefit is, we may suppose, not drinking.

VI. Temporary Reversals in Rankings

I am skeptical, then, about strong and moderate resolution.[27] But I also think that sophistication is too simple.

Consider Ann. She enjoys a good read after dinner but also loves fine beer at dinner. However, she knows that if she has more than one beer at dinner she cannot concentrate on her book after dinner. Prior to dinner Ann prefers an evening of one beer plus a good book to an evening with more than one beer but no book. Her problem, though, is that each evening at dinner, having drunk her first Pilsner Urquell, she finds herself tempted by the thought of a second: for a short period of time she prefers a second beer to her after-dinner read.[28] This new preference is not experienced by her as compulsive. If asked, she will say that right now she really prefers to go ahead this one time and have the second drink, despite the impact on her ability to concentrate later, though she will also acknowledge that even now she prefers that she resist similar temptations on future nights. As she knows all along, this change in ranking will be short-lived: after dinner she will return to her preference for a good read.

Prior to dinner on Monday Ann prefers

(1) one beer at dinner on Monday plus a book after dinner

to

(2) more than one beer at dinner on Monday and no book after dinner.

In the middle of dinner, after her first beer, this preference reverses, and she prefers (2) over (1). By the end of dinner, she again prefers (1) over (2), though by then this preference will express itself either in relief or in regret. Throughout dinner, however, Ann continues to prefer

(3) one beer at dinner and a book after, for all nights,

to

(4) more than one beer and no book for all nights.

But it is also true that during dinner on Monday Ann temporarily prefers

(3') more than one beer and no book on Monday, but one beer and a book on all other nights

to (3).[29]

What is Ann to do? We might say to Ann: "You should settle in advance on a policy of having at most one beer at dinner and then stick with that policy in the face of expected temptations. In that way you will achieve (3) rather than (4), thereby satisfying a preference you will have throughout. Granted, on each night there will be a slightly modified policy you will prefer to (3). On Monday, for example, you will prefer (3') to (3). But this will be only temporary. The preference that will persist throughout is for (3) over (4). By settling on a policy in favor of (3), that is what you can achieve."

Might this be sensible advice? Might Ann rationally settle on such a policy and then rationally stick with it in the face of a diverging preference?

Note that we are not asking whether it is always rational to resist all temptations. Nor are we supposing that if, in a particular case, it would be rational to stick with such a prior policy, that very fact ensures that one does. Note finally that I am understanding evaluative rankings as aspects of the real, explanatory story of action. Although such rankings are susceptible to a broadly functional characterization, they are not merely the reflection of actual choice and action. In this sense of "ranking" it is possible for Ann intentionally to stick with her policy and to act contrary to her present ranking (even though there is also a sense in which, if she so acts, that is what she most wanted).[30] Our question is whether this may be rational.

Sophistication answers in the negative. Despite her prior one-beer policy, at dinner Ann prefers a second beer. So, given the standard view, that is what instrumental rationality requires. A sophisticated Ann cannot even settle on the one-beer policy in the first place.

Such a blanket prohibition on settling on and sticking with such policies in the face of temporary rankings to the contrary seems to me mistaken. It seems to me that instrumentally rational willpower sometimes involves sticking with a sensible prior policy in the face of a diverging temporary preference. Can we make theoretical room for rational willpower of this sort?

We might distinguish here between a reversal of a mere preference and a reversal of an evaluative ranking.[31] Only the latter, we might say, trumps a prior policy. This may work for some cases of temptation, but I do not think that it does justice to all that is at stake. First, some versions of Ann's case may involve temporary changes in evaluative ranking. And second, for reasons that will emerge, there remain important issues about a planning agent's concern with her own future assessments.

Ann's case is in some respects similar to the toxin and reciprocation cases. In all three cases there is a prior plan or policy settling on which is best in prospect. And in all three cases the agent knows that when the occasion for action arrives her rankings of then-present options will argue against following through. But there is also a significant difference between the cases. The underlying desires and values that argue for abandoning a plan to drink toxin, or a plan to reciprocate, are stable. Ann's preference for two beers, in contrast, is temporary. I want to see whether an account of instrumentally rational planning agency should exploit this difference and, if so, how. But first I need to look at a different kind of case.

VII. Slippery-Slope Intransitivities

Consider Warren Quinn's example of the potential self-torturer who agrees to allow an extremely tiny medical device to be permanently attached to his body. The device generates a constant electric current of varying levels, from 0 (no current) to 1,000 (extremely high and extremely painful current). Each increment, from setting n to setting $n + 1$, is so small that he cannot feel the difference, though he can of course feel the difference between setting 0 and setting 1,000. The device begins at setting 0, and the potential self-torturer is given an initial ten thousand dollars for allowing it to be attached. He is also offered ten thousand dollars for each advance in the setting (something he can choose once each week) from setting n to setting $n + 1$, though he knows that once the device is advanced to a higher setting it cannot be returned to a lower setting.

This poses a problem:

> Since the self-torturer cannot feel any difference in comfort between adjacent settings, he appears to have a clear and repeatable reason to increase the voltage each week. The trouble is that there *are* noticeable differences in comfort between settings that are sufficiently far apart. Indeed, if he keeps advancing, he can see that he will eventually reach settings that will be so painful that he would then gladly relinquish his fortune and return to 0.[32]

This potential self-torturer has intransitive preferences.[33] He prefers setting 1 to setting 0, setting 2 to setting 1, and so on. But he prefers setting 0 to setting 1,000. Further, these intransitive preferences are there all along. This is not a case of preference change over time, though, once the process gets going, different preferences are engaged at different times.

What is the potential self-torturer to do? Quinn suggests he should decide in advance on a "*reasonable* stopping point" and then stick with it when he gets there.[34] In that way he gets more than enough money to compensate for the discomfort but does not find himself in unacceptably extreme suffering.[35]

This is good advice. But to follow this advice the agent will need to stick with his prior decision in the face of a stable preference to go on. Suppose that he prefers 15 to 0, and 0 to 16: 15 is, so to speak, the *switch point relative to 0*. Suppose that for this reason the agent decides in advance to stop at this switch point – to stop at 15.[36] When he gets to 15 he will prefer to move to 16, and that is a preference that was there all along. In order to stick with his prior decision he must act contrary to his ranking of 16 over 15, and that would violate the standard view and so sophistication.

I have rejected strong and moderate resolution as applied to our autonomous-benefit cases. For these cases sophistication is a superior response to the fact that our agency is located temporally and causally. But as a view about cases of temptation, and of slippery-slope intransitivities, sophistication seems overly simple. We need to steer a path between resolution and sophistication.

VIII. Planning Agency and Future Regret

Ann prefers, at the time of action, to drink a second beer; I prefer at the time of action not to drink toxin. Given, in each case, a prior intention to the contrary, why should Ann's drinking a second beer be a potential candidate for rational criticism whereas my refraining from drinking toxin is not? Why should rational intention stability distinguish in this manner between toxin and temptation?

Suppose that you are an adviser to Ann, or to the potential self-torturer. You might well say: "Stick with your plan or policy. If you do, you will be glad you did. And if you do not, you will wish you had." We can spell this out as an argument offered at the time of action:

(a) If you stick with your prior intention, you will be glad you did.
(b) If you do not stick with your prior intention, you will wish you had.

So, other things being equal,

(c) Though you now prefer to abandon your prior intention, you should nevertheless stick with it.

Statement (a) says, roughly, that the agent would not regret sticking with her prior intention; (b) says, roughly, that she would regret not sticking with her intention. Let us say that when (a) and (b), suitably interpreted, are true, following through with one's prior intention satisfies the *no-regret condition*.[37] Sophistication (since it accepts the standard view) holds that in our no-unanticipated-information cases it is instrumentally rational to follow through with one's prior intention to A at t only if one's evaluative ranking at t favors A over one's other options at t. But consideration of the no-regret condition suggests an alternative view: in the kind of no-unanticipated-information cases we are considering, the agent's reasonable anticipation at the time of action that follow-through would satisfy the no-regret condition can sometimes make follow-through rational even in the face of a present ranking to the contrary.[38]

The agent, then, is to ask at the time of action, t_2, about her attitude at some appropriate later time, t_3, concerning options still available at t_2. I will say more shortly about what counts as an appropriate later time. Note, though, that the anticipated attitude at t_3 that is at issue concerns options still in one's power at t_2. We are not considering one's anticipation at t_2 of an assessment at t_3 of overall courses of action beginning *earlier* than t_2. We want the options being assessed to be options still available to the agent at the time of plan follow-through, t_2, for we are trying to be responsive to the fact that agency is located temporally and causally.

Such a view would continue to subscribe to the linking principle, but it would reject the standard view for some cases like that of Ann or of Quinn's potential self-torturer. I want to spell out how such a view would work.

Begin with Ann. She knows that she will be glad after dinner if she has stuck with her policy and had only one beer; and she knows that after a second beer, faced with the later part of the evening, she will wish that she had stuck with her one-beer policy. So she knows that in following through with a one-beer policy she would satisfy the no-regret condition.

The case of the potential self-torturer is more complicated. We need first to ask how far into the future he is to look. After all, very shortly after moving from 15 to 16, he may still be glad he gave up on a prior intention to stop at 15. However, at the time of his choice between 15 and 16, he can ask: "If I abandon my prior decision to stop at 15, what will then transpire?" And it seems he may reasonably answer: "I would then follow the slippery slope all the way to 1,000." His prior decision to stop at 15 was his best shot at playing the game without going all the way; if he does not stick with that decision, there is little reason to think he would stick with any other decision short of the bottom of the slippery slope.[39] Further, he can anticipate that were he to slide all the way to 1,000 he would then wish that he had instead stopped at 15: he would then wish he had earlier followed through with his yet-earlier decision and stopped at 15 rather than abandoning that decision and sliding all the way to 1,000. This line of reasoning can reasonably lead him to accept versions of (a) and (b), appropriately interpreted, concerning his following through with his plan to stop at 15: he would be glad later if he stuck with his plan and would regret it if he did not. So he can conclude at the time of action that his following through with his intention to stop at 15 satisfies the no-regret condition.

Now consider the toxin case. Suppose on Wednesday you try saying to me: "I know you prefer not to drink toxin, despite your prior intention to drink. But you will later be glad if you did drink it, and if you do not drink it you will later wish you had." I think I would surely object. On Wednesday I already either have the money or not. If I have the money and yet abandon an intention to drink, I will be *glad* I abandoned that intention and so avoided the pains of the toxin!

It might be replied that even after Wednesday I still prefer money and drink to no money and no drink. So perhaps I would later be glad I had stuck to my intention and drunk the toxin, given my preference for the package of toxin plus money. But recall that we are considering my reflections at the time of action, on Wednesday. By this time the first part of the package – whether I have the money or not – is already fixed. My choice at that time – what remains under my control then – concerns the second part of the package: to drink or not to drink. What I want on Wednesday to know is how I will later assess *these* options. And it seems that I will reasonably conclude on Wednesday that at the end of the week, and holding fixed the past prior to my Wednesday decision, I would regret following through and drinking the toxin. Granted, if I did follow through I might later be glad that I am that kind of guy – the kind of guy who wins the money in such cases. But that is not later to favor the option on Wednesday of drinking over the option on Wednesday of not drinking, given that the money is, by Wednesday, already in the bank. So following through with an intention to drink toxin would not satisfy the no-regret condition, properly interpreted.

A similar point can be made for the case of reciprocation, as we have understood it. Suppose I intended to reciprocate, you have helped me with my luggage, and I am now considering reciprocating. Given the special assumptions we are making about the case, I will see that, after all is done, I would later favor not following through, for then I would have thereby gotten the benefit without the burden. As in the toxin case, if I did follow through I might be glad I am that kind of guy, but that seems a different matter.

The no-regret condition, then, seems to divide the cases in the manner we anticipated: It is reasonably believed by the agent at the time of action to be satisfied by follow-through in some cases of temptation and of slippery-slope intransitivity, but not to be satisfied by follow-through in our cases of toxin and reciprocation. In our temptation case, the agent can anticipate that looking back later she will be glad of earlier follow-through. In the toxin case the agent can anticipate that looking back later he would regret earlier follow-through.[40]

To deepen our discussion we need to reflect further on regret. Regret should be grounded in some appropriate evaluative ranking. In particular, the agent's regret at t_3 concerning abandoning her prior intention at t_2 is, we may suppose, grounded in some appropriate evaluative ranking. What ranking?

In our temptation case, the answer is clear: Ann's later regret that earlier she had a second beer is grounded in her later ranking of one beer over two – a ranking she did not have at the time of drinking the second beer. Matters are more complex, however, for the potential self-torturer. He can see that if he abandons his intention and opts for 16 there is good reason to expect that he will continue all the way to 1,000. And he can see that when he gets to 1,000 he will wish he had stuck at 15: he will regret having abandoned his intention to stop at 15. But this regret is not grounded in a ranking of 15 over 16: there is no reason to think that he has reversed his ranking of 16 over 15. In what ranking, then, is the regret grounded?

Well, 15 is the switch point relative to 0. Is the relevant ranking his ranking of 0 over 16?[41] But we want the regret to concern what is still available to the agent at the time of choice between 15 and 16; for we want to respect the way in which agency is temporally and causally located. And 0 is no longer available at the time of choice between 15 and 16. This suggests that the ranking that is critical is, instead, his ranking of 15 over where he ends up, 1,000,[42] for both of those remain available at the relevant time. Perhaps, then, we can understand the relevant anticipated regret as grounded in *that* ranking: if he opts for 16, he will end up at 1,000; if he sticks with his intention, he will stay at 15; and he will regret his failure to stick with his intention to stop at 15 because he ranks 15 over 1,000.

But if that is the ranking that grounds the relevant regret, we have a puzzle about this case that does not arise in the temptation case. The ranking that grounds the later regret relevant to Ann's case is not a ranking that Ann has when she is faced with the temptation. But if the potential self-torturer ranks 15 over 1,000, that is a ranking that is there all along. In particular, it is there at the time of the choice between 15 and 16. If this ranking is relevant to the rationality of that choice, why isn't it relevant in a straightforward way, at the time of the choice itself? Why is there a need to look to later regret?

There is a good reason why this ranking, at the time of action, of 15 over 1,000 would not by itself support the choice of 15 over 16. The choice of 16 is *evidence* that one will go all the way to 1,000: it is, we are supposing, evidence that one's underlying psychology is such that one will likely go all the way. But the choice of 16 does not itself *cause* one's going all the way to 1,000; it is, rather, itself an effect of the mechanisms that will cause one's going all the way. There are large issues here, issues associated with "Newcombe's problem."[43] For present purposes let me just say that it seems to me that it is normally not a reason in favor of a choice that it is merely evidence of, and does not contribute to, something that is valued. At the time of the choice between 15 and 16 the agent could reasonably appeal to the ranking of 15 over 1,000 if he thought that the choice of 16 would cause his going all the way to 1,000. But that is not what the potential self-torturer thinks: he only thinks that a choice of 16 would be evidence that he will go all the way.

That explains why we cannot appeal to the ranking, at the time of action, of 15 over 1,000 to explain why it might be rational to stick with the intention to stop at 15. But if we cannot appeal to that ranking at the time of action, how can we appeal to it at the end, when the agent is in the throes of pain experienced at setting 1,000?

The answer seems to be that there is a kind of regret that is grounded in a ranking of what would have resulted from certain past conduct as compared with what has actually transpired.[44] At the end of the day the self-torturer sees that, indeed, after choosing 16 he did go on all the way to 1,000, and he sees that that would not have happened if he had stuck with his intention to stop at 15. If he had stopped at 15, he would, as a result, not have ended up at 1,000. He therefore regrets not having stuck with his intention to stop at 15. This regret seems to be grounded in his ranking of 15 over 1,000, even though he does not see his choice, instead, of 16 as causing his ending up at 1,000. Given his ranking of 15 over 1,000, it is enough to support this regret that he believes that if he had stuck with his intention to stop at 15 he would (as a result) not have ended up at 1,000 (which is in fact where he did end up). It is the potential self-torturer's anticipation of such later regret that supports the argument that it may be rational for him to stick with his intention to stop at 15.[45]

IX. Why Future Regret Can Matter

Why should anticipated satisfaction of the no-regret condition matter to an instrumentally rational planning agent? Let us reflect on the very idea of a planning agent. Planning is future oriented. In being engaged in planning agency, one seems to be committed to taking seriously how one will see matters in the relevant future. One seems, in particular, to be committed to taking seriously how one will see matters at the conclusion of one's plan, or at appropriate stages along the way, in the case of plans or policies that are ongoing.[46] This gives anticipated future regret or nonregret on relevant future occasions a special significance to an agent engaged in settling on and following through with plans. That is a major reason why the anticipated satisfaction of the no-regret condition matters to an instrumentally rational planning agent. This also helps somewhat to clarify how far into the future the agent is to look. Implicit in one's planning is, normally, a rough conception of what counts as – as we might say – plan's end.[47]

The idea is not simply that anticipation of future regret or nonregret can change one's present evaluative ranking, though no doubt it can. The idea, rather, is that anticipation of future regret or nonregret can be relevant to the stability of a prior intention of a planning agent; it can be relevant to the question of when it is reasonable to reconsider and abandon a prior intention, and when not.[48] Our concern with stability, recall, is a concern with when it is rational to stick with a prior intention, given that one already has it; it is not simply a concern about the formation of a new intention from scratch.

This clarification helps defuse a possible objection. I have argued that anticipated future regret or nonregret can have a special relevance to a planning agent. But, faced with temptation, why couldn't an agent simply abandon any relevant planning and thereby escape the rational pressures of such anticipations?[49] The answer is that the agent comes to the temptation with relevant prior intentions, and so there is already an issue about whether she may rationally simply give them up. This is the issue of rational intention stability that we have been addressing. And so long as she has these intentions she is a planning agent in a manner that makes salient relevant, anticipated future regret.

In some cases, granted, one will reasonably side with one's present ranking and abandon one's prior plan, while recognizing that one will later regret it. Perhaps one now sees one's anticipated later regret as deeply misguided, or perhaps one anticipates that one's later regret will itself not be stable. The inference from

(a) and (b) to (c) in the earlier argument is defeasible. Indeed, at the level of generality at which we have been proceeding there may be no simple principle that sorts out those cases in which this inference goes through from those in which it does not. But this inference can still have force in certain cases for a planning agent: that is what sophistication fails to see, and that is the key to our explanation of how rational intention stability distinguishes between toxin and temptation.

My claim is not that the no-regret condition has force simply because, in the words of Thomas Nagel, one sees "oneself as a temporally extended being for whom the future is no less real than the present."[50] Nagel argued that such a conception of oneself as temporally extended supports a concern with one's future desires. But that is not my argument. The force of the no-regret condition is not grounded simply in the recognition that one is a "temporally extended being." It is grounded, further, in one's actual engagement in relevant planning agency, and in the resulting significance to one of how one will see matters specifically at plan's end.

I am appealing to certain later attitudes toward now-available options, later attitudes one now anticipates that one will actually have if one proceeds with one's plan and completes it in a certain manner (or, alternatively, if one abandons one's plan). My appeal is not merely to some ranking one would have if one were to step back from pressures of present choice, nor is my appeal to regret or nonregret at the time of plan follow-through concerning one's earlier decisions, nor is it to a ranking made from some detached perspective on the whole of one's life.[51] Finally, the relevant, anticipated later attitudes concern courses of action that are still available to the agent at the time of the anticipation, at the time of plan follow-through. They are not rankings of general traits of character or of general procedures of deliberation.[52]

Earlier I indicated my endorsement of a broadly pragmatic, two-tier approach to plan stability and rational reconsideration in the face of resource limits and unanticipated new information. My main concern here, however, has been with perplexities about certain no-unanticipated-information cases in which one's ranking at the time of action argues against follow-through, and in which issues of resource limits are not germane. For some of these cases I have rejected the standard view, and so sophistication. But in doing this I have not appealed to a pragmatic, two-tier theory of plan stability; for I have argued that such an appeal in these kinds of cases would not do justice to the fact that our agency is temporally and causally located. Instead I have appealed to a planning agent's concern with how she will see her present decision at plan's end. It is this concern, not an appeal to a two-tier pragmatic structure, that supports a distinctive kind of intention stability in certain no-unanticipated-information cases, and thereby a path between resolution and sophistication.[53]

Resolution does not do full justice to the way in which our agency is located temporally and causally. Sophistication does not do full justice to the way in which our engagement in planning agency normally bestows a special significance on how we will see our now-present action at plan's end. By avoiding both extremes we arrive at a view of instrumentally rational planning agency that does justice both to the fact that we are planners and to the fact that we are temporally and causally located agents. Instrumental rationality does limit access to certain kinds of autonomous benefits, even for a planning agent. Nevertheless, there are no-unanticipated-information cases in which an instrumentally rational planning agent can reasonably commit herself in advance to a plan or policy and then reasonably follow through, rather than simply conform to her rankings at the time of action.

Notes

1. This is a major theme in my *Intention, Plans, and Practical Reason* (Cambridge, MA: Harvard University Press, 1987).
2. This is in the spirit of work by Herbert Simon. See, e.g., his *Reason in Human Affairs* (Stanford: Stanford University Press, 1983).
3. A similar point is made by J. David Velleman in his *Practical Reflection* (Princeton: Princeton University Press, 1989), pp. 225–6.
4. Jordon Howard Sobel emphasizes the possibility that an agent may "put a premium on steadfastness"; see his "Useful Intentions" in his *Taking Chances: Essays on Rational Choice* (Cambridge: Cambridge University Press, 1994), pp. 237–54, esp. p. 249. Wlodek Rabinowicz, in a complex and subtle discussion, also emphasizes that a rational agent may "assign value to resoluteness and to commitment to previously chosen plans." "To Have One's Cake and Eat It Too: Sequential Choice and Expected-Utility Violations," *Journal of Philosophy* 92 (1995), 586–620, at p. 611. Matters here are delicate: Such valuations may lead to odd forms of bootstrapping, as I argued in my *Intention, Plans, and Practical Reason*, ch. 2. But here I want simply to put such views to one side, for my interest is in an account of instrumentally rational planning agency that does not begin by presupposing such intrinsic valuations.
5. "Instrumental" is here understood broadly: it is not limited solely to causal means to an end. For example, my going to a concert tonight might be promoted by my going to hear the Alma Trio, though my going to hear the Alma Trio is not a causal means to my going to a concert. (See Bernard Williams, "Internal and External Reasons," in his *Moral Luck* [Cambridge: Cambridge University Press, 1981], p. 104.) The crucial point is that I am trying to discuss structures of planning agency in a way that appeals to the nature of such agency and to demands of instrumental reason but does not depend on arguing that practical reason, by itself, mandates certain ends.
6. This problem is similar to the problem posed by the trilemma I discuss in *Intention, Plans, and Practical Reason*, p. 5. See also Paisley Livingston, "Le dilemme de Bratman: Problèmes de la rationalité dynamique," *Philosophiques* 20 (1993), 47–67.
7. Much of the model to be described is discussed in my *Intention, Plans, and Practical Reason*, which also provides other details.
8. These were a primary concern in my discussions of stability in my *Intention, Plans,*

and Practical Reason, esp. chs. 5–6. See also my "Planning and the Stability of Intention," *Minds and Machines* 2 (1992), 1–16.

9. Gregory S. Kavka, "The Toxin Puzzle," *Analysis* 43 (1983), 33–6.
10. Gregory S. Kavka, *Moral Paradoxes of Nuclear Deterrence* (Cambridge: Cambridge University Press, 1987), p. 21.
11. This assumes that on Monday my mere intention, even in the special, science-fiction circumstances of the toxin case, does not by itself amount to an assurance to the billionaire of a sort that induces an obligation to drink the toxin. It also assumes that my intention to drink the toxin is not itself an intrinsic desire to drink toxin, an intrinsic desire of a sort that would give me an instrumental reason for drinking. Both assumptions are implicit in standard discussions of the toxin puzzle, and here I follow suit.

    In his comments at the March 1995 Pacific Division meeting of the American Philosophical Association, Gilbert Harman challenged the second of these assumptions. (This challenge is also presented in his chapter "The Toxin Puzzle" in this volume, an essay that derives from his comments at the meeting.) Harman argues that the intention to drink toxin would be an intrinsic desire adopted for instrumental reasons. In this respect, he suggests, it would be like a new intrinsic desire to win a game, adopted because it is more fun to play when you care about winning.

    I agree that if one does somehow come to have such a new intrinsic desire to drink, that may make it instrumentally rational to drink. But I do not see that an intention to drink toxin would generally be like this. After all, in coming to have the intrinsic desire to win, you come to care about winning – winning is now something that matters to you, if only temporarily. In intending to drink toxin in the kind of case we are discussing you would not in the same way care about drinking it.
12. Kavka writes that "you cannot intend to act as you have no reason to act, at least when you have substantial reasons not to act" ("The Toxin Puzzle," p. 35). My remark in the text is in the same spirit, though it is offered as a remark about rational intention, rather than about intention *simpliciter.*
13. I refer to versions of this principle also in my "Planning and Temptation," in *Mind and Morals,* ed. Larry May, Marilyn Friedman, and Andy Clark (Cambridge, MA: Bradford/MIT, 1995), pp. 293–310, and in "Following through with One's Plans: Reply to David Gauthier," in *Modeling Rational and Moral Agents,* ed. Peter Danielson (Oxford: Oxford University Press, 1998), pp. 54–65. Both Brian Skyrms, in remarks at the conference held in honor of Gregory Kavka, and Gilbert Harman, in his comments on my paper at the 1995 Pacific APA meeting, have suggested that the linking principle is challenged by cases of rational irrationality. (See Derek Parfit, *Reasons and Persons* [Oxford University Press, 1984], p. 13, and Thomas Schelling, *The Strategy of Conflict* [Cambridge, MA: Harvard University Press, 1980], p. 18.) These are cases in which it seems to be rational to cause oneself to have an intention to do something one knows it would be irrational to do. Now, it does not follow from the fact that it would be rational to cause oneself to intend to *A* if *C* that it would be rational so to intend. But in any case the formulation I have offered here of the linking principle is intended to circumvent these worries by limiting the cases to occasions on which the agent expects to retain rational control. These are, after all, the cases that are central here. (On this point I am in agreement with David Gauthier's remarks about rational irrationality in his "Commitment and Choice: An Essay on the Rationality of Plans," in *Ethics, Rationality, and Economic Behavior,* ed. Francesco Farina, Frank Hahn, and Stefano Vannucci [Oxford: Oxford University Press, 1996], pp. 217–43, at pp. 239–40.) My formulation also aims at forestalling

complexities raised by Alfred Mele's case of Ted in his "Intentions, Reasons, and Beliefs: Morals of the Toxin Puzzle," *Philosophical Studies* 68 (1992), 171–94.

    Both Skyrms and Harman indicated a preference for a principle that instead links a rational intention to *A* with a belief that one will *A*. I agree that a full story will include some appropriate belief condition (see my *Intention, Plans, and Practical Reason,* pp. 37–8), but I do not see this as precluding the linking principle formulated here.

14. In *Intention, Plans, and Practical Reason* I wrote that "in . . . deliberation about the future the desire-belief reasons we are to consider are reasons for various ways we might *act* later" (p. 103). This precluded appeal to autonomous benefits in deliberation. I have changed my mind about this in response to criticisms from David Gauthier in his "Intention and Deliberation," in Danielson, *Modeling Rational and Moral Agents,* pp. 40–53. The linking principle I formulate here aims to retain a tight connection between rational intention and supposed rational execution of that intention, without precluding appeal to autonomous benefits in deliberation. T. L. M. Pink has offered a different criticism of my cited remark. See his "Purposive Intending," *Mind* 100 (1991), 343–59, and in more detail in his *Psychology of Freedom* (Cambridge: Cambridge University Press, 1996). Pink supposes that my remark disallows an appeal in deliberation to certain kinds of coordination benefits of a prior intention. Suppose, for example, that if I intend to go running tomorrow my intention will insure that I get a new pair of running shoes before then, thereby making my running more attractive. Pink thinks that my remark precludes appeal to this fact in my deliberation now about whether to run tomorrow. I am not sure that my remark has this implication. (In the example, note, the benefit of running with new shoes is a benefit of the act of running.) In any case I agree with Pink that we should allow appeal in deliberation to such coordination benefits.

15. Examples along these lines have figured prominently in the work of David Gauthier. See for example his "Assure and Threaten," *Ethics* 104 (1994), 690–721.

16. We could make this more realistic by assuming only that I know that a sincere assurance is considerably more likely to be successful than an insincere one.

17. Recall that I am assuming in both of these cases that simply by forming the intention concerning t_2 I do not newly come to have a reason-giving intrinsic desire so to act.

18. These last two paragraphs draw (with changes) from my "Following through with One's Plans: Reply to David Gauthier." For a trenchant discussion leading to a similar conclusion about the toxin case, see Daniel Farrell, "Intention, Reason, and Action," *American Philosophical Quarterly* 26 (1989), 283–95.

    There is a possible complication concerning the reciprocation case (pointed out to me in different ways by Meir Dan-Cohen and David Gauthier). Suppose I do not follow through and so do not reciprocate even though you have helped me. I get the benefit of your help without the burden of my helping you. But I also get evidence about myself – evidence that I tend not to follow through in such cases. This evidence may make me in the future more skeptical than I would have been if I had followed through that I would follow through with such intentions in the yet farther future, and thereby make me less likely in the future to form intentions to reciprocate. I would, then, be in the future less likely to achieve associated autonomous benefits. So perhaps in those cases in which I expect to be in an indeterminate number of future situations of potential cooperation (even with different potential partners) I do have reason now to follow through and reciprocate.

    This argument cites what we might call a *reflexive* reputation effect. I tried to abstract away from reputation effects in my characterization of our reciprocation case. But it might be objected that if we preclude even such reflexive reputation effects we are imposing an overly severe limitation on our discussion.

My response is, first, that if this argument succeeds, we should just grant that it is only a limited range of cases of potential reciprocation that are our concern here, namely, those cases that really do have the structure of the toxin case, a structure in which the primary consideration in favor of follow-through derives from the autonomous benefit of the prior plan rather than from the future effects of follow-through. But, second, I am skeptical that the argument succeeds. The argument depends in part on the claim that if I do follow through and reciprocate this time, I will as a result have reason to be more confident that I would follow through in the future and so will, as a result, achieve such self-confidence. But we are assuming that I am, and know I am, generally an instrumentally rational agent. So, for my present follow-through to support a rational belief in my own future follow-through, it needs to support the belief that such future follow-through would be instrumentally rational; otherwise I will tend to infer that my present follow-through is not a good predictor of my future conduct. But it is not clear how the appeal to the reflexive reputation effects of my present follow-through supports a claim about the rationality of future follow-through. (Perhaps what is crucial is not the reflexive reputation effects of my present follow-through but rather that my present follow-through gives me evidence that later follow-through would itself have certain reflexive reputation effects that would tend to make that later follow-through rational. But if my present follow-through only gives me evidence of that – if the rationality of later follow-through is not itself an effect of my present follow-through – it is not clear how this helps the argument.) A related concern is that the linking principle says that I can in the future rationally intend to reciprocate only if (roughly) I judge then that it would be *rational* in the farther future to follow through. It will, again, not be enough for me just to expect that I would (perhaps not rationally) follow through. And it is not clear how appeal to reflexive reputation effects of present follow-through can show that such follow-through in the farther future would be rational.

19. I learned this terminology, and much else, from Edward F. McClennen, *Rationality and Dynamic Choice: Foundational Explorations* (Cambridge: Cambridge University Press, 1990).

20. Ibid. See also Laura DeHelian and Edward F. McClennen, "Planning and the Stability of Intention: A Comment," *Minds and Machines* 3 (1993), 319–33. I do not try to do justice to the complexity and subtlety of McClennen's detailed views here. In particular, his defense of his version of resolute choice is limited in important respects. My broad characterization of strong resolution will, I think, suffice for the purposes of the present discussion.

21. See his "Assure and Threaten," "Commitment and Choice," and "Intention and Deliberation."

22. This is a change from Gauthier's earlier views about deterrence. See his "Deterrence, Maximization, and Rationality," *Ethics* 94 (1984), 474–95. Gauthier's views about following through with a failed threat are complicated and involve consideration of general policies of issuing and carrying out certain kinds of threats. For a probing discussion and criticism see Joe Mintoff, "Rational Cooperation, Intention and Reconsideration," *Ethics* 107 (1997), 612–43.

23. Gauthier writes: "in deliberating rationally, one considers whether one's course of action is best . . . where a course of action is distinguished and demarcated by its intentional structure." "Assure and Threaten," p. 717.

24. What about the sequence: Sincerely assure at t_1; do not reciprocate at t_2? This is not a sequence that one could decide on at t_1, since the intention not to reciprocate would mean that the assurance is not sincere. So it is not a "course of action" available beginning at t_1.
25. Compare Bernard Williams's remark that "The correct perspective on one's life is *from now.*" *Moral Luck* (Cambridge: Cambridge University Press 1981), p. 13.
26. Gauthier, "Assure and Threaten," p. 701.
27. In a recent essay David Velleman tries to anchor a Gauthier-like view about reciprocation and assurance in a fundamentally different line of argument, one that appeals to the idea that action has a constitutive aim. I do not try to assess Velleman's alternative strategy here. See David Velleman, "Deciding How to Decide," in *Ethics and Practical Reason,* ed. Garrett Cullity and Berys Gaut (Oxford: Clarendon Press, 1997), pp. 29–52.
28. I assume that there really is a preference shift, that she is not merely confused about what her preferences are. My discussion of the case of Ann owes much to George Ainslie, *Picoeconomics: The Strategic Interaction of Successive Motivational States within the Person* (Cambridge: Cambridge University Press, 1992).
29. Ainslie, in *Picoeconomics,* tries to show that temporary preference reversals like Ann's would occur in agents who have certain – as he believes, extremely common – highly bowed temporal discount functions. But we do not need to discuss here Ainslie's diagnosis of such cases to agree that they are common. Our preferences for certain goods – be they beer, mystery novels, chocolates, or others you can cite from your own experience – do seem susceptible to this kind of temporary shift.

   I consider Ainslie's views in "Planning and Temptation," where I discuss a wine-drinking pianist whose problem is similar to Ann's, except that whereas Ann's preference reversal is triggered by her drinking the first beer, the pianist's preference reversal is triggered by the arrival of dinnertime. Given this difference, Ann's case may not cohere with Ainslie's claim that the primary mechanism underlying such preference changes is generally one of temporal discounting.
30. Here I agree with similar remarks of Gauthier's in "Commitment and Choice," pp. 238–9. For a different approach to preference see Sarah Buss, "Autonomy Reconsidered," *Midwest Studies in Philosophy* 19 (1994), 95–121.
31. Compare Gary Watson, "Free Agency," *Journal of Philosophy* 72 (1975), 205–20. This appeal to Watson's distinction was a suggestion of J. L. A. Garcia, in conversation.
32. The example is from Warren Quinn, "The Puzzle of the Self-Torturer," in his *Morality and Action* (Cambridge: Cambridge University Press, 1993), pp. 198–209, at p. 198. Quinn provides references to relevant literature. Thanks to Liam Murphy for bringing Quinn's essay to my attention.
33. Quinn says that such intransitivities bar the potential self-torturer from saying that each setting is better than the preceding one, for *better than* is, Quinn says, a transitive relation. But Quinn also says that the preferential ranking may be thoughtful and informed, and so an appropriate candidate for shaping choice (ibid., p. 199). So we may allow it to provide evaluative rankings in the sense relevant here.
34. Ibid., p. 206.
35. In his discussion Quinn seems to endorse "the principle that a reasonable strategy that correctly anticipated all later facts (including facts about preferences) still binds" (ibid., p. 207). We need to be careful, however, not to interpret this principle in a way that would justify sticking with a plan to drink toxin. (In an earlier essay Quinn had indicated that he would not welcome such a result. See "The Right to

Threaten and the Right to Punish," in his *Morality and Action* [Cambridge: Cambridge University Press, 1993], pp. 52–100, at p. 98.)

36. I owe to David Gauthier the suggestion that such a switch point relative to 0 is a reasonable point at which to settle in advance on stopping. (In the absence of some such argument the agent might be in a Buridan situation: he might know that there is reason to decide in advance on a stopping point, but there might be no single point such that there is reason to decide to stop there rather than at some competitor.) Note that in reaching a decision to stop at the switch point relative to 0 the agent may know that there is also a later switch point *relative to 15* – a later point that is preferred to 15 but whose successor is dispreferred to 15.

37. Note that this no-regret condition includes both the absence of regret at having followed through and the presence of regret if one did not follow through.

38. Versions of the idea that anticipated future regret, or its absence, can matter to the rationality of present conduct appear in a number of studies. See, e.g., Graham Loomes and Robert Sugden, "Regret Theory: An Alternative Theory of Rational Choice under Uncertainty," *Economic Journal* 92 (1982), 805–24. (Note, though, that the regret that is central to the Loomes and Sugden theory is the result of new information that was not available at the time of the (regretted) action; my focus, in contrast, is on anticipated later regret that does not depend on such new information.) See also John Rawls, *A Theory of Justice* (Cambridge, MA: Harvard University Press, 1971), pp. 421–3.

39. He need not think that his descending the slippery slope all the way to 1,000 would be *caused* by his failure to stop at 15. It is enough that he believe that if he does not stick with his plan to stop at 15 he will go all the way to 1,000. I return to related matters at the end of this section.

40. Consider the much-discussed case of Ulysses and the Sirens. (See, in particular, Jon Elster, *Ulysses and the Sirens: Studies in Rationality and Irrationality,* rev. ed. [Cambridge: Cambridge University Press, 1984].) Suppose Ulysses decides in advance to sail by the Sirens, but when he hears them his ranking changes in just the way he had anticipated. Ulysses is like Ann in one respect: he knows that if he sticks with his prior decision to sail by he will be glad he did. But on some versions of the Ulysses case, and unlike the case of Ann, it is also true that if he does not stick with his prior decision he will be glad he did not! So follow-through would satisfy one but not *both* parts of the no-regret condition. So there will be important cases of temptation and the like that are similar in certain respects to the one I have discussed but will need a different treatment.

41. A suggestion of Gideon Yaffe's.

42. I am assuming that this is indeed a ranking of our agent.

43. See, for starters, Robert Nozick, "Newcombe's Problem and Two Principles of Choice," in *Essays in Honor of Carl G. Hempel,* ed. Nicholas Rescher et al. (Dordrecht: Reidel, 1969).

44. I do not say: "a ranking of what certain past conduct would have been evidence for (but not a cause of) as compared with what has actually transpired."

45. Gideon Yaffe has wondered whether there is an instability here. The potential self-torturer, let us suppose, sticks with his prior intention to stop at 15 in part because he believes that if he instead goes on to 16 he will (likely) go on to 1,000. But if he does stop at 15 he can, perhaps, reasonably believe that if he instead intended to stop at the (later) switch point *relative to 15* (supposing there is one) he might well pull that off. (After all, we have given reason to think it would then be rational to do so.) Suppose the agent had earlier decided on 15, the switch point relative to 0. Faced

with the choice of 15 or 16, he wonders whether to stick with his prior decision. He sees that if he *does* stick with it, he *would* (probably) stick with a decision to stop at the (later) switch point relative to 15. So why not go on to that later switch point? The answer seems to be that if he does go on past 15 he will not have this evidence that he will stop at the later switch point. That seems sufficient to support his stopping at 15. Having stopped at 15, it may seem that one has available an argument for going on to the next switch point, but that argument would be undermined by one's going on and so seems not to have practical force.

46. This qualification concerning ongoing plans or policies should be understood throughout the discussion that follows.

47. These last two sentences benefited greatly from conversation with Elijah Millgram. For some suggestive remarks broadly in the spirit of this paragraph, see Gerald J. Postema, "Morality in the First-Person Plural," *Law and Philosophy* 14 (1995), 35–64, at pp. 56–7. See also Thomas E. Hill, Jr., "Pains and Projects," in his *Autonomy and Self-Respect* (Cambridge: Cambridge University Press, 1991). Hill writes that "the commitment to make my choices justifiable to myself later seems implicit in any project of deep deliberation" (p. 186). I am suggesting that a somewhat analogous commitment is implicit in planning agency more generally.

48. Of course, it may be that anticipated regret can play other roles in practical reasoning as well. See, for example, Robert Nozick, *The Nature of Rationality* (Princeton: Princeton University Press, 1993), p. 185, n. 21.

49. Tim Schroeder suggested an objection along such lines.

50. Thomas Nagel, *The Possibility of Altruism* (Oxford: Oxford University Press, 1971), p. 69. See also Rawls's remarks about seeing oneself "as one continuing being over time." *A Theory of Justice,* p. 422.

51. David Velleman emphasizes the significance of those evaluations of a person that "are relative to the perspective of his life as a whole" in his "Well-Being and Time," *Pacific Philosophical Quarterly* 72 (1991), 48–77, at p. 67.

52. I am not saying that at the time of follow-through one might not anticipate such later assessments – including forms of regret – concerning general character traits, or courses of action that began well before the time of follow-through. I am only saying that it is not one's anticipation, at the time of follow-through, of those later attitudes that is critical to plan stability, for those later attitudes are not focused on what is now, at the time of follow-through, in one's control.

53. I do not claim this is the only source of the cited intention stability. My concern is only to identify a major source of such stability, one that responds differently to toxin and to temptation, and one that is not grounded in a two-tier pragmatic structure. In my discussion of the toxin case in *Intention, Plans, and Practical Reason,* ch. 6, I argued, as I do here, that rationality stands in the way of follow-through. But my argument there assumed that our approach to stability in such no-new-information cases should stay roughly within the two-tier framework I had developed primarily for new-information cases in which our resource limits play a central role and in which the crucial issue is whether or not to reconsider one's prior intention. I no longer accept that assumption.

Remarks in this and the preceding paragraph in the text are intended to indicate briefly what seem to me to be some significant differences between my view here and ideas about temptation and related cases in Gauthier's "Resolute Choice and Rational Deliberation: A Critique and a Defence," *Noûs* 31 (1997), 1–25. Concerning cases of temptation, Gauthier contrasts preferences that the agent has at the time of action with "(temporal) *vanishing point* preferences that he acknowledges when choice is not imminent" (p. 20). The notion of a vanishing-point preference is in some respects similar to, but is not the same as, my notion of one's attitude at plan's end: vanishing-point preferences are preferences, either earlier or later, when "choice is not imminent," not specifically at plan's end. Gauthier's view about cases like Ann's is "based on a comparison of the effects on an agent's overall prospects of different modes of choice" (p. 23). I have here, in contrast, eschewed such a two-tier pragmatic approach to such cases and appealed instead to the significance to a planning agent of anticipated regret or nonregret at plan's end. Finally, Gauthier appeals (p. 24) to possible regret, at the time of action, concerning an earlier decision. The regret I appeal to is regret one anticipates at the time of action that one will have later, at plan's end.

The Toxin Puzzle

GILBERT HARMAN

I. The Puzzle

Here is "a vial of toxin that, if you drink it, will make you painfully ill for a day, but will not threaten your life or have any lasting effects." An "eccentric billionaire . . . will pay you one million dollars tomorrow morning if, at midnight tonight, you *intend* to drink the toxin tomorrow afternoon."[1]

The case is designed to distinguish between having reasons to intend to do something and having reasons for doing it. You have reasons to intend to drink the toxin tomorrow, but do you or will you have reasons actually to drink the toxin tomorrow? You can see that if you do not and will not have reasons actually to drink the toxin tomorrow, you will not do it. But, if you can see that you will not actually drink the toxin tomorrow, because you will not have any reason to drink the toxin at that point, it is going to be difficult now to intend to drink the toxin tomorrow. It is certainly going to be harder to get the $1 million in this case than in the easier case in which you would get the money only for actually drinking the toxin, not just for intending to do it.

I want to discuss whether you will have any reason actually to drink the toxin tomorrow in the first case – Kavka's toxin case, the case in which you get the $1 million for the intention alone. I will argue that if you do form the intention to drink the toxin, that intention can give you a reason actually to drink the toxin tomorrow afternoon, a reason similar to that provided by an intrinsic desire. If it is a strong enough reason, then you will drink the toxin, and, if you foresee that it will be a strong enough reason, you will be able to form the intention to drink the toxin.

II. Instrumental Rationality

I am concerned entirely with "instrumental rationality," which has to do with reasons that derive from your own desires and concerns. I claim that intentions

The present essay derives from comments that I offered at a symposium with David Gauthier and Michael Bratman entitled "The Stability of Intentions" at the Pacific Division meeting of the American Philosophical Association in San Francisco on March 31, 1995.

are sometimes to be included in the relevant desires and concerns. But what are the relevant desires and concerns?

III. Intrinsic Desires

Only intrinsic desires are relevant to instrumental rationality. Otherwise, there is double counting.

Double Counting: Suppose you have equivalent intrinsic desires for X and for Y, where Y can be obtained directly, and X can be obtained only indirectly. Your desire for X leads you to desire W, which is a means to X, and so to desire V, which is a means to W. If you pursue X, you satisfy three desires, and if you pursue Y you satisfy only one desire. But that difference gives you no reason to pursue Y rather than X, since your instrumental desires for V and W do not provide you with additional reasons over and above the reason provided by your intrinsic desire for X.

Roughly speaking, a desire for G is an intrinsic desire, in the relevant respect, to the extent that you do not desire G only as involving something else that you desire. There are at least three ways in which a desire for G might fail to be an intrinsic desire: (1) G might be desired only as a means to something else that you desire; (2) G might be desired only as good news – that is, as a sign of something else that is desired; (3) G might be desired only as a component of a larger whole that is intrinsically desired.[2]

IV. Instrumental Reasons for Intrinsic Desires

Suppose you have instrumental reasons to form a long-lasting, stable intrinsic desire for X (where these are not reasons actually to have X). Suppose further that, consequently, you get yourself to have such a long-lasting intrinsic desire. Once you have it, your future instrumental reasons do not need to be entirely based on satisfying your original desires. You can at that stage have instrumental reasons based on the anticipated satisfaction of the new intrinsic desire, even when the original desires are not satisfied.

You often form intrinsic desires in the manner just described. You take an interest in trying to win a game, because the game is more interesting, and so therefore more enjoyable, if you do; the expected benefits are not benefits of actually winning, but of playing with the goal of winning.

Similarly, you take an interest in a topic of conversation. You do not expect to learn anything about that topic that advances your prior interests, but the conversation is more enjoyable if you are interested in its subject. Furthermore, you may retain an intrinsic interest in that topic even after the conversation has ended, perhaps for quite a long time.

More generally, you have reasons to acquire a variety of intrinsic desires, because happiness consists at least in part in the satisfaction of such desires, and you have reasons to try to be happy.

It is possible that someone who starts without any intrinsic concern for the welfare of others may have a self-interested reason to acquire such a concern. It is conceivable that a good part of your interest in the welfare of others arose in this fashion.

V. Reasoning about Ends and Second-order Desires

Can there be reasons for ultimate ends or intrinsic desires? In recent years a number of philosophers have observed that it is possible to have "second-order desires," desires to have certain first-order intrinsic desires. Some philosophers have argued that certain second-order desires are especially relevant to freedom of the will; others have argued that certain second-order desires constitute your values.[3] I will not discuss any of these proposals except to point out that second-order desires to have certain intrinsic first-order desires can provide reasons for adopting those intrinsic first-order desires. As Christian Piller has observed, this indicates one way in which it can be possible to reason about ends.[4]

VI. Using Intrinsic Desires to Solve the Toxin Case

Now consider the following way to obtain the $1 million in Kavka's toxin case: you form a stable and enduring intrinsic desire to drink the toxin in celebration of the payment. If you can form such an intrinsic desire and if having that desire would then give you sufficient instrumental reason to drink the toxin, you can expect your intention to drink the toxin to be successful, and so you can form the intention.

VII. "Sophisticated" versus "Resolute" Solutions

This sort of response to the toxin problem is an instance of what Gauthier has called a "sophisticated" response – you see to it that you will have appropriate intrinsic desires at the time of the later action, where your later action is motivated solely by your intrinsic desires at the later time. Gauthier distinguishes such a sophisticated response from a "resolute" response, in which you do not add new intrinsic desires but can count on simply carrying through with the intention to do the later action because you have firm dispositions to carry through in that manner.[5] However, it is not clear to me that there is any real difference between the two responses, sophisticated and resolute, in this particular case.

First, an intention always counts as a desire, even if not all desires count as intentions. If you intend to do something, then it is correct to say that that is what you want or desire to do.

Second, your intention to drink the toxin in the present instance would be a concern to drink the toxin neither in order to produce certain other desirable effects, nor as part of a larger intrinsically desirable whole,[6] nor as a concern for good news.

Third, an intention always has a reason-giving force that is not just a summary result of the reasons for forming the intention. This is especially clear to the extent that the intention is the result of an arbitrary decision among several methods of accomplishing certain goals. Having formed the intention to take route 1 rather than route 2, you have a reason to take route 1 rather than route 2 that you may not have had prior to forming that intention. A similar point must hold for the intention to drink the toxin as conceived by the resolute strategy; that intention, like any other intention, must be conceived as having independent reason-giving force.

So, the resolute intention to drink the toxin counts as an intrinsic desire with independent reason-giving force and the second, resolute, solution of the toxin puzzle is a special case of the first, sophisticated, solution.

VIII. When Desires and Intentions Should Be Given Up

Suppose you desire G solely as a means to H. Suppose you then obtain H in some other manner, so that your desire for H is completely satisfied. Then you should abandon your desire for G, since that desire is a desire *for G as satisfying the desire for H*. If the desire for H goes away – for example, because it is completely satisfied – then you cannot rationally continue to have the desire *for G as satisfying the desire for H*. Similarly, an intention *to satisfy the desire for H by means of G* cannot rationally survive the disappearance of the desire for H.

The situation is different if you desire G solely because you take the desire for G (but not G itself) to be a means to H, or you intend to get G solely because the intention (but not G itself) is a means to H. It would be a mistake to suppose that the principle of rationality just mentioned, which applies to instrumental concerns, also applies to intrinsic concerns that are adopted for instrumental reasons. When an intrinsic concern for G is motivated by a concern for H, the content of the concern does not allude to H, and there is not the same rational incoherence in continuing to have the concern for G after your concern for H has been satisfied. There may be nothing irrational in continuing to take an intrinsic interest in a subject after the end of the conversation that was made more interesting by virtue of your taking an intrinsic interest in its subject.

Similarly, there may be nothing irrational in continuing to have an intrinsic desire or intention to drink the toxin after you receive the reward for having formed that desire or intention.

IX. When Intrinsic Concerns Can Be Given Up

You are not rationally required to abandon intrinsic concerns simply because the forming of those concerns was a means to something that you have now achieved. On the other hand, rationality does not require you to retain intrinsic concerns, either desires or intentions, once your original reason for having those concerns has lapsed. Once the conversation has ended, you may lose any intrinsic interest in its topic, and once you have received the money in the toxin case you may lose any intrinsic interest in celebrating by drinking the toxin – in either case without violating any real principles of rationality.

Indeed, once you have received the money for having formed the intention, the intention and desire to drink the toxin will be in conflict with your strong desire not to experience painful illness. So there may be reasons to abandon that desire, just as there may be reasons to abandon your intrinsic interest in a given subject if that interest conflicts with other important interests.

Certain variants of the intention and desire to drink the toxin may have more strength – for example, the desire and intention to drink the toxin in order to celebrate receiving the money for having formed an intention to drink the toxin. That intention might better survive conflict with other strong desires.

X. Conclusion

The issue in the toxin case is not about rationality. The issue is whether you can adopt a firm, strong-enough, long-enough-lasting intrinsic concern (desire or intention) to drink the toxin to celebrate receiving the money. Will the concern, if adopted, continue to remain after you have received the money? If you can adopt such a concern and can expect it to last long enough, you can adopt the concern by forming the intention to drink the toxin.

Notes

1. Gregory S. Kavka, "The Toxin Puzzle," *Analysis* 43 (1983), 33–6, at p. 33.
2. Gilbert Harman, "La valeur intrinsèque," in French translation by Laurie Calhoun, *Revue de Métaphysique et de Morale* 99 (1994), 245–55.
3. For references and discussion, see Gilbert Harman, "Desired Desires," in *Value, Welfare, and Morality,* ed. R. G. Frey and Christopher W. Morris (Cambridge: Cambridge University Press, 1993), pp. 138–57.
4. Christian Pillar, "The Limits of Humeanism," typescript.
5. E.g., David Gauthier, "Stabilizing Intentions: When It Pays to Be Resolute," a con-

tribution to a symposium with Michael Bratman entitled "The Stability of Intentions" at the Pacific Division meeting of the American Philosophical Association in San Francisco on March 31, 1995. Gauthier's terminology ("sophisticated" vs. "resolute") derives from Edward F. McClennen, *Rationality and Dynamic Choice* (Cambridge: Cambridge University Press, 1990).

6. I discuss the somewhat complicated conditions under which you can desire something as part of a larger intrinsically desirable whole in "La valeur intrinsèque."

Religion and Morality in Hobbes

EDWIN CURLEY

I. Prelude on Religion and Morality

In "Religion and the Queerness of Morality,"[1] George Mavrodes has argued that a religious view of the world is a necessary presupposition of morality, that morality makes sense only on a religious view. "Religion" here means at least a generic theism, incorporating doctrines common to Judaism, Christianity, and Islam. Specifically, unless you believe that you have been created by a God who will judge your actions in this life and mete out punishments and rewards in an afterlife, you will not find it rational to recognize and honor moral obligations. Moral obligations frequently require us to forego certain this-worldly goods. Telling the truth is (in most circumstances at least) a moral obligation, but often it carries a cost which seems to make it imprudent. Why should we pay that cost unless there is a system of divine justice, involving otherworldly goods, which can make up for the deficiencies of human justice? Mavrodes' position is a counterfactual version of that taken by Hobbes' Fool, who says in his heart that there is no God, and that, since there is no God, we have no reason to be just.[2] Mavrodes says that if the Fool were right about there not being a God, he would also be right about the reasonableness of morality.

Mavrodes canvasses various ways a philosopher might try to show that moral obligations make sense even on a nonreligious view of the world, giving most attention to a line of argument he finds in Kurt Baier, but which has, as he recognizes, roots in Hobbes. So Hobbes appears, in his argument, as representative of a way you might defend morality, even if you did not believe in a theistic religion. I think this is typical of the way philosophers who have not specialized in the study of Hobbes think of him.[3] The view of Hobbes held by most "philosophers in the street" – that is, philosophers who know enough

This essay is the final version of a paper I presented at the conference in honor of Gregory Kavka entitled "Rationality, Commitment, and Community," held at the University of California at Irvine on Feb. 10–12, 1995. In the interim I presented versions of it at the University of Colorado at Boulder and at Dartmouth College. By now I am indebted to more people for their comments than I can clearly recall, but those who stand out in my memory are David Gauthier, Brian Skyrms, Steve Darwall, Margaret Wilson, Walter Sinott-Armstrong, and Barbara Tovey.

about Hobbes to have some view about what might be important in his work but are not Hobbes specialists – is very like that held by many of Hobbes' contemporaries: that he was an atheist (or perhaps merely a thorough religious skeptic), but, in any case, someone in rebellion against the dominant religious tradition of his times, and so a suitable precursor for modern secularists.

II. Philosophers in the Street vs. Hobbes Specialists

It may come as a surprise to the philosopher in the street to know how frequently, in this century, Hobbes scholars have taken a different approach to Hobbes. It began, I think, with an influential article by A. E. Taylor,[4] arguing that Hobbes was a deontologist whose moral theory could not be adequately understood without recognizing his theological commitments. Howard Warrender took a similar line in his book on Hobbes, as did F. C. Hood.[5] Then there was a lull in theistic interpretation, as people took time to digest the work of Taylor and Warrender. David Gauthier, in his book on *Leviathan*,[6] conceded that Hobbes was a theist but argued that his moral and political theory is independent of any theistic suppositions. Jean Hampton took a similar line,[7] as did Gregory Kavka.[8]

Now we are seeing a new wave of theistic interpretation, represented by the books of A. P. Martinich and Sharon Lloyd,[9] both of which argue that Hobbes was a theist and that recognizing this fact about him is essential to understanding his moral and political theory. Martinich holds an extreme version of this line: he thinks Hobbes was not merely a theist but a Christian, and an orthodox one at that (specifically, a Calvinistic Anglican). Lloyd's view is more moderate. She avoids controversy about Hobbes' orthodoxy, on the plausible ground that the term "orthodox" is too ill defined to be useful in discussion[10] and does not try to identify Hobbes with any particular denomination. But she does think that he was a Christian – indeed, that he had "an unshakable belief in the truth of the Christian religion," that he was trying to make a version of Christian belief appear reasonable to modern man, and that seeing that this was his project is essential to understanding *Leviathan*.[11]

So you have, broadly speaking, two schools of thought among the specialists, one holding that Hobbes was a theist, but that it does not matter, because his moral and political philosophy is independent of his religious beliefs, the other holding that he was a theist, and that this matters a great deal, that you cannot properly understand his moral and political thought without recognizing its religious component. I hold what seems to be a minority view among the specialists.[12] I think Hobbes was probably an atheist, but that at a minimum he was deeply skeptical about Christianity, and about theism in general, and that seeing *that* is essential to understanding *Leviathan*. I see Hobbes as one member of an underground movement, which also included Spinoza and Hume, whose purpose was to subvert the dominant religion of their culture and to free people from the authority of the priests and their sacred texts. So I think that with respect to this issue the philosopher in the street is nearer the mark than the majority of recent Hobbes specialists seem to be. I have argued this elsewhere,[13] without, so far as I know, persuading anyone yet. But here I intend to have another go at it, to try to show that a theistic interpretation of *Leviathan* is not plausible on the evidence, and that we miss something important about Hobbes if we do not see this.

III. Methodology

Most English-language writers who specialize in the history of early modern philosophy these days concentrate on the history of metaphysics and epistemology and leave the study of early modern moral and political philosophers to those who specialize in moral and political philosophy, people who frequently do not have broader interests in the history of the early modern period and are often political theorists first and historians second.[14] This fact about the discipline can have unfortunate consequences.

It is not that the people who write books on Hobbes' moral and political philosophy are not capable of producing work that makes a major contribution to our understanding of Hobbes' thought. The work of Gregory Kavka, whom we are honoring in this volume, is a splendid example to show that they can. I yield to no one in my admiration for his contributions to Hobbes scholarship. He did as much to help me understand Hobbes as any other scholar I have read (and much more than most). But he did not claim to approach Hobbes as an historian would: He focused on certain aspects of the text of *Leviathan* and had little to say about others (particularly those parts of the work dealing with religious issues); he made only occasional use of Hobbes' other works; and as he himself said, he "largely ignored" the historical context of the work, aiming to provide "a model of how a classic text can be used to contribute to contemporary debate."[15] I think he achieved that goal, which is no small accomplishment. I think, in addition, that he was unduly modest about his historical skills. He did write about Hobbes in a way which not only made him an interesting contributor to contemporary debates but also was extremely useful to the historian trying to figure out what the best reading of the text is. His brilliance enabled him to transcend the limitations of his official methodology.

That said, one of my goals in this discussion is to argue that there is also value in a more historical approach, and that such an approach need not make Hobbes any less interesting for contemporary philosophers.[16] The methodological principles which will guide this study are familiar enough: Looking at the historical context of the author's work is important; so is looking at the contemporary reception of the work, looking at other works by the philosopher, looking at biographical data and correspondence, and looking at variant versions of the text. I suppose many people would be prepared to grant these principles, even if they are not prepared to act on them. What needs argument here, I assume, is the claim that if you do not attend to these maxims of historical scholarship, you may miss something really interesting about Hobbes.

One of the great difficulties in understanding *Leviathan* is that you need to be alert to the presence of irony in this work. Irony is often a difficult thing to be sure about. Hearing its presence requires not taking the text at face value, and many interpreters are understandably reluctant to do that. But some readers of *Leviathan* seem to me to be tone deaf when it comes to hearing clear notes of irony. Recognizing irony requires having some sense of what it was possible for an author of a certain period to think and to say. I hope to show that an understanding of the Renaissance and Reformation debates about religion – combined with a knowledge of other matters which seem mainly to interest historians – may help you to detect irony in *Leviathan,* and (if your interpretation of that text has been unduly influenced by the recent secondary literature) alter your perception of this masterwork. Theistic interpretations of Hobbes often seem to assume that it was just not possible for anyone in seventeenth-century Europe to be as critical of Christianity as I think Hobbes was, and that if Hobbes had been that much at odds with the dominant religion of his time and place, he would have had to keep quiet about it, since he could not have found a receptive audience for his critique. To write that critically of Christianity, it will be said, would have alienated his readers and undermined his political project of persuading people that the sovereign needed, and was entitled, to absolute obedience. A little history should clear us of these illusions.

IV. Reflections on Anticlericalism

Theistic interpreters of Hobbes will probably concede that he was profoundly anticlerical. They could hardly deny it. Hobbes may have had dear friends among the clergy, men like Mersenne and Gassendi, but he did not like the clergy as a class. Here is an anecdote Aubrey tells in his biography of Hobbes:

Mr. Edmund Waller said to me, when I desired him to write some verses in praise of him [Hobbes], that he was afraid of the churchmen. He quoted Horace – "Incedo per ignes suppositos cineri doloso." ["I tread on fire still smouldering underneath deceptive ash." *Odes* 2.1] – that what was chiefly to be taken notice of in his elegy was that he, being but one, and a private person, pulled down all the churches, dispelled the mists of ignorance, and laid open their priest craft.[17]

Waller knew Hobbes pretty well, as the recent edition of Hobbes' correspondence makes clear,[18] and his judgment about what was to be taken notice of in Hobbes' elegy deserves our attention.

Now it may be said that to be anticlerical is not necessarily to be irreligious; to be critical of the Christian clergy, for example, is not necessarily to reject the religion they represent. Martinich makes this point.[19] I concede the point. Indeed, I made it myself in the article Martinich criticizes, citing the example of Milton.[20] Now I would add the examples of Erasmus and Luther, both of whom had scathing things to say about the clergy of their day. There is an entertaining illustration of this in the dialogue Erasmus wrote just after the death of Pope Julius II,[21] called *Julius Excluded from Heaven.*

In this work Erasmus imagines Julius presenting himself at the gates of heaven and being denied admission by Saint Peter. (Julius has neglected to bring the Keys to the Kingdom with him.) At the end of the dialogue, Saint Peter says to Julius's "genius" (i.e., his guardian angel): "Are you the one who stirred him up to such atrocious crimes?"

Julius's genius replies: "I did hardly anything; he was so eager in his vices that even with wings I could hardly have followed him."

To which Saint Peter responds: "Well, I'm not surprised that we get so few candidates for admission, when monsters like this are in charge of governing the church. But perhaps the common people may be curable – or so I conjecture from the fact that because of the mere empty title of pope, they gave honor to such a filthy piece of garbage as this."[22]

Erasmus is also quite critical of the clergy in his better-known work, *The Praise of Folly,* though in that work – which, unlike *Julius Excluded from Heaven,* he acknowledged having written – he is careful not to name any of the popes he mocks.[23] His idea is that if the objects of his satire are not named, they can take offense only by admitting that they are guilty of the offenses he criticizes. There may be some doubt about Erasmus's orthodoxy,[24] but I would not question his commitment to Christianity. (We will have an example from Luther later.)

That conceded, I think it is difficult psychologically to sustain a faith in Christianity, or any other organized religion, and at the same time reject the official representatives of that religion as thoroughly corrupt and disreputable. If you are a Christian, in the early modern period at least, one of the things you are apt to believe is that God revealed himself to man through Christ, and that the Church is the vehicle through which that revelation has been preserved and propagated. After the Reformation you may have some doubts about just which church is that vehicle, but if you come to regard that church's clergy as thoroughly corrupt, and your faith is not shaken, you will at least suffer what we now call "cognitive dissonance," a certain tension in your beliefs which is difficult to live with, and which, when resolved, may not be resolved in favor of the faith.

Hobbes himself makes a point very like this in his discussion of religion in Part I of *Leviathan* when he writes:

For seeing all formed religion is founded at first upon the faith which a multitude hath in some one person, whom they believe not only to be a wise man, and to labour to procure their happiness, but also to be a holy man, to whom God himself vouchsafeth to declare his will supernaturally, it followeth *necessarily,* when they that have the government of religion shall come to have either the wisdom of those men, their sincerity, or their love suspected, or that they shall be unable to show any probable token of divine revelation, that *the religion which they desire to uphold must be suspected likewise;* and (without the fear of the civil sword) contradicted and rejected.[25] (L xii, 24, my emphasis)

Hobbes seems to go further here than I would. He says that disillusionment with the clergy *must* shake your faith in the religion they profess; I claim only that it *may* do so.[26] But perhaps Hobbes' point is more epistemological than psychological: not that it is a necessary law of human nature that all who suspect the clergy will suspect the religion the clergy represent, but that they *ought to,* given the grounds they have for belief in the religion. I leave this interpretive issue undecided.

Hobbes goes on, after this passage, to list various things which take away the clergy's reputation for wisdom, for sincerity, for love, and for having a divine calling. If they enjoin belief in contradictory statements, fail to practice the moral doctrines they teach, are detected in private ends, and are unable to perform miracles or make true prophecies, their credit will suffer. He concludes by commenting that the sole cause of change in religion is "unpleasing priests, and those not only amongst Catholics, but even in that church which hath presumed most of reformation" (L xii, 32). So even the most reformed of churches has its share of unpleasing priests. Perhaps this is one passage Waller had in mind when he said that Hobbes had "pulled down all the churches."

V. Anticlerics and Antichristians

There are anticlerics and anticlerics. Machiavelli, like Erasmus, is also strongly anticlerical. I suggest that Hobbes is closer to Machiavelli than to Erasmus, and that Machiavelli is no Christian. There are important differences between Hobbes and Machiavelli, of course, but the similarities are interesting enough to be worth pursuing.

You will not know much about Machiavelli's anticlericalism if you have read only *The Prince,* because the criticism of the clergy in that work is very mild. *The Prince* was not published in Machiavelli's lifetime, but it was dedicated to (and evidently sent to) Lorenzo de' Medici, whose uncle had just ascended the throne of Saint Peter as Leo X (successor to Julius II). The discussion of the clergy comes primarily in chapter xi, where Machiavelli discusses ecclesiastical states; it appears first as what I take to be ironic praise: only the rulers of ecclesiastical states can maintain their power without either ability (*virtù*) or luck (*fortuna*), because they are "sustained by ancient religious institutions, which have been sufficiently strong to maintain their rulers in office however they live or act."[27] Then, after a cool, non-judgmental analysis of the political policies of Alexander VI (pope from 1492 to 1503) and Julius II (pope from 1503 to 1513), and of how they used money and military force to increase their power, Machiavelli concludes by expressing some optimism about Leo: "His Holiness Pope Leo has found the Papacy very powerful indeed; and it is to be hoped that, just as his predecessors made it great by their military activity, he, by his goodness and countless other virtues, will make it both very great *and worthy of reverence*" (my translation and emphasis). The implication is that the papacy was not worthy of reverence under Alexander and Julius. Machiavelli had gone into exile after the republican government he served was overthrown. In *The Prince* he is hoping he can get a place in the new political order by making himself useful to the Medici, who have replaced the republican government. Mild criticism of Alexander and Julius will be acceptable, and a little flattery of Leo will not be amiss.

In *The Discourses,* which also were not published during Machiavelli's lifetime but may have reached members of the Medici family indirectly,[28] the criticism of the Church is much sharper.[29] Machiavelli holds the Church responsible for the decline of both religion and morality in Italy:

The wicked examples presented by the papal court have caused the whole of Italy to lose all piety and all religious devotion . . . Just as respect for religion has a whole range of beneficial consequences, so contempt for religion has a whole range of evil consequences. We Italians owe this much to our Church and our clergy: they have made us irreligious and wicked.[30]

Notice that Machiavelli anticipates the Hobbesian principle that disrespect for the clergy leads to disrespect for the religion they represent. And Machiavelli is no friend of the clergy as he knows them in the Italy of his day.

Does he also reject their religion? I think he does, though this is a matter of dispute. He certainly does not reject it openly and unequivocally, and he is not hostile to all religion as such. He thinks a religion of the right kind is a good thing, because it is very useful politically. So in the *Discourses* he credits Numa – the second of the kings of Rome and successor to Romulus, the founder of Rome – with having done foundational work comparable in its importance to that of Romulus by establishing a religion in Rome:

The Romans of his day were completely wild, not domesticated; he wanted to train them to live a sociable life and to practice the arts of peace. So he turned to religion, because it is essential for the maintenance of a civilized way of life, and he founded a religion such that for many centuries there was more fear of God in Rome than there has ever been anywhere else. Such piety was of considerable assistance whenever the senate or one of Rome's great leaders undertook any enterprise. (I, xi, p. 114)

One reason religion was valuable to the Romans was that it made them very fearful of breaking oaths, and this was good both for civil order and for military discipline. But the Roman religion also served the public good by encouraging men to do great deeds, by defining the supreme good as "boldness of spirit, strength of body, and all the other qualities that make men redoubtable" (II, ii, p. 168). The Roman religion did not make men completely domesticated; rather, it taught them to save their savagery for the enemies of the state.

Two points need emphasis here. Though religion does, in Machiavelli's eyes, serve the interests of the rulers, enabling them to get their proposals accepted by adding the luster of divine sanction to their authority (I, xi, p. 115), it does not serve only their interests. In Rome religion also served the interests of the community as a whole. The Roman state which this religion was so instrumental in forming and preserving was the most durable and powerful republic ever known, the best historical example of the best kind of government, self-government. Machiavelli sees republican government (in the Roman sense) as the only stable form of government in which people are free; for him, liberty is a very important value. He does not mind that this religion was not a true religion, and that its acceptance involved deception of the people by their rulers. Numa claimed that his actions were authorized by the gods: he "pretended," as Machiavelli puts it, "to be on friendly terms with a nymph who advised him on everything before he made recommendations to the people" (I, xi, p. 115). Machiavelli does not for a moment credit those claims. For that matter, neither did his source, the Roman historian Livy. (Cf. Livy, I. 18–21.) Hobbes reminds us of this story from Livy in chapter xii, paragraph 20 of *Leviathan,* where he adds other examples (from Islam and the religion of the Incas) in support of the general proposition that the first founders of "gentile commonwealths" (or "heathen religions," as the marginal summary says) always claim divine authority for their edicts.[31]

Though Machiavelli thinks the right kind of religion is a good thing, it does not appear that he thinks Christianity is the right kind of religion. In some respects Christianity is like the religion of pagan Rome: it provides divine authority for the actions of human rulers and gives people reason to think that if they commit a crime and escape the power of human justice, they are still not home free. So far, Christianity is a good thing. But Machiavelli does not seem to think that it teaches the right virtues. He says in the *Discourses:*

Our religion, by contrast [with the religion of ancient Rome], glorifies men who are humble and contemplative, rather than those who do great deeds. In fact, it regards humility, self-abasement, and contempt for worldly goods as the supreme virtues . . . It is true our religion requires that you be strong, but it wants you to demonstrate your strength by undergoing suffering without complaint, rather than by overcoming resistance. This set of values, it would seem, has turned the men of our day into weaklings and left them unable to defend themselves against the ravages of the wicked. The wicked have no difficulty in handling their fellow men, for they know the average individual wants rather to endure their blows than to strike back, for he hopes to go to heaven. (II, ii, pp. 168–9)

Notice that Machiavelli speaks of Christianity here as "our religion." Elsewhere in the same chapter he says that "our religion has taught us the truth and the right way to salvation" (p. 168). Some scholars infer that Machiavelli was a sincere Christian.[32] I do not. It seems clear from both *The Prince* and *The Discourses,* that, *if* Machiavelli believed that Christianity teaches *these* virtues as the proper route to heaven, he does not believe in practicing them. He certainly does not preach those virtues; he may not be the amoralist he is reputed to be, but he did not get his reputation for nothing.

Machiavelli does provide a way out of the conclusion that he rejected Christian ethics. He makes a distinction in the *Discourses* between Christianity as commonly taught and Christianity properly interpreted:

Although it seems we have all been made effeminate, and God himself allows injustice to flourish, it is of course the fault of the sinful nature of mankind, which has caused them to interpret the teachings of our religion as suits their lazy temperament, and not as brave men would have done. For if they had taken into account the fact that our religion allows us to praise and defend our homeland, they would have realized that if we are religious we ought to love and honor our country, *and to prepare ourselves to be the sort of people who will be capable of defending it.* (p. 169; my emphasis)

I emphasize that last phrase because I think that if you reflect on the kind of person Machiavelli thinks it is necessary to be in order to be capable of defending your homeland, and then reflect on the teachings of Christianity, you will find Machiavelli's "interpretation" of Christianity too implausible to be credible as an interpretation.[33]

For authentically Christian theorists in the sixteenth century, it was hard to see how to combine Christianity, which preaches nonresistance to evil (Matt. 5:39), with political authority, which inherently involves the use of force to resist evil. Luther, for example, wrestling with this problem in his treatise *On Secular Authority,* concluded that it was not impossible, but still a rare and difficult thing, to be both a Christian and a prince at the same time.[34] Similarly Erasmus advises his Christian prince to "do violence to no one . . . tolerate injuries rather than avenge them at great cost to the state [even if] your empire is likely to be reduced to some extent," and to abdicate rather than defend his kingdom by violating justice, incurring much bloodshed, or damaging the cause of religion.[35]

For authors whose Christian commitments are less clear, the Gospel teaching was a serious ground of objection to Christianity. Sometime in the 1590s Jean Bodin, who was at least nominally a Catholic, wrote a dialogue, the *Colloquium heptaplomeres,* in which the representatives of various religious points of view appear: a Catholic, a Lutheran, a Calvinist, a Jew, a former Christian converted to Islam, a defender of natural religion, and a skeptic.[36] The dialogue form makes it a matter of speculation which party (if any) represents Bodin's point of view. Bodin did not publish this dialogue even posthumously, and it did not appear in print until the nineteenth century, but it had considerable clandestine circulation before that. Seventeenth-century authors who knew it often regarded it as an attack on Christianity,[37] perhaps because of the critique of Christian ethics that Bodin puts in the mouth of some of his non-Christian interlocutors. A central theme of the critique is that it is contrary to human nature, and hence impossible, to adhere consistently to the injunction to return good for evil.[38]

For the most part Hobbes' *Leviathan* does not use the dialogue form. Instead he uses a strategy like Machiavelli's. He advocates a pagan morality and then alleges that it is Christian. His second law of nature requires

That a man be willing, *when others are so too,* as far forth as for peace and defence of himself he shall think it necessary, to lay down this right to all things, and be contented with so much liberty against other men, as he would allow other men against himself. (L xiv, 5; my emphasis. Cf. xv, 36.)

This prescription to divest yourself of your natural right to all things is, as I emphasize, conditional on others being willing to do the same. No sooner has Hobbes said this than he has the cheek, as I would call it, to identify this principle with the Golden Rule, as if the Golden Rule taught that we should do unto others as we can reasonably expect them to do unto us.[39]

In the Renaissance there was a tendency, in reaction against the complexity – some would say, absurd subtlety – of scholastic theology, to reduce Christianity to its moral teachings. Erasmus is representative of this tendency, which is one reason Luther is so hostile to him in *De servo arbitrio*.[40] There was a battle going on in the sixteenth century over the soul of Christianity. I take it that if the moral teachings of Jesus do not constitute the essence of Christianity, they are at least essential to it. So if you reject moral teachings which are central to the Gospel message, you reject the religion.[41]

It seems to me that both Machiavelli and Hobbes teach a doctrine fundamentally incompatible with Christian ethics, and that it is, therefore, a mistake to regard them as Christians. They both, of course, present their doctrine as an interpretation of Christian ethics. But I do not take that claim very seriously. In the period in which they were writing, someone in fundamental disagreement with Christian teaching could hardly be open about his disagreement with any safety. Machiavelli and Hobbes represent one way in which it was possible for a Renaissance humanist to resolve the conflict between Christianity and classical culture, a way very different from the way Erasmus chose. If we are not conscious of the historical context in which Hobbes is working, we may take much too seriously his assimilation of his second law of nature to the Golden Rule.

VI. Hobbes and Spinoza on Miracles

Let us come back to another favorite passage of mine from Aubrey's biography, which reports Hobbes' reaction to reading Spinoza's *Theological-Political*

Treatise (1670). Waller had sent Lord Devonshire (Hobbes' patron) a copy of the work and asked him what Hobbes thought of it. Hobbes replied cautiously to Lord Devonshire, citing Matthew 7:1 ("Judge not that ye be not judged"), and more informatively to Aubrey: "He told me he [Spinoza] had out thrown him [Hobbes] a bar's length, for he durst not write so boldly."[42] Theistic interpreters of Hobbes tend not to like this remark. Hood, for example, casts doubt on Aubrey's reliability as a reporter. Martinich asks how we can hope to determine what Hobbes might have meant by this. Perhaps Hobbes just admired Spinoza's prose style.

An earlier article of mine[43] asked what Hobbes might have meant, recognizing that any answer must be conjectural, but arguing that if we find Hobbes and Spinoza taking up the same topics, and if we find Spinoza consistently taking a bolder position than Hobbes on those topics, we have some reason both to trust Aubrey's reporting and to suppose that Hobbes might have wished that he had felt free to make such claims himself. We can never be certain what Hobbes meant – and that may be one reason why some interpreters of Hobbes will not venture into this swamp – but I suggest that if there are enough affinities, and they seem deep enough, we may properly conclude that Spinoza, in some respects, represents what Hobbes himself saw as a logical development of his thought.

In that earlier article I took up three topics: prophecy, miracles, and the authority of Scripture, each of which Hobbes discusses, in what seems a rather skeptical vein, in Part III of *Leviathan,* and each of which Spinoza takes up more fully (and I would say, much more boldly) in the *Theological-Political Treatise.* These topics are closely connected: a prophet, in traditional theology, is the initial vehicle of divine revelation, an intermediary between God and man; miracles constitute one of the criteria for distinguishing true prophets from false ones; and Scripture is the record of the revelation the prophets conveyed. These three topics are central to the claim of Christianity to be based on a divine revelation.

I will not repeat what I said in my earlier article. But I would like to enlarge on one of its themes and then add a new one to the list. The old theme is the issue of miracles. Hobbes' discussion of miracles is complex, and we cannot go into all its subtleties, but he concludes that because "mankind [are apt] to give too hasty belief to pretended [i.e., alleged] miracles, there can be no better, nor I think any other, caution, than that which God hath prescribed [e.g., in Deut. 13:1–5] . . . that we take not any for prophets that teach any other religion than that which God's lieutenant . . . hath established" (L xxxvii, 13). When Deuteronomy was written, "God's lieutenant" was Moses. When Hobbes was writing, God's lieutenant was "the head of the Church," whose identity, of course, varied with the identity of the church (and in England, the identity of the monarch or other secular ruler). So that person, and the doctrine she[44] has established, are to be consulted before we give credit to a pretended miracle or prophet. And when that is done, the thing they pretend to be a miracle, we must both see it done, and use all means possible to consider whether it be really done or no; and not only so, but whether it be such as no man can do the like by his natural power, but that it requires the immediate hand of God. And in this also we must have recourse to God's lieutenant . . . So also if we see not, but only hear tell of a miracle, we are to consult the lawful Church, that is to say, the lawful head thereof, how far we are to give credit to the relators of it. (Ibid.)

Hobbes does not exclude the possibility of a contemporary miracle and generally implies the existence of bona fide miracles in the past, but he sets demanding criteria for accepting contemporary claims that a miracle has occurred, and he leaves all doubtful cases to the decision of the sovereign. He emphasizes human gullibility and the possibility of priestly deception in a way which foreshadows Hume. Why, if reports of present-day miracles are untrustworthy, should we credit reports of past miracles, when it is so much more difficult to investigate claims about past miracles?

Still, Spinoza takes a more radical position: miracles in the strict sense are a logical impossibility; in the strict sense a miracle would be a violation of a law of nature; but the laws of nature are an expression of the power of God, God's decrees concerning nature, so any occurrence contrary to those laws would be an occurrence contrary to the will of an omnipotent being, which is absurd. Spinoza acknowledges a loose sense of the term "miracle," in which it signifies an occurrence which we, at a certain point in the development of human knowledge, cannot understand in terms of the laws of nature. But acceptance of miracles in this sense is merely recognition of human ignorance, which cannot be made the foundation of any knowledge of God.

Now it may be said that many perfectly good Christians have been skeptical about many alleged miracles, even when those miracles are alleged to support (some form of) the Christian religion. Luther is a case in point. In his *Appeal to the Ruling Class of German Nationality* he first rejects the use of miracles to support the authority of the pope: "If an authority does anything against Christ, it is due to the power of the Antichrist and of the devil, even if that authority makes it rain and hail miracles and plagues. Miracles and plagues prove nothing, especially in these latter days of evil, for specious miracles of this kind are foretold everywhere in Scripture." Later Luther criticized, as one of the abuses of the Roman Church, the establishment of "extra-parochial chapels and churches" as the goal of pilgrimages. He thinks pilgrimages are just one of many corrupt methods the clergy have found to get money out of the laity:

It is useless to argue that miracles are seen in these places, for the Evil Spirit can also work miracles, as Christ declared (Matthew 24:24). If they got to work in all seriousness and forbade things of this kind, the miracles would soon cease . . . these things are indications of great unbelief among the people; for if their faith were as it should be, they would find everything needful in their own churches . . . Each bishop is only thinking how he can start one of these pilgrimages in his own province, not caring whether the people believe and live as they should . . . [their aim] is to draw crowds and cause money to flow.[45]

It is dangerous, I think, for Christian authors to acknowledge that people are easily taken in by miracle stories, particularly if in doing so they attribute corrupt motives to the Christian clergy. They may encourage more doubts than they intend to. The admission – indeed, insistence – that human gullibility and greed have operated even within the Christian world simply feeds the doubts of those humanists whose acquaintance with classical historians, and with the uses religion was put to in the pagan world, has already encouraged them to be suspicious.[46] If Christianity is to be a convincing exception to the general run of religions, its clergy ought to be more virtuous than that.

VII. Hobbes and Spinoza on Natural Law

One of Spinoza's more revolutionary conclusions in the *Theological-Political Treatise* is that God cannot be a lawgiver. In Chapter iv, on the strength of an argument similar to his argument concerning miracles, Spinoza contends that if God were a lawgiver (in the relevant sense of the term "law"), he would have to prescribe to men rules that they are capable of either obeying or disobeying, as it seems good to them, taking into account the possible consequences of obedience or disobedience. But one thing which God, in spite of his omnipotence (or rather, precisely because of his omnipotence), *cannot* do is to prescribe laws in that sense of the term. For a law, in that sense, is a command, that is, an expression of the will of the commander. And if God wills, say, that Adam not eat the apple, then Adam will not eat the apple, indeed, will not be able to eat the apple. When we speak of law in connection with God, the only thing we can coherently mean is a necessary truth about how things actually behave, and must behave; we cannot mean a command that they are capable of disobeying. To suppose otherwise is to confuse the power of God with the power of human monarchs.[47]

I conjecture that this may be one of the things Hobbes found interesting in Spinoza. The doctrine does, later in Spinoza's work, lead to some rather Hobbesian-sounding conclusions about the status of obligations in the state of nature. In the *Theological-Political Treatise* (xvi, 9) Spinoza concludes that the law of nature "prohibits nothing except what no one desires and what no one can do: not disputes, not hatreds, not anger, not deception; without qualification, it is not averse to anything which appetite urges." This is certainly reminiscent of the doctrine of Chapter xiii, paragraph 13, of *Leviathan:* that in the war of all against all which characterizes the state of nature "nothing can be unjust. The notions of right and wrong, justice and injustice, have there no place. Where there is no common power, there is no law; where there is no law, no injustice."

Students of Hobbes' reception will know that many of his readers found this statement troubling.

Leibniz is a case in point. He wrote Hobbes a letter in 1670,[48] inviting him to clear his theory of the consequences which certain unsympathetic interpreters had attached to it:

If anyone . . . applied your theory of the complete licence which exists in the state of nature to the dealings which take place between all the citizens of various republics, he would, I think, fall far wide of your own opinion . . . For you recognize that . . . given the existence of a ruler of the world, men cannot live in a pure state of nature outside all republics, since God is the common monarch of all men. So when some people accuse your hypotheses of licentiousness and impiety, they are wrong. Having . . . always understood your theories [in this way], I confess that they have kindled a great light in my mind.[49]

You might conclude from this that Leibniz was the originator of the Taylor–Warrender thesis, but I think he is being slightly disingenuous here.

In the same year Leibniz also wrote to Jacob Thomasius in rather different terms, reporting that he had "recently seen an article . . . in which you treated according to its deserts an intolerably licentious book on the liberty of philosophizing." Leibniz is referring here to Spinoza's *Theological-Political Treatise,* which argues, among other things, for freedom of thought and expression. He continues,

The author seems to follow not only Hobbes' politics, but also his religion, which he has outlined so adequately in his *Leviathan,* a work monstrous even in what its title suggests.[50] For Hobbes, in a whole chapter of *Leviathan* [xxxiii], has sown the seeds of that very smart critique which this bold man carries out against Sacred Scripture.[51]

Because Spinoza's rejection of natural law, and of the associated concept of God as a lawgiver, is clear and unequivocal, Leibniz's claim that Spinoza follows Hobbes' politics as well as his religion suggests that he does not take the theistic natural law theory of *Leviathan* at face value. I suggest that in the letter he wrote to Hobbes Leibniz is trying to draw Hobbes out on the question of the relation between God and natural law. So far as we know, Hobbes never replied to Leibniz's letter – so he did not endorse the Taylor–Warrender interpretation of his natural law theory when Leibniz gave him the opportunity to do so.

In Chapters xiv and xv of *Leviathan,* Hobbes enumerates some nineteen "laws of nature." Given what he has said in Chapter xiii, the appearance of laws of nature at this point is anomalous. At the end of Chapter xv Hobbes either clarifies the situation or muddies the waters, depending on how you take it:

These dictates of reason men use to call by the name of laws, but improperly; for they are but conclusions or theorems concerning what conduceth to the conservation and defence of themselves, whereas law, properly, is the word of him that by right hath command over others. But yet if we consider the same theorems, as delivered in the word of God, that by right commandeth all things, then are they properly called laws.[52] (L xv, 41)

Now Taylor and Warrender[53] regarded this passage as extremely important, because they saw the last sentence as cancelling the apparently anarchic implications of Chapter xiii, and as saying, in effect, "If you are an atheist, you can only regard these so-called laws as hypothetical imperatives; it is only if you are a theist that you can see that they really are laws, which impose a genuine obligation independently of any human legal system."

I, on the other hand, hold that at heart Hobbes does not think his laws of nature are properly called "laws," in the sense defined by this passage, that he regards them as a (very special) kind of hypothetical imperative. I hold that he is (probably) an atheist (or at least a thorough skeptic about theistic religions), who is content to permit his theistic readers to interpret his laws of nature as laws in the strict sense, but who, for his part, regards them as being "merely" a very special kind of hypothetical imperative.

Why? For one thing Hobbes does not seem to attach as much importance to the last sentence of paragraph 41 in Chapter xv as he ought to, on the Taylor–Warrender interpretation. He omits it from the Latin *Leviathan*. He also ignores it when he paraphrases the final paragraph of Chapter xv in paragraph 8 of Chapter xxvi. And if this should be dismissed as a mere argument from silence, in Chapter xxvi he denies that the laws of nature are actually laws until a commonwealth has been established and the sovereign commands obedience to them.[54]

These textual and biographical data are not decisive. No such information ever is. They are simply interesting data, which may add up to something, if there are enough of them, and which may prompt us to ask related questions, which may have interesting answers. What would Hobbes have thought about Spinoza's argument that God cannot be a lawgiver? Could that argument be one of the acts of boldness Hobbes admired in Spinoza?

Perhaps Hobbes approved of the argument as he found it in Spinoza; perhaps not. One reason for doubt is that, as Spinoza states his argument, it depends on the theological doctrine that in God, will and intellect are identical. It is not obvious what that means or why a theist must accept that assumption. In reformulating Spinoza's argument earlier in this section I deliberately avoided introducing that assumption, because it seemed to me obscure and inessential. Hobbes may have found it both obscure and essential.

But Hobbes did have the materials for his own argument to the same conclusion. He never states that conclusion – but he does state premises from which that conclusion can easily be derived. The Hobbesian argument, like Spinoza's, would rely crucially on a definition of "law":

(1) Law in general is not counsel, but command; nor a command of any man to any man, but only of him whose command is addressed to one formerly [i.e., by a prior act of consent] obliged to obey him. (L xxvi, 2)

Consider next the definition of the term "command":

(2) Command is where a man saith *do this,* or *do not this,* without expecting other reason than the will of him that says it. (xxv, 2)

In both these passages Hobbes seems to be treating laws and commands as prescriptions from one human being to others. Let us take that apparent limitation to be inessential. (Otherwise we get too quickly to the conclusion that there cannot be a divine law.) From his definition of command Hobbes draws the following conclusion:

(3) He that commandeth pretendeth thereby his own benefit; for the reason of his command is his own will only, and the proper object of every man's will is some good to himself.

From this we may conclude that

(4) If there is such a thing as a divine law (in the prescriptive sense of "law"), it must be a command which God issues for the purpose of securing his own benefit.

I then observe that, according to Hobbes,

(5) God has no ends (L xxxi, 13).[55]

But if God cannot have as his object any good to himself, then on Hobbesian principles

(6) There can be no such thing as a divine law (in the prescriptive sense of the term "law").

The fact that this argument is available to Hobbes – and is indeed a fairly easy deduction from premises he explicitly adopts within a relatively short stretch of *Leviathan* – encourages me to think that one of the things Hobbes liked about the *Theological-Political Treatise* was its conclusion that God cannot be a lawgiver.

VIII. Sifting out Disinformation

So far, if I am right, we have the following result: Hobbes was an anticleric who thought that anticlericalism entailed rejection of the religion the clerics represent; he did, in fact, reject central elements of Christian moral teaching; he was also quite skeptical about the miracle stories on which the claim of the Christian Scriptures to be a record of divine revelation is based; and there are grounds for thinking that he rejected the Christian conception of God as a lawgiver, who would distribute punishments and rewards in an afterlife. Other scholars may read these passages differently than I do, particularly where my reading involves, not just reporting what Hobbes says, but inference from what he says.[56] But suppose, for the moment, that I am right. Does this entail that Hobbes was, in a strict sense, an atheist, someone who denies that there is any legitimate sense in which it can be said that there is a God?

Of course not. If I have Spinoza right, he was a Hobbesian in all the relevant respects, and I do not think (contrary to what Martinich, for example, assumes) that Spinoza was an atheist. I think Spinoza is sincere when he says that he believes in God. It is a very different God from the God of Abraham, Isaac, Jacob, and Jesus. Spinoza's God is an impersonal set of principles immanent in the universe: it has no intellect, no will, no purposes, no affects like love, hate, or anger. But Spinoza's austere God is evidently, for him, an object of love, and when he says that the love of this God is man's highest good, I think he means it. So I consider Spinoza a religious thinker of a very unconventional sort. I see no sign of this kind of philosophical religiosity in Hobbes. It is possible that Hobbes was a kind of nondenominational theist, who believed in God, without believing in any of the major religions of his day. But I see no reason to think so.

A full discussion of this issue would require discussion of various passages in which Hobbes affirms a belief in God and offers arguments for God's existence. This is a subject I have written about elsewhere,[57] and I have no desire to repeat myself. But I would like to reprise one theme of that discussion, with an embellishment or two.

Hobbes does not claim merely to be a theist. He claims to be a Christian, and, indeed, an Anglican who "favored the episcopal side."[58] If we attempt to defend a compromise position according to which Hobbes was a theist but not specifically a Christian, we must discount some, at least, of the things he says about his religious views. The only question is, how much? If, when we say that Hobbes was disingenuous in his avowals of conventional religious views, we impute some moral fault to Hobbes – say, dishonesty, or cowardice – then the compromise position is also involved in that imputation (though not to the degree that a more radical interpretation would be). I do not myself think that there would be any moral fault in Hobbes' being disingenuous on this subject, given the circumstances in which he was operating. Whatever fault is to be found lies with those who persecute unorthodox opinions. But theistic interpreters frequently act as if they were defending Hobbes' honor. I reject the suggestion that his honor is at issue here and insist that, if it were, it would also be at issue when Hobbes is read as a nondenominational theist.

In 1642 Hobbes wrote, in *De cive,* that man can know that there is a God by the light of nature (ii, 21) or by natural reason (xiv, 19; xv, 14). He does not actually say there what arguments reason can use to come to know that God exists, but it seems fair to suppose that he would have used some form of the argument from a first cause, since that is the argument he uses in *The Elements of Law* (I, xi, 2), written two years earlier than *De cive,* and in *Leviathan* (xi, 25), which Hobbes was beginning to write around the time of the second edition of *De cive* in 1647. *De cive* is a work Hobbes published and is well known to Hobbes scholars.

In 1642 Hobbes also wrote, but did not publish, a work called *An Examination of Thomas White's* De mundo. White was a friend of his who had written a cosmological treatise attempting to reconcile the new science with the foundations of the Christian religion.[59] Hobbes' critique of White lay in the Bibliothèque Nationale for some three hundred years, unrecognized as a Hobbesian work, until Jean Jacquot and Harold Whitmore Jones identified it and made it available.[60] Though this work is a major find, knowledge of it seems to have been slow to penetrate the world of Hobbesian scholarship. Perhaps because it is primarily a scientific treatise and the interests of most Hobbes scholars lie elsewhere, I know only one recent writer on Hobbes who takes notice of it: David Johnston in his book *The Rhetoric of* Leviathan.[61]

What is interesting about this work, for our purposes, is that in it Hobbes takes quite a different line about arguments for the existence of God than he takes in his published works of the period. One thing White had claimed to do was to demonstrate the existence of God by positing God as a necessary first cause to explain the existence of motion. This is a familiar enough line of argument, one which, judging by his published works, you might expect Hobbes to be sympathetic to. But in the *Examination of White* Hobbes contends that White's attempt is both unphilosophical and antireligious: unphilosophical because it shows a misunderstanding of the nature of demonstration to suppose that questions of existence or nonexistence are capable of demonstration (xxvi, 2); antireligious because the attempt to prove the articles of faith necessarily weakens both faith and religion (xxvi, 4). Rulers should not allow their subjects to claim to demonstrate such matters as the existence of God and the immortality of the soul. The attempt to prove such theses will only cause ordinary people to consider them false, "because those who wished them to be true could not demonstrate that they were" (xxvi, 6).

Indeed, there is an even greater danger: the philosopher who inquires into the nature and cause of motion may come upon some proposition now held by the Christian faith which seems to contradict something he has previously proven. He may be tempted to conclude that the Christian doctrine is false. The proper conclusion is that he does not understand in what sense it is true (xxvi, 7). But those who subject incomprehensible matters of divinity to their own metaphysical speculations almost inevitably come into conflict with Christianity at every step (xxviii, 3) – so it is best to avoid such speculation.

Hobbes' position in the *Examination of White* involves quite a strong form of fideism: not merely that the Christian faith requires belief in propositions inaccessible to human reason, but that it requires belief in propositions *prima facie* contrary to reason. Now it should be said immediately – and loudly and clearly, so that there can be no mistake – that there is nothing inherently atheistic or irreligious or un-Christian about adopting a fideism of this strength. Certainly there have been Christians whose faith I would not dream of questioning who have held similar positions. In this context Luther seems the most apt example.[62] But a fideism this strong does seem surprising in an author capable of writing that men set "themselves against reason as oft as reason is against them" (L xi, 21) and that enjoining belief in contradictory propositions takes away "the reputation of wisdom" and is "an argument of ignorance" (xii, 25).

The issue, though, is not whether a strong, antirationalistic fideism is inherently an irreligious view, or even whether it is credibly a Hobbesian view, but what explanation we can give of Hobbes' adoption of a strongly fideistic position in the *Examination of White*. Since Hobbes wrote this work during a period when he was repeatedly proclaiming in his published work that we can know by natural reason at least that God exists, it does not seem possible to explain the variation in position by postulating a change of view. My conjecture is that in the *Examination of White* Hobbes was experimenting with a position which he was tempted to adopt, as his way of dealing with the religious issue, when he wrote the foundational work which he thought his political philosophy demanded. But he hesitated to take such a strongly fideistic line in print, because he thought it too dangerous to represent Christian belief as irrational (rather than merely nonrational). I note that later, in *De corpore* (xxvi, 1), Hobbes does adopt a weaker form of fideism, according to which God's existence is merely not demonstrable by natural reason. Taking this line brought him grief enough from critics like Wallis.[63] In the three major political works Hobbes takes a more traditional line. An author who is advocating unconventional views, at a time when such authors face the most fearsome of penalties, must make nice judgments about what it is safe to say.

This is, of course, merely a conjecture on my part. But it does seem to me that if theistic interpreters of Hobbes are going to give much weight to his claims that God's existence is knowable by natural reason, then they owe us some plausible explanation of the discrepancy between the published work and the unpublished work. So far I have not seen any of them attempt this task.

IX. Hobbes and His Audience

One feature of *Leviathan* any interpreter must explain is the fact that so much of it is devoted to religious issues. This seems particularly puzzling if you think Hobbes is trying to show how morality can be reasonable on secularist principles. It will not do simply to say that Hobbes needs to cover his secularist tracks by pretending to take Christianity seriously, for the space he devotes to religious topics is out of all proportion to what would be needed for that. I gather that

Sharon Lloyd wrote her book *Ideals as Interests* partly because she thought there was a glaring deficiency in the works of her most prominent recent predecessors: They made a good half of the text seem quite mysterious.[64]

Lloyd has an explanation for Hobbes' preoccupation with religious issues. She thinks he was a sincere Christian, who nevertheless rejected much of what passed for Christianity in his day, because it had been corrupted by the introduction of alien doctrines. So his project is to "rationalize" Christianity by paring away some of the irrational but illegitimate accretions.[65] I think there is some truth in that, but not enough. I take Hobbes' view to be that Christianity is probably a part of our culture which cannot, given human nature, be eliminated in the short term, and that given that fact, it is desirable to try to make it as undemanding as possible, both theologically and morally.

One reason Lloyd thinks my kind of reading of Hobbes[66] must be wrong is that she thinks that Hobbes' readers were all committed Christians, that Hobbes knew this, and knew that it would be futile to try to discredit Christian belief. So even if Hobbes had not been a Christian, he would not have tried to write an anti-Christian tract:

> In addition to his believing Christianity to be true, and a properly conceived Christianity to be invaluable in procuring civil obedience, Hobbes also recognized that *his readers* believed Christianity to be true, and thus he had a third reason for attempting to rationalize, rather than to discredit, Christian belief: Hobbes could *never* have hoped to succeed in persuading his audience to *give up* Christianity; so to have made an argument whose success depended upon their doing this would have been utterly vain. Had Hobbes tried to delegitimize Christianity itself, he would likely have been summarily dismissed and his theory ignored.[67] (Her emphasis)

I think this supposes more homogeneity in Hobbes' audience than we are entitled to assume.

No doubt many of Hobbes' readers were so committed to Christianity that a frontal attack on their beliefs would simply have alienated them, would have caused Hobbes' book to be dismissed summarily and ignored. For that part of his audience Hobbes makes his criticism in an indirect way, which makes it *possible* for a committed Christian not to think that Christianity itself is under attack.[68] For that part of his audience Hobbes' message is just that they should suspend judgment about much of what they have believed, that much of what seventeenth-century Christians believe is not essential to their religion, and that they should interpret their religion so that it is a support for, not a threat to, the social order. Hobbes does regard Christianity as a very dangerous religion, because some of its sacred texts appear to say that if there is a conflict between the will of God and the command of the sovereign, we must obey God rather than the sovereign. Much of *Leviathan* aims to defuse that threat by arguing that we have to rely on the sovereign to know what to treat as a sacred text, and how to interpret it. On Hobbes' preferred conception of Christianity, only two things are ultimately necessary for salvation: belief that Jesus is the Christ, and obedience to the laws of the civil society.[69] This seems to me to take the minimalist tendencies I noted in Erasmus about as far as you can without passing into a view which no longer deserves to be called Christian. Indeed, if any Christian thought it crossed this line, she would not get an argument from me.

But there is, Hobbes believes, another part of his audience which is not so committed, which is at least uncertain about the theology, and not strongly inclined to accept the rather demanding moral requirements of Christianity. For this part of his audience Hobbes has a different message: he encourages their doubts about Christian theology, provides them with ammunition, and tries to give them a secular ground for practising those elements of Christian morality which are rationally defensible.

To see that there was such an audience out there, we might do various things. We might read Montaigne's *Essais,* and raise again the question whether Montaigne was as skeptical about Christianity as he has often seemed to subsequent readers. The current trend in Montaigne scholarship seems to favor reading him as a sincere fideist.[70] But the older interpretation, stemming from Pascal, is still alive, and I think Pascal got Montaigne right: that his skepticism was deep, his fideism superficial, and his commitment to Christian values very suspect.[71]

Since the example of Montaigne is a controversial one, we might do better to look at Bodin's *Colloquium heptaplomeres,* which clearly illustrates one consequences of the Reformation: the need to decide which version of Christianity is correct can easily lead to wondering whether any version of Christianity is the true religion, and from there to the question whether any historical religion is the true religion. Whatever doubts we may entertain about Bodin's personal convictions, it is at least the case that his dialogue forcefully raises all these questions.[72]

But perhaps the most helpful thing would be to read Pascal. After all, Hobbes wrote *Leviathan* in Pascal's Paris, as one of many expatriate Englishmen. Pascal certainly thinks that irreligion is widespread in his society. The famous wager argument (fragment 418, Krailsheimer; 233, Everyman) is addressed to someone who is unpersuaded by traditional arguments for the existence of God but remains open to an argument which appeals to his self-interest. What Pascal says, essentially, is this: let it be as uncertain as you like that God exists, as long as it is not impossible. Now consider what you stand to gain if you wager that God exists and win: eternal bliss in heaven. Compare that with your costs if you wager that God exists and lose: a few trivial pleasures.[73] Surprisingly, Pascal does not actually call our attention to the fact that if we wager that God does not exist *and lose,* we lose very big: We go to hell for eternity. But I assume that that thought is in the subtext.[74] His conclusion is that, however improbable it may be that God exists, we do best to believe that he does. This argument is clearly addressed to an audience Pascal thinks is quite prone to skepticism – and to a strong variety of skepticism at that, one which holds that God's existence is at best no more probable than his nonexistence, and, at worst, that his existence is highly improbable.

Hobbes' reply to the Fool (L xv, 4–8) has an interestingly similar structure. It is useful to point this out, if only to rebut those who find it anachronistic to use game-theoretic or decision-theoretic analyses in the interpretation of Hobbes. But it is also a helpful reminder when we are worrying about Hobbes' audience. He considers an opponent who has resolved the question of God's existence in the negative but is still uncertain how he ought to conduct his life.[75] If there is no God to make up for the deficiencies of human justice, why should this man not pursue his own advantage without regard for justice, breaking his covenants when it seems conducive to his benefit, as it must sometimes be?

Hobbes' reply is that in the state of nature you are under no obligation to keep covenants that require you to perform first, trusting the other party to perform later; to do that would merely be to make yourself a prey to the ambition and avarice, etc., of others (L xiv, 18; xv, 36). But if the other party has performed first, you no longer have any reason to fear that he will take advantage of your trust, and you ought to keep your covenant (L xiv, 27).[76] There may be circumstances in which it is highly improbable that you will pay any penalty for covenant breaking (particularly in the state of nature, where there is no sovereign to enforce covenants). You may, in those cases, expect significant gains if you opt for injustice. Still, it is not reasonable to order your life by trying to maximize your payoffs in that way. It will never be certain that you pay no penalty, and the costs of guessing wrong are disastrous. The price you may pay, if you are wrong, is exclusion from civil society. For if a civil society should form (or if an already formed civil society, of which you are not a member, should contemplate taking you in), the members of that society may learn of your unreliability; if they do, you cannot reasonably expect them to overlook it. And exclusion from civil society is the worst evil Hobbes can imagine. For Hobbes, hell is not other people, but the absence of other people, and of the benefits which cooperative living can bring.

Hobbes makes no assumption here about the probability of your acquiring a reputation for unreliability, except that it is not 0.[77] What he does assume is that the disutility of exclusion is sufficiently great that no rational person will take even a very small risk of that outcome.[78] Hobbesian prudence is highly risk averse when the disutility of the less favorable outcome is very great. It was Gregory Kavka, with his talk of disaster avoidance in the reply to the Fool, who helped me to see the similarity between Hobbes' reasoning and Pascal's.[79] Kavka, of course, did not make the comparison with Pascal; that was not his style.

X. Religion and Morality in a Hobbesian World

If the argument of this essay is correct, a Hobbesian world is the kind of world in which, as Mavrodes has argued, morality is queer, difficult to make sense of. There is no God, and no hope of reward or fear of punishment in an afterlife. So if we have prudential reasons to be moral, those reasons must rely only on the benefits and costs of this life.

Mavrodes' critique of modern-day Hobbesians is that their attempt to justify morality is fallacious. Their argument, as he presents it, begins with the assumption that

(A) It is in everyone's best interest (including mine) for everyone (including me) to be moral.

From this the modern-day Hobbesian is supposed to infer that

(B) It is in my best interest for everyone (including me) to be moral.

And from (B) it is concluded that

(C) It is in my best interest for me to be moral.

To this Mavrodes has two replies.

First, (C) certainly does not follow from (B). Even if, for the sake of argument, we grant (B), the most that would follow from (B) is

(C') It is in my best interest for me to be moral, *provided everyone else is moral.*

And the need to make this proviso betrays a fatal weakness in the argument. A defense of morality should not be conditional on such an unrealistic assumption.

Second, if (B) is to follow from (A), we must take (A) distributively rather than collectively (i.e., as meaning that each individual's interests are best served when everyone is moral, and not merely that the utility of the group as a whole is maximized, perhaps at the expense of certain individuals). But if we interpret (A) distributively, it is obviously false. Surely – assuming, of course, that we do not take into consideration possible costs and benefits in an afterlife – my best interests will be maximized in a world in which everyone else is moral and I act immorally when it suits me (e.g., when I can escape detection).

Now it seems to me pretty clear what Hobbes would say to this. Regarding the first point, he would not think that the principles of morality (his laws of nature) require us to make sacrifices of self-interest except when we have reasonable assurance of reciprocity (e.g., when there is a sovereign available to enforce covenants or when, in the state of nature, the other party has already performed). This is the point of the distinction between obligation *in foro in-*

terno and obligation *in foro externo* (L xv, 36). There is a substantive difference between the morality Hobbes is trying to justify and the morality Mavrodes expects secularists to justify. As far as actual conduct is concerned, Hobbesian morality does not require any more of us, in the state of nature, than an earnest endeavor to leave that state by establishing conditions under which we will have a reasonable assurance of reciprocity (L xiv, 5). So Hobbes will concede to Mavrodes that he cannot justify promise keeping in the full range of cases in which Mavrodes might think it is obligatory, but he will not concede that he has to justify it in those cases, because he does not think that this is unconditionally an obligation. The differences between Hobbesian morality and Christian morality make it easier for Hobbes to justify that part of traditional morality which he thinks is valid.

As regards Mavrodes' second point, I think Hobbes would concede that (A) is false in its distributive interpretation. He must concede that, I think. For although it is plausible to hold that

(A') Everyone is better off in a world in which everyone follows the laws of nature than they would be in a world in which everyone pursues her own self-interest, without regard to those laws,

it does not follow from that fact that

(A") Everyone is better off in a world in which everyone follows the laws of nature than they would be in any other world.

Hobbes must, I think, concede to the Fool that he would be better off in a world in which everyone else followed the laws of nature while he pursued his own self-interest, without regard to the laws of nature, and without being detected. But if I have understood Hobbes correctly (i.e., if I am right in the Kavkaesque reading that I have given of Hobbes' reply to the Fool), the essential point is that, though each of us might be better off in a world in which everyone else obeyed the laws of nature while we pursued our own self-interest, than we would be in any world in which everyone followed the same rules (either the laws of nature or the laws of self-interest), it does not follow that it would be rational for us to act in the hope of living in such a world. Rationality does not consist in maximizing individual utility[80] but in minimizing the risks of really bad outcomes. If we attempt to live according to the Fool's rules – follow the laws of nature when you think you must, pursue self-interest by disobeying those laws when you think you can (without detection) – we risk an appalling outcome: exclusion from civil society. So even though (A) and (A") are false, it is nonetheless rational for me to behave morally, as Hobbes understands that concept. The Fool identifies rationality, not with disaster avoidance, but with individual utility maximization. That's why he's a fool.

Notes

1. George Mavrodes, "Religion and the Queerness of Morality," appeared first in *Rationality, Religious Belief and Moral Commitment,* ed. Robert Audi and William Wainwright (Ithaca: Cornell University Press, 1986), and subsequently in Louis Pojman's *Philosophy of Religion* (Belmont, CA: Wadsworth, 1994).
2. See Thomas Hobbes, *Leviathan,* ch. xv, par. 4. I shall make all references to *Leviathan* hereafter in the text, in parentheses, by chapter and paragraph, following the system of paragraph numbering given in the edition of *Leviathan* which I published with Hackett in 1994, and abbreviating the title as L. Hobbes first published *Leviathan* in 1651 in English. One premise of my edition is that there are important differences between the English *Leviathan* and the Latin version which first appeared in 1668, in Amsterdam, during a period when there was a prohibition on reprinting the English *Leviathan* in England. My edition attempts to give an account of those differences.
3. For example, Kai Nielsen, in his *Ethics without God* (Amherst, NY: Prometheus, 1990), ch. 7, presents Hobbes as developing one of the two main ways in which a secular humanist might try to make sense of morality.
4. A. E. Taylor, "The Ethical Doctrine of Hobbes," *Philosophy* 13 (1938), 406–24. I have let the text stand as I originally wrote it. But in the interim I have learned from Paul Cooke that John Hunt anticipated Taylor in his *Religious Thought in England,* published in 1870. See Cooke's *Hobbes and Christianity* (Lanham, MD: Rowman & Littlefield, 1996), p. 22.
5. Howard Warrender, *The Political Philosophy of Hobbes* (Oxford: Clarendon Press, 1957); F. C. Hood, *The Divine Politics of Thomas Hobbes* (Oxford: Clarendon Press, 1964).
6. David Gauthier, *The Logic of* Leviathan (Oxford: Clarendon Press, 1969).
7. Jean Hampton, *Hobbes and the Social Contract Tradition* (Cambridge: Cambridge University Press, 1986). Unlike Gauthier, Hampton never raises the issue of Hobbes' theism in a way which suggests that she considers the hypothesis of his atheism to be worthy even of consideration. She writes as if his theism were a settled matter and holds that the way to rebut Taylor and Warrender is to show how Hobbes gets from his psychological assumptions to his moral and political conclusions.
8. Gregory S. Kavka, *Hobbesian Moral and Political Theory* (Princeton: Princeton University Press, 1986). See particularly pp. 361–3.
9. A. P. Martinich, *The Two Gods of* Leviathan (Cambridge: Cambridge University Press, 1992); Sharon Lloyd, *Ideals as Interests in Hobbes'* Leviathan (Cambridge: Cambridge University Press, 1992).
10. That's her view on pp. 112 and 345–6 of *Ideals as Interests,* at least. But cf. p. 17.
11. Ibid. See particularly pp. 272–4 and 278.
12. Not to paint too bleak a picture of isolation: Raymond Polin, *Hobbes, Dieu et les hommes* (Paris: Presses Universitaires de France, 1981), David Johnston, *The Rhetoric of* Leviathan (Princeton: Princeton University Press, 1986), and David Berman, *A History of Atheism in Britain: From Hobbes to Russell* (London: Croom Helm, 1988), have all published views which at least tend to question Hobbes' religious commitments. Quentin Skinner's recent book, *Reason and Rhetoric in the Philosophy of Hobbes* (Cambridge: Cambridge University Press, 1996), pp. 13–14, dismisses the interpretations of writers like Martinich as insensitive to the irony in Hobbes' discussions of Christianity. I also find Paul Cooke's *Hobbes and Christianity* very congenial.

13. Most fully in "'I Durst Not Write So Boldly' or, How to Read Hobbes' Theological-Political Treatise," in *Hobbes e Spinoza, Scienza e politica,* ed. Daniela Bostrenghi (Naples: Bibliopolis, 1992), pp. 497–593. (Since this volume is not widely available in American libraries, I plan shortly to put a version of it on my Web site, *http://www-personal.umich.edu/-emcurley.*) See also the introduction and annotation to my edition of *Leviathan* and "Calvin and Hobbes," *Journal of the History of Philosophy* 34 (1996), 251–77. These pages include a reply by Martinich, and my reply to his reply.

14. Notable exceptions to this generalization are Quentin Skinner, Richard Tuck, and Johann Sommerville.

15. Kavka, *Hobbesian Theory,* p. xiii.

16. This seems to have been Sharon Lloyd's worry in *Ideals as Interests,* p. 323, n. 2.

17. See pp. lxx–lxxi in my edition of *Leviathan* and, for a similar anecdote (no. 12), p. lxviii. (Aubrey gives the quotation from Horace in Latin. The translation is mine.)

18. *The Correspondence of Thomas Hobbes,* 2 vols., ed. Noel Malcolm (Oxford: Oxford University Press, 1994), 2:913–15.

19. In the appendix of *Two Gods* in which he criticizes my article, "'I Durst Not Write So Boldly'. . . ."

20. "'I Durst Not Write So Boldly' . . . ," p. 506.

21. Julius had a very bad press in the sixteenth century. Rabelais not only consigns him to hell (along with many of his fellow popes), he also makes him an especially pathetic creature. See *The Histories of Gargantua and Pantagruel,* tr. J. M. Cohen (Harmondsworth, Middlesex: Penguin, 1955), II, xxx, p. 269.

22. See *The Praise of Folly and Other Writings,* ed. Robert Adams (New York: Norton, 1989), p. 173. In the text I had assumed, in company with most previous students of Erasmus, that he was indeed the author of the anonymously published *Julius Excluded.* But a recent article by Patrick Collinson in the *Times Literary Supplement* (Dec. 26, 1997) alleges that Dr. Cathy Curtis has established that this work was actually written by Richard Pace. Apparently Erasmus was not pleased that its authorship was ascribed to him. I have chosen to let the text stand as it is, since I have not been able to examine Dr. Curtis' arguments.

23. Cf. *The Praise of Folly,* pp. 70–2, with the Letter to Martin Dorp (May 1515), defending his *Folly* (esp. pp. 230–4 in Adams' edition).

24. Erasmus was accused of Arianism, for rejecting, on text-critical grounds, a verse in 1 John 5:7, which was the best scriptural support for the doctrine of the Trinity. See Cornelis Augustijn, *Erasmus, His Life, Works, and Influence* (Toronto: University of Toronto Press, 1991), pp. 93–4. His comments on the Trinity in his treatise *On the Freedom of the Will* (in *Luther and Erasmus: Free Will and Salvation,* ed. E. Gordon Rupp and Philip S. Watson [Philadelphia: Westminster, 1969], p. 40) suggest at least a certain uneasiness about the doctrine.

25. Hobbes makes an analogous point in L vii, 7: "When we believe that the Scriptures are the word of God, having no immediate revelation from God himself, our belief, faith and trust is in the church, whose word we take." It seems fair to infer that if we take away trust in the church, we take away trust in Scripture as the word of God.

26. That it need not is the joke behind the Second Story of the First Day in Boccaccio's *Decameron.* Giannotto, a Christian merchant living in Paris, wished to convert his Jewish friend, Abraham, to Christianity. After much argument Abraham finally agreed to become a Christian, but only if he could first visit Rome and observe firsthand the behavior of the man whom Giannotto claimed was God's vicar on earth. Giannotto objected to this condition, thinking that if Abraham witnessed the con-

duct of the Roman clergy, he would never accept baptism. But his argument was unavailing, and Abraham went to Rome. When he returned to Paris, he told the surprised Giannotto that he had resolved to become a Christian – not because he had not witnessed great wickedness in Rome, but because he thought that any religion which could flourish when its clergy were so corrupt must be preserved by divine providence. I do not know whether or not Hobbes read Boccaccio. But he had clearly thought about the issue Boccaccio's story raises.

27. Here I cite the translation of *The Prince* by Russell Price (Cambridge: Cambridge University Press, 1988), p. 40. But I have not found a translation of this work which I am consistently pleased with. Sometimes I will cite other translations. Sometimes, under the guidance of the many existing translations, I venture my own version.

28. They circulated privately among the members of a circle who met in the Oricellari Gardens, some members of which were affiliated with the Medici party. (See J. R. Hale, *Machiavelli and Renaissance Italy* [London: English Universities Press, 1961], pp. 168–73.)

29. *The Prince* does seem to have won Machiavelli some favor from the Medici. After the death of Lorenzo they invited him to advise them on the best form of government for Florence (he recommended a republican government) and later commissioned him to write his *History of Florence* (Sebastian de Grazia, *Machiavelli in Hell* [Princeton: Princeton University Press, 1989], pp. 13, 114).

30. Here I follow David Wootton's translation, in Machiavelli, *Selected Political Writings* (Indianapolis: Hackett, 1994), p. 118. Wootton's introduction to this edition contains the most plausible attempt I have seen to reconcile the politics of *The Prince* with those of *The Discourses*.

31. It is a nice question whether Hobbes thinks Moses is genuinely different from the other founders of commonwealths. According to L xii, 12, he is supposed to be. But this may be undermined by xxvi, 40–1. Interesting here is chapter vi of *The Prince*. The subject is new kingdoms acquired by one's own skill (*virtù*). Machiavelli first lists four figures as outstanding examples: Moses, Cyrus, Romulus, and Theseus. He then says that we should not discuss ("ragionare di," so perhaps, following Mansfield, "reason about") Moses' skill, since "he was a mere agent, following the instructions given him by God." But he does proceed to 'discuss' Moses, in the course of arguing that the other founders of states did not behave any differently from Moses, "who had such a great teacher." What Moses evidently learned from God was to use force when necessary, without being deterred by the fact that he would have to kill a great many people. Romulus is reported to have killed two people to establish his authority. Moses is reported to have killed three thousand. Cf. *Discourses* I, ix, III, xxx, and Exodus 32:28.

32. Cf. de Grazia, *Machiavelli in Hell,* p. 89. For a more subtle view of Machiavelli's relation to Christianity, see Isaiah Berlin, "The Originality of Machiavelli," in *Against the Current,* ed. Henry Hardy (New York: Penguin, 1982), pp. 45–56. Although I think Berlin is wrong (p. 47) to take at face value the passage I quote in the next paragraph, he is surely right to say, in the end (p. 54), that Machiavelli is rejecting Christian ethics in favor of pagan morality.

33. Consider, for example, *Discourses* I, xxvi, where Machiavelli advises that, if we want to opt for being good, we should remain private citizens; if we want to hold political power, we must be prepared to adopt evil methods. Cf. his account of Giovampagolo Baglioni, the tyrant of Perugia, who passed up his opportunity to assassinate Julius when Julius entered Perugia with only his personal guard to protect him (and with the evident intention of removing Giovampagolo as ruler of Perugia).

Machiavelli expresses regret that Giovampagolo did not have the courage to take advantage of his chances: "He would have won eternal fame for being the first person to show the clergy just how little one should respect people who live and govern as they do" (*Discourses*, I, xxvii, Wootton, pp. 132–3). Cf. also Quentin Skinner, *Machiavelli* (New York: Hill & Wang, 1981), pp. 30, 38, 62–4. At the Hanover conference Barbara Tovey called my attention to a parable in Boccaccio (*Decameron*, I, ix), which questions whether rulers act properly when they adhere to the Christian principle which requires us not to resist evil.

34. See Luther and Calvin, *On Secular Authority*, ed. Harro Höpfl (Cambridge: Cambridge University Press, 1991), p. 36.

35. *The Education of a Christian Prince*, vol. 27 in *Collected Works of Erasmus*, ed. A. M. T. Levi (Toronto: University of Toronto Press, 1986), p. 217. Readers who are familiar with the life of the prince to whom this advice was given (Charles V) may judge the extent to which he followed it.

36. See Jean Bodin, *Colloquium of the Seven about Secrets of the Sublime*, tr. M. D. L. Kuntz (Princeton: Princeton University Press, 1975).

37. For Oldenburg's reaction see Richard Popkin, "The Dispersion of Bodin's Dialogues in England, Holland and Germany," *Journal of the History of Ideas* 48 (1988), 157–60, and "Could Spinoza have known Bodin's *Colloquium heptaplomeres?*", *Philosophia*, 16 (1986), 307–14. For Leibniz's reaction, see his letter to Jacob Thomasius, April 1669, in Leroy Loemker, *Leibniz's Philosophical Papers and Letters* (Dordrecht: Reidel, 1969), p. 102.

38. Bodin, *Colloquium*, pp. 343–6, 431–3.

39. In *The Elements of Law* Hobbes writes: "The sum of virtue is to be sociable with them that will be sociable, and formidable to them that will not" (I, xvii, 15). Not quite the Golden Rule, I think.

40. Luther, *De servo arbitrio*, in Rupp and Watson, *Luther and Erasmus: Free Will and Salvation*, p. 114.

41. In discussion at the Dartmouth conference Margaret Wilson reminded us that there is a long tradition of just war theory within Christianity, and that many authors, whose commitment to Christianity should not be questioned, have argued that the use of force is sometimes legitimate. I would not be thought to deny that. (The debates over the toleration of heretics would provide another example. Cf. Joseph Lecler, *Toleration and the Reformation* [London: Longman Group, 1960], bk. 1.)

But it seems to me that there is a great difference between someone like Grotius, say, for whom the Gospel teachings make any use of force profoundly problematic, requiring elaborate rationalization, and someone like Hobbes or Machiavelli, who contemplates the use of force with equanimity, provided that the end for which force is used is a sufficiently good one. But I have some sympathy with Tolstoy's view, that the Christian rationalizers of the use of force are not being true to the authentic teaching of their master. Cf. the excerpts from *My Religion* presented in Walter Kaufmann's *Religion from Tolstoy to Camus* (New York: Harper, 1961), pp. 45–66.

42. I quote the text as given in my edition of *Leviathan*, p. lxviii, which incorporates an emendation by V. de S. Pinto. The emendation has some importance, since it removes one reason Hood had for skepticism about Aubrey's reporting.

43. "'I Durst Not Write So Boldly' . . ."

44. That this person might in fact be a woman was one ground of objection to Hobbes' erastianism. In L xlii, 78a (a passage which occurs only in the Latin *Leviathan*) Hobbes defends the right of the queen to be the head of the church.

45. Martin Luther, *Appeal to the Ruling Class of German Nationality*, in *Martin Luther,*

Selections from His Writings, ed. John Dillenberger (New York: Doubleday/Anchor, 1961), pp. 417, 457.

46. Previously I cited L xii, where Hobbes reminds us that, according to Livy, Numa used false claims of divine revelation to establish his authority. Also interesting is a passage in L vii, 7, where Hobbes writes: "If Livy say the Gods once made a cow speak, and we believe it not, we distrust not God therein, but Livy." There is a passage in Livy (III, 10) where he talks about a cow's speaking; but he does not there say that the Gods made a cow speak. He says that in one year it was believed that a cow had spoken, and that similar stories had not been believed in the preceding year. Hobbes' point is counterfactual: if Livy had reported such a miracle, believing in its occurrence, Christians could reject his claim without impiety. They would be mistrusting only a human historian.

   I assume that Hobbes will accept (indeed, wishes to encourage) the obvious extension of this point: if non-Christians reject the reports of miracles in the Christian Scriptures, they are not being impious, they are just mistrusting the humans who made the reports. Later Hobbes' discussion of Scripture will emphasize that for much of Scripture we have no idea who wrote it (L xxxiii). All we know is that many of the books of the Bible were *not* written by the people traditionally thought to be their authors. So we do not know whom we would be trusting if we believed the stories in those books.

47. I summarize here a fuller discussion of this argument in my article, "The State of Nature and Its Law in Hobbes and Spinoza," *Philosophical Topics,* 19 (1991), 97–117.

48. I.e., just after the *Theological-Political Treatise* appeared, and at a time when he was much concerned about this work of Spinoza's. See my "*Homo audax:* Leibniz, Oldenburg and the TTP," in *Studia Leibnitiana, Supplementa, Leibniz' Auseinandersetzung mit Vorgängern und Zeitgenossen,* ed. Ingrid Marchlewitz and Albert Heinekamp (Stuttgart: Steiner, 1990), pp. 277–312.

49. Leibniz to Hobbes, July 1670, in *Correspondence of Hobbes,* 2:717.

50. As I note in my edition of *Leviathan,* Aquinas had associated the biblical Leviathan with the devil, in his *The Literal Exposition on Job: A Scriptural Commentary Concerning Providence,* ed. Anthony Damico, tr. Martin Jaffe (Atlanta: Scholars Press, 1989), p. 448. See also Bodin's *Colloquium of the Seven,* pp. 105, 110, 118, 217. It would be interesting to know whether or not Hobbes had read Bodin's *Colloquium.*

51. I quote Leibniz's letter to Jacob Thomasius, September 23, 1670, Akademie ed., II, i, p. 66.

52. In the phrase "men use to call," near the beginning of this quotation, the received text is correct, *pace* Martinich (pp. 123–4). "Use" is a present tense verb, meaning "are accustomed to"; it is not a misprint for "used" (and hence a way of forming the past tense).

53. Taylor, "Ethical Doctrine," pp. 418–20; Warrender, *Political Philosophy,* pp. 98–100.

54. David Gauthier pointed this out in discussion during the conference at Irvine, and Steve Darwall made the same point in his review of Martinich, *Philosophical Review* 103 (1994), 748–52.

55. Readers of Spinoza will recall that he argues for a similar conclusion in the Appendix to Part I of the *Ethics.* But he does not make that claim in the *Theological-Political Treatise.*

56. It was, of course, one of Hobbes' first lines of defense against the charge of atheism that the only ground on which a person can legitimately be accused of atheism is if he has straightforwardly denied that God exists. Cf. Thomas Hobbes, *The English*

Works of Thomas Hobbes, ed. William Molesworth, 9 vols. (London: John Bohn, 1839), 4:75–6, on "atheism by consequence." But those who are inclined to press that passage should consider also the appendix to the Latin *Leviathan,* ii, 36, and my annotation of that passage in the Hackett edition.

57. In "'I Durst Not Write So Boldly' . . .", pp. 572–88.

58. See excerpts [3] and [5] from his Latin Autobiography, in my edition of *Leviathan,* pp. lxiv – lxv.

59. See Thomas Hobbes, *Critique du* De mundo *de Thomas White,* édition critique d'un texte inédit par Jean Jacquot et Harold Whitmore Jones (Paris: Vrin-CNRS, 1973), p. 49.

60. The first public identification of the work as Hobbesian was Jacquot's "Notes on an unpublished work of Thomas Hobbes," *Notes and Records of the Royal Society of London* 9 (May 1952). This was followed by the critical edition of the Latin text cited in the previous note, and an English translation by Whitmore Jones, *Thomas White's* De mundo *Examined* (London: Bradford University Press, 1976).

61. David Johnston, *The Rhetoric of* Leviathan (Princeton: Princeton University Press, 1986).

62. Cf. Luther, *De servo arbitrio,* in Rupp and Watson, *Luther and Erasmus: Free Will and Salvation,* pp. 138, 230, 244.

63. See "'I Durst Not Write So Boldly' . . . ," pp. 574–9.

64. See Lloyd, *Ideals as Interests,* pp. 15–23.

65. Ibid., pp. 272–4.

66. She does not discuss any of my work on Hobbes, of course. None of it was in print at the time she was writing, so she had no reason to be aware of it. But she does discuss the similar views of David Johnston.

67. Ibid., p. 273.

68. Many committed Christians did, of course, think their religion was under attack, and did, as Lloyd knows, leap to its defense. She suggests that some (perhaps many) of the contemporary accusations of atheism were just abusive name calling and did not reflect an authentic assessment of Hobbes' position (p. 273). Martinich takes a similar line. No doubt the motivations of Hobbes' critics are complex and sometimes obscure. But I think the outrage of critics like Clarendon was genuine and shows a perceptive reading of Hobbes. See Edward Hyde (Lord Clarendon), *A Brief View and Survey of the dangerous and pernicious Errors to Church and State, in Mr. Hobbes's Book Entitled Leviathan* (Oxford, 1676).

69. See the final chapter of Part III, and particularly xliii, 3–5, 11. It helps Hobbes' case greatly that he can treat those troublesome imperatives from the Sermon on the Mount as merely counsel, not command; hence, not law; hence, not binding. Cf. xliii, 5, with xxv, 10–11, and the annotation there. The status of these imperatives was a major issue in the Reformation, with the leading reformers insisting that they were commands, and the Catholic Church replying that they were merely counsel. Cf. Calvin, *Institutes,* pp. 29–30, and 249 in the Battles translation of the 1536 edition.

70. See, for example, M. A. Screech's introduction to his edition of Montaigne, *The Complete Essays* (New York: Penguin, 1991), or his *Montaigne and Melancholy* (Penguin, 1991). This was also the view advocated by Screech's predecessor as a translator of Montaigne, Donald Frame, in "Did Montaigne Betray Sebond?" *Romantic Review* 38 (1947), 297–329.

71. For Pascal on Montaigne, see §§780, 680, and 649 in the Penguin edition of the *Pensées,* ed. by Krailsheimer (§§62, 63, and 65 in the Everyman edition). For a defense of reading Montaigne as an atheist, see D. L. Schaefer, *The Political Philosophy of*

Montaigne (Ithaca: Cornell University Press, 1990). Those who think it must be anachronistic to question the religious convictions of any author in this period should read the following works by David Wootton: "Lucien Febvre and the Problem of Unbelief in the Early Modern Period," *Journal of Modern History* 60 (1988): 695–730; "New Histories of Atheism," in *Atheism from the Reformation to the Enlightenment,* ed. Michael Hunter and David Wootton (Oxford: Clarendon Press, 1992); and *Paolo Sarpi* (Cambridge: Cambridge University Press, 1983). In Montaigne's case one thing which persuades me is that the professed fideism of the "Apology for Raymond Sebond" is of the strong, antirationalist kind, which proclaims the Christian faith to be, not merely beyond, but contrary to reason.

72. Of course, we might not need the Reformation to get this line of questioning going. Barbara Tovey pointed out to me that there is a version of it in Boccaccio's Parable of the three rings (*Decameron,* First Day, Third Story). But the Reformation made the issue more urgent.

73. I simplify considerably here. For a more complex and accurate presentation of the argument see chapter 8 of Ian Hacking's *The Emergence of Probability* (Cambridge: Cambridge University Press, 1975). Hacking's article is also included in *Gambling with God,* ed. Jeff Jordan (Lanham, MD: Rowman & Littlefield, 1994), which contains a number of interesting articles on the wager. See particularly: Edward McClennen, "Pascal's Wager and Finite Decision Theory," and Roy Sorensen, "Infinite Decision Theory."

74. I think Pascal is widely assumed to have argued in this way. Cf. the anecdote about John von Neumann, *Gambling with God,* p. 1. The infinite disutility of failing to believe in God in case God does exist is part of the version of the wager argument which appears in the *Port Royal Logic,* as McClennen notes, *Gambling with God,* p. 133.

75. As with Pascal I simplify considerably, focusing on the *prima facie* hardest case for Hobbes: covenant breaking in the state of nature by an atheist. Hobbes also replies in this passage to theists in civil society who think breach of faith with their sovereign may earn them eternal felicity in heaven. To them Hobbes replies, that they cannot rationally act on that belief, since we can have no natural knowledge of man's estate after death. This implicitly denies that revelation can be a ground of rational belief and action.

76. So I do think Hobbes recognizes obligations in the state of nature, though I think that they cannot be obligations in quite the usual sense of that term. Earlier I spoke of Hobbes' laws of nature as being a "special kind of hypothetical imperative." My thought (which goes back to Watkins) is this: normally when we speak of a hypothetical imperative we have in mind a conditional whose antecedent is contingent. But Hobbes' laws of nature are conditionals which have the form "If you want to preserve yourself, then do X." And he assumes that the desire for self-preservation is both natural and necessary.

It may be objected that we do not always choose to preserve ourselves when faced with a life-or-death situation. (This is an objection which Jean Hampton made in the discussion in Irvine, and which Bernard Gert made in the discussion in Hanover; presumably it is also an objection Sharon Lloyd would make. There is a nice summary of the conflicting evidence in Greg Kavka's book, in the section on Death Avoidance.) I think the best way to understand Hobbes may be to construe him as holding that we (must) always desire to avoid death, though that may not always be our strongest desire. The desire to avoid shame, for example, or to avoid excruciating pain, may override it. Whether such a position would be sufficient to account for the force of these imperatives is a matter I leave to be decided later.

77. It seems to me that this comes out somewhat more clearly in the Latin version of the argument than in the English. Cf. my edition, p. 91, n. 6, p. 92, n. 8.

78. I do not suppose he thinks, as Pascal presumably would regarding hell, that the disutility is infinite. Whether it makes sense to admit infinite utilities is a matter of controversy among decision theorists (cf. the articles by McClennon and Sorenson cited earlier), but it seems desirable to avoid them if possible.

79. Kavka, *Hobbesian Moral and Political Theory,* pp. 137–44.

80. Or even, I think, in maximizing expected utility, though Kavka holds that out as one possible interpretation of the reply to the Fool. I think Hobbes was too skeptical about the possibility of attaching any precise values to the probabilities of other people's actions to rely on expected utility maximization as a conception of rationality.

Contemporary Uses of Hobbes's Political Philosophy

S. A. LLOYD

Aristotle thought that the best sort of human life would have to include friendships, for the reason, among others, that engaging in common activities with our friends helps us to sustain a livelier and more continuously active interest in those projects that give meaning and substance to our lives.[1] John Cooper points out[2] that we need not be officially collaborating with friends in order to reap this benefit of friendship; when, for instance, as philosophers we work on the same problem as our friend and view our individual works as contributions to solving the problem we share, we enjoy the goods of friendship Aristotle is describing.

Those who find this Aristotelian claim plausible will understand why I have been alarmed by the state in which Gregory Kavka and I were forced to leave our Hobbes dispute. After years of wrangling over the content of Hobbes's political theory, he had just come to a conclusion he expressed this way: "Well, Sharon, you're probably right about the historical Hobbes. But *my* Hobbes is more *interesting!*" Now, this pronouncement could describe a satisfactory state of affairs only if one supposes us engaged in two quite different projects – mine to uncover the actual Hobbes, in the way that interests the intellectual historian, and Kavka's to construct a philosophically interesting and useful Hobbes, in the way that interests the political philosopher. These would be parallel projects, not unrelated perhaps, but also not the joint enterprise of friends. But I take it that as friends and fellow Hobbes enthusiasts, we were *not* engaged in two such different projects. Rather, we shared the aim of uncovering what really is philosophically interesting about what Hobbes really did. And on that understanding of our project, Kavka's pronouncement represents, not a satisfactory settlement, but a provocation of the highest order.

I intend to take up his challenge in this essay, by explaining why I think the quite philosophically interesting positions some have claimed to be Hobbesian are not Hobbesian, let alone Hobbes's own, and by trying to show why the philosophical problem that the real Hobbes addressed is an extraordinarily interesting and important one for us.

I believe that Kavka thought that what makes a political theory philosophically interesting is that it speaks to continuing human concerns in a way that might inform and improve our own theories. In this context, it is striking that the two most celebrated analytical approaches of present-day political philosophy – namely John Rawls's "political liberalism,"[3] and David Gauthier's "moral contractarianism"[4] – do both claim Hobbes as their first illustrious ancestor.

At first it seems clear enough why both of these approaches should be regarded by their creators as descended from Hobbes: despite their essential antipathy, each is a variety of social-contract theory, and we understand Hobbes to have undertaken the contractarian task of justifying political arrangements by appeal to the agreement that informed and rational occupants of a prepolitical state would make to advance their interests by the means that reason specifies. This generally accepted characterization of Hobbes's project is sufficiently neutral to render Hobbes a resource for both Rawls and Gauthier. "Political liberalism" emphasizes Hobbes's use of what Rawls calls "reasonable" (as opposed to merely "rational") constraints on the setup of the contractors' choice situation and on their reasoning in it, such as the presumption of equality in the contractors' moral standing and bargaining position, and the requirements of reciprocity, mutual benefit, and fairness in the terms agreed to that are imposed by Hobbes's laws of nature – his laws forbidding, for example, injustice, iniquity, and partiality – where these laws are conceived as reasonable directives. In particular, Hobbes's requirement of reciprocity among persons understood as free and equal,[5] in the face of disagreement in interests, beliefs, and judgments as to the correct conduct of common life[6] (which Rawls calls "the fact of pluralism"), invites the suspicion that Hobbes may have developed a fledgling political liberalism.

Gauthier, in calling Hobbes the greatest advocate of what he terms "moral contractarianism," instead stresses Hobbes's atomistic conception of the person as moved by sociable precepts like the laws of nature only to the extent that those are recommended by the self-interested calculations of a maximizing rationality. In contrast to political liberalism, Gauthier's moral contractarianism characterizes Hobbes's moral norms as consequences, rather than conditions, of the contractors' deliberations. "In Hobbes we find the true ancestor of the theory of morality we shall present," writes Gauthier, but "to the conceptual underpinning that may be found in Hobbes, we seek to add the rigor of rational choice" (*MA*, p. 10).

Hobbes would probably have been pleased to imagine twentieth-century philosophers fighting to claim him as one of their own; in his own day he was called everything from "supercilious dogmatist" of "magisterial pomposity" to purveyor of "horrid and execrable opinions" and "pander to bestiality." But, as I shall argue, a careful consideration of Hobbes's views shows both Rawls's and Gauthier's patrimony suits to be indefensible. Exposing the difficulty with moral contractarianism's claim depends upon showing that the theory it purports to take from Hobbes is not in fact Hobbes's, and that Hobbes's theory, properly understood, renders inapplicable the particular model for rational choice Gauthier defends. Disinheriting political liberalism involves showing that Hobbes's actual view prohibits the use of an argumentative device that political liberalism cannot do without. In the process of arguing that what is of real philosophical interest in Hobbes's view cannot be what Gauthier (and following him, Kavka) thought it to be, nor quite what political liberalism would take it to be, I hope to provide a persuasive alternative account of the philosophical interest of Hobbes's political theory.

I

Gauthier's doctrine in *Morals by Agreement* employs what has become over the last several decades the standard philosophical interpretation of Hobbes's political theory. That is not surprising, since Gauthier himself was a major contributor to this interpretation, introducing the refinements of game theory into the interpretive tradition passed from John Laird through Leo Strauss, J. W. N. Watkins, Thomas Nagel, and John Plamenatz, and, via Gauthier's innovation, developed to what must surely be its zenith by Jean Hampton and Gregory Kavka.[7] This interpretation identifies Hobbes's solution to the problem of social disorder as the erection of a political power that coerces obedience by credibly threatening to punish disobedience. The power to punish operates to secure order because, says the standard interpretation, humans are egoists who care above all about self-preservation and the avoidance of bodily harm to themselves. Given this preservation-centered conception of human nature, the fear of death, and of the punishments that may well lead to death – wounds, imprisonment, or the deprivation of livelihood – may be expected to motivate compliance with the sovereign's commands. Denuded then, of its game-theoretic fancy dress, the standard interpretation's central claim is that "might plus fright makes order."

It asserts further that Hobbes derives his preservation-centered conception of human nature from a mechanistic materialism that analyzes men as bits of matter in motion, attracted or repulsed by external stimuli proportionately to the increase or decrease of internal vital motion produced by the impingement on them of these stimuli. "From this account of vital and voluntary motion it follows," writes Gauthier, "that each man seeks, and seeks only, to preserve and strengthen himself. A concern for continued well-being is both the necessary and sufficient ground of human action. Hence man is necessarily selfish."[8]

The standard interpreters take this to imply that no irreducibly moral or religious consideration can motivate action. For example, Watkins writes that "since the vital motions of the heart can only be excited by the prospect of some bodily change in its owner . . . merely moral considerations unrelated to such a change cannot affect behavior."[9] This suggests something the standard interpretation goes on to assert, namely, that Hobbes will have to hold a subjectivist and personally relativist moral theory that analyzes moral utterances in terms of personal affinity or aversion. And it suggests further that theism will be irrelevant to Hobbes's system, since the requirements of religious duty per se will also be motivationally inert, as will even the requirements of what might be called "special prudence" – of salvation – if these involve the death of one's present physical body. Thus we have, on the standard interpretation, a theory that attempts to move from a physical-scientific account of man as matter in motion to a preservation-centered egoism that precludes the motivational efficacy of religious and moral requirements as such, to a "might plus fright makes order" solution to social unrest. Such a reading might naturally attract those who believe that only a materialist and nontheistic political theory can have any real philosophical interest in the modern world.

II

There are a couple of striking *prima facie* reasons for thinking that the theory just sketched is improperly attributed to Hobbes. The first is that it fits extremely poorly with Hobbes's text, the second that it makes Hobbes's theory conceptually incoherent.[10] Perhaps some will think that these problems do not settle the case against the standard interpretation, but all should agree that they warrant more careful attention to alternative interpretations.

Textual Inadequacy

The first *prima facie* reason for thinking that Hobbes did not espouse the theory that the standard interpreters attribute to him is that fully half of Hobbes's masterwork, *Leviathan,* where he expresses his political theory in its mature form, is devoted to a detailed discussion of religious doctrine, practice, and history, a fact for which the standard interpretation cannot adequately account. The theory that it ascribes to Hobbes does not attend to religion, and it makes no reference to material contained in the half of *Leviathan* devoted to discussion of religion. But because so much of *Leviathan* is about religion it is fair to ask: Why does Hobbes obsess about religion?

It is not plausible to suppose that Hobbes included the discussion of religion in order to make an essentially irreligious political theory easier for a religious audience to swallow, because the content of that discussion was highly inflammatory, drawing the most scathing attacks from Hobbes's contemporaries, and Hobbes quite clearly anticipated that reaction. We can see this from his remarks in *Leviathan* concerning its religious views: "I confess they are very hardly to bee reconciled with all the doctrines now unamimously received" (L 347), they "will appear to most men a novelty" (L 241), and "That which perhaps may most offend are certain texts of Holy Scripture alleged by me to other purpose than ordinarily they used to be by others" [L, "Epistle Dedicatory"]. Had Hobbes been intending his discussions of religion as "window dressing," an effort to prettify the theory by disguising its atheism, he would surely have had the sense to employ a less scandalous religious position.

It is marginally more plausible to imagine that the half of the book that Hobbes devotes to religion is included solely to address people's self-interested concern to secure their own salvation. It is unfortunate that this account, which reduces all religious motive to special prudence, seems to rely on an impoverished conception of what it is to have religious concerns and sits poorly with the fact that many of Hobbes's intended readers were Calvinist predestinarians who did not believe it possible for them to affect their own salvation and thus would not have been open to persuasion by a reductionist argument. But unfortunate or not, if the standard interpretation hoped to include the half of *Leviathan* on religion as a working part of Hobbes's theory, its egoism assumption would compel it to understand that half as concerning a longest-run self-interest in salvation, despite the obvious tension between that account and its assumption of mechanistic materialism. The larger difficulty for the standard interpretation is that if it were true that Hobbes had devoted half his book to the issue of salvation, that would suggest that he regarded people's interest in their own salvation as an *extremely important source of social disorder.* But how could that be so, given the state's threats of capital punishment, unless the interest in personal salvation were often and widely given priority over people's interest in securing their temporal bodily preservation? Obviously, if the interest in salvation did not override fear of bodily harm, then it would not need to be dealt with in order for Hobbes's "might plus fright makes order" solution to work. But if the interest in salvation does need to be confronted, then it must be that people's action on that interest can jeopardize order, which could happen only if their interest in salvation could override their concern to avoid bodily harm. If the concern to secure one's own salvation were overriding in this way, then the sovereign's threat to inflict such comparatively minor harms could not possibly provide the fundamental foundation for political obedience, as the standard interpretation insists it does.

Notice that this will be true even if the society in question includes many people who themselves have no religious interests and who would indeed be deterred by a credible threat of capital punishment. So long as others with overriding religious concerns are numerous enough that they can disrupt social order, the reasons for obedience of even atheistic egoists are undermined. If the state can neither protect them nor credibly threaten to punish them, as it may not be able to do if religious resisters impede its functioning, then they have no reason from narrow prudence to obey it, even though they themselves have no religious interests. (In homely terms, a few rotten apples can spoil the whole barrel.) So the standard interpretation is in a bind. If religious interests do not pose any serious threat to social order, then Hobbes's extended treatment of them becomes an inexplicable mystery. It could not have served as window dressing, and it is no working part of the theory. But if those interests do pose a serious threat, it is because they can override fear of the bodily harm that the sovereign's punishments threaten, and this would make the standard interpretation's proffered solution for social disorder no solution at all. So it appears that if that interpretation renders the half of *Leviathan* on religion a working part of the theory, its foundation crumbles. This may explain why the standard interpreters line up behind Leslie Stephen's claim that Hobbes's system "would clearly be more consistent and intelligible if he simply omitted the theology altogether."[11]

Still, and here is the point, *Hobbes* did not think so: after acknowledging in the "Epistle Dedicatory" that his unorthodox interpretations of Scripture are likely to offend, he explains, "but I have done it with due submission, *and also (in order to my subject) necessarily;* for they [the orthodox understandings] are the outworks of the enemy, from whence they impugne the civill power" (emphasis added). And later, in the *Six Lessons,* commenting on the writing of *Leviathan* and speaking of the clergy, Hobbes says explicitly that "The cause of my writing that book was the consideration of what the ministers before and in the beginning of the civil war, by their preaching and writing did contribute thereunto." And later still, in his *Seven Philosophical Problems,* he says of *Leviathan,*

It was written in a time when the pretence of Christ's kingdom was made use of for the most horrid actions that can be imagined; and it was in just indignation of that that I desired to see the bottom of that doctrine of the kingdom of Christ, which divers ministers then preached for a pretence to their rebellion.[12]

Conceptual Incoherence

The second *prima facie* reason for doubting that the view the standard interpretation ascribes to Hobbes really is his is that on no plausible construal of the problem Hobbes was addressing could that problem be solved by the solution the standard interpreters attribute to Hobbes. The standard reading represents the disorder of the state of nature as the product of rational egoists trapped in a prisoner's dilemma, to be solved, as we have seen, by erecting a sovereign power to change the payoffs of noncooperation through threat of punishment. If this were right, Hobbes's solution would be capable of originally establishing order from the anarchy of the state of nature. But what analysis shall we give of recurrent disorder – of the recurring collapses of order within established societies? This, after all, is the problem Hobbes was addressing. He writes:

long time after men have begun to constitute commonwealths, imperfect, and apt to relapse into disorder, there may principles of reason be found out, by industrious meditation, to make their constitution (excepting by externall violence) everlasting. And such are those which I have in this discourse set forth. (L 176)

These principles of reason are principles to prevent domestic rebellion, for, as Hobbes writes, "in those nations whose commonwealths have been long-lived, and not been destroyed but by forraign warre, the subjects never did dispute of the sovereign power" (L 107). So recurrent disorder caused by rebellious subjects is the problem that engages Hobbes. Can the standard interpretation give a plausible account of rebellion compatible with the solution it attributes to Hobbes?

If original disorder were the result of the actions of rational egoists trapped in a prisoner's dilemma, then once the payoff matrix is changed, disorder ought to have been permanently eradicated. Rational egoists will be deterred from rebellion by the sovereign's threatened punishments. That is just what it means to say that the payoff matrix has been changed. If, then, subjects rebel in the face of the sovereign's credibly threatened punishments, bringing a state of order to collapse (and if we assume that none of those "externall factors" that Hobbes has excluded from his discussion – foreign invasion, natural disaster, plague – occurs, rebellious subjects must be experiencing either a failure of rationality or the intrusion of extrarational forces that undermine or override their rational self-interest. If the proper account of recurrent disorder is a failure of rationality pure and simple, then one could hardly expect the standard interpretation's solution to restore order – the threat of punishment will motivate only self-interested persons who correctly identify their self-interest; it cannot be expected to have any salutary effect on self-interested individuals who are so irrational as to fail to see the imprudence of rebellion even in the face of credibly threatened punishments of sufficient severity.

On the other hand, if rebellion results from "perturbations" of reason, such as the passions associated with religious zeal, moral indignation, and personal pride, these must be forces capable of overriding rational self-interest (that is assuming, as the standard interpretation does, that the avoidance of punishment is in one's rational self-interest), and be forces capable also of overriding one particular sort of passion, namely the fear of death. Otherwise they could not motivate disobedience in the face of credibly threatened capital punishment. But we can see that if recurrent disorder is caused by forces that override rational self-interest and fear of death, the standard interpretation's solution by appeal to rational self-interest and fear of death cannot be expected to solve the problem. For the standard interpretation, changing the payoff matrix ought to do it – for good; and if it does not, that interpretation has nothing further to offer. Given the solution it attributes to Hobbes, and the analyses of Hobbes's problem available to it, the problem of recurrent disorder is either negligible or insoluble, and Hobbes's solution is either unnecessary or useless. So unless we are to conclude that Hobbes himself was, to use his own favorite term of abuse, an "egregious blockhead," a conclusion that the principle of charity in interpretation requires us to resist, we have to exercise caution in embracing the standard interpretation.

III

Suppose we look, then, with fresh eyes at what Hobbes actually says. Although he thinks that disruptive actions are usually irrational, he never says that irrationality is the cause of disorder. What he does say is this:

The most frequent praetext of sedition and civil war, in Christian commonwealths hath a long time proceeded from a difficulty, not yet sufficiently resolved, of obeying at once both God and man, then when their commandments are one contrary to the other. (L 321)

And in *Behemoth,*[13] Hobbes's history of the English Civil War, Hobbes writes:

If it be lawfull then for subjects to resist the king, when he commands anything that is against the Scripture, that is, contrary to the command of God, and to be judge of the meaning of Scripture, it is *impossible* that the life of any King, or the peace of any Christian kingdom, can long be secure. (B 50)

These remarks strongly suggest that people's opinions may contribute to disorder.

Hobbes confirms this suspicion in *Leviathan:*

the actions of men procede from their opinions, and in the well governing of opinions, consists the well governing of mens actions, in order to their peace and concord . . . It belongeth therefore to him that hath the soveraign power, to be judge, or constitute all judges of opinions and doctrines, as a thing necessary to peace, thereby to prevent discord and civill warre. (L 91)

Because people's opinions about their religious duty are particularly problematic, stability requires that the sovereign must control religious doctrine, since, "if he give away the government of doctrines, men will be frighted into rebellion with the feare of spirits" (L 93). So people's religious beliefs can cause rebellion.

But can't the sovereign prevent rebellion by threatening punishment? The sovereign's rights, Hobbes insists,

cannot be maintained by any civil law, or terrour of legal punishment. For a civill law that shall forbid rebellion . . . is not . . . any obligation, but by virtue onely of the law of nature that forbiddeth the violation of faith; which naturall obligation if men know not, they cannot know the right of any law the sovereign maketh. And for the punishment, they take it for an act of hostility; which when they think they have strength enough, they will endeavour by acts of hostility, to avoyd. (L 175–6)

In a Christian commonwealth like Hobbes's, the sovereign's civil power depends "on the opinion men have of their duty to him, and the fear they have of punishment in *another* world" (L 296, emphasis added) – not, that is, on their sovereign's coercive threats, but rather on their opinions of what God expects of them. They must be brought to see civil obedience as their duty, for, as Hobbes asks, "If men know not their duty, what is there that can force them to obey the laws? An army, you will say. But what shall force the army?" (B 59). Hobbes presumably thinks that nothing shall force the army, and so that order cannot be maintained by force, all the way down, so to speak. This explains his view that "The power of the mighty hath no foundation but in the opinion and belief of the people" (B 16).

If order depends on the subjects' believing themselves duty bound to obey their sovereign, responsibility for disorder is, it seems, naturally to be laid at the door of those who persuade subjects that obedience is not due to their sovereign or is instead due to someone else. This is precisely where Hobbes deposits this responsibility, the lion's share with ecclesiastics who urge that fulfilling our supreme duties to God may require disobedience to the civil sovereign. In his *Behemoth* account of the cause of the English Civil War, Hobbes primarily blames the Presbyterian ministers who, aided by (as he calls them) "Papists" and various Independent sects, promulgated religious doctrines inimical to the sovereign's authority, for example, the doctrine that "the present church now militant on earth is the kingdom of God" and so that its commands have priority over the civil sovereign's; that "whatsoever a man does against his conscience is sinne," making each man's own judgment in matters of religion authoritative; and that "every private man is judge of good and evil actions," including the actions of his sovereign. All of these doctrines encourage subjects to regard some judgment other than the sovereign's as authoritative (i.e., to regard some *private* judgment as authoritative), and to obey it in defiance of constituted public authority.

Once subjects believe these disruptive doctrines, the sovereign's coercive threats will be useless. In *Leviathan* (L 384) Hobbes writes that

the emperours, and other Christian soveraigns, under whose government these errours and the like encroachments of ecclesiastics upon their office, at first crept in to the disturbance of their possessions, and of the tranquillity of their subjects . . . might have hindered the same in the beginning: But when the people were once possessed by those spirituall men, there was no humane remedy to be applied, that any man could invent.

It is essential that civil sovereigns establish their authority in religious matters, because

It is impossible a commonwealth should stand, where any other than the soveraign, hath a power of giving greater rewards than life; and of inflicting greater punishments than death . . . [And] eternall life is a greater reward, than the life present; and eternall torment a greater punishment than the death of nature . . . (L 238)

For this reason, we cannot expect to avoid rebellion in Christian common-wealths like Hobbes's until "preaching be better looked to, whereby the inter-pretation of a verse in the Hebrew, Greek, or Latin Bible, is oftentimes the cause of a civil war" (B 181). It matters what preachers preach, "for ambition can do little without hands, and few hands it would have, if the common people were as diligently instructed in the true principles of their duty, as they are terrified and amazed by their preachers, with fruitless and dangerous doctrines" (B 70). It begins to sound very much as though preventing rebellion requires overcom-ing any division between civil and religious authority.

There is quite a lot of textual evidence that this division is in fact what *Leviathan* is all about, including one fairly striking piece never discussed by proponents of the standard interpretation. It is the anonymous engraving for *Leviathan*'s frontispiece that Hobbes comissioned in order to depict the content of his book (Figure 1).

Certainly everyone has noticed that the figure of the king is wearing armor composed of many small people, signifying that the sovereign's power consists in the combined strength of his subjects. He holds the civil sword in his right hand and the church staff in his left. Above him is written a quotation from Job 41:33, in the Vulgate Latin, which means in English "Upon earth there is not his like," referring to God's creature Leviathan. This kingly figure represents the human approximation to Leviathan.

But notice now the two sets of smaller drawings on either side of the title banner. These, I suggest, represent the division of authority with which the book is primarily concerned, the opposition of temporal and spiritual rule that Leviathan overcomes. The first depicts the seat of power, with the temporal cas-tle on the left and the spiritual church on the right. The person in whom au-thority is vested is signified in the second frame by the crown on the temporal side and the bishop's miter on the spiritual. The third set of drawings contrasts the types of force exercised in temporal rule – physical force, as symbolized by the cannon, with the wrath of God, the threat of excommunication and damna-tion, symbolized by lightning bolts.

The fourth set of pictures takes as its subject the weapons and equipment of war: temporal rule uses guns, bayonets, standards, and drums; spiritual warfare is conducted by means of arguments and distinctions. The figure at the far left in the spiritual frame has the word "syllogisme" written on it, divided into three parts, to correspond to the structure of a syllogism. The next three figures in the top of this frame are what Hobbes calls "verbal forks." Verbal forks are "dis-tinctions that signify nothing, but serve only to astonish the multitude of igno-rant men," which the "schoolmen" used for "the trick of imposing what they list upon their readers, and declining the force of true reason" (B 41; cf. L 171). The verbal forks depicted here are the temporal–spiritual distinction, which, Hobbes insists, "makes men see double, and mistake their lawfull soveraign,"

Figure 1. Hobbes's *Leviathan* (1651), title page. By permission
of the British Library, (BL) 1476.d.23.

and the direct–indirect [power] distinction, which was used to assert the church's authority over those civil matters thought to affect spiritual matters. In his *Leviathan* reply (ch. 42) to Cardinal Bellarmine's *De summo pontifice,* Hobbes sarcastically criticizes Bellarmine's use of the direct–indirect distinction: "'That the pope has (in the dominions of other princes) the supreme temporall power INDIRECTLY' . . . is denied; unless hee [Bellarmine] mean by indirectly, that he has gotten it by indirect means [e.g., fraud or theft]; then is that also granted" (L 314). But he adds in earnest that "this distinction of temporall, and spirituall power is but words. Power is as really divided, and as dangerously to all purposes, by sharing with another indirect power, as with a direct one" [L 315].

The verbal fork on the right is the *esse reale–esse intentionale* distinction that makes possible the Roman Catholic Church's use of the Aristotelian doctrine of separated essences to support its doctrines of the immortality of the soul, transubstantiation, and the infusion of qualities, all of which Hobbes attacks as diminishing the civil authority. In the bottom center of the frame we have Hobbes's wry editorial comment on these distinctions: he has labeled a set of *horns* from which the temporal–spiritual distinction springs "Di-lem-ma."

The final set of scenes depicts the battlefield on which each side struggles – the site of its conquests. The temporal frame shows an ordinary battlefield, with soldiers engaged in combat. The spiritual frame is a scene from a university disputation among divines, where doctrines conducive to the church's independent power are developed and their supporting verbal forks devised. In the "Epistle Dedicatory" to *Liberty and Necessity,* Hobbes inquires,

What, I pray, is the effect of so many . . . disputations, conferences, conventicles, printed books, written with so much distraction and presumption upon God Almighty, and abuse of his Holy Word? Marry this: it is the seminary of many vexatious, endless, and fruitless controversies, the consequence whereof are jealousies, . . . the introduction of factions and national quarrels into matters of religion, and consequently all the calamities of war and devastation.[14]

Clausewitz famously remarked that war is the continuation of politics by other means. The frontispiece to *Leviathan* shows Hobbes to have affirmed a kind of twisted anticipation of that celebrated dictum: according to Hobbes, ecclesiastical politics is the continuation of war by other means.

The frontispiece is, then, a symbolic representation of Hobbes's theory of social disorder, disorder as generated by conflict between civil and religious authorities. Hobbes tells us in the *Six Lessons* that "though the competition of the papal and civil power be taken away now, yet the competition between the ecclesiastical and the civil power hath manifestly enough appeared very lately."[15] And so, Hobbes concludes,

When therefore these two powers oppose one another, the common-wealth cannot but be in great danger of civill warre, and dissolution. For the civill authority being more visible, and standing in the cleerer light of naturall reason cannot choose but draw in all times a very considerable part of the people: And the spirituall, though it stand in the darknesse of schoole distinctions, and hard words; yet because the fear of darknesse, and ghosts, is greater than other fears, cannot want a party sufficient to trouble, and sometimes to destroy a common-wealth. (L 171–2)

The problem here is not one of merely superstitious fears, of some irrational pneumatophobia. Our religious duties should indeed trump our civil duties when the two are in conflict. "It is manifest enough," Hobbes writes, "that when a man receiveth two contrary commands, and knows that one of them is God's, he ought to obey that, and not the other, though it be the command even of his lawfull soveraign," and "if the command [of the Civill Soveraign] bee such . . . as cannot be obeyed without being damned to eternall death, then it were madnesse to obey it" (L 321).

IV

In this light we can see that Hobbes's problem of social disorder cannot be solved by threatening civil punishment for disobedience. People simply are not the bodily preservation–centered egoists needed to make that sort of threat motivationally reliable. Rather, they are religious believers who count salvation and the fulfillment of their duties to God as a part of their good, and who may embrace martyrdom for their faith or resist their government on the ground of conscience. They have interests that may *transcend* their interest in temporal bodily preservation, interests for the sake of which they may be willing to risk death, or even to embrace death. Hobbes says of the clergy that "by the canonization of saints, and declaring who are martyrs, they assure their power, in that they induce simple men into an obstinacy against the laws and commands of their civill soveraigns *even to death*" (L 383, emphasis added). That makes proper management of these transcendent interests indispensable to the maintenance of order. And that means that

the right of judging what doctrines are fit for peace and to be taught to the subjects, is . . . inseparably annexed . . . to the soveraign power civill . . . For . . . men that are once possessed of an opinion that their obedience to the soveraign power will bee more hurtfull to them, than their disobedience, will disobey the laws, and thereby overthrow the commonwealth, and introduce confusion, and civill war. (L 295)

So the bodily preservation–centered conception of human nature that the standard interpretation attributes to Hobbes is not in fact Hobbes's. This snag is a serious problem for that interpretation, because if we pull on this thread we can watch the standard interpretation unravel in both directions. The bodily preservation–centered egoism was said to be derived from Hobbes's physical-scientific account of man as matter in motion, and together with it to form the account of man from which the political theory is derived. But that psychological conception is not derived from Hobbes's physical science. Hobbes insists that

in this naturall kingdome of God, there is no other way to know any thing, but by naturall reason; that is, from the principles of naturall science; which are so farre from teaching us any thing of Gods nature, *as they cannot teach us our own nature,* nor the nature of the smallest creature living. (L 191, emphasis added)

Preservation-centered egoism receives no support from Hobbes's natural science because that natural science cannot in practice ground *any* conception of human nature, nor through it a political philosophy.

Could it do so in principle, at least? If we look at Hobbes's own chart of the sciences (Figure 2), we can see that civil philosophy, that is, the science of politics, is a distinct branch of philosophy and not a subfield of the study of bodies, including men, and their natural properties, physical or psychological.

Of course, in some sense a study of the properties of states would have to be related to a study of the properties of human beings, because states are in some sense composed of human beings. But if, as Hobbes's chart indicates, a science of politics is not a branch of the science of natural bodies, then it seems likely that Hobbes's natural science is not meant to provide what we would think of as deductive grounding for his political argument. If that were Hobbes's intention, we would expect the chart to be configured quite differently.

If, upon seeing this, we are curious to know why the natural science is included at all, we have only to pay attention to what Hobbes actually does with it. He uses it to correct mistaken accounts of sense perception, dreams, and visions, because

This nature of sight having never been discovered by the ancient pretenders to naturall knowledge . . . it was hard for men to conceive of those images in the fancy, and in the sense, otherwise than of things really without us . . . Daemons. As if the dead of whom they dreamed were not inhabitants of their own brain, but of the air, or of heaven, or hell . . . and by that means have feared them. (L 352–3)

This bad natural science made plausible the Scholastics' doctrine, importing Aristotle, of "separated essences," which Hobbes declares

would fright them [men] from obeying the laws of their countrey with empty names . . . For it is upon this ground, that when a man is dead and buried, they say his soule (that is his life) can walk separated from his body; and a great many other things that serve to lessen the dependance of subjects on the soveraign power of their countrey. (L 373)

Such erroneous doctrines, made plausible only by a misunderstanding of natural science, position the church to claim that it has jurisdiction over men's spirits or souls at the very same time that men's bodies are under the sovereign's civil jurisdiction. This duplication of authorities over men is precisely what Hobbes is concerned to avoid.

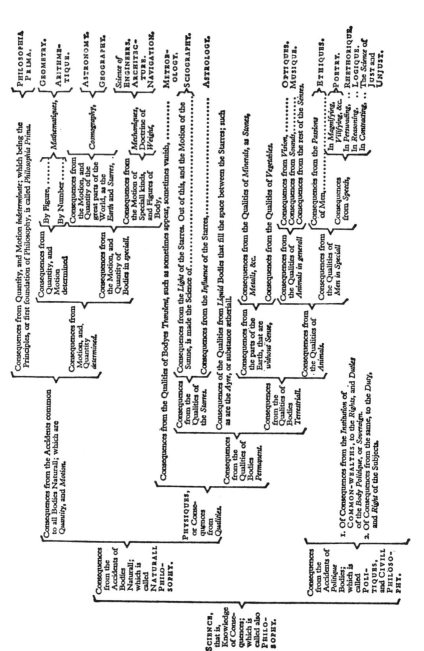

Figure 2. Hobbes's *Leviathan* (1651), table entitled "Chart of the Sciences." By permission of the British Library, (BL) 1476.d.23.

In short, Hobbes's remarks on natural science are present in order to correct several identifiable disruptive religious errors, and not, as the standard interpretation would have it, to ground some general psychological theory and, through that, a political theory. That is why Hobbes's physical science is so thin and patchy and is abandoned after only a few short chapters. And it also explains why in each revision of his political theory, though Hobbes vastly expands his religious discussion – from 29 pages, or about 12 percent, of *The Elements of Law,* to 116 pages, or 36 percent, of *De cive,* to a whopping 357 pages, exactly 50 percent, of *Leviathan* – he never feels the need to develop the rudimentary physical science that serves in his political writings. It is not that Hobbes is generally uninterested in science; he wrote many scientific works and engaged in many scientific debates. But not in the service of his political theory. There the science had a sharply limited, nonfoundational, role.

As for the standard interpretation's claim that Hobbes must have affirmed a subjectivist and personally relativist moral theory, because that is implied by bodily preservation–centered egoism, once the egoism goes, the nonobjectivism is no longer necessary, unless there is compelling independent textual evidence for it. As it happens, there is not. Even a fleeting look at Hobbes's text shows Hobbes to *disapprove* of subjective or relativized uses of moral terms. He criticizes the Greek philosophers on this ground:

Their morall philosophy is but a description of their own passions. For the rule of manners, without civill government, is the Law of Nature; and in it, the law civill; that determineth . . . what is good and evill: whereas they make the rules of good and bad by their own liking and disliking: By which means, in so great diversity of taste, there is nothing generally agreed on; but every one doth (as far as he dares) whatsoever seemeth good in his owne eyes, to the subversion of commonwealth. (L 369–70)

Hobbes is here indicating that it is incorrect to suppose that private appetite is the measure of good and evil. In a state of nature the proper measure of good and evil is the law of nature, and in a commonwealth the proper measure of good and evil is the civil law, because the law of nature requires us to take it for such. We may observe that in a state of nature people do in fact use their differing private appetites as the measure of good and evil (partly because there are difficulties in applying and enforcing the laws of nature), but even there it is not the correct measure. It is never the correct measure.

In fact, Hobbes's famous state of nature argument is best understood as a *reductio* of the use of private judgment; he writes in *Leviathan,* "And therefore so long a man is in the condition of mere nature, (which is a condition of war), as private appetite is the measure of good and evill" (L 80). Note carefully that this passage does not say (as the standard interpretation would have it) that *so long as* people are in the condition of mere nature, their private appetites *are* the measure of good and evil; what it says is that so long as private appetite is the *measure* of good and evil, people will remain in the condition of mere nature, which is a state of war. What it *is* to be in a state of nature is to be every man measuring good and evil by his own private appetite. Government by individual appetite – private judgment of good and evil – is the *defining* characteristic of a state of nature in which, as we all know, life is supposed to be "solitary, poore, nasty, brutish and short." Such a state can obtain in the absence of all government, but it can also occur in the presence of government if there is another authority, say a church, which challenges the government's authority so that individuals must use their private judgment to decide which authority to obey, with the prospect of them deciding, some of them one way, others another, in a dispute that cannot be settled by peaceful means.

In fact, a state of nature can obtain even in the presence of a single, sovereign authority, if people reserve to themselves a right to decide whether or not to obey their government, since they may withhold their obedience, to the paralysis of effective government. Hobbes warns,

> Take away in any kind of state the obedience (and consequently the concord of the people), and they shall not onely not flourish, but in short time be dissolved. And they that go about by disobedience to doe no more than reforme the common-wealth, shall find they thereby destroy it; like the foolish daughters of Peleus (in the fable), which desiring to renew the youth of their decrepit father, did by the counsell of Medea, cut in him pieces, and boyle him together with strange herbs, but made not of him a new man. (L 177)

Both divided sovereignty and limited sovereignty necessitate the use of private judgment to adjudicate or evaluate the claims of pretenders to authority. That is why Hobbes disapproves of them.

"And thus," concludes Hobbes (L 169), "wee fall again into the fault of taking upon us to judge of good and evill; or to make judges of it, such private men as pretend to be supernaturally inspired, *to the dissolution of all civill government*" (emphasis added). Taking it upon ourselves to judge of good and evil is imprudent, but it is not merely imprudent; it is also explicitly prohibited by God's positive laws as revealed in Scripture, for "the Scripture teacheth [that] it belongeth . . . to the soveraigne to bee judge, and to praescribe the rules of discerning good and evill" (L 105–6). The text thus shows that personal relativism is out.[16]

Hobbes's remarks on science, morality, and language must be taken in context. What appears at first to be a motley hodgepodge of disconnected topics in Part I of *Leviathan* turns out to be a catalog of most of the root sources of disorder in Hobbes's commonwealth and a first pass at correcting disruptive errors at their source. Not all errors stem from bad natural science, but some do; hence an early four chapters on errors grounded in faulty science. Numerous other disruptive errors rely on mistakes about the use of language and a failure to distinguish distinct ideas from one another; hence another seven chapters on errors from the abuse of language. Religious errors are a major source of disorder, so Hobbes includes a preliminary corrective discussion of religion. The natural tendencies toward pride, fearfulness, and acquisitiveness, when we make private judgment the rule of our actions, can cause disorder; hence an exposé of the perils of private judgment. A misunderstanding of the most basic norms of social life causes people to offend one another and to advance contentious moral claims, so Hobbes devotes two chapters on the laws of nature to clarify these norms. A misunderstanding of persons and authors leads subjects to resist their public representative, sometimes on the ground that they will be held responsible for the sinful actions he commands, other times on the ground that they have not authorized the powers he exercises; hence Hobbes includes a corrective chapter on authorization.

These are the primary sources of disorder identifiable by unaided natural reason. The remainder of the sources of disorder are presented in Part IV, where Hobbes discusses the root causes of those religious errors that most severely threaten order, a task that could not be completed until Hobbes had established (in Part III) what true religion properly involves, and so what should be counted as an error.

Parts II and III of *Leviathan* carry out the "compositive," or constructive, portion of Hobbes's project. In Part II, he aims to derive the rights and duties of subjects and sovereigns from the concept of a commonwealth,[17] and by the end of Part II Hobbes sums up his accomplishment thus far in these words:

That subjects owe to sovereigns simple obedience in all things wherein their obedience is not repugnant to the laws of God, I have sufficiently proved in that which I have already written. There wants onely, for the entire knowledge of civill duty, to know what are those lawes of God. For without that, a man knows not when he is commanded any thing by the civill power, whether it be contrary to the law of God or not; and so, either by too much civill obedience, offends the divine majesty, or through feare of offending God, transgresses the commandements of the commonwealth. To avoid both these rocks, it is necessary to know what are the lawes divine. (L 186)

That project is carried out in Part III. So Parts I and IV discuss the causes of disorder, whereas Parts II and III devise a remedy. Parts I and II employ exclusively natural knowledge, whereas Parts III and IV make additional use of prophetic or supernatural knowledge. The parts have different functions, but none of the parts is dispensable to Hobbes's project. *Pace* Stephen, it is not the case that Hobbes's system would be more consistent and intelligible if he omitted the theology altogether.

The textual evidence indicates that the standard interpretation, with its attribution to Hobbes of an attempted logical progression from mechanistic materialism to preservation-centered egoism to personal relativism to the "might plus fright makes order" remedy for rebellion stalls on each count. Its Hobbes is a fiction – a reassuringly modern and in many respects philosophically interesting one, but a fiction nonetheless.

V

And now the reason why Gauthier's moral contractarianism cannot properly claim Hobbes as an ancestor is clear. It relies on the standard interpretation's Hobbes to model the deliberations of its contractors – on a narrowly egoistic Hobbes, devoid of overriding religious concerns that impose constraints on bargaining strategies and desirable ends. Ruling out these kinds of interest is required by the rational bargaining model, which seeks to generate, rather than to import, normative constraints on action. But in Hobbes, everything depends on acknowledging the existence of such constraints and their effect on the reasonableness of social cooperation.

For Hobbes, to imagine narrowly egoistic interest-maximizing deliberators stripped of their transcendent, nonnegotiable, religious commitments would be to abstract away from the very features of persons that generate the most serious problems for social stability. To appreciate Hobbes's point, consider not just Christian martyrs in ancient Rome or various medieval sects but today's Hamas, engaged in the project of Islamic Jihad. Members of such groups identify their religious interests in ways that can make the sacrifice of their temporal (bodily) self-preservation acceptable, so long as they judge their actions to substantially contribute to their transcendent ends. These interests may threaten social order, since if those who have them are willing to die in pursuit of them, it is difficult to see how they could be deterred from destabilizing action by the threat of state force.

We can give greater rigor to our intuitive understanding of this point. The more fastidious way of putting it is that Hobbes analyzes social disorder as primarily the result of transcendent religious interests, which divide into two basic interests: the interest in fulfilling one's duty to God, and the interest in obtaining salvation and avoiding damnation. But the model of rational choice that Gauthier employs and wishes to credit, at least embryonically, to Hobbes, cannot accommodate interests of this transcendent (i.e., temporal, bodily preservation–overriding) character. Gauthier insists that one of the necessary conditions on preference required for an interval measure of the satisfaction of preferences is "continuity": that for three possible outcomes, A, B, and C, such that A is preferred to B and B to C, there is one (and only one) lottery, with A and C as prizes, that is indifferent to B. That is, assuming these preferences, there exists a probability, p, such that

$$pu(A) + (1 - p)u(C) = u(B).$$

But this continuity condition is not met by the preference orderings of those who have transcendent religious interests, as Hobbes conceives of these. It is true that in Hobbes's view the seventeenth-century Christian believer might prefer eating fruit to eating gruel and will prefer eating gruel to experiencing eternal damnation, but she is certainly not understood to be indifferent as between the certainty of eating gruel and a gamble with fruit and damnation as the stakes. Similarly, the believer will prefer attaining salvation to eating fruit, and fruit to gruel, but she is not understood to be indifferent as between fruit now and some gamble on salvation. To be indifferent between these sorts of things – culinary preferences versus eternal prospects – would be certifiably insane, in Hobbes's view. So continuity is not assumed to hold for these kinds of cases.

Gauthier's response to cases like this, which indicate the failure of continuity, is to say (in *Morals by Agreement*) that they are "perhaps best handled by limiting the contexts in which continuity is expected to hold by exempting 'extreme' cases" (MA, p. 46). This response might do fine for some purposes, but for Hobbes's project, the "extreme" cases are central. They are ineliminable from his account of disorder, and so cannot be excluded from any model of rational cooperation adequate to address that problem. No model that required their exclusion could be in a relevant sense Hobbesian.

The same can also be said of the transcendent interest in fulfilling one's duty to God, which also fails to satisfy the continuity condition, though apparently for a different reason. The most natural account of the failure of continuity for the case just considered of interests concerning salvation and damnation is that to these outcomes we attach an infinite utility or disutility, in the specific sense that we are unwilling to consider any bargain at all concerning them. (The problem there was not that one could not, in principle, do the mathematics, since in nonstandard analysis one can deal with such quantities, but rather that some possibilities, such as damnation, are ruled out of court – absolutely unacceptable – no matter what the result of the mathematician's calculation.) The difference in this case of transcendent interests in fulfilling our duties to God is that given Hobbes's view that when it comes to fulfilling one's duties to God, "the will is the deed," the probability of achieving that outcome, if chosen, can never be less than 1, so no point of indifference between it and the next-best outcome can ever be established.

Hobbes argues for the view that "the obedience required at our hands by God, that accepteth in all our action the will for the deed, is a serious endeavour to obey him . . . Whosoever therefore unfeignedly desireth to fulfill the commandements of God . . . hath all the obedience necessary to his reception into the kingdome of God" (L 322). And again, "[the laws of nature/God], because they oblige onely to a desire and endeavour . . . , are easie to be observed. For in that they require nothing but endeavour; he that endeavoureth their performance, fulfilleth them; and he that fulfilleth the law, is just" (L 79).

This means that if one selects to do one's duty to God, one automatically succeeds, with complete certainty, in doing so. Uncertainty, or risk, is eliminated. So it is impossible to assign to one's most preferred outcome, A, a probability that could allow for indifference between B and a lottery between A and C. If

A is chosen, the probability of achieving it is 1, and so the expected utility of that action must, by hypothesis, be greater than that of the next preferred outcome, B. If A is not chosen, the probability of achieving it is 0, and so the expected utility of one's action is just the utility of C, which is, by hypothesis, less than that of B. But in neither case can it be equal to that of B. Continuity fails.

So the continuity condition, which Gauthier insists is essential to his model for rational choice (the refinement he intends to introduce into Hobbes's theory), is one that Hobbes's central problem requires him to reject. And seeing this gives us a more precise way of explaining why the standard interpretation of Hobbes was not equipped to give an account of disorder that could, even in principle, be solved by the remedy it attributed to Hobbes. Its suggested solution is to increase the probability of bodily harm (via punishment) in order to alter the payoff matrix for disobedience, but no such increase will be adequate to force a reordering of preferences if continuity fails. And it does fail, where transcendent interests of the character Hobbes describes are what generate disorder.

Hobbes would thus have judged Gauthier's facile elimination of the "extreme case" of transcendent religious interests from his model of human deliberation to be a particularly egregious example of throwing out the baby with the bathwater. Hobbes is no forefather, nor even friend, to Gauthier's moral contractarianism.

VI

In contrast, our emerging sense of Hobbes's actual concerns makes it easier to understand why the political liberal would see a friend in Hobbes. Hobbes was addressing the problem of maintaining social order in the face of fundamental religious and moral disagreement over how people should live, and thus over the state's proper ends and operations. Hobbes's problem, to use the modern parlance of Rawls's political liberalism, was one of how to ensure stable social cooperation in the face of competing comprehensive doctrines. Rawls's political liberalism addresses a closely related problem, the problem of discovering how a stably just system of social cooperation might be maintained among those who affirm competing and irreconcilable comprehensive doctrines. Both philosophers are attempting to respond to the fundamental problems posed by pluralism – Hobbes to the problem of order *simpliciter,* and Rawls to the problem of establishing a just social order that could endure. And both problems arise when people within a society disagree in their comprehensive doctrines and either cannot or will not allow each person free rein to act on his or her own comprehensive doctrine. Indeed, we can see both problems as generated by the same pair of conditions:

  (1) A collapse of consensus on values, interests, and ends. (Rawls, who assumes that this condition is a permanent feature of democratic societies, calls this the "fact of pluralism.")

(2) The unwillingness to tolerate others' pursuit of comprehensive doctrines of which one disapproves, along with the willingness to use state power to enforce compliance with one's own comprehensive doctrine.

Together these conditions give rise to problems both of social order and of social justice, for both Hobbes and Rawls. So we can understand why Rawls might find a resource in Hobbes.

Nonetheless, although their problems are related, it is their approaches to a solution that distinguish them, and these are what matter for our purposes. Hobbes's strategy for resolving his problem of order is to overcome condition (1), diversity in comprehensive doctrines, by reconciling them through a process of correcting disruptive religious errors and by redescribing religious duty so that formerly competing religious factions can be brought to affirm one and the same substantive conception of their religious duties, a conception that reinforces social order. This is a complicated process, to which Hobbes devotes some three hundred pages of *Leviathan,* and I shall not attempt to recount it here.[18] It involves identifying commonly acceptable resources for settling doctrinal disagreement and then arguing that these support a unique conception of religious duty fully compatible with civil obedience. Through this process, Hobbes aims to move all of his intended audience from their idiosyncratic beliefs to a single comprehensive doctrine, and then to use the full force of the state's power to enforce and to reproduce allegiance to that comprehensive doctrine. Clearly, this is a fundamentally illiberal strategy.

In contrast, the liberal solution to the problem of justice focuses on overcoming, or limiting, condition (2), people's intolerance of competing doctrines. It attempts this by appealing to the political values of reciprocity among equals, liberty, and individuality; by separating church and state, the public and associational realms; and – critical in the case of Rawls's political liberalism – by emphasizing the primacy of citizens' interest in securing the necessary conditions for the exercise of their capacities to form, revise, and pursue a conception of the good and to have and act from a sense of justice (what Rawls calls their "powers of moral personality"). Rawls gives greater emphasis to citizens' interest in securing conditions for the exercise of these powers than to their interest in pursuing the substantive comprehensive doctrines they affirm at any given time. Citizens' representatives in the "original position" select principles of justice that best protect the exercise of these capacities, but they do so in ignorance of the content of the comprehensive doctrines affirmed by those whom they represent. Roughly speaking, instead of pressing for the requirements of your comprehensive doctrine, they press for conditions that would allow you to pursue the requirements of any reasonable comprehensive doctrine you may affirm, or may come to affirm.[19]

So Hobbes takes aim at the problem of pluralism, seeking to forge uniformity in belief, whereas Rawls, assuming the fact of pluralism, seeks to delegitimize the use of state power in enforcing intolerance of differing, though reasonable, comprehensive doctrines. Given their fundamental difference in approach, should Rawls's political liberalism claim Hobbes as one of its own?

Insofar as overcoming intolerance requires Rawls to rely on the distancing device of the "veil of ignorance" to abstract away from the particular content of people's transcendent interests, his theory is, like Gauthier's, dancing around the very problem that Hobbes thought an adequate political philosophy must grapple with directly. Hobbes firmly believed that "the devil is in the details" – that political instability is generated by the details of the particular religious views citizens in fact affirm, and that remedying disorder requires direct attention to these particularisms. Hobbes demonstrates the required attention in the half of *Leviathan* that he devotes to religious issues. Indeed, the painfully thorough way in which he works through every competitor to his own interpretation of religious duty may partially explain why so few contemporary readers have the patience to study the half of *Leviathan* devoted to religious argument. Hobbes allows himself no broad brushstrokes of high theory, no abstractions that gloss over the points of contention among combatants.

But Rawls's use of a veil of ignorance to defuse the problem posed by intolerance precisely precludes doing what would be necessary to eliminate diversity. One cannot expect to move people from the views they hold without dealing with the content of those views, yet Rawls's device prevents his deliberators from even knowing what those views are, except in the most general terms, let alone engaging those views on their own terms. This is not a problem for Rawls, because his project does not require forging consensus on comprehensive doctrine, but it would be fatal to Hobbes's project. So, if some such distancing device as the veil of ignorance is indispensable for defending the kind of principles of justice Rawls seeks (namely, principles that could gain the support of an overlapping consensus in a society well ordered by them), then Hobbes's theory, which must disallow this sort of abstraction, is fundamentally incompatible with Rawls's. This incompatibility would be a deep one, in the specific sense that Hobbes could not carry out his project were such abstraction from the content of contested comprehensive doctrines allowed, and Rawls could not carry out his project were such abstraction *dis*allowed.

I do not insist that the use of a device like the veil of ignorance is necessary to the successful completion of Rawls's project; we might think of the "original position" as just an expository aid to an argument that can be mounted independently, without reliance on any substitute distancing device. But, given all that Rawls says to justify his use of the veil of ignorance, I think that the burden of proof must rest with those who would claim that Rawls's principles of justice could be defended without any abstraction from the content of contested comprehensive doctrines.[20] Nor has my discussion reflected how subtle are the differences between Hobbes and Rawls, since Hobbes cannot escape resort to a distancing device of his own. Hobbes argues that our religious duties are properly specified by the judgment of a religious authority, and that we ought to profess and practice as the appropriate authority in matters of religion dictates (whatever the content of his dictates). This is an abstraction of sorts, because it transforms the question of what religious doctrines are true into the question of whose judgment God requires us to regard as authoritative on religious questions.[21]

But one important difference between Rawls's distancing device and that employed by Hobbes is that Hobbes's distancing move away from characterizations of religious duty as requiring particular profession and practice toward one requiring whatever profession and practice the appropriate religious authority may dictate is argued to be sanctioned by, rather than foreign to, the comprehensive doctrines it seemingly disempowers. It is not at all clear that the same can be said of Rawls's distancing device, and this seems to me to be a very important difference. Even should Rawls's principles of justice find direct support in the comprehensive doctrines that make up an overlapping consensus, it is still highly unlikely that all of Rawls's machinery, including, especially, the original position with its veil of ignorance, will enjoy such support. So, if the use of the original position (with the veil of ignorance) is required in order to settle on Rawls's principles of justice, his political liberalism will depend upon an abstraction that Hobbes would have viewed as impermissible. The two views do have other affinities,[22] but on the basis of the considerations just advanced, we should conclude that Hobbes was not the first "political liberal."

So the real Hobbes cannot be used to support the admittedly philosophically interesting projects of Gauthier or Rawls, because his project requires paying attention to transcendent interests in ways that their projects cannot permit. But there is, to my mind, a philosophical problem at least as interesting as theirs to which the real Hobbes speaks directly, and that is the problem of how to address disorder generated by transcendent interests. This, it seems to me, is perhaps the most pressing problem of our world. Many of the religious conflicts, and ethnic conflicts, and pride and blood feuds we confront every day seem to have the "force-resistant" character of transcendent interests. So we need a theory that addresses disorder generated by transcendent interests, and Hobbes was the first to have made significant progress toward designing such a theory.[23] The real Hobbes brought an astounding intellect to bear on one of the most pressing problems of human life and suggested what, to my knowledge, is the most promising strategy for solving it.

I think Gregory Kavka would have agreed that the problem of how we might overcome disorder generated by transcendent religious and ethnic interests is of great philosophical interest, and that he would have appreciated the power of Hobbes's strategy. I do not know whether he would have agreed that what is of greatest philosophical interest in Hobbes is Hobbes's contribution to this problem, but I think it is clear that Kavka and I *were* engaged in a common project. Until others take up his part in our conversation, as I hope they will, I have the undeserved, and undesired, advantage of having the last word.

Notes

1. See, e.g., Aristotle's *Nicomachean Ethics,* 9.9. 1170a4–11 and 9.9.1170b7–14.
2. John Cooper, "Aristotle on Friendship," in *Essays on Aristotle's Ethics,* ed. Amelie Oksenberg Rorty (Berkeley and Los Angeles: University of California Press, 1980), p. 326.
3. See esp. John Rawls, *Political Liberalism* (New York: Columbia University Press, 1993). Here I assert that Rawls claims Hobbes as an ancestor, despite the fact that in his writings to date Rawls has done no more than acknowledge Hobbes as a founder of the social-contract tradition, within which he includes his own view; and perhaps it seems surprising that Rawls would afford special standing to Hobbes. Rawls has told me that he suspects, for a number of reasons that should become clear in what follows, that Hobbes may have been the first political liberal, and he has asked me to investigate this suggestion. So I hope to discharge this commission while answering Kavka's challenge.
4. David Gauthier, *Morals by Agreement* (Oxford: Clarendon Press, 1986), cited hereafter in parentheses in the text, as *MA,* with page number.
5. On this requirement see *Leviathan,*

   > The question who is the better man, has no place in the condition of meer nature; where, (as has been shewn before,) all men are equal . . . If nature therefore have made men equall, that equalitie is to be acknowledged: or if nature have made men unequall; yet because men that think themselves equall, will not enter into conditions of peace, but upon equall termes, such equalitie must be admitted. And therefore for the ninth law of nature, I put this, That every man acknowledge other for his Equall by Nature. (L 76–7)

   and Hobbes's second law of nature, requiring reciprocity,

   > That a man be willing, when others are so too . . . to lay down [his] right to all things; and be contented with so much liberty against other men, as he would allow other men against him-selfe. (L 64–5)

   References to Hobbes's *Leviathan* are to the original Head edition (1651) page numbers as these are indicated in square brackets in C. B. Macpherson's Pelican edition of *Leviathan* (Harmondsworth, UK: Penguin, 1968), from which I quote, cited hereafter as L, in parentheses in text.
6. E.g., at L 79: "And divers men, differ not onely in their judgement, on the senses of what is pleasant, and unpleasant to the tast, smell, hearing, touch, and sight; but also of what is conformable, or disagreeable to reason, in the actions of common life."
7. See David Gauthier, *The Logic of Leviathan* (Oxford: Oxford University Press, 1969), and, for the tradition, John Laird, *Hobbes* (London: Ernest Benn, 1934); Leo Strauss, *The Political Philosophy of Hobbes* (Chicago: University of Chicago Press, 1952); J. W. N. Watkins, *Hobbes's System of Ideas* (London: Hutchinson, 1965), and his "Philosophy and Politics in Hobbes," in *Hobbes Studies,* ed. K. C. Brown (Cambridge, MA: Harvard University Press, 1965); Thomas Nagel, "Hobbes's Concept of Obligation," *Philosophical Review* 68 (1959), pp. 68–83; John Plamenatz,

"Mr. Warrender's Hobbes," in *Hobbes Studies,* ed. K. C. Brown (Cambridge, MA: Harvard University Press, 1965); Jean Hampton, *Hobbes and the Social Contract Tradition* (Cambridge: Cambridge University Press, 1986); Gregory S. Kavka, *Hobbesian Moral and Political Theory* (Princeton: Princeton University Press, 1986).

8. Gauthier, *The Logic of Leviathan,* p. 7.

9. Watkins, "Philosophy and Politics in Hobbes," p. 252.

10. Both of these lines of objection are developed in S. A. Lloyd, *Ideals as Interests in Hobbes's Leviathan: The Power of Mind over Matter* (Cambridge: Cambridge University Press, 1992), ch. 1.

11. Leslie Stephen, *Hobbes* (Ann Arbor: University of Michigan Press, 1961), p. 152.

12. Thomas Hobbes, *Six Lessons,* and *Seven Philosophical Problems,* in *The English Works of Thomas Hobbes,* ed. William Molesworth, 9 vols. (London: John Bohn, 1839), vol. 7, quotations at p. 345 and p. 5, respectively.

13. Thomas Hobbes, *Behemoth or the Long Parliament,* ed. Ferdinand Tonnies, intro. by Stephen Holmes (Chicago: University of Chicago Press, 1990), cited hereafter as *B*, in parentheses in text.

14. "Epistle Dedicatory" to *Liberty and Necessity,* in Hobbes, *English Works,* ed. Molesworth, 4:233.

15. Hobbes, *Six Lessons,* p. 345.

16. Nor should we imagine that Hobbes took moral judgment to be relative to at least one person, namely the sovereign, and that sovereigns, by their pronouncements, define good and evil. If sovereigns defined good and evil, it would be impossible for them to err in their moral judgments. But Hobbes says in plain language that it is possible for sovereigns to make moral mistakes: "there is no judge subordinate, *nor sovereign,* but may erre in a judgment of equity" (L 144, emphasis added). Cf. L 330, where Hobbes indicates that Christian kings may issue mistaken religious directives. Hobbes's point is not that one's sovereign defines right and wrong or is for some other reason normatively infallible; it is rather that one ought to accept one's sovereign's judgment as authoritative, whether or not it is correct. For the full argument, see S. A. Lloyd, "Coercion, Ideology, and Education in Hobbes's *Leviathan,*" in *Reclaiming the History of Ethics: Essays for John Rawls,* ed. Andrews Reath, Barbara Herman, and Christine M. Korsgaard (Cambridge: 1997), esp. the section entitled "The Hobbesian Responsibility Puzzle."

17. For an account of how this is done, see my *Ideals as Interests,* ch. 2.

18. I offer a detailed account of Hobbes's argument in *Ideals as Interests,* ch. 3.

19. See, for example, Rawls's discussion in his 1980 Dewey Lecture, "Rational and Full Autonomy," of the contrast between our highest-order interests in realizing and exercising our powers of moral personality and our merely higher-order interest in protecting and advancing our determinate conception of the good. The latter interest is "in essential respects subordinate to the highest-order interests," which are "supremely regulative." "Kantian Constructivism in Moral Theory: The Dewey Lectures, 1980," *Journal of Philosophy,* 78 (1980), 525.

20. In *A Theory of Justice,* Rawls writes that the purpose of the original position is to "nullify the effects of specific contingencies which put men at odds," and that "in order to carry through the idea of the original position, the parties must not know the contingencies that set them in opposition" (136–7). Such contingencies must be rendered invisible by a veil of ignorance. But among the most important such contingencies are the comprehensive doctrines that citizens in fact affirm, for, "The most intractable struggles, political liberalism assumes, are confessedly for the sake of the highest things: for religion, for philosophical views of the world, and

for different moral conceptions of the good" (*Political Liberalism*, p. 4). So citizens' comprehensive doctrines must be set behind the veil of ignorance.

Rawls confirms this conclusion in answering the objection that his veil of ignorance is made "too thick" by its inclusion of citizens' comprehensive doctrines. He insists that, given the fact of reasonable pluralism,

> if all citizens are freely to endorse the political conception of justice, that conception must be able to gain the support of citizens who affirm different and opposing though reasonable comprehensive doctrines . . . This suggests that we leave aside how people's comprehensive doctrines connect with the content of the political conception of justice . . . We model this by putting people's comprehensive doctrines behind the veil of ignorance. This enables us to find a political conception of justice that can be the focus of an overlapping consensus and thereby serve as a public basis of justification in a society marked by the fact of reasonable pluralism. (Ibid., pp. 24–5, n. 27)

So the inclusion of citizens' comprehensive doctrines behind the veil of ignorance is further justified by the requirements of achieving an overlapping consensus.

This is connected with the proper role of a conception of justice:

> In order to explain why the veil of ignorance excludes certain kinds of beliefs . . . I have cited the public role that a conception of justice has in a well-ordered society. Because its principles are to serve as a shared point of view among citizens with opposing religions, philosophical and moral convictions, as well as diverse conceptions of the good, this point of view needs to be appropriately impartial among those differences. (Dewey Lectures, 1980, pp. 542–3)

And related to these considerations is the role of the veil of ignorance in modeling appropriate restrictions on acceptable reasons for favoring one conception of justice over another. Given our shared normative conceptions of citizens as free and equal moral persons and of society as a system of willing cooperation on fair terms for mutual benefit among such persons (as these conceptions are gleaned from our public political culture),

> The fact that we affirm a particular religious, philosophical, or moral comprehensive doctrine with its associated conception of the good is not a reason for us to propose, or to expect others to accept, a conception of justice that favors those of that persuasion. To model this conviction in the original position, the parties are not allowed to know the . . . particular comprehensive doctrine of the person each represents. (*Political Liberalism*, p. 24)

Taken together, these considerations strongly suggest that the use of some such device as the veil of ignorance in the original position to abstract from the content of citizens' comprehensive doctrines will be necessary to the successful completion of Rawls's project. So, it seems to me, the burden of argument will lie with those who would maintain that no such abstracting device is necessary to Rawls's project.

21. For the details of this argument, see my *Ideals as Interests*, ch. 3.
22. There is some similarity in the reasoning behind Rawls's insistence on a "free-standing" justification for his principles of justice and Hobbes's care to provide a multiplication of reasons from different comprehensive views for adherence to his principle of political obligation; after all, to show one's principles justified without dependence on any comprehensive doctrine at all, and to show them justifiable from within many comprehensive doctrines, are different ways of showing one's principles to be not dependent upon the affirmation of some privileged comprehensive doctrine. On the confluence of reasons for supporting Hobbes's principle of politi-

cal obligation, see my *Ideals as Interests,* p. 279; for a discussion of the requirement that the argument for principles of justice be freestanding, see Rawls, *Political Liberalism,* pp. 10–12, 140, 144.
23. I try to explain how we might adapt Hobbes's general method to the particular features of the conflicts that concern us in *Ideals as Interests,* ch. 9.

The Knavish Humean

JEAN HAMPTON

The title of this essay is not meant to impugn Humeans; it is only meant to recognize a kind of person that some Humeans might have thought impossible, namely, someone with a full complement of other-regarding sentiments who possesses those "useful" natural virtues (such as benevolence) of the sort described by Hume but who nonetheless behaves like a "knave" (to use Hume's own word) in situations where he can exploit another with impunity. In the *Second Inquiry*,[1] Hume regards such knavishness as resulting from of a lack of concern for, and integrity with respect to the treatment of, one's fellow human beings. Hume represents the knave's point of view as follows:

> And though it is allowed that, without a regard to property, no society could subsist; yet according to the imperfect way in which human affairs are conducted, a sensible knave, in particular incidents, may think that an act of iniquity or infidelity will make a considerable addition to his fortune, without causing any considerable breach in the social union or confederacy. That *honesty is the best policy,* may be a good general rule, but is liable to many exceptions; and he, it may perhaps be thought, conducts himself with most wisdom, who observes the general rule, and takes advantage of all the exceptions. (Enq, ix, ii, pp. 282–3)

The knave is essentially saying that he will cooperate if and only if it is advantageous for him to do so, and thus will not do so in situations (such as the "prisoner's dilemma" game) where it is not advantageous, despite the existence of a moral convention to perform the cooperative act in that sort of situation. And what does Hume say to this sensible knave?

> I must confess that, if a man think that this reasoning much requires an answer, it will be a little difficult to find any which will to him appear satisfactory and convincing. If his heart rebel not against such pernicious maxims, if he feel no reluctance to the thoughts of villainy or baseness, he has indeed lost a considerable motive to virtue; . . . But in all ingenuous natures, the antipathy to treachery and roguery is too strong to be

I wish to thank Paul Hurley, Ken O'Day, and Andrews Reath for comments and discussions on the ideas of this essay. If Gregory Kavka were alive, I would have sent a copy to him, and I know that he would have given me highly valuable comments and we would have enjoyed a very fruitful and pleasant exchange of ideas. How I miss him.

counter-balanced by any views of profit or pecuniary advantage. Inward peace of mind, consciousness of integrity, a satisfactory review of our own conduct; these are circumstances, very requisite to happiness, and will be cherished and cultivated by every honest man, who feels the importance of them. (Enq, ix, ii, p. 283)

Hume's answer admits that if the knave has no sentiments pressing him to embrace moral behavior, reason cannot persuade him to do so when the consequences of immoral behavior are better. Hume lists those sentiments as a rebellion against "pernicious maxims," a reluctance at the "thought of villainy or baseness," an "antipathy to treachery and roguery," and the experience of "inward peace of mind" and "consciousness of integrity" at the thought of resisting the temptation to exploit (which he says is associated with a satisfactory review by the agent of his own conduct), all of which Hume says are "very requisite to happiness, and will be cherished and cultivated by every honest man, who feels the importance of them." These are rather special "sentiments," and I will want to elaborate in detail on their content. (They are certainly more than feelings, and seem highly idea-ridden.) For now, I will simply refer to them as "exploitation-blocking sentiments."

If such sentiments are common, it seems Hume can argue that most of us have within us motivators that block the drive to exploit. Therefore it seems that knavery would be less common in the Humean world than in a world full of purely rational egoists, precisely because Humean people are more likely to have motivations that press them to behave morally, even when rational self-interested concerns fail to do so or oppose such action.

I want to argue in this essay, however, that the exploitation-blocking sentiments that Hume defines are relatively useless in preventing knavery if one accepts the rest of the Humean portrait of our nature as human beings. If this argument is right, it shows that nonexploitative behavior – a particularly important example of moral behavior – can rarely be explained or justified by appeal to the kind of sentiments Hume is prepared to recognize. And this, I go on to argue, casts doubt on the strategy of explaining or justifying moral behavior by using a sentimental model.

I. Deriving Other-regard from Self-regard

In many respects, Thomas Hobbes's theory of human psychology and his approach to morality form the basis of Hume's view of humankind and morality, although Hume is clearly interested in supplementing the Hobbesian theory with a richer (and more other-regarding) conception of motivation and value. But that enrichment still builds upon a Hobbesian foundation, which must be understood before we can proceed farther.

One of the most notorious aspects of Hobbes's view of human beings is the extent to which he thinks that individuals can be defined as human beings apart from their connection with other people. This is demonstrated by the fact that he thinks it is possible to imagine individuals without connection to one another, existing in a "state of nature," defined not only as a prepolitical state but also a presocial state.

I have called this way of thinking about the nature of human beings "radical individualism."[2] This position has two components. First, it holds that all those characteristics, skills, and desires that are distinctive of the human species are "intrinsic" properties of human beings, not properties that are "interactive" in the sense that they have developed through interaction between the human being and her (social or natural) environment. So, for example, the capacity to perform certain bodily functions, to reason, and even to speak a language are held to be definitive of the human species. For Hobbes such capacities are not features that emerge in a human being only after interaction with the environment – in particular, a social environment – but are instead features that emerge inevitably under normal conditions because of how we are built as a species. Contrast these capacities with, say, the ability to speak a particular language, or to ride a bike, or to do calculus: these are examples of features of human beings that are interactive in that they are created in a human being through the interaction of the environment – in particular, a certain kind of social environment – with that human being's intrinsic capacities and characteristics.

Second, radical individualism holds that the intrinsic properties defining us as human beings make no essential reference to other members of our species, so that we are able to conceive of each member of the species in his or her full humanity, without thinking of such individuals as members of a social group. To use Hobbes's terminology, because the human-making features of each of us are nonsocial in nature, we can perform a thought experiment in which we conceive of human beings as "sprung out of the earth, and suddenly, like mushrooms, come to full maturity, without all kind of engagement to each other."[3]

Among the features that are intrinsic to us, Hobbes lists certain self-regarding desires, such as the desire to preserve our life, obtain food, and have sex. If we understand "self-regard" as defined by the set of desires that have some aspect of the self and its well-being as their object, then many of the most powerful and important desires in this set will be intrinsic rather than interactive in nature.

What about desires that have as their object the well-being of other people? Such desires make essential reference to other selves, so that to posit them as intrinsic desires would be to define our humanity in a manner that makes us intrinsically social. However, consistent with his commitment to radical individualism, Hobbes recognizes the existence of these desires but explains them in a manner that makes them interactive rather than intrinsic features of human beings. Consider, for example, that he defines the emotion of pity as "Griefe, for the Calamity of *another*" and says that it arises "from the imagination that the like calamity may befall himselfe; and therefore is called also COMPASSION, and in phrase of this present time is a FELLOW-FEELING."[4] Note in this definition that there is a distinction between the object of the passion, which is the well-being of another human being, and the cause of its origination, which has to do with the self. The idea seems to be that via some sort of imaginative identification we put ourselves in someone else's place, imagine what she is suffering, and (if it is calamitous) feel pity for her as a result. Note that we really do feel pity for her, so the object of the passion is genuinely other-regarding. But the origin of the passion has to do with a psychological process that makes reference to the self.

So here we have a theory of the origination of an other-regarding passion: and insofar as this theory says that this sort of passion arises out of a process of imaginative identification, it construes all passions generated in this fashion as interactive rather than intrinsic. That is, the passion originates only after interaction with other members of the species, because its generation requires an imaginative procedure that involves identifying with the plight of another human being (where, presumably, the ability to engage in this imaginative identification is an intrinsic feature of each human being). Moreover, note that this theory of the origination of other-regarding passions predicts that they would exist in human beings only minimally in a state of nature, because such people would not, by hypothesis, be interacting with one another enough (or in the right kind of way) to allow the process of sympathetic identification to produce very many of these other-interested passions (or maybe any at all).

By relying on what he calls "sympathy," Hume has an analogous mechanism available to him to derive many, perhaps even all, other-regarding passions from the operation of sympathy. As he explains in *A Treatise of Human Nature,*

'Tis evident, that the idea, or rather impression of ourselves is always intimately present with us, and that our consciousness gives us so lively a conception of our own person, that 'tis not possible to imagine, that any thing can in this particular go beyond it. Whatever object, therefore, is related to ourselves must be perceived with a like vivacity of conception, according to the foregoing principles; . . .

Now 'tis obvious, that nature has preserv'd a great resemblance among all human creatures, and that we never remark any passion or principle in others, of which, in some degree or other, we may not find a parallel in ourselves . . . There is a very remarkable resemblance, which preserves itself amidst all their variety; and this resemblance must very much contribute to make us enter into the sentiments of others, and embrace them with facility and pleasure.[5]

So, like Hobbes, Hume explains the origin of certain kinds of sentiments within us by appeal to a psychological process in which we "enter into the sentiments of others" and, as a result, develop certain desires and feelings with respect to them.[6] Thus Hume accepts an explanation of the origin of other-regarding passions that has the same basic structure as the Hobbesian account. That is, both accounts insist that self-regarding concerns are the (mere) source of certain other-regarding passions and sentiments; these concerns are involved in explaining how such passions and sentiments are generated within us; but both accounts also insist that once the other-regarding passions are generated the objects of these passions are for and about others.[7]

How many of our other-regarding passions does Hume wish to derive using the mechanism of sympathy? Clearly, the mechanism itself is intrinsic to human beings, but the passions generated from it would count as interactive, by virtue of the fact that they arise because of the interaction between that mechanism and the (human-populated) environment in which the agent exists. The more passions Hume derives from sympathy, the more he is thinking about us as individuals, defined by intrinsic characteristics that make no reference to other human beings. Conversely, the fewer other-regarding passions he derives from sympathy, the more other-regarding passions must be understood as intrinsic to our nature, in which case that nature would be understood to include features (in this case, passions) that do make essential reference to other people.

Interestingly, the *Treatise* is not entirely clear on how many other-regarding passions come from the operation of sympathy. It is as though Hume is of two minds about this issue. In Book II, Hume speaks of some of the calm passions as "certain instincts originally implanted in our natures, such as benevolence or resentment, the love of life, and kindness to children; or the general appetite to good, and aversion to evil, consider'd merely as such" (II, iii, p. 417). Clearly this passage suggests that at least some important other-regarding passions are intrinsic to us and not generated by sympathy. Similarly, he says later in Book II that passions such as the desire to punish our enemies, the desire to give happiness to friends, and hunger, lust, and other bodily appetites are "natural impulses" (II, iii, ix, p. 439). Both passages therefore recognize the existence of inborn (and non-sympathy-induced) other-regarding passions.

However, in Book III Hume sings a different tune. In the process of arguing that there is no such thing as the "love of mankind, merely as such, independent of personal qualities, of services, or of relation to oneself," he says:

'Tis true, there is no human, and indeed no sensible creature, whose happiness or misery does not, in some measure, affect us, when brought near to us, and represented in lively colors: But this proceeds merely from sympathy, and is no proof of such an universal affection to mankind, since this concern extends itself beyond our own species. (III, ii, i, p. 481)

And in his discussion of natural virtues, later in Book III, he insists that "we have no such extensive concern for society but from sympathy; and consequently 'tis that principle, which takes us so far out of ourselves, as to give us the same pleasure or uneasiness in the characters of others, as if they had a tendency to our own advantage or loss" (III, iii, i, p. 579). Note that even Hobbes could have agreed with these last remarks, insofar as Hobbes believed that we are "taken out of ourselves" only by identifying with the plight of another.

Given these passages, we cannot decisively say how much of Hobbes's individualism Hume was prepared to accept. In Book III he seems prepared to accept the entire Hobbesian view, whereas in Book II he suggests only a partially individualistic conception of human beings. However, all readers of the *Treatise* and the *Second Enquiry* know that Hume takes sympathy very seriously as the source of our concern for others. And as long as sympathy is an important source of fundamental other-regarding passions, Hume is thinking along very Hobbesian lines, seeing self-concern as "basic" or "primary" to human psychology and other-concern as often – maybe even always – "derived" from self-concern by the mechanism of sympathy. So, although Hume may not be a radical individualist, he is at the very least a "moderate individualist," that is, one who holds that most (albeit not all) characteristics definitive of our humanity are (1) intrinsic in nature and (2) do not make reference to other human beings.

Note that both the moderate and radical forms of individualism treat self-regard as basic, and thus relatively unproblematic, but other-regard as motivationally much less strong and, either entirely or in part, something that one works hard both to create and to strengthen in young human beings, who are viewed as instinctively concerned with self but who seem to have to be taught to show any substantial concern for others. This primacy of self-regard has seemed highly plausible to generations of philosophers since the seventeenth century; hence, the Humean–Hobbesian view of other-regarding passions as derived from a self-referring mechanism has struck many philosophers ever since as sensible and likely true.

Of course, whether or not either approach to understanding human beings is correct is certainly debatable. And, as we shall see, the problem of the knave is essentially born once either of these individualistic conceptions of human beings is assumed.

II. Knaves

Hobbes's theory of morality, put forward in Chapters xiv and xv of *Leviathan,* explains and justifies moral behavior by showing how moral actions can be commended in hypothetical imperatives dictating peace. If morality is peace securing, then it is in our interest to behave morally – as long as others are willing to do so too. In this way, Hobbes attempts to represent the moral point of view as the point of view of enlightened rational self-interest. Hobbes's imperatives were relatively simple and not terribly detailed, but there have been many attempts subsequent to *Leviathan* to make these imperatives more complex and detailed and to understand both moral behavior and its advantages for human beings in a psychologically richer fashion. Indeed, as I see it, Hume's discussion of the artificial virtues is one attempt to refine and further develop this Hobbesian approach. Hume offers a more detailed and more explicitly convention-based version of Hobbes's laws of nature, enhancing the Hobbesian model by showing the manner in which, for example, appeal to other-regarding passions can make peace-preserving conventions more stable. Hobbes himself would be dubious about some of these enhancements, not convinced that human beings have the psychological or cognitive mechanisms to pull them off, but that may be Hobbes's problem.

Of course, one mechanism in Hume's theory that Hobbes would like is sympathy. But Hume relies upon it much more and takes the motivational efficacy of the passions produced by sympathy much more seriously than Hobbes, seeing them as crucial to understanding what morality really is. Even if Hume's sympathy-based derivation of many of our other-regarding passions makes them interactive rather than intrinsic and belies an individualistic conception of human beings, it would still seem that because his theory relies far more than Hobbes's theory upon other-regarding passions, the Humean theory is, in many respects, non-Hobbesian in its portrayal of our moral life. Moreover, because Hume is more of a believer in the extensiveness and strength of the other-regarding passions than Hobbes, it would seem that he has the resources to handle better than Hobbes the thorny problem of following the artificially created laws of nature even in those cases when it is not in one's interest to do so.

It is essentially this last problem that Hume is reflecting upon when he describes his knave. The clearest way of stating the problem of the knave is this: there seem no rational grounds to persuade a purely instrumentally rational person to cooperate in a single-play prisoner's dilemma game. Of course, any sensible knave will cooperate in iterated prisoner's dilemma games, as will any rational Hobbesian person, so cooperation in such iterated games is not a problem. Note that iteration does not necessarily mean "iteration with the same partner." If my ability to reap cooperative benefits from a future game with some player depends upon whether or not I cooperate with you in a game right now, then this present game and that future one with another person are linked, and I have a self-interested reason to cooperate with you now to get the cooperative reputation I need to reap those future rewards, assuming some assurance is available to both my partner and me that each of us is rationally disposed to cooperate. (This is where Hume's institution of promise keeping can come in handy; it acts as an assurance device, which is itself conventionally established and supported because of its self-interested benefits.) Any smart knave understands all this. But any smart knave also understands that when he is in a prisoner's dilemma game that is not linked to any other prisoner's dilemma game in the future (and therefore is really and truly a single-play game), then he is rational not to cooperate. And were he to meet some cooperative person, he would happily take advantage of him – and would deserve no criticism from the standpoint of reason – or from Hobbesian morality – since for the Hobbesian, the moral standpoint must also be a rational standpoint (insofar as a Hobbesian insists that the moral must be rational). And yet we do not approve of knaves, and we consider them immoral. So where does this criticism come from? Because it does not come from the standpoint of (instrumental) reason, we must search for some other source for it, which means admitting that, *contra* Hobbes, we do not really get the moral standpoint from enlightened self-interest alone.

Note that the problem of the knave is precipitated by an individualistic conception of human beings. The prisoner's dilemma game numbers can be "overcome" and cooperation in the game secured only if an individual is able to commit herself to securing the well-being of her partner as well as herself (even while aware that her partner's well-being is not the same as her own well-being, so that the numbers in the boxes of the matrix game do not change in a manner that transforms the prisoner's dilemma game into another, more easily solved game). Although the interests generating the numbers for each player might not be entirely self-regarding (e.g., I might value the situation where you cooperate and I do not because I can gain resources not only for myself but also for my family), nonetheless, as long as neither player has any capacity to identify with and work to secure the well-being of her partner in the game, the two players cannot solve this game cooperatively.

However, if, consistent with Hume's individualism, each player had an interactive desire motivating him or her to be concerned with the welfare of the other, perhaps the game could be solved. Hume's exploitation-blocking sentiments might seem to be examples of such interactive desires, particularly if they were indebted to sympathy for their creation. So how much knavery can these sentiments really prevent? The sentiments that Hume lists can be reduced to two kinds. The first sort can be characterized, overall, as an antipathy to exploitation, and the second sort can be characterized, overall, as a concern for one's own integrity. We shall examine the content and efficacy of each of these types.

Consider the first sort. What is the explanation of, or reason behind, someone's having an antipathy to exploitation?

One obvious possible explanation of this antipathy is that it is generated by beneficent feelings: I feel benevolence toward other people, and thus I hate the idea of cheating them. But this explanation is unsatisfactory. Consider that Hume himself insists that the rules of justice, which nonexploitative people would believe they ought to follow in their dealings with their fellow human beings, are necessary precisely in those situations where other-regarding sentiments are too weak (if they exist at all) to insure cooperative behavior. Hence Hume cannot rely on these sentiments to give – by themselves – a motive for eschewing exploitation and treachery, and thus obeying the rules of justice, because, by the very nature of the situation, such sentiments are too weak to succeed (otherwise the rules of justice would not be necessary to effect cooperation) and can therefore be no match for self-interest when breaking the rules is clearly to one's advantage.

Nonetheless, Hume might argue that these sentiments, when added to the self-interested desires supportive of just action (that are insufficient by themselves to motivate justice) could tip the balance in favor of performing justly. That is, because Hume believes people have more other-regarding desires than Hobbes thinks they have, Hume might argue that there would be more times when these desires, after being factored into a calculation about whether or not to be just, would make the calculation come out in favor of justice.

How many more times? It is hard to say. In order to test Hume's theory, we would have to do empirical studies to see whether he, rather than Hobbes, was right, not only about the strength of other-regarding passions such as benevolence, but also about how often such passions could tip the balance in favor of justice. But given, as I have pointed out, Hume's admission that these passions are rather weak, and given the rather substantial benefits of injustice in many situations, he has offered us no reason to believe that such passions would provide a significant cure for knavery. Knavish exploitation would still be a fact of life in a Humean world among people with beneficent passions, because the costs of justice would often be too high to be outweighed, even when other-regarding passions supplemented the self-interested desires supportive of justice.

If benevolence is not sufficient to stop knavery, what else might do so? Perhaps Hume might propose that an antipathy to exploitation could be generated by effective socialization. He could either try to argue that this antipathy could be generated *de novo* by society in its members, or he could argue that certain passions (such as benevolence) could be augmented and developed by society into this kind of antipathy. In any case, it would be a matter of society trying to inculcate within us a desire to behave in a certain socially useful manner. Such a suggestion is not explicitly made, but readers might think that it is at least hinted at in one passage of the *Treatise,* where Hume says that after the institution of justice is created, the manner in which the institution benefits people in the community can excite within us other-regarding passions that are not only supportive of the institution but also a source of additional motivation to be just:

Thus self-interest is the original motive to the establishment *of justice; but a* sympathy *with public interest is the source of the* moral approbation, *which attends that virtue.* (III, ii, iii, pp. 499–500; Hume's emphasis)

Yet later Hume amended this last passage in order to explicitly deny that moral approbation was, by itself, a motive for justice in such a case. The amended passage (made by Hume to the first edition), which is reprinted in the textual notes of the Selby-Bigge edition, reads as follows:

Thus *Self-interest* is the original Motive to the *Establishment* of Justice: but a Sympathy with *public* Interest is the Source of the *moral* Approbation, which attends that Virtue. This latter Principle of Sympathy is too weak to controul our Passions: but has sufficient Force to influence our Taste, and give us the Sentiments of approbation and blame. (p. 670)

This Humean amendment tells us that the sympathy-induced sentiments supportive of justice are motivationally ineffective, only determining whether or not we approve of actions but not affecting what we do – a position that would make the moral judgments emanating from these sentiments epiphenomenal – completely removed from what actually gets us to act justly.[8]

However, there are other passages in the *Treatise* in which Hume seems to reject this epiphenomenal role for sentiments supporting justice and tries to get some motivational purchase from them. In these passages Hume suggests that society can instill certain exploitation-blocking passions in a way that enables them, at least sometimes, to motivate moral behavior when self-interest gives out. Consider, for example, the following passage:

As publick praise and blame encrease our esteem for justice; so private education and instruction contribute to the same effect. For as parents easily observe, that a man is the more useful, both to himself and others, the greater degree of probity and honour he is endow'd with; and that those principles have greater force, when custom and education assist interest and reflexion: For these reasons they are induc'd to inculcate on their children, from their earliest infancy, the principles of probity, and teach them to regard the observance of those rules by which society is maintain'd, as worthy and honourable, and their violation as base and infamous. By this means the sentiments of honour may take root in their tender minds, and acquire such firmness and solidity, that they may fall little short of those principles, which are the most essential to our natures, and the most deeply radicated in our internal constitution. (III, ii, iii, pp. 500–1; see also III, ii, i, p. 479)

Because there is nothing in the *Treatise* or the *Enquiry* that sets out the details of how such socialization would work, Hume's belief in the power of socialization to cultivate these "sentiments of honour" is more a matter of faith than anything else – and a deeply un-Hobbesian faith.

But is it also deeply un-Humean? Does Hume's view have room for a kind of socialization that will instill such powerful passions in people?

Hume cannot argue, consistent with the rest of his psychological views, that socialization can create these passions *de novo*: he himself notes in the *Treatise* that "if morality had naturally no influence on human passions and actions, 'twere in vain to take such pains to inculcate it" (III, i, i, p. 457). Consistent with the rest of his views, can he say that socialization strengthens an existing passion supporting institutions of justice that not only makes us desire to act so as to benefit others when self-interest gives out but also produces this desire such that it is strong enough to compete and win against those self-interested desires dictating noncooperation? The problem is that we do not really know what such a desire could be. As we have already seen, it cannot be benevolence; indeed, Hume specifically says that a general desire to benefit the public good "is a motive too remote and too sublime to affect the generality of mankind, and operate with any force in actions so contrary to private interest as are frequently those of justice and common honesty" (III, ii, i, p. 481). This remark essentially discounts the possibility that socialization could strengthen a beneficent impulse enough to enable it to block the temptation to exploit when it is rational to do so. However, Hume might be able to propose, consistent with his other views, that society can take advantage of the associative principles of the human mind to link, in the minds of its members, "honorable" nonexploitative conduct with social approval, in a way that plants within them a motivationally efficacious sentiment to engage in such conduct. Because the conduct is useful to others, it would have some attraction to them; socialization builds upon that attraction and links the behavior to additional, more self-interested concerns, so as to dispose people to engage in it (starting when they are very young). Let us examine how far this theory explains and justifies nonknavish conduct.

In order to work as a descriptive account of why, in fact, people eschew knavery, the account would have to show that socialization not only cultivates sentiments of honor, but also renders them powerful enough to combat the voice of self-interest in a single-play prisoner's dilemma game. Because it is a single-play game, its players need fear no reputation effects. (As an example of such a game, imagine a situation where it will be impossible for anyone to know whether or not either player reneged or cooperated.) So any fear of what "others will think" will play no role in their decision about what to do here. Hume has to propose that society is somehow able to get a "hold" on them, in a way that makes them want to behave honorably even when self-interest dictates that each of them refrain from doing so. Because Hume is a powerful respecter of self-interest, it is difficult to see how he could believe that society could mold us in ways that enable us not to take the self-interested course. Perhaps he could argue that we can sometimes take that course, but surely he would be forced to admit that for each person honor has its price, and that if the self-interested temptations were powerful enough the society-induced sentiments of honor could not compete with them. This suggests that the socialization theory could provide, at most, only a partial cure for knavery.

But the more important problem with the socialization theory is that it fails as a justification of nonknavish behavior, in a way that has implications for its success as a descriptive theory. According to this account, society would be trying to use tactics of habituation and conditioning to implant in people a social norm, with some kind of sentimental force giving it motivational power, not to behave knavishly. But once implanted, such a norm is grounded neither in any person's self-interest nor in her benevolent feelings toward others: indeed, it is actually opposed by each person's self-interest, and the norm's effect on people is far greater than the effect that mere benevolence is able to have. So consider how each person would view the "sentiments of honour" in a single-play situation: he would know that his self-interest opposed them, and he would know that he had no substantial other-regarding feelings toward his partner in the prisoner's dilemma game. Yet he would feel himself disposed to cooperate because of the effects of socialization. So why not regret the socialization? Why not see it as social manipulation, which disposes one to perform in a collectively rational but individually irrational manner? I am reminded of a friend of mine, reared in a certain religious tradition, who changed her view of her disposition not to have sex before marriage: "I was reared to think it was a sin," she said, "but I couldn't figure out why it was wrong, and I began to resent the fact that people made me think I shouldn't do this." After a while, she abandoned the teachings of her childhood, because they made no sense to her and interfered with what she wanted. The Humean person socialized to eschew knavery would be in the same position were he to reflect upon his disposition to cooperate. In the end, he would see that it came from a process of habituation that had implanted within him something to combat rational self-interest, and that went beyond any benevolent instinct, insofar as the disposition tells him to cooperate with people about whom he may care little or nothing. So why should he not regret the socialization that has implanted this disposition in him? Why shouldn't he see it as social trickery and do what he can to remove its effects, so that he can better serve his authentic desires, which, among other things, direct him to behave knavishly in a single-play prisoner's dilemma game?

In the end, the problem with the socialization argument is that, were it not for the socialized disposition to cooperate, the exploitative action, rather than the cooperative action, would be rationally justified. Indeed, the whole reason why society presumably undertakes such socialization is precisely that it believes knavery rather than that cooperation is rational in this situation. But once people appreciate this fact, they will have reason not only to regret, but also to try to remove, the effects of that socialization.[9]

This failure of justification has implications for Hume's descriptive account of why, in fact, many of us eschew knavery. As long as exploitation remains the rational action in a single-play prisoner's dilemma game, absent the existence of the socialized desire, then the socialized desire not to exploit will not be stable under reflection. That is, once people figure out, upon reflection, that the socialized desire directing them to behave nonexploitatively is contrary to the dictates of rationality, they will want, and be rational to attempt, to rid themselves of this manipulative programming. But this means that a socialized desire that directs them to behave irrationally is unlikely to remain effective for very long in a society once people realize that its directive is irrational. Of course, Hume might recommend that a society do its best to prevent such reflection, but such a policy is sufficiently morally repulsive, and sufficiently likely to have a variety of other bad consequences, that he could not reasonably suggest it in order to shore up his socialization view.

Finally, note that such reflection would destroy any effect such a socialized desire might have to produce the "inward peace" that Hume says one who has eschewed knavery will experience because of his awareness of his own integrity. Upon reflection, one is more likely to experience the sense that, having eschewed knavery, one has been a fool, compliant with the wishes of one's society in a manner that harms one's ability to pursue one's own desires. (Compare the view of my friend, who now regrets losing the opportunities that her prudish upbringing caused her to pass up.)

There is a deep issue lurking in all this: Hume has the sense that we ought to eschew knavery – that it is somehow authoritative over other competing desires. The problem with the socialization argument, however, is that it explains our disposition to cooperate as arising from an "implanted" sentiment, which has neither the authenticity nor the authority to survive any reflective challenge to it.

Can we do better than this argument on Hume's behalf? Let us try a third explanatory theory of these sentiments, which is related to, but more straightforward than, the socialization account. One of the lessons we should have learned from the failure of the socialization account is that in order to construct a better account we need to link the disposition to cooperate with other desires, even if socialization may play some role. We would seem to be able to make this link, however, by connecting the desire to cooperate with our concern for our reputation. (Hume himself might be thought to suggest this idea when he refers to nonknavish people as those who are "conscious of their integrity.") The idea behind such a theory is this: suppose we posit a (self-regarding) desire to be well thought of by our fellow human beings (a desire that is, arguably, akin to Hobbes's desire for glory). This desire could, one might argue, be the foundation for an antipathy toward exploitation, on the grounds that if other people dislike such behavior, they will dislike us if we perform it; hence, we develop an antipathy to exploitation because we associate this behavior with a state of affairs we dislike, namely social ostracism, rejection, and criticism. Good socialization might also be thought to encourage such an association in order to increase the strength and motivational efficacy of the antipathy to exploitation, but such socialization is not necessary for the creation of this antipathy, which comes instead from the natural associative mechanisms of the human mind. This theory also seems to be able to explain how the eschewal of knavery could bring the "inner peace" and consciousness of integrity of which Hume speaks, because, insofar as it is the sort of behavior that will bring us the good opinion of others, it allows us to have a good opinion of ourselves.

It is important to appreciate exactly how this argument works with respect to a single-play prisoner's dilemma game. In that game, noncooperation will (by definition) have no effect on any person's reputation, because the game is (by definition) not linked with any other game in the future, so that there will be no reputation effects from any action one takes in such a game. Hence, we cannot say that our concern for our reputation directly motivates us to cooperate in such a game; if it did, we would be in an iterated, not a single-play, game. Instead, the argument has to be that, in our minds, cooperative action is invariably associated with a good reputation, so that we develop an antipathy to exploitation. As I have said, given that this association might be thought to be "natural" and inevitable, it is not an association that can be construed as "implanted" by society, although clearly, as I have noted earlier, good socialization could presumably strengthen this associative process and the sentiments against knavery that it produces.

This theory seems to "ground" the sentiments against exploitation in authentic interests of the agent in ways that might make it stable under reflection. (It is not some alien disposition that society tries to "implant.") Moreover, it does so in a way that seems consistent with the rest of Hume's theory; in particular, it uses an associative mechanism that, like sympathy, is self-referring but that seems, like sympathy, to be able to produce sentiments in us that have genuine other-regarding content. (Hence this theory need not be construed as an instance of an Epicurean or "Hobbist" account, of the sort that Hume attacks.) Does this theory succeed where the previous socialization account did not?

One problem with this account is that by claiming we would develop a desire to cooperate because of the association of this conduct with the good opinion of others, the account presupposes that other people have sentiments that produce pleasure at the contemplation of moral traits. But not only might these sentiments not be particularly strong in others; more worryingly, such sentiments might be opposed in them by nonmoral sentiments that produce pleasure at the contemplation of nonvirtuous and exploitative action. (I once overheard an undergraduate telling a friend about a person she knew, "She was so cool – totally out for herself. I really want to be like her.") So the account yields a desire to cooperate that is only as strong as the rest of the population's approval of that conduct.

Suppose, however, for the sake of argument, that people did generally approve of cooperation. Why shouldn't they approve of cooperative behavior only in iterated prisoner's dilemma games but *not* in a single-play game? Although, other things equal, they are likely to welcome cooperative rather than exploitative action in a single-play game, insofar as the former is better for the community than the latter, nonetheless, if it is true that exploitation is individually rational in this situation, then it would seem that the rest of the community would regard those who cooperated anyway as useful but irrational. That is, it would seem the rest of the community would reason: "Given our interests, we would prefer it if Patsy didn't behave exploitatively toward Edina, but it's clearly rational for Patsy to behave exploitatively, so if she did not behave exploitatively we would regard her as irrational, foolish – a sucker."

Being regarded as a fool is hardly to have a "good" reputation: indeed, if you were to have such a reputation, it would be very dangerous for you, because it would encourage other people to treat you exploitatively. For example, they would reason with respect to you, "If she really does cooperate in single-play prisoner's dilemma situations with her partner, maybe her disposition to cooperate is something that I can take advantage of, in which case I can exploit her and come out the winner."[10] Of course, in a single-play prisoner's dilemma game, there are no reputation effects (by definition), so, in fact, no one (except the other player in the game) would know that you were a cooperator in such a game. There would therefore be no real reputation effects from cooperation in that game. But a reflective person would realize that were people to know what you had done, they would regard you as having behaved irrationally and this, in turn, would likely lower their opinion of you rather than raise it. So even if, prereflectively, you were disposed to cooperate in this sort of game, given the association between cooperation and people's good opinion of your cooperation in many common situations (such as iterated prisoner's dilemma games), nonetheless, after reflection you would realize that such an association was unjustified in this type of game. To cooperate in a situation where it is individually irrational to do so would be to earn the contempt, not the respect, of other people who are committed to commending only rational behavior.

The real problem with the reputation argument is that it assumes what it is supposed to explain: to be precise, it assumes that people's good opinion of you will be associated with cooperation in a single-play prisoner's dilemma game. But it would seem instead that when such behavior is individually rational, their opinion of you should be negative. Knaves do not do anything "wrong" – in the sense of irrational – if they behave knavishly; indeed, they would be doing something wrong – in the sense of irrational – if they did not behave knavishly. To the extent that I appreciate this fact after reflection, then any sentiments I may have to cooperate that owe their existence to my desire to earn the good opinion of others will be modified so that I do not cooperate in this particular situation, where my cooperation would (if they only knew) earn their contempt.

But surely, a Humean might argue, other people would welcome rather than condemn my cooperation in a single-play prisoner's dilemma game, because such behavior is good for their society. Were they to know what I did, shouldn't I view them as rewarding me with their good opinion of me for my collectively rational behavior?

There is something to this, because they would indeed be happy at the results of my behavior. Nonetheless, their evaluation of *me* would be quite different.

This Humean analysis does not, and cannot, challenge the idea that knavish behavior in a single-play prisoner's dilemma game is individually rational. Hence it cannot dispute the fact that one who eschews knavery in this situation is behaving irrationally. On reflection, I will realize that this must be their evaluation of me, in which case I know very well what my reputation would be if my cooperative behavior were revealed to others. Any antipathy to knavery generated through an associative mechanism via a concern for reputation is therefore not reflectively stable.

The failure of this reputation account points squarely to the resources that a theory must have to succeed as a description and justification of the basis for any eschewal of knavery. It must make that eschewal *rational upon reflection.* But Hume has no theoretical resources available to him to say that the nonknave is rational. Of course, a theory that appeals to a Kantian-style sense of justice inherent in each person, which is part of our reason and also motivationally powerful enough to get people to act in a morally virtuous manner despite passions opposing such behavior, can offer a reason-based description of, and justification for, the eschewal of knavery. But Hume spends considerable time in the *Treatise* disparaging the idea that any such sense of justice exists.

III. The Nonknavish Kantian

Why, then, do those of us who eschew knavery do so? How is it that (at least much of the time) most of us manage to resist any temptation to exploit our fellow human beings?

In a way, although he cannot ground it successfully within his larger theory, Hume's surface explanation is on the right track: it makes sense to me to think that we do it because we have an "antipathy to treachery" and because we are conscious of a kind of integrity within us that precludes this kind of behavior. Recently, for example, I found two hundred dollars on the street and managed (I confess, with some difficulty) to turn it in to the police, enabling them to return it to its owner. "What a non-Hobbesian thing to do," I marveled to myself; "How did I manage to pull it off?" Well, it was not because there was any self-interested reason to do so; self-interest was screaming at me to put the money in my purse. And it certainly was not because of any other-regarding sentiments toward my fellow human beings, as a Humean might propose, because I had no idea whose money this was and, for all I knew, it belonged to somebody odious and disreputable. In any case, I had no sentiments, favorable or unfavorable, toward the money's owner. The only explanation I could come up with was that "morality required it." ("Well, it was the right thing to do," I kept saying to myself, in part to comfort my self-interested side, that persisted in protesting against the virtuous action. So much for the "inward peace" at the consciousness of virtue of which Hume speaks.) Such an answer posits a kind of reason-based commitment to the eschewal of exploitation, even in situations where one can cheat another with impunity, a commitment that can move us to action and that we recognize as authoritative over action. Because I think this sort of account explains (and justifies) the phenomenon, I must say that it is hard for me, admittedly a Kantian sympathizer, not to conclude that Hume's theory fails as an explanation and normative defence of morality because it cannot accommodate the components of that account. Hume's theory is missing both a reason-based foundation for impartial judgment and a notion of moral duty defined independently of desire and convention that can (and should) combat the opposing forces of self-seeking desires in ways that enable us to resist any motive to exploit our fellows.

What about the role of sentiment? Does the Kantian-style theory preclude sentiment from playing any role in encouraging us to eschew knavery? It need not be understood to do so. Part of the reason I believe Hume's analysis goes wrong is that it persists in making a sharp separation between rationality, understood instrumentally and in service to our passions, and the passions themselves. Using a noninstrumental notion of reason, we might develop a reason-based understanding of our commitment to cooperate with our fellows that could be linked with certain sentiments that might give such a commitment considerable power. Moreover, rethinking the individualism basic to Hume's (and Hobbes's) theory can also reintroduce sentiment into the moral point of view: if I do not think of myself as radically separate from my fellow human beings, then in situations where I might have an opportunity to exploit them I may well see myself – and indeed, believe I am rationally required to see myself – as "related to" them in a fashion that makes such behavior painful to me, thereby engaging sentiments, with respect both to myself and to this larger group of which I believe myself to be a part, that empower me to refuse the chance to exploit the other person.

To be believable, any such theory would still have to reckon with the reality of the temptation to knavery. (Giving up two hundred dollars is not effortless, I found to my chagrin.) Fantastic claims about our communal nature or about the amazing authority and motivational efficacy of moral reason fly in the face of human reality. Hume and Hobbes are certainly right about that. But both of them, as we have seen, systematically keep missing an aspect of the "good" side of ourselves that enables us to live well with one another, with integrity and a good conscience.

Notes

1. David Hume, *An Enquiry Concerning the Principles of Morals,* ed. L. A. Selby-Bigge, rev. P. H. Nidditch ([1751] Oxford: Clarendon Press, 1975). Often referred to as the *"Second Enquiry."* Cited hereafter as *Enq* in parentheses in the text, with section, part, and page number.

2. See Jean Hampton, *Hobbes and the Social Contract Tradition* (Cambridge: Cambridge University Press, 1986), pp. 6–11. The definition here is based upon, but in certain respects goes beyond, the definition of radical individualism there.

3. See *De cive* in *The English Works of Thomas Hobbes,* ed. William Molesworth ([1642] London: John Bohn, 1840), ch. 8, sec. 1, 2:109.

4. See Thomas Hobbes, *Leviathan,* ed. C. B. Macpherson ([1651] Harmondsworth, UK, Penguin, 1968), vi, 26, p. 27 (emphasis is added), and Thomas Hobbes, *De homine,* in *Man and Citizen,* ed. B. Gert (Atlantic Highlands: Humanities Press, 1968), xii, 10, p. 61.

5. David Hume, *A Treatise of Human Nature,* ed. L. A. Selby-Bigge, rev. P. H. Nidditch ([1739–40] Oxford: Clarendon Press, 1978), II, i, xi, pp. 317–18. Hereafter cited in parentheses in the text with book number, part number, chapter number, and page number.

6. It may be that the details of those accounts are not exactly the same. Consider one account: via the operation of sympathy we imagine ourselves in the position of others, form an idea of the passions they are experiencing by imagining what we would experience in that situation, and that idea is then converted into the impression of the passions of the other. Consider a second account (suggested to me by Andrews Reath): we form an idea of the passions of the other insofar as we see the other as resembling us (where the mechanism precipitating this reaction, given the resemblance, might be taken to be virtually inevitable), and these ideas are then converted into the passions of the other. Both accounts generate the passions of self-regard, but in completely different ways: the first makes my self-concern the *cause* of my acquiring the ideas (and eventually the impressions) of the other's experience; the second makes the acquiring of those ideas and impressions simply the result of a mechanism that is not motivated by self-concern but only the other's resemblance to me. Hobbes certainly suggests the former account; Hume may have meant the latter. (But note that the two accounts are not inconsistent and could be held together.) I shall not have time here to explore which of these accounts is really the Humean one, but for my purposes it does not really matter which of them is correct. But note that both accounts have the same structure: that is, both explain other-regarding passions as derived from an innate psychological mechanism that involves reference to the self.

7. Hume suggests that he does not hold a "Hobbist" position on other-regarding sentiments, but he misrepresents Hobbes's position. See *Enq,* pp. 296–7.

8. I am indebted to Ken O'Day for suggesting this line of interpretation.

9. Part of the point of Gregory Kavka's *Hobbesian Moral and Political Theory* (Princeton: Princeton University Press, 1986), and my *Hobbes and the Social Contract Tradition* (Cambridge: Cambridge University Press, 1986) was to determine whether the institution of the sovereign was similarly reflectively unstable or, even worse, irrational. Both of us concluded, for different reasons, that it was not.

10. This theoretical argument has a real-life analogue: the feminist legal theorist Carol Rose has argued that one reason why women have become disadvantaged in terms of property holdings in our society is that they have been perceived as more cooperative than men, so that they have become targets of exploitation more than men. See Carol Rose, "Women and Property: Gaining and Losing Ground," *Virginia Law Review* 78 (1992), 421–59.

Some Considerations
in Favor of Contractualism

GARY WATSON

The rights and responsibilities that we recognize in our critical moral practices serve human interests in deep and pervasive ways; that is part of their point. At the same time, they do this by constraining our pursuit of those interests; that is how they work. These utterly familiar features of our practices turn out to be troublesome for moral philosophy; they have seemed in serious tension with one another. One of the chief appeals of contractualist moral theory is its capacity to accommodate these features in a straightforward manner. In this essay, I want to articulate this theoretical virtue more fully.

I

The connection between morality and general human well-being gives some credibility to the long-standing notion that morality is in some sense an expression of love or benevolence.[1] This notion belongs, of course, to one strand of Christian teaching, but utilitarians have traded on this truth as well, especially when seeking to put their doctrine in a high-minded light. "In the golden rule of Jesus of Nazareth," John Stuart Mill assures us, "we read the complete spirit of the ethics of utility. 'To do as you would be done by,' and 'to love your neighbor as yourself,' constitute the ideal perfection of utilitarian morality."[2] More recently, J. J. C. Smart put utilitarianism forward as the unique theoretical expression of "generalized benevolence," the outlook of those who have the "welfare of humanity at heart."[3] The idea is given a more ghastly twist by Joseph Fletcher, who speaks of the "vast scale of 'agapeic calculus' [on which] President Truman made his decision about [dropping] the A-bombs on Hiroshima and Nagasaki."[4]

However, utilitarians are not the only secular moralists to embrace this no-

Over the years, I have presented various versions of this material to a number of audiences. I want to thank them collectively.

I was encouraged early on by discussions of this essay with my late colleague, Gregory Kavka, to whose friendship and philosophical work I owe a very great deal. This latest version is all the worse for not having had the benefit of his criticism. The penultimate draft did benefit from comments by Amy Lara and Christopher Morris, to whom I am grateful.

tion. Schopenhauer, for example, held that morality could be codified by a two-part principle: "Injure no one; help others as much as you can." Each part of this principle corresponds to one of the two cardinal moral virtues, justice and "loving-kindness," both of which are rooted, according to Schopenhauer, in "compassion."[5] Rodger Beehler and A. I. Melden are contemporary nonutilitarians who see benevolence as, in some sense, underlying moral practice. Beehler declares: "if human beings did not care about one another there could not be what we speak of as morality, for the reason that morality is a manifestation of that caring."[6] Melden connects benevolence with rights in particular: "Far from it being the case that a consideration of the rights of persons occupies a separate moral domain from that of benevolence, it depends on it; for in the absence of a concern for the well being of others there could be no sense of the important role that the rights of persons . . . play in our lives."[7] The truly just person cares about rights at least partly because of a concern for the human good that rights foster and protect. Without such concern, the concern for justice lacks sense.

Thus, any satisfactory moral theory must provide for the connection of rights with vital human goods.[8] Respect for certain rights (for example, the right to be secure against aggression, the right to pursue one's ends without interference, rights arising from special relationships or undertakings) is essential to human cooperation and (hence) to flourishing. This truth is acknowledged every day in moral casuistry, where disputes about the existence or interpretation of rights often turn on the interests at stake. To illustrate, judgments about the content of the right to privacy inescapably involve balancing interests protected by that right with other concerns. We do not recognize a right not to be viewed as one walks down the street, since that would be too invasive of other interests.[9] (Privacy is not just a legal matter. Other things being equal, it would be wrong of you knowingly to look at my diary without permission, even though I might have no legal recourse.)

Furthermore, the relative gravity of rights corresponds to the importance of the interests concerned. Killing or assaulting another is generally worse than failing to repay a small loan. Hence the corresponding rights are relatively more stringent, their violation a graver matter.

The connections between rights and goods, then, do not appear to be accidental; they are part of the *function* of rights and responsibilities. The moral justification of rights and responsibilities depends upon their manifold connections to central human ends. I will call this the *teleological connection*.

Philippa Foot has suggested that what makes utilitarianism so "compelling" is its consequentialism, the "thought that it can never be right to prefer a worse state of affairs to a better."[10] But I think that the teleological connection is the source of its specific appeal; in contrast both to nonconsequentialist views and to other forms of consequentialism, utilitarianism takes the link between morality and well-being as its starting point. The teleological connection is, as T. M. Scanlon puts it, "the incontrovertible insight of the classical utilitarians."[11]

But as we will see, this connection is a theorem of any plausible form of contractualism as well. I want, in what follows, to consider the teleological connection from a contractualist point of view. What initially seems a strength of utilitarianism is, I shall argue, better accommodated by a nonconsequentialist theory.

II

Although utilitarianism seems to handle the teleological connection in a straightforward way, it comes to grief, notoriously, over another and equally conspicuous feature of our moral practice: its *deontological character.* Rights not only foster goods but constrain our pursuit of them. This feature of rights has been explored by many writers.[12] Much of modern moral philosophy has been an attempt to articulate a theory that can accommodate both of these features of rights. This is not a simple task. It is arguably not even coherent, for they appear to be in tension with one another.

Despite the teleological connection, rights are not reducible to reasons of beneficence, that is, to considerations of the benefits to be achieved and the harms to be avoided in particular actions. This point does not depend upon the rare case in which respecting a right does no good at all. Even if reasons of beneficence typically stand against the infringement of rights, they do not explain the moral force of rights in specific circumstances.

Although we might agree with Beehler that morality is in *some* sense a "manifestation" of a concern for human well-being, we should not accept his explanation of why "lies ought not to be told or promises broken," namely that "pain will be given."[13] For avoiding the pain to one person caused by a second person's lie, theft, or broken promise is equally a reason for a third person to prevent these things or to do what was promised herself, if possible. If I do not keep my promise to help you move on Saturday, you might be in a serious jam. But avoiding that consequence is equally a reason for a third person to help you move when she notices your plight. So to invoke the pain I would cause you will not explain *my* special obligation. To promise is to grant rights, and to do this is to grant moral authority over a limited range of one's life. In promising to help you, I thereby forswear (within limits) the appeal to considerations that would otherwise have been available to me – for instance, that I might help another just as much.[14]

Similarly, any bystander has a moral reason to warn you of the banana peel in your path, namely, to prevent your injury. But if I negligently drop a banana peel and create the risk, my reason has a different source (and perhaps weight); it derives from my causal responsibility, and hence is not a consideration that is neutral for all agents.

Rights, then, are not reducible to reasons of beneficence. They place constraints on one's response to such reasons. It is these features of rights and responsibilities that I am calling *deontological constraints.* Such constraints are ubiquitous in everyday life. They appear throughout legal and other institutional contexts of authoritative regulation. Laws against assault say "Do not attack others," not "Minimize physical attacks on others." Your obligation is to pay your tax bill, not to use that money in whatever way is best designed to minimize tax evasion (say, by evading your tax payments and using the money you owe to hire a detective to expose more serious evasions). When such laws have legitimate authority over us, they are sources of deontological reasons. So are legislators, judges, military commanders, department chairs, parents, teachers, mayors, employers, police officers, when they have rightful jurisdiction over us. It is essential to the role of these rules and the function of these offices that they yield such constraints.

Less institutionalized contexts are saturated with nonconsequentialist reasoning as well. As bearers of moral rights, we each hold a moral office, as it were, and as such each is a source of deontological reasons. To have a moral right is to have a certain kind of authority, a sphere of discretion in which what others may properly do depends upon one's consent.[15] (This is not to say that one may not wrongly consent.) The notion of authority bears its deontological character on its face.

III

These familiar points about moral practice give rise, then, to a theoretical problem. On the one hand, the connections between rights and goods are deep and pervasive. They exert a strong teleological pull on moral theory. On the other hand, rights restrict our pursuit of human good in distinctive ways. The problem is to make these connections perspicuous without reducing rights to reasons of beneficence in particular cases. The problem is to accommodate the teleological connection in a theory that at the same time accounts for the deontological character of moral rights. I shall call this the *problem of accommodation.*[16]

This problem is exacerbated by the fact that we do not in general take most deontological constraints to be *absolute;* they may sometimes be overridden not only to prevent the infringement of more serious rights, but to prevent sufficiently bad consequences of other kinds. Most deontological theorists would agree, for example, that one may lie to protect innocent lives. Although this position seems morally correct, it enhances the initial obscurity of the phenomenon. For how can reasons of beneficence interact in this manner with deontological considerations? How can such disparate considerations be "balanced" in an intelligible way? Doesn't this balancing require ordering principles that are ultimately teleological? Once again, the pressure is to collapse deontological constraints into reasons of beneficence or to deny that deontological constraints can be overridden. Though it seems to be true of our practice, the mixed position seems difficult, in theory, to occupy.[17]

A perpetual philosophical temptation is to try to dissolve the problem by abandoning one of its elements. At one extreme, we find proposals to view rights as merely useful rules of thumb or else to reject deontological constraints as somehow paradoxical. At the other extreme, we find philosophers[18] who would repudiate the teleological connection altogether.

Both responses seem unsatisfactory. The teleological connection is too deep and important to ignore, but the deontological aspect of our thought cannot be dismissed just because it is theoretically inconvenient. One of the greatest achievements of contractualism is its capacity to bring these two features of rights together in a coherent and straightforward way.

IV

First, let me say more about the possibilities for utilitarianism. My aim in these remarks is not to advance original objections but to set up the discussion of contractualism as an attractive alternative treatment of the problem of accommodation.

Clearly, this problem has been the primary theoretical impetus of rule utilitarianism and other two-level consequentialist views. The idea is to accommodate the teleological and deontological character of rights by distinguishing different levels of justification and evaluation.[19] Systems of rules and rights are justified by their "general acceptance utility" relative to other systems. The connection between rights and human well-being appears at this level. However, particular actions or policies are justified by reference to the applicable rules. The set of rules with the greatest acceptance utility is likely to call for conduct in isolated cases that differs from the dictates of act utilitarianism. Therefore, complying with the best set of rules will constrain one's pursuit of benefits in particular cases. Hence deontological constraints are explained as well.

Rule utilitarianism has not, however, succeeded in explaining how these two levels of justification cohere with one another.[20] If what justifies the rule or the right are just the effects on well-being of general compliance, then the effects on well-being should be decisive in deciding whether or not to comply in particular cases. To follow the rules in these counterutilitarian cases looks like "rule worship,"[21] in which one's concern for consequences has become fixated on general compliance.

Therefore, rule utilitarians face a dilemma: either the requirements of the rule completely coincide with what has the most utility, in which case rule utilitarianism is equivalent to act utilitarianism and deontological constraints are denied, or else those requirements diverge from straightforward utilitarian reasoning in some instances, in which case obedience has no consequentialist justification. Either rule utilitarianism collapses into act utilitarianism, or it ceases to be utilitarian.[22]

Other responses to the problem of accommodation have been inspired by Henry Sidgwick's observation that it is probably best, from a utilitarian point of view, that most people are not utilitarians. The rule-utilitarian insight was that the observance of deontological constraints is very useful because of the abuses to which utilitarian thought is liable in practice. The best results are most likely to ensue if we are not wholehearted utilitarians. The best means of accomplishing this is to take rule worship (within limits) as a virtue, something to foster and encourage. In this way, utilitarianism endorses its own rejection. This argument is said to be coherent because the endorsement and rejection take place at different levels of moral thought. One question concerns the ideal form of reasoning for beings who are fully informed, impartial, and rational. A different question is how we are to raise children, who never will be perfect in these respects. We need to inculcate moral sensibilities and dispositions for beings who are imperfect in these ways. Since we never fully outgrow these liabilities, we are never in a position to kick over the deontological traces altogether.[23]

Perhaps this is the most coherent utilitarian response to deontological constraints. And it *is* a kind of accommodation. But it remains troubling. The chief trouble, in my view, concerns the gap between theory and practice; practice must be to a significant degree benighted. There is much to be said on this question.[24] I will emphasize just one point. The reason why the gap is disturbing is not that it requires too much psychological complexity on the part of moral agents, but that it precludes the realization of a certain kind of value in the moral life. Just people (those who among other things are deontologically sensitive) must be to a certain extent deluded about the grounds of their own virtue.[25] The charge of rule worship is not so much evaded as turned into a form of praise. But the praise is faint; attachments that are necessarily deluded cannot be fully admirable in a mature human being, and therefore the trait that involves that attachment cannot be affirmed unambivalently as a virtue.

This criticism concerns the moral adequacy of two-level utilitarianism, not its conceptual or psychological coherence. The complaint is that it excludes some of our deepest moral aspirations. We might live with this implication, if this were the best philosophy we could get. But contractualism can do better.

V

Contractualism comes in both a Hobbesian and a Kantian form.[26] Hobbesian versions attempt to explain moral constraints in terms of individual advantage. It is to the advantage of each of us to submit to agreements that constrain our individual pursuit of advantage. Morality is thereby derived from nonmoral interests.[27] In contrast, on Kantian versions, morality involves a form of practical reason that is independent of the rationality of maximal advantage. Practical reason expresses itself as a fundamental commitment to act in accordance with principles to which all rational beings could agree.

These preliminary characterizations allow for significant refinements within each type. For now, I wish to bring out some common issues and advantages.

One issue is whether a determinate content can be given to morality just by appealing to the relevant notion of agreement. There must be a solution, or at least a definite range of solutions, to the hypothetical choice problem as the theory defines it. Call this the problem of content. Moreover, the theory must justify its definition of the choice situation without invoking moral considerations of the kind the theory is designed to explain; that definition cannot be justified merely by the fact that it leads to such and such (intuitively plausible) moral principles. This point is related to the second issue, which is how the fact that certain principles would be agreed to can be a reason for endorsing those principles in the actual world. Call this the problem of compliance.

These issues will be more difficult for some versions of contractualism than for others; I shall take up some aspects of them shortly. However, we can already see the connection between these issues and the problem of accommodation. For, any contractualist theory that has a reasonable response to these issues will thereby accommodate both the teleological connection and deontological constraints. To begin with the former, in a contractualist account, each individual is to agree upon principles at least partly from the standpoint of her own interests. (On some types, that will be the parties' only concern; on others, this concern will be qualified in certain respects.) The resultant set of principles is bound to reflect some concern for each person's well-being; the agreement point will necessarily represent something like the common good. Therefore, on any plausible contractualist view, the rights, duties, and responsibilities that are the product of the agreement will serve to protect certain central interests.

At the same time, on any plausible view, the agreement will include rights-conferring principles restricting how we may treat others without their consent. That is, they entail deontological constraints. Therefore, contractualism of either form will support two claims: that rights are pervasively and nonaccidentally linked to human good, and that the moral reasons to which rights give rise do not all reduce to reasons of beneficence.

The problem of commensurability that we identified in our examination of mixed positions (section III) also seems manageable on a contractualist view. There are obvious reasons why it would not be in the common interest to adopt principles that accorded absolute rights; rather, the adopted principles would likely contain provisos for their permissible infringement. This conclusion would have to be shown in detail. But it can be seen why reasons of beneficence and deontological constraints are not incommensurably disparate, as they might initially appear.

What gives force to the problem of accommodation and the subsidiary problem of commensurability is the idea that teleological reasons must be explained by some version of *outcome* ethics, according to which moral reasons come from the value of particular outcomes, in this case the enhancement of human good. In contrast, on a contractualist approach, considerations of beneficence, deontological constraints, and the conditions of their infringement all have a common source in the principles defining the basic agreement. (I take up a related point in section IX.)

For the same reasons, contractualism has no difficulty with the "self–other asymmetry" discussed by Michael Slote, who takes this asymmetry to cast suspicion on ordinary morality.[28] Given the circumstances that define the hypothetical choice situation, namely the need for a framework for interpersonal cooperation, it is not surprising that moral requirements would include mutual aid but not self-regard.[29] This asymmetry will seem puzzling only on a theory that derives all moral reasons from the value of outcomes.

VI

If any form of contractualism is adequate, then the problem of accommodation is resolved. That is, of course, a very large "if." Any acceptable form of contractualism must deal with the issue of compliance as well. Why should we be concerned to comply with principles that have the feature of being choiceworthy under certain hypothetical circumstances? How does the reason for choosing principles in the hypothetical situation transfer to one's choices here and now? This issue is worrisome in different respects to the two general forms of contractualism we have distinguished.

The main worry for Hobbesian views is the "free-rider" problem. The reason for agreement – namely, long-term advantage – is not necessarily a reason for compliance with the agreement. The agreement will include deontological constraints only if it restricts individuals' pursuit of their long-term advantage. It is clear that a concern for one's long-term advantage could rationally motivate one to agree to limit one's pursuit of one's long-term advantage if others did so as well. But that reason cannot intelligibly lead one to comply with deontological constraints when doing so can be expected to frustrate one's interests overall.

Note the instructive parallel here to the problem of rule utilitarianism. Hobbesianism and utilitarianism are rival interpretations of the same truth: that moral constraints serve the common good. In the common good, the ends of both benevolence and self-interest are realized. Nonetheless, in order to explain reasons for compliance with moral constraints, we must go beyond the austere resources of both theories; we must appeal, apparently, to fairness or some similar moral concern.

To continue the parallel, Hobbesians can also respond to the problem of compliance by recourse to a two-tier view, a kind of character "egoism"; it can be rational, in terms of one's own advantage, to develop character traits that lead one to comply with deontological constraints. The parallel objection would be that such self-sacrificing compliance would still be irrational, on Hobbesian criteria. So a two-tier theory would not succeed in explaining how moral conduct can be rational; it would show at most that it might be rational to become the kind of person who is disposed to behave irrationally in certain contexts.

This problem is what makes David Gauthier's appeal to constrained maximization tempting. Gauthier argues against the received Hobbesian interpretation of practical rationality. The rationality of an action is not a simple function of its expected utility. It is enough if the action manifests a "disposition" that it is rational (in terms of expected utility) to acquire and maintain. The rationality of acquiring and maintaining the disposition to limit the pursuit of one's advantage in accordance with deontological constraints transfers to the actions that exercise those dispositions. Thus, a choice can be rational not because it maximizes expected utility but because it is an exercise of a disposition that it is rational to have. Thus Gauthier proposes to "identif[y] practical rationality with utility-maximization at the level of dispositions to choose."[30]

This view agrees with Kantians that compliance with moral constraints cannot plausibly be motivated in particular cases by a concern to maximize one's advantage. But to explain such compliance we need not invoke a distinctly moral interest nor appeal to a form of practical reason other than rational advantage. All that is needed is rational consistency, where this is understood to include consistency with the dispositions that it is advantageous for one to possess.

VII

Gauthier's proposal has turned out to be very controversial. It seems clear, in any case, that a Hobbesian solution will invoke some kind of two-level view.[31] On the other hand, compliance is not an issue for Kantian versions of contractualism. Actions are right or wrong, on this approach, if they are allowed or disallowed by principles that it would be unreasonable to reject as a basis for cooperative arrangements.[32] The reason for compliance with such principles is not the advancement of one's ends (though that concern is important in determining what principles one could reasonably reject); it is, rather, the concern to pursue one's ends only in ways that can be justified by reasons that others can accept as free and rational persons. I shall call this concern *respect*.[33] It involves a readiness to acknowledge the points of view of others, which in turn involves a concern to take others' aims and interests into account. This attitude is an acknowledgment of others as in this way moral equals.

Thus, Kantian contractualism works with two motivational assumptions. It assumes that individuals are motivated both by self-regard and by respect for others. It assumes (1) that each individual is concerned to advance his or her own ends, but (2) that moral persons will do this only in ways that can be justified to others on the basis of reasons the others can accept from their own points of view (assuming that they too respect others).[34] Respect delimits the form of practical reason, but the content of judgments of right and wrong is determined by the agreement of individuals so conceived. Determinate moral principles and judgments are constructed by mutual deliberation, not given directly by the notion of respect. Hence, the fact that respect is a moral notion does not entail that the notion of a hypothetical agreement is a dispensable expository device.[35]

These assumptions distinguish this form of contractualism from both Hobbesianism and utilitarianism. Self-regard[36] is not the sole source of practical reasons. Nor is there any foundational commitment here to general benevolence. "Individual well-being will be morally significant," as Scanlon puts it, "not because it is intrinsically valuable or because promoting it is self-evidently a right-making characteristic, but simply because an individual could reasonably reject a form of argument that gave his well-being no weight."[37] Self-regard, rather than benevolence, makes the teleological connection a theorem of contractualism.

VIII

The appeal to respect enables Kantians to avoid the compliance problem. But to Hobbesians, the appeal is a cheat. To understand this complaint, we must distinguish two general forms that a Kantian doctrine can take. In what might be called the "classical" or stronger version, the readiness to submit to impartial constraints is somehow a constitutive commitment of practical reason; to lack this virtue is a failure of reason. In contrast, neo-Kantians (such as Scanlon) view respect as a rationally more contingent matter. On both views, one has a (nonhypothetical) reason to take the interests of others into account. The concern to conform one's conduct to the hypothetical-choice situation – to reason morally – is part of what it is to be "reasonable." But whereas classical Kantians think that the commitment to moral virtue can be derived from a more general account of reason, neo-Kantians do not take reasonableness to be something that can be demonstrated outside the moral point of view.

Hobbesians find these versions of Kantianism objectionable in different respects. Ironically, perhaps, the Hobbesian shares the classical Kantian ambition to find a universal and "sure grounding" for morality in reason. As Gauthier puts it, the Hobbesian wants to "demonstrate the rationality of impartial constraints on the pursuit of individual interest to persons who may take no interest in others' interests." But this demonstration must rely on "a weak and widely accepted conception of rationality,"[38] not on the notoriously controversial notion favored by Kantians. Hobbesians suspect that this notion depends for its appeal upon an antecedent commitment to impartial morality.

The Hobbesian complaint against the neo-Kantians is precisely that they abandon the classical project. They take as basic what ought to be securely grounded: moral rationality. They give us no reply to the Foole.

My own sympathies lie with the neo-Kantians here. I suspect that the Hobbesian project can support at best a seriously revisionist conception of moral practice. Nor am I optimistic about the Kantian version of the project. The Hobbesian worries, however, bring out an important truth: that Kantianism cannot be contractualist at its foundations.

A moral theory is contractualist at its foundations, I take it, if it claims to account for the significance of all moral phenomena in terms of the notion of agreement.[39] But the moral significance of respect cannot itself be understood in this manner. For respect – the readiness to act only on principles to which others could agree – is itself something we demand of one another. It might be called an *ur*-demand, a metarequirement to deliberate from a point of view from which all other moral requirements are constructed. The demand to submit to the standpoint of impartial deliberation (what Scanlon himself calls the "most general moral demand")[40] cannot itself derive its authority from that standpoint.[41]

So contractualism on its own does not get to the bottom of things. The *ur*-demand itself must be understood in a different way. On classical Kantian theories, as I have said, respect will be founded in the commitments of rational agency more generally. That theory will be contractualist if moral requirements (other than respect itself) are understood in terms of an interpersonal hypothetical choice situation.[42]

There are a number of possibilities for neo-Kantian theories. For example, respect might be based on a widely shared and deeply rooted cultural ideal[43] or tradition. A neo-Kantian account could even be grounded in a theory of virtue, in which respect was explained as just one among a number of central virtues.[44] In any case, a satisfactory neo-Kantian view must explain why respect has a deep motivational place in our lives and further how (and in what sense) it is something that we can demand of one another.[45]

IX

I have tried to show how a contractualist view (or any view that includes contractualism) can readily accommodate both the deontological and the teleological features of rights. Some philosophers have argued that any moral outlook that includes deontological constraints will have an "air of paradox." In this concluding section, I want to respond to this argument.

This challenge to deontological constraints has been pressed especially forcefully by Samuel Scheffler. Moral requirements can claim our allegiance, Scheffler argues, only if their violation is highly "objectionable" and "undesirable" from a moral point of view. Then how, Scheffler asks, "can it be rational to forbid the performance of a morally objectionable action that would have the effect of minimizing the total number of comparably objectionable actions that were performed and would have no other morally relevant consequences? How can the minimization of morally objectionable conduct be morally unacceptable?"[46] One may not kill an innocent person just because that would prevent two other deaths, or even two other murders. The usual "rationales" for these restrictions do not dispel the puzzle, Scheffler claims. To say that deception or homicide violates the victim's autonomy, for example, does not explain why we recognize deontological limits rather than the aim of minimizing violations of autonomy.

Of course, it is no objection to say that deontological constraints restrict one's pursuit of various outcomes. That is what they are supposed to do. To take this as an objection is already to assume a consequentialist position. Scheffler's argument is rather that deontological theories cannot do without goals, and that this threatens their coherence.[47] In order to have sufficient authority to override our own interests, Scheffler thinks, moral violations must be seen as "objectionable or undesirable" in the sense that "it is morally preferable that no such actions should occur than that any should."[48] So, deontological theories are committed to at least one agent-neutral, impersonal goal: the nonviolation of the restrictions they imply. To have a goal is to have a reason, *ceteris paribus*, to choose those options that promise to realize that goal. These reasons reflect an elementary commitment of practical rationality, not an antecedent commitment to a particular moral theory.

Although this argument helps to bring out what is at stake, it does not establish a presumptive case against deontological theories. What it shows, at most, is this: if deontological theories are coherent, then they must explain how maximizing rationality interacts with other alleged features of practical reason. But this is of course the starting point of anticonsequentialist theories since Kant, who took the main task of moral philosophy to be to show how the hypothetical and categorical imperatives can be unified in practical reason. That Scheffler takes his conclusion to present an apparent "paradox" rather than to describe a philosophical project simply expresses his pessimism about the enterprise. By itself, it is no argument against it.

To be sure, Scheffler's challenge raises interesting questions for contractualism. A theory that admits deontological goals (that is, to minimize violations of constraints) must explain why they should in general be subordinate to the constraints. One could view the constraints as themselves agent-relative *goals*,[49] but as Scheffler says, it is hard to see why agent-relative deontological goals should generate stronger reasons than the impersonal ones.

But I am not convinced that contractualism is committed to deontological goals, or that such a commitment would be a problem. This issue recalls the problems of mixed theories we considered in section III. Everything depends on how these goals are construed. If the point is that the theory must have a foundational commitment to the idea that moral violations constitute intrinsically bad states of affairs and are therefore "objectionable" or "undesirable," the reply is that contractualism need have no such commitment.[50] If instead the question is whether there is a *derivable* commitment to minimize violations, the answer depends on the upshot of moral deliberation. Arguably, if no one could reasonably reject principle P, then no one could reasonably reject a *ceteris paribus* commitment to prevent violations of P. The same contractualist reasoning that establishes a constraint against homicide, for example, would establish a general reason to prevent others from violating this principle. So the answer is plausibly yes.

The weight of this reason (and the permissible means by which it could be acted upon) would probably vary somewhat with the principle in question (would be stronger in the case of homicide, say, than in the case of deception). More importantly, the reasons would operate like moral goals rather than restrictions. They correspond to what were traditionally called "imperfect duties." Although we are required to give some weight to these goals in our decisions, we may choose to forego them in particular circumstances if their pursuit would violate a constraint or would seriously interfere with our attaining important personal ends.

The crucial point here is to distinguish the status of moral goals in a contractualist view from their role in outcome ethics. On the former view, I have a reason to minimize moral violations, not *because* they are morally objectionable or impersonally undesirable, but because no one could reasonably reject a principle that gave some deliberative importance to this consideration.[51] To be sure, moral violations *are* morally undesirable and impersonally objectionable, on this view, but that is to say that the prohibitions in question are derivable from the hypothetical choice situation. This judgment is an implication, rather than a ground, of my contractualist duties.[52]

X

Our practical and theoretical lives might be simpler if a concern to maximize valued outcomes were the sole determinant of moral reasoning. But it appears not to be. Morality both enjoins and restricts the pursuit of goals. This complexity is not puzzling from a (Kantian) contractualist point of view. It is just what we should expect of the practice of human beings who are concerned to advance their good under conditions of mutual respect. This constitutes, I have argued, a considerable theoretical merit.

Notes

1. Of course, to Nietzsche and some others, this connection is a mere pretense.
2. John Stuart Mill, *Utilitarianism* ([1861] Hackett: Indianapolis, 1979), ch. 2, p. 16. To treat these two ideals as equivalent is, as we will see, problematic. The contractualist sees the Golden Rule as an expression of a concern for reciprocity rather than love.
3. J. J. C. Smart, *Utilitarianism: For and Against* (Cambridge: Cambridge University Press, 1973).
4. Joseph Fletcher, *Situation Ethics* (Philadelphia: Westminster, 1966), p. 98.
5. Arthur Schopenhuuer, *On the Basis of Morality* ([1841] Indianapolis: Bobbs-Merrill, 1965), pp. 135–8.
6. Rodger Beehler, *Moral Life* ([1848] Oxford: Blackwell Publisher, 1978), p. 1.
7. A. I. Melden, *Rights and Persons* (Berkeley and Los Angeles: University of California Press, 1977), p. 145.
8. My discussion in the next few paragraphs of the role of rights follows T. M. Scanlon, "Rights, Goals and Fairness," in *Public and Private Morality*, ed. Stuart Hampshire (Cambridge: Cambridge University Press, 1978), pp. 93–111; reprinted in *Consequentialism and Its Critics*, ed. Samuel Scheffler (New York: Oxford University Press, 1988). For further remarks on Scanlon's relation to utilitarianism, see note 32 in the present chapter.
9. Some will insist that these rights are restricted not by interests but by others' rights – your right to privacy by my right to noninterference. This response is suggested by John Hospers' declaration: "Every human being has the right to act in accordance with his own choices, unless those actions infringe on the equal liberty of other human beings to act in accordance with *their* choices." "What Libertarianism Is," in *The Libertarian Alternative*, ed. Tibor Machan (Chicago: Nelson Hall, 1974), p. 3. Presumably this principle is meant to restrict my right to punch you when I feel like it. But it can be applied in a noncircular manner only when it is supplemented by background assumptions about what interests are more worthy of protection. For your claim not to be punched also interferes with my liberty to punch. We do not consider that an infringement, because we do not take the right to punch someone to be a general interest worth protecting.
10. Philippa Foot, "Utilitarianism and the Virtues," *Mind* 94 (1985), 196–209. The quoted passage is from the reprinted version in Scheffler, *Consequentialism*, p. 227.
11. Scanlon, "Rights, Goals and Fairness," p. 93. One of the best discussions of these connections from a utilitarian point of view is in chapter 5 of Mill's *Utilitarianism*.
12. My account follows especially Thomas Nagel, *The View from Nowhere* (New York: Oxford University Press, 1986), ch. 9. See also Robert Nozick, *Anarchy, State and Utopia* (New York: Basic Books, 1974), pp. 28–35.
13. Beehler, *Moral Life*, p. 17.
14. On this feature of promising, see John Rawls, "Two Concepts of Rules," *Philosophical Review* 64 (1955), 3–32.
15. To characterize rights in terms of authority will be circular, if authority cannot be explained without invoking rights. Nevertheless, a circular characterization can be philosophically helpful by locating a term in its conceptual network.

16. The problem of accommodation is relevant to what Gregory Kavka called "the rec-onciliation project," "The Reconciliation Project," in *Morality, Reason, and Truth: New Essays on the Foundations of Ethics,* ed. David Copp and David Zimmerman (Totowa, NJ: Rowman & Allanheld, 1984), pp. 279–319. In one version, this is the project of showing that morality is compatible with "self-interest." Because self-interest is then identified with (practical) rationality, this project is transformed into the attempt to reconcile morality with rationality. The problem of accommodation is related but distinct; it is not to reconcile morality with the independent claims of reason, but to accommodate two features *of* morality, neither of which is on its face self-interested. Nevertheless, the problem can also be seen as arising from a tension within practical reason: that morality at once requires and restricts "maximizing rationality." I return to this notion later in this essay.

17. For an attack on the mixed position, see Shelly Kagan, *The Limits of Morality* (New York: Oxford University Press, 1989).

18. For instance, H. A. Prichard. Because he identifies morality with the realm of de-ontological constraints (in his term, the realm of "obligation"), Prichard takes the search for the "role" of such constraints to be a misguided attempt to ground moral-ity in nonmoral considerations. Since moral philosophy is conceived to be the the-ory of such constraints, the very enterprise "rests on a mistake." See "Does Moral Philosophy Rest on a Mistake?", *Mind* (1912), reprinted in Prichard's *Moral Obligation* (New York: Oxford University Press, 1949). For a valuable discussion of Prichard's view, see James Wallace, *Virtues and Vices* (Ithaca: Cornell University Press, 1978), ch. 4.

19. For a related attempt to "reconcile deontological intuitions with consequentialist in-sights," see the very suggestive essay by Conrad D. Johnson, "The Authority of the Moral Agent," *Journal of Philosophy* 82 (1985), 260, reprinted in Scheffler, *Consequentialism,* pp. 261–87. As an alternative to two-level views, Johnson proposes a "division of labor" view, which distinguishes judicial and legislative points of view within morality. He appears to think that his view remains fundamentally conse-quentialist; he speaks of reconciling "consequentialism with agent-centered con-straints" (p. 263) rather than developing an alternative to consequentialism.

20. My discussion abstracts from substantial differences among versions of rule utili-tarianism. A valuable discussion of rule utilitarianism and its varieties is to be found in David Lyons, *The Forms and Limits of Utilitarianism* (Oxford: Clarendon Press, 1965). See also Donald Regan, *Utilitarianism and Co-operation* (Oxford: Claren-don Press, 1980), Rawls, "Two Concepts," and Wallace, *Virtues and Vices.*

21. This is Smart's criticism of what he calls "indirect utilitarianism" in *Utilitarianism: For and Against.*

22. Hence, as Scanlon puts it, rule utilitarianism "strikes most people as an unstable compromise." See "Contractualism and Utilitarianism," in *Utilitarianism and Be-yond,* ed. A. Sen and B. Williams (Cambridge: Cambridge University Press, 1982), pp. 103–28.

23. R. M. Hare defends a view like this in *Moral Thinking* (Oxford: Clarendon Press, 1981). A similar view is expounded, though not endorsed, by Robert Adams, "Mo-tive Utilitarianism," *Journal of Philosophy* 73 (1976), 467–81.

   A subtle version of consequentialism has been advanced by Peter Railton. See "Alienation, Consequentialism, and the Demands of Morality," *Philosophy and Public Affairs* 13 (1984).

24. See, e.g., Michael Stocker, "The Schizophrenia of Modern Ethical Theories," *Jour-nal of Philosophy* 73 (1976), 453–66; Thomas Nagel, "The Limits of Objectivity,"

in *The Tanner Lectures on Human Values,* ed. S. McMurrin (Salt Lake City: University of Utah Press, 1980), esp. pp. 129ff.; and various contributions to *Hare and Critics: Essays on Moral Thinking,* ed. D. Seanor and N. Fotion (Oxford: Clarendon Press, 1990).

25. Hare responds to some of these worries in *Moral Thinking* and in "Ethical Theory and Utilitarianism," in *Utilitarianism and Beyond,* ed. Sen and Williams, pp. 23–38. See also his replies in Seanor and Fotion, *Hare and Critics.*

26. Hobbesian and Kantian theories are so different at their foundations that they might better be treated as generically different. For this point, see Will Kymlicka, "The Social Contract Tradition," in *A Companion to Ethics,* ed. Peter Singer (Oxford: Blackwell Publisher, 1993). I would propose "consentualism" as an apt term for Kantian-type theories. I treat them together just the same, because each promises to resolve the problem of accommodation via some notion of agreement.

27. I shall assume that Hobbesian theories aspire (with David Gauthier) to generate morality as "a rational constraint from the non-moral premises of rational choice." David Gauthier, *Morals by Agreement* (Oxford: Clarendon Press, 1986), p. 4. This book contains an excellent presentation of the two forms of contractualism; see esp. chapter 1. See also Jean Hampton, "Two Faces of Contractarian Thought," in *Contractarianism and Rational Choice: Essays on Gauthier,* ed. P. Vallentyne (Cambridge: Cambridge University Press, 1990), pp. 31–55, and Christopher Morris, "A Contractarian Account of Moral Justification," in *Moral Knowledge? New Essays in Moral Epistemology,* ed. Walter Sinnott-Armstrong and Mark Simmons (New York: Oxford University Press, 1996), pp. 215–42.

28. In "Morality and Self–Other Asymmetry," *Journal of Philosophy* 81 (1984), 179–92. In "The Authority of the Moral Agent," p. 284, Johnson notes the capacity of two-level views to accommodate this asymmetry.

29. Conversely, it is arguably a problem that self-neglect and self-development cannot even be regarded as moral issues by contractualism. This points to one of the ways in which contractualism can be at most an adequate theory for a part of morality, the part having to do with moral requirement. (I return to a related issue at the end of this essay.)

30. Gauthier, *Morals by Agreement,* p. 187.

31. See the essays by Michael E. Bratman and Daniel M. Farrell in this volume. See also Gregory S. Kavka, "A Paradox of Deterrence Revisited," in his *Moral Paradoxes of Nuclear Deterrence* (Cambridge: Cambridge University Press, 1987), pp. 33–56, esp. 43–7. For a development of a two-tier view that does not rely on a revision of maximizing rationality, see Eric M. Cave, *Preferring Justice: Rationality, Self-transformation, and the Sense of Justice* (Boulder, CO: Westview, 1997).

32. Here I follow Scanlon, "Contractualism and Utilitarianism." It is a reasonable conjecture, I think, that Scanlon's transitions from an earlier Kantian stage, through his flirtation with a two-tier consequentialism in "Rights, Goals and Fairness," to the contractualism of this essay are influenced by his evolving assessment of the capacities of these theories to handle the problem of accommodation.

33. Scanlon himself does not use this term, but it is a fair characterization of what he has in mind. In certain contexts, at least, the refusal to consider one's actions from the perspective of others is called "unreasonable." We call the opposite "fair-mindedness." The connection between these notions is brought out by Rawls, who links being reasonable (as distinct from rational) with a concern for "fair terms of cooperation," that is, "terms which participants may reasonably be expected to

accept provided that everyone else likewise accepts them." "Kantian Constructivism (The Dewey Lectures)," *Journal of Philosophy* 77 (1980), 515–72, at p. 528.

    Cp. Rawls, in *A Theory of Justice* (Cambridge, MA: Harvard University Press: 1971): "respect for persons is shown by treating them in ways that they can see to be justified" (p. 586). Respect is shown in "our willingness to see the situation of others from their points of view, from the perspective of their conception of the good; and in our being prepared to give reasons whenever the interests of others are materially affected" (p. 337).

34. A circularity problem looms here. Respect is the concern to justify one's actions to others, assuming that they have the same attitude. But what is the content of that attitude? This arises for Scanlon's formulation as well. He characterizes the con-tractualist motivation as the "desire to be able to justify one's actions to others on grounds they could not reasonably reject." "Contractualism and Utilitarianism," p. 116. He goes on to explain: "The intended force of . . . 'reasonably' . . . is to ex-clude rejections that would be unreasonable *given* the aim of finding principles which could be the basis of informed, unforced general agreement . . . The only pres-sure for agreement comes from the desire to find and agree on principles which no one who had this desire could reasonably reject." Ibid., p. 111. Scanlon addresses this and other issues in his manuscript "What We Owe to Others."

35. Contrary to Alan Donagan, *The Theory of Morality* (Chicago: University of Chicago Press, 1977), sec. 7.2. Cp. Rawls once again: "While the principles of justice will be effective only if men . . . respect one another, the notion of respect . . . is not a suitable basis for arriving at these principles. It is precisely these ideas that call for interpretation." *A Theory of Justice*, p. 337.

    In Rawls's terms, because respect frames the structure of the original position, it gives the outcome of otherwise self-regarding reasoning a moral significance. But the frame does not by itself supply the content. Similarly, in Scanlon's version, the concern to satisfy the terms of reasonable cooperation frames the concern to find principles that will advance one's interests.

36. The term "self-regard" is meant to refer to a concern to advance one's ends, what-ever they may be; the term does not imply that one's ends themselves are specifi-cally self-regarding or "egoistic." The same goes for talk of "advantage." The issue between Kantians and Hobbesians is whether self-regard in this sense is directly or indirectly (as with Gauthier) the ultimate standard of practical reason.

37. Scanlon, "Contractualism and Utilitarianism," p. 119.

38. Gauthier, *Morals by Agreement*, p. 17.

39. See Scanlon, "Contractualism and Utilitarianism," pp. 118–19.

40. T. M. Scanlon, "The Significance of Choice," in *The Tanner Lectures on Human Values*, ed. Sterling McMurrin (Salt Lake City: University of Utah Press, 1988), pp. 149–216, at p. 174.

41. That is not to say that this requirement would not itself be endorsed from that stand-point. It is plausible to suppose that the requirement to constrain one's deliberations by the hypothetical-choice situation would itself be chosen in that situation.

42. Thomas Nagel's enterprise in *The Possibility of Altruism* (Oxford: Clarendon Press, 1970) is a contemporary example of a "classical" Kantian theorist in my loose sense. His view might also be given a contractualist turn. He argues that prudential reasoning involves a conception of objective reasons that yield impartial other-regarding reasons as well. To put the claim in explicitly Kantian terms, the force of the hypothetical imperative as a principle of practical reason depends upon a point of view that implies "categorical reasons." Objective reasons do not depend on any

notion of hypothetical agreement, but Nagel entertains the suggestion that conflicts among objective reasons are properly decided by recourse to a hypothetical-choice situation; thus, all-things-considered moral "ought" judgments would have, on this suggestion, a contractualist interpretation.

In a bold new work, *The Sources of Normativity* (Cambridge: Cambridge University Press, 1996), Christine Korsgaard pursues the classical project without making any foundational use of contractualist notions.

43. This idea is congenial to a Rawlsian view. Samuel Scheffler elaborates a view of this sort in "Moral Skepticism and Ideals of the Person," *Monist* 62 (1979), 288–303, though he does not give it contractualist construal.

44. Foot's "Utilitarianism and the Virtues" suggests to me the possibility of a view of this kind.

If contractualism were grounded in a theory of virtue in this manner, then it might be committed to benevolence (as a virtue) after all. Although respect would be a virtue distinct from benevolence, it would not follow that respect is intelligible *as* a virtue independently of the concerns of benevolence. For, on this theory, the account of what makes respect a virtue (say, its role in human flourishing) might entail that benevolence (a concern for the well-being of individuals) is a virtue as well. See section VII in the present chapter.

45. The latter requirement is not met by showing that a failure of respect involves a failure of reason, as the classical Kantians would have it. To say that someone is under a moral demand is not just to say that she has acted contrary to reason; it is to say that she is *answerable* to us in certain ways.

46. Samuel Scheffler, "Agent-centred Restrictions, Rationality, and the Virtues," reprinted in his *Consequentialism,* pp. 243–60 at p. 244.

47. Ibid., p. 254.

48. Ibid., p. 252.

49. For the development of this idea, see Amartya Sen's important essay "Rights and Agency," *Philosophy and Public Affairs* 11 (1982), 3–39 (also reprinted in Scheffler, *Consequentialism*).

50. It is possible that a commitment to goals should appear in the foundations of a particular version of contractualism, but there is no general reason to suppose that it must.

51. This remark parallels what Scanlon says about duties of beneficence; see section VII of the present chapter.

52. This reverses Scheffler's claim that agent-relative deontological goals would be "derivative from, and given life by" the impersonal deontological goal, a claim that betrays his predilection for outcome theories. "Agent-centred Restrictions," p. 256.

Justice, Reasons, and Moral Standing

CHRISTOPHER W. MORRIS

> The notions of right and wrong, justice and injustice, have there no place.
> *Leviathan,* ch. xiii

The best account of the virtue of justice, I have long thought, is that offered by a certain type of contractarianism. This sort of approach seeks to base justice in mutual advantage. The implications it yields are clearly revisionist. As David Gauthier acknowledges, "No doubt there will be differences, perhaps significant, between the impartial and rational constraints supported by [contractarian morality] . . . and the morality learned from parents and peers, priests and teachers."[1] To many moral philosophers these sorts of revisionist implications are the basis for rejecting the whole approach.

Gregory S. Kavka has identified a particular source of these revisionist implications, and he has dubbed it "the problem of group egoism." He notes that these sorts of contractarian theories "appeal, in one form or another, to reciprocity: compliance with moral constraints benefits you because it facilitates the cooperation (and like compliance) of others, and you – like everyone else – need such cooperation to get along in the world." This approach, however, gives rise to this problem of group egoism.

Everyone does need the cooperation of others to get by in this world. But not *all* others. Only enough suitably placed. Hence, if the only rational ground of compliance with moral constraints is reciprocity, the scope of moral protection would seem to extend only to cover potential reciprocators. More specifically, while all individuals may need cooperation from other individuals in their group, members of powerful groups may not need the cooperation of the members of weak groups. The weak may have nothing to

I presented earlier versions of this essay at the conference in honor of Gregory Kavka entitled "Rationality, Commitment, and Community," Feb. 10–12, 1995, University of California, Irvine, and at the Virginia Commonwealth University, Richmond. I am very grateful to members of these audiences for interesting and useful comments. I am indebted as well to the discussion of a related paper at a conference on distributive justice sponsored by the International Economics and Philosophy Society and by the Murphy Institute of Political Economy of Tulane University, especially to Gerald Gaus. For earlier conversations or suggestions I am grateful as well to David Brink, R. G. Frey, Arthur Ripstein, and David Schmidtz.

offer, or what they have to offer may be gotten more cheaply by coercion than by cooperation.[2]

Kavka is tempted to conclude, from the seriousness of this problem and from
the difficulties with various responses to it, that some of the ambitions of the
contractarian project must be abandoned. Specifically, he suspects that "the
drive toward unanimity, the ambition of showing adherence to moral norms to
be rational for everyone, must – despite its attractions – be abandoned."[3]
      I have not thought that contractarian theory could show that everyone has a
reason to be just. Rather, I thought that contractarianism could generate reasons
for all who are bound by justice – but that not all human beings will be so bound.
The scope of contractarian justice is thus restricted; certainly it is not likely to
include all human beings or even all persons. And this is how I read the accounts
of classical contractarians such as Hobbes and Rousseau, as well as contemporaries such as David Gauthier, Gilbert Harman, and Jan Narveson, and others.
The restricted scope of contractarian justice has always concerned me. But the
ways in which the group egoism problem compounds and complicates this feature of contractarianism are striking and make me think that the theory recom-
mends an unworkable conception of justice. These worries, then, have led me
to rethink this way of understanding justice, and I have come to believe that it
is mistaken in certain respects. It may be possible to reconcile justice and rationality by restricting the scope of the former, but I have come to think that this
may be an error. This essay proposes to explore that possibility.

I. Contractarian Justice

As I said, I have thought that the best account of the virtue of justice has been
contractarian. I am not thinking only of distributive justice, the focus of so much
recent attention. Rather, I am thinking of justice in a broad sense, as the virtue
that would have us respect the rights of others, refrain from harming and de-
frauding them, provide whatever positive services we owe them, and the like.[4]
I have never supposed that contractarianism could offer an account of virtues
such as benevolence, courage, or temperance, much less wisdom or prudence
(if we count these as moral virtues). But it seemed that it could offer an account
of justice in this broad sense. Indeed, the account seemed ideally suited to address the concerns that Philippa Foot famously raised years ago about justice:

For while prudence, courage and temperance are qualities which benefit the man who
has them, justice seems rather to benefit others, and to work to the disadvantage of the
just man himself . . . We will be asked how, on our theory, justice can be a virtue and injustice a vice, since it will surely be difficult to show that any man whatsoever must need
to be just as he needs the use of his hands and eyes, or needs prudence, courage and temperance?

... [If this question] cannot be answered, then justice can no longer be recommended, as a virtue. The point of this is not to show that it must be answerable, since justice is a virtue, but rather to suggest that we should at least consider the possibility that justice is not a virtue.[5]

Contractarianism seemed to offer an account of justice that would show justice to be beneficial to the just person (as well as to others). If supplemented by a revisionist account of practical rationality of the sort David Gauthier and others have developed, contractarian theory promised as well to show that justice provides reasons for action and, *contra* many critics, reasons of the right sort. As we shall see, it could not plausibly be thought that this kind of account could make the scope of justice universal, that is, applicable to all human beings or even all persons. So I accepted that justice was restricted. By contrast, Foot eventually gave up the requirement that justice must provide reasons.[6] I am now inclined to think that her abandonment of the reasons requirement was right.

The assumption that I propose to question is commonly called "internalism" in the contemporary literature. The version that I shall focus on is the one that would have moral requirements provide reasons for action (though not necessarily motives). The sort of contractarianism that I believed could account for justice is committed to this condition. I shall see if it can do without.

Contractarianism we may think of as a family of views that seeks to justify morality or political institutions by reference to rational agreement. The general idea is that a morality or a form of political organization (e.g., a state) is to be justified by being shown to be the outcome of the rational agreement of the individuals over whom it has authority. This general idea may take many different forms, and there are many different kinds of contractarian theory, as well as different purposes to which it may be put. Our interest will be confined to particular versions of *moral* contractarianism: the attempt to justify morality – or, as I propose, justice – in agreement.[7]

The "agreement" that is to ground justice I shall understand as hypothetical, even though some contractarians, especially those offering accounts of the polity, invoke actual agreement.[8] Contractarianism may thus be understood to be a kind of discovery or decision procedure; we are to determine what justice asks of us by ascertaining what we would agree to under certain conditions. But contractarianism is not merely a method for determining the nature and content of the requirements of justice; it may also give us a way of providing reasons for accepting and complying with justice. Thus, we may say, with John Rawls, that "The theory of justice is a part, perhaps the most significant part, of the theory of rational choice."[9] The difference between the two aims – a discovery procedure and a method for generating reasons to be just – is important, especially for the discussion at the end of this essay. Both aims may be understood to presuppose a view of morality or of political society as a "cooperative venture for mutual advantage," to use another of Rawls's useful phrases.[10] But mutual advantage and cooperation can signify several different things. One might think, as John Harsanyi and Rawls do, that the outcome of hypothetical rational agreement determines the nature and content of certain fundamental moral principles, without thinking that agents are necessarily provided thereby with reasons for action.[11] Compliance may be another matter, for agreement will not always suffice to ensure that individuals in certain situations have reason to act in accord with mutually advantageous principles. For instance, the "free-rider problem" – the temptation of rational agents in certain situations to take advantage of the cooperative behavior of others – remains.[12] By contrast, other theorists think that rational agreement can provide reasons for compliance; this seems to have been the view of Hobbes in his answer to the Foole, and it certainly is the view of Gauthier.[13] The two aims of contractarianism are somewhat independent, and one does not entail the other. Gauthier would espouse both aims. Harsanyi and Rawls, as mentioned, would use contractarian agreement only as a discovery procedure.

A social contract, whatever it is, is a type of agreement. However, "agreement" here is ambiguous: it can be a species of consent or something else. It is hard to see, though, how hypothetical agreement could count as genuine consent. Actual agreement will normally so count, barring certain conditions (e.g., coercion or duress, lack of relevant information), but hypothetical consent does not engage the will in the requisite manner to be consensual.[14] Hypothetical agreement, however, can be, just like genuine consent, evidence of advantage or of reasonable compromise. As such, these "agreements" will be purely heuristic and need not have any independent normative force.[15]

The fact that agreement constitutes consent only if morally constrained in certain respects suggests another distinction, one that will be especially relevant at the end of the essay. In political theory, an obvious difference between Hobbes and Locke is that for the latter contractarian agreement is morally constrained (by natural law), whereas for the former it is not – or so his theory may be read. For Locke, consent can generate obligations only if the constraints imposed by the laws of nature are respected, which is to say only if certain moral constraints are not violated. For Hobbes, on this reading, there are no *moral* conditions that constrain the sort of consent that can create obligations. Rawls has made it clear that his theory is to be understood as one where agreement is morally constrained.[16] By contrast, Gauthier's theory is a morally unconstrained form of contractarianism.[17] As the examples show, this distinction applies equally to moral and to political forms of the theory. Contractarian agreement, then, may be morally constrained (e.g., Rawls) or unconstrained (e.g., Gauthier). What is important for our purposes about the distinction between these two contractarianisms is that it cannot be claimed of the former that agreement is the ground of all of justice, for morally constrained contractarianism presupposes moral constraints that are prior to and independent of agreement.[18]

More importantly, this kind of contractarianism cannot provide reasons to be just that are independent of the moral elements of the construction. The sort of contractarianism that I had thought provides an account of justice must be morally unconstrained.[19]

We may ask generally, about the scope of the agreement that is to generate moral norms, Who are the parties to the agreement? The simple answer, offered by many contractarians, is, all those who are to be bound by the norms, namely, all those who find themselves in "the circumstances of justice" in question. For these contractarians, the circumstances of justice are the conditions that give rise to the particular virtue of justice.[20] The circumstances include two sorts of conditions: (1) rough equality of physical and mental powers, vulnerability to attack, moderate scarcity, and (2) consciousness of the latter, and awareness of conflict as well as of some identity of interest. Moderate scarcity is relative to individual ends and is understood to include variability of supply, thus allowing the possibility of mutually beneficial cooperation. People may usually find themselves in the "circumstances of justice," that is, in situations where cooperative, constrained behavior is mutually beneficial. But as Kavka's description of the problem of group egoism reveals clearly, this need not always be. This problem, and many related objections to contractarianism, stem from the limited scope of justice that appears to be entailed by this doctrine of the circumstances of justice.[21]

The picture of justice that emerges from the view I have sketched is quite different from many, if not most, ordinary conceptions of the virtue. Justice on this view turns out to be rather complex. It may consist in multiple sets of norms and ideals, rather than a single set of principles. And these norms will have limited and varying scope, rather than applying universally to the class of human beings or persons. The sets may also overlap in various complicated ways, just as the legal norms from different legal systems can overlap. The general picture one gets is of a kind of particularism, without complete relativism.[22] We shall explore some of the implications of this picture for the matter of moral standing.

II. Moral Standing

David Gauthier claims of his contractarian theory that it "denies any place to rational constraint, and so to morality, outside the context of mutual benefit." He notes that "Only beings whose physical and mental capacities are either roughly equal or mutually complementary can expect to find co-operation beneficial to all. Humans benefit from their interaction with horses, but they do not co-operate with horses and may not benefit them. Among unequals, one party may benefit most by coercing the other, and on our theory would have no reason to refrain." The implications are clear, he thinks: "we may agree that the moral constraints arising from what are, in the fullest sense, conditions of mutual advantage, do not correspond in every respect to the 'plain duties' of conventional morality. Animals, the unborn, the congenitally handicapped and defective, fall beyond the pale of a morality tied to mutuality."[23]

The implications, in fact, are less clear and simple than may at first appear. Let me introduce some terminology that will enable me to sketch fairly quickly the implications of this sort of account.[24] Something has "moral standing," I shall say, insofar as it is owed (some) moral consideration. Typically, we think that people have moral standing but artifacts and natural objects, albeit valuable, lack it. (Some environmentalists contest this claim; I put it forward merely for illustrative purposes.) We need to distinguish, then, moral standing from another sort of moral value that objects may possess. Something has moral standing, let me say, if it is a *direct moral object,* something *to* which moral consideration is paid. By contrast, an *indirect moral object* is something *about* or *concerning* which moral consideration is paid. For instance, we may think that Yosemite National Park, the Louvre, or a national flag are indirect moral objects. We may not damage them, but the considerations we owe concerning them are not owed *to* them. They are, as it were, mere "third-party beneficiaries" of our relations to one another; not everything of moral *value* has moral *standing.* Again, I do not mean to make a claim about the moral status of nonliving things or to advance substantive positions, merely to illustrate an important distinction.

It is possible that animals, the unborn, the congenitally handicapped and defective – to use Gauthier's examples – lack moral standing but are indirect moral objects. Just as we owe it to one another not to trash Yosemite or the Louvre, so, one may argue, one ought not to harm animals or certain people. It may seem that this is all that contractarian justice can do for beings who are not in certain respects our equals, that is, who do not find themselves in the circumstances of justice with us. But this conclusion, I have argued elsewhere, is mistaken. Someone who is not able to reciprocate may nevertheless acquire moral standing through his or her relations to us. Consider simply the case of children. No normal human being would interact cooperatively with someone who was not ready to accord genuine moral standing to one's children. No one would be satisfied with cooperative relations that merely accorded one's children the status of indirect moral objects, or so I have argued elsewhere.[25]

In the contractarian framework I have sketched, someone can acquire moral standing in relation to certain others by being in the circumstances of justice and by being able and willing to cooperate. But an individual can also acquire moral standing if others with moral standing care sufficiently about him or her not to be willing to cooperate with others unless this individual is also accorded (genuine) moral standing (not merely the status of an indirect moral object).[26] So it need not be the case that "animals, the unborn, the congenitally handicapped and defective" lack moral standing. As Kavka points out, reciprocity is not, then, necessary throughout.[27]

I do not labor these distinctions and complicated relations in order to exonerate contractarianism. It is just that the standard sorts of (counter)examples found in the literature are too quick and easy. The implications of the theory are rather more complicated. This said, it certainly cannot be denied that some creatures, who we ordinarily believe have at least some moral standing – and are not mere indirect moral objects, like artifacts – will lack that status, on this contractarian view. This conclusion seems inescapable, even if there are fewer such beings than the critics of contractarianism usually suggest. Additionally, as Kavka points out, the dependence of moral standing on the contingent pattern of people's interests may seem too arbitrary. "For, even on his [Morris's] interpretation, the moral standing of individuals (and groups) is contingent upon whether anyone (and if so, who) in other groups happens to care about them. And it seems to assign moral standing in a rather arbitrary way: two entities may be just alike except with regard to possession of the fortuitous relational property of being cared for by me, yet – on this account – one of them has moral standing for you and the other does not."[28] Kavka concludes that "Morris has not solved the group egoism problem for Gauthier in a satisfactory manner."

Kavka, however, does not really explain the way in which groups make these implications of contractarianism especially worrisome. The theory would accord moral standing to all who stand to benefit from cooperation, as well as to others who gain standing by being the object of the former's caring. But one need not suppose that we ascertain who is in this situation – the circumstances of justice – by examining individuals. Rather, it is groups of varying size that will be crucial. For most individuals will stand to benefit from cooperation with virtually all members of their group, if the latter is relatively small (e.g., a clan, a village, a small community). But the particular group(s) of which one is a member will determine the prospects of mutually beneficial cooperation. By oneself one may be as helpless as the solitary souls in Hobbes' or Rousseau's states of nature, but as a member of a powerful and prosperous group, one may be in little need of cooperation with others less well placed.

There are two problems here that I wish to distinguish, both serious for contractarian theory, though in different ways. One is a problem of indeterminacy. The membership of the "social contract," as it were, depends on the groups that form. And there seems to be no theoretical method for determining the relevant groups. Certainly we cannot turn to the theory of rational choice, because coalition theory, on which the sort of contractarian theory we are examining depends, is one of its least developed areas.[29] The problem is that without such a method contractarian theory will be indeterminate; it will have few implications for our world. This may not be a criticism; it depends on the appropriate aims of moral theory. I merely note this problem of indeterminacy, and I shall have a few words to say about it at the end of the essay.

The second problem is more worrisome. It is not merely that the distribution of moral standing is arbitrary and offensive in certain respects, once the effects of coalition formations are taken into account. It is that the implications are particularly nasty. Consider classical slavery, where slaves typically were war captives. Slaves in these societies were not always noticeably different from the bulk of the population in terms of what we now think of as cultural or "ethnic" attributes, so it might be possible for these slaves or their descendants to escape their condition and acquire the political status of other lower-class members of the society. But contrast this situation with American slavery. Here "a distant people," perceived to be different, with no cultural connections to the place to which they were brought, were enslaved. Given the salient differences between enslaved Africans and free Americans, the exploitation of one by the other was facilitated and more easily maintained. Status distinctions could be preserved with less difficulty than with classical slavery.

Suppose that a group enslaves another and that there are no salient features distinguishing members of one from members of another. This is what I have just supposed for many instances of classical slavery. As Thomas Jefferson notes, "Among the Romans emancipation required but one effort. The slave, when made free, might mix with . . . his master."[30] From a contractarian perspective, individuals who are not distinguishable in any systematic manner more easily acquire moral standing than those who are. It is not, of course, the distinguishing attributes that have this effect – they are relatively arbitrary. Rather, it is that these features are used as the basis for the formation and maintenance of exploitative coalitions.[31] Once formed, these coalitions cannot always be condemned by the moral theory, insofar as it lacks the resources to judge the exploitation as unjust. Bernard Boxill argues that "if people are going to be unjust it is likely that they will restrict their greatest injustices to 'barbarians' and 'outlanders.'"[32] But contractarians will not usually be able to call these practices *unjust* (or just). For, between such groups, "The notions of right and wrong, justice and injustice, have . . . no place."[33]

This world is a very nasty one. Many of our distant ancestors were not bothered by these features of moral conventionalism or of group moralities. For them, relations to members of other groups were much like what many take to be our relation to nonhuman animals. For most of us today it does not seem possible to view members of other groups in that manner. We may quarrel about the extent of our positive duties to members of less well-placed groups, but virtually none of us doubts that we have negative duties – for instance, not to enslave people so placed. Yet no such negative duties emerge if our analysis of the problem of group egoism is right.

I do not want, or have not wanted, to say that the problem is one of a moral theory generating implications that are "contrary to our moral intuitions." For, as I have argued elsewhere, it is hard to see what independent weight such moral "intuitions" would have at this stage of theory construction. The project is to determine what the requirements of justice are, so it is difficult to understand how common opinion about justice could have any independent weight.[34] It might be said that this sort of theory does not "capture our concept of morality." It most likely does not, though again it is hard to see what force this has. (I am also skeptical that "we" have a univocal or particular clear conception of the moral, but this is another matter.) What is one – or am I – to say?

III. Interactions among the Virtues

Morality we may think of as consisting in sets of norms, ideals, and dispositions. We have already relied on traditional, though not unproblematic, distinctions among virtues (e.g., justice, benevolence, courage). I have supposed that these virtues have different claims and effects on us. I believe, in addition, that some of these norms, specifically those of justice, are "artificial" in a particular sense. They are dependent for their force on the existence of certain conventions and practices. This is clear – or rather, less controversial – in the case of property: whether walking or flying across someone's land constitutes trespass depends on the moral and legal conventions of the setting. This is the feature of justice that classical contractarians seemed to be highlighting in their denials that justice is natural. Hume argues that "the sense of justice and injustice is not deriv'd from nature, but arises artificially, tho' necessarily from education, and human invention."[35] These matters are complicated, so I do not want to rest much on this claim of artificiality. I merely want to suggest the possibility that, just as with other systems of conventional norms (e.g., etiquette, the law), we might anticipate the existence of conflict among the parts or members of any such system. We might expect the laws of nature, whether established by an omniscient, benevolent deity or by nature itself, to form a consistent set.[36] But we should have no such expectation of any set of conventional norms. Just as we expect to find conflicts among different laws or different parts of the law, so we might expect to find conflicts among different norms of justice or among different virtues. The conflicts may not be deep or may only be apparent, but we have no reason to expect human-made conventions, developed over a long time, in varying settings, to be consistent. James Griffin thinks that

Our norms are unlikely to have grown in a way that would make them a system; they have grown, by fits and starts, in response to pressing, heterogeneous practical needs. They have taken their shape partly from the kinds of circumstances we found ourselves in, from the sorts of problems that we faced. Since the problems were different – sometimes large-scale political, sometimes small-scale personal, sometimes about dispositions for facing moral life generally, sometimes about the way to decide out-of-the-way cases – it would not be surprising for different clusters of norms to have emerged . . .

I think we come to ethics with a false assumption. We expect the content of morality to derive from one kind of source – namely, from principles of one sort or another. We expect it to derive from the good, or from the right, or from fairly normative standards of rationality. The reality seems to me quite different. When we understand the forces shaping moral norms of property, say, we see how heterogeneous the forces are.[37]

To suggest that different parts of morality can conflict is, in effect, to challenge the classical thesis of the unity of the virtues. It is not a thesis that I wish to deny just yet. Let us consider another suggestion, namely, that different virtues can have different scope, and that this may shed some light on our common reaction to the appalling implications of contractarian justice. Consider the possibility that benevolence, for instance, could require kind treatment where justice is silent.[38] This was, in fact, Hume's view of the situation of nonhuman animals.[39] In some such situations, the demands of benevolence may be similar in scope to the minimal demands of justice. Cruel treatment, say, of nonhuman animals, may seem unjust because it offends benevolence so; the demands of justice, were there any in this case, would require (perhaps) little more. We might naturally suppose that our objection from benevolence is in fact an objection from justice. Similarly, we might conjecture that our reaction of horror to the supposition that we have no obligations of justice to significant numbers of human beings or persons because we do not stand to benefit from cooperation with them might be a judgment motivated by benevolence. So it is not that the virtues are at odds here. Rather, the suggestion is that our sentiments of benevolence create a cognitive illusion that justice has something to say when it is in fact silent.

There is much more to be said here. I think both ideas discussed in this section worthy of exploration. Still, it is hard to believe the first, the idea that confusion or conflict among the virtues, or some cognitive illusion, is at the heart of our problem. I shall return later to the second, the idea that our norms and ideals may not all be consistent, having been formed by heterogeneous forces, as Griffin suggests. For now, I shall pursue another hypothesis.

IV. Internalism in Moral Theory

The real culprit, I think, is the internalism to which this sort of contractarianism is often committed. "Internalism," in this sense, is roughly the view that there is some sort of necessary connection between moral considerations and motivation or reasons. Usually the focus is on motivation, but I prefer to formulate the condition in terms of reasons: moral considerations provide agents with reasons (though not necessarily motives) for action. The issues at hand have to do with the normative, and motivation, occurrent or dispositional, is a different, perhaps more complicated matter.[40] The view I have been presupposing would have it that the moral considerations themselves, independently of the agent's affirmation or recognition, provide reasons. This view has been called "existence internalism" or "agent internalism," contrasted with versions that would have agents provided with reasons insofar as they have the requisite moral beliefs or judgments.[41] (But much of my discussion will apply to the latter as well.)[42]

Internalism is often thought to be a "conceptual" claim (though it may also be a metaphysical claim). Internalism may be a conceptual claim, though I am not entirely clear on how one establishes conceptual connections such as these. As I understand the tradition, contractarianism has a practical understanding of morality, especially justice. Justice is a framework of norms and ideals that is one of the means – perhaps the most important – whereby we secure the necessary social conditions for well-being, such as security of person and possessions, control of conflict, and expansion of systems of mutual aid. Justice, in order to achieve its purpose, must be practical; that is, it must be effective.

There are two important modern traditions that maintain that these conditions – security, mutual aid – can be more or less secured by institutions, namely, the state or the market (or some combination). The first tradition is exemplified by Hobbes, the second by certain classical and neoclassical political economists. Champions of these traditions are mistaken insofar as they believe that these conditions can be secured solely by political or economic means (narrowly understood), especially in the circumstances of the modern world – large, anonymous societies, characterized by considerable religious, cultural, and material conflict – in the absence of morally motivated self-restraint.[43] The project of developing a contractarian account of justice is governed by this practical conception, and the latter is the primary motivation, on my view, for internalism.

Our contractarian account of justice, as I have noted, is wedded to (existence) internalism (with regard to reasons). It is this that I wish to question. I shall do so by having us consider two different worlds, or, if you wish, two different characterizations or ways of speaking of our world. These two worlds differ essentially only in that in one of them considerations of justice give reasons and in the other they need not. We shall examine the implications of this difference for the matter of moral standing.

In both worlds there are the same individuals, with the same dispositions, and the circumstances of justice do not differ. In each there are three groups of people. There is a set of agents who are able and willing to cooperate with one another ("cooperators"), another set the members of which are not willing ("noncooperators"), and a third set who have little to offer that would make cooperative activity with them advantageous ("the disadvantaged"). We may think of the last two sets as "nonreciprocators." These three sets of cooperators, noncooperators, and disadvantaged jointly exhaust the membership of these worlds. These sets of people are highly idealized, and unrealistically so (e.g., no nonreciprocator stands to cooperate mutually with anyone at all). But it will be useful to set up the problem in this artificially simple manner.

In the first world, justice applies to members of the set of cooperators; they are bound by the norms of justice, and these give them reasons to act. (We shall assume away problems of compliance.) The noncooperators, by contrast, lack reasons to act justly. In this (internalist) world, considerations of justice provide reasons, so it follows that noncooperators are not governed by justice. Justice, I shall say, does not "apply" to them; by this I mean that justice does not bind or obligate them, and the norms of justice do not, as it were, address them. The notion of jurisdiction will be useful here. In this world, the jurisdiction of justice is limited. Each and every cooperator is under the jurisdiction of the norms of justice, but none of the noncooperators is. Internalism would have it that justice provide one with reasons if (but only if) one is under the jurisdiction of justice.

It follows from our contractarian account of justice that the noncooperators in this first world lack moral standing. They are not obligated by justice, and they are not protected by justice. Cooperators are bound not to act unjustly to one another, but justice is silent concerning their treatment of noncooperators (except as that treatment affects the cooperators). Noncooperators, of course, are not constrained by justice in their relations to cooperators, or to anyone else in this world.

The disadvantaged are in a position similar to that of the noncooperators, though not through any unwillingness on their part. They may be both able and willing to cooperate, but they have nothing much to offer. Cooperators will not cooperate with them – it not being advantageous to do so – and noncooperators will treat them as they treat anyone else. The disadvantaged, then, will not fall under the jurisdiction of justice and will lack moral standing. Were someone to treat the disadvantaged justly they might have reason to abide by justice,[44] but, this possibility aside, they will also lack reasons.

This first world is an instance of the contractarian account of justice we have been considering. I have given no flesh and blood to the parties and have said little about their concrete situation, so we do not yet know how much to fret over the fate of the two groups of nonreciprocators. The noncooperators may be supermen or possess rings like Gyges', or be cold-hearted contract killers, or be simply unable to constrain their behavior. And the disadvantaged may be the unfortunate weak and unproductive that contractarians let in only insofar as they are the object of someone's affections (i.e., secondary moral standing). (The differences between these two kinds of nonreciprocators will be significant.) This lack of detail is intentional; I wish to examine some of the formal or structural implications of internalism, and these appear clearly in the contrasting worlds, independently of the detail needed for flesh and blood.

The second world is similar to the first, but there is an important difference. The people are the same; they divide into sets of cooperators, noncooperators, and disadvantaged in exactly the same ways, for exactly the same reasons (whatever these happen to be). The big difference is that whereas in the first

The Two Worlds Compared

Relation	World 1	World 2
$C \Rightarrow C$	O, R	O, R
$C \Rightarrow N$		O
$C \Rightarrow D$		O
$N \Rightarrow N$		O
$N \Rightarrow C$		O
$N \Rightarrow D$		O
$D \Rightarrow D$		O
$D \Rightarrow C$		$O, (R?)$
$D \Rightarrow N$		O

world justice provides reasons, in the second world it need not. This has two significant implications. First, in this world, even though noncooperators (still) lack reasons to act justly, they remain under the jurisdiction of justice. Justice applies to them, in the sense that the norms of justice address and obligate them (and all other inhabitants of this world). Secondly, the disadvantaged will be protected by justice; if we allow considerations of gratitude and the like, then the disadvantaged may, as a consequence, have reasons to be just, at least toward cooperators. Additionally, cooperators will not generally have reasons to be just toward members of the two sets of nonreciprocators.

So, in this world, all agents are obligated to be just toward all other agents. The norms of justice address everyone, and everyone is bound by them. The connection with reasons is, however, severed. In this world, not all under the jurisdiction of justice have reasons to be just. The noncooperators, situated in the same way as before, lack reasons. And cooperators will lack reasons in their relations with nonreciprocators. So, to maintain that they are obligated nevertheless, we must abandon internalism.

We can summarize the picture of our two worlds in the accompanying table, where C, N, and D represent respectively the (disjoint) sets of cooperators, noncooperators, and disadvantaged; $C \Rightarrow N$ represents the relation of cooperators toward or with respect to noncooperators, and O and R stand for "obligations" and "reasons," respectively. The main differences between the two worlds are that in the second, noncooperators and disadvantaged have moral standing and are obligated by justice. In both worlds noncooperators lack reasons, and in the second world cooperators and disadvantaged will sometimes lack reasons in their dealings with other groups.

The question I wish to ask is this: What do these differences amount to? Should we prefer one world to the other? The question I am trying to get at concerns the world(s) we live in. Why should we characterize the relevant features of our world in one of these ways rather than another? These two worlds, as I mentioned, are highly idealized and simplified. Not only, as I mentioned, has the flesh and blood been left out, but so have many other features that may turn out to be relevant to our inquiry. But, as I said, I am interested in certain formal or structural features of these possible worlds; I trust that the picture is sufficiently detailed that I can proceed. Why, then, favor one characterization over another?

The virtue of justice that concerns me, we should recall, is the broad one. Our recent preoccupation with the narrow virtue of distributive justice may have us focus our attention on different aspects of the problem. A theorist preoccupied by distributive matters will notice not only that the scope of the obligations of cooperators in the second world is larger – they are now obligated to nonreciprocators – but that there are distributive differences as well, and I did not mention these. The *content* of the norms of justice may well differ from world to world, depending on factors such as the size of the total population, their productivity, and the like. Depending on the treatment that cooperators are required to accord nonreciprocators, the justly acquired advantages of the former may be lessened by extending the scope of their obligations. So the difference in the scope of justice is not distributively neutral between the two worlds.

This point has to be accepted. There is, then, a relevant difference between the two worlds that I had not mentioned initially and that may influence our evaluation. I propose, however, to bracket these distributive considerations for the moment, at least as much as we can. For the considerations I wish to raise can, I think, be made independent (though perhaps not).

The practical considerations that I discussed previously seem to favor the first world. These considerations are what drove us to accept internalism in the first place. What considerations would have us favor the second world? One might say – as I have heard people say – that in the second world, at least it is the case that justice has some "grip" on noncooperators. In the second world, justice applies to them – that is, addresses and binds them – whereas in the first world that is not so. But this comparison does not seem right. For what grip does justice have in the second world? Noncooperators lack reasons to be just in this world (as in the first). The "grip" in question is elusive. I should have thought that, in the relevant sense, justice has no grip on these people in either world. (In addition, justice will not always provide reasons for others.)

One might think the second world preferable because it would enable cooperators to justify their treatment of noncooperators – treatment such as avoidance, ostracism, or preventive detention. But this apparent comparative advantage may be overestimated. After all, in the first world cooperators do not need to justify to noncooperators their treatment of the latter, for nothing they do to the noncooperators will be unjust (or just). (There is more to be said here.)

There are some other reasons why we might favor the second world over the first, which may be appealing to the internalist contractarian. Given our characteristically fallible judgments and uncertain motivations, there may be good reasons not to allow cooperators to judge who is or is not a cooperator. First, there is simply too much ambiguity. Second, in our world actual noncooperators will usually cooperate with some people at least some of the time; our artificially simple and disjoint sets are not representative of real agents. In the first world, noncooperators have the status of moral outlaws.[45] Relations among cooperators might be too precarious if individual cooperators are allowed to judge to what category others belong.

If we enrich our two worlds in various other ways, additional reasons for relaxing internalism may be offered. Not only is human motivation uncertain and ambiguous – making it difficult to decide whether to classify some criminals as noncooperators or merely as weak-willed – people change. (Consider only that most violent crime is the act of young males.) Certainly wants and interests change and are affected by social settings. It may be that if we offer noncooperators moral standing and the protection of justice, some will change sufficiently to become agents for whom cooperation is advantageous.[46] The "scope" distinctions of the sort that need to be made in the first world will be hopelessly complex in our world. We might imagine a situation where there would be a presumption that everyone has moral standing until his or her behavior indicates otherwise, but, given the uncertainty and ambiguity of human motivation, and given our characteristic weaknesses, it is hard to imagine that the system would be workable; I suspect that it would be hopelessly complex.

I shall not explore this line of thought, because for now I do not wish to enrich the two simple worlds I have sketched.[47] As idealized and simplified as they are, they possess all the information that we need to argue for a rejection of internalism. The main, and by itself sufficient reason, to reject internalism, I shall suggest, is that justice in our world(s) is not like justice in the first world. For us, justice does not always provide reasons. We consequently get a better picture of our justice by relaxing the internalism requirement imposed by (most) contractarians.[48] The main reason to favor the second world, then, is that it is more like our world; that is, it offers a more accurate picture of our world. Our ordinary moralities, the ones we use and appeal to, are very much like justice in the second world. Everyone falls under their jurisdiction. The norms are addressed to all and bind all, but it often seems that some, like our noncooperators, lack reasons to be just. For us justice is rarely completely silent – even in love and war – but sometimes it provides no reasons. The revisionism of contractarianism in effect changes the subject; it no longer has *our* moralities in sight.[49]

Consider for a moment some analogies, namely, norms of etiquette and legal norms. Both apply to everyone, that is, address and bind all. This is most obvious about law. The law presents itself as addressing all within its jurisdiction and as obligating them.[50] On some accounts the law claims a certain type of authority, one that is overriding.[51] But recognizing this does not require that we think the law's claim always justified. So, although the law presents itself as having a certain authority, we do not think that it in fact always has this authority. We may, for example, believe (correctly) that we have an obligation to come to a complete stop at a stop sign on a deserted country road in broad daylight, but few of us think we have a (sufficient) reason to do so.[52] Etiquette similarly makes demands of us. These are not withdrawn when it is learned that we do not care for such things.[53] The rules of etiquette apply to us, that is, address and bind us, whether or not we in fact have reason to respect them.

Internalism with respect to the law or etiquette is an exceedingly hard position to maintain. For it would have us deny that the law or etiquette applies to us whenever we lack reasons, which may be quite frequently. (The alternative, even more absurd, would be to say that we always have reason to obey the law and follow the norms of etiquette.) So why should justice be different? In her famous attack on moral judgments as categorical imperatives, Foot argues for the analogy:

The conclusion we should draw is that moral judgments have no better claim to be categorical imperatives than do statements about matters of etiquette. People may indeed follow either morality or etiquette without asking why they should do so, but equally well they may not. They may ask for reasons and may reasonably refuse to follow either if reasons are not to be found.[54]

There is more to be said about the analogy, but this seems right; justice does not, in fact, always provide reasons.

What is to be said for taking up this suggestion and for opting for the second world? Let us return to our practical conception of justice. Justice, I said, is a framework of norms and ideals that is one of the means, perhaps the most important, whereby we secure the necessary social conditions for well-being (e.g., basic security, control of conflict, mutual aid). Justice, in order to achieve its purpose, must be practical; that is, it must be effective. Hence, internalism. On reflection, however, it is not obvious that this practical concern requires internalism. All that it requires is comparative or relative efficacity. Justice satisfies this practical aim if a sufficiently large number of people have reasons and act on them and if the number of defectors is sufficiently small. As long as the proportion of cooperators is large relative to the proportion of noncooperators and there are not too many disadvantaged, justice will help secure the conditions for our well-being. Additionally, justice can work in conjunction with, be supplemented by, other practices and institutions, such as governments, cultural identifications, and markets.[55] There is no reason why we may not supplement justice with other practices and institutions, however imperfect these may be. Internalism requires that each and every agent bound by justice have reasons. The practical conception of justice does not require this, only that a sufficiently large number of individuals be given such reasons.[56]

Justice will satisfy the practical conception as much as we need, then, if the relevant sets of cooperators are large compared to the sets of noncooperators and there are not too many disadvantaged. In addition, it must be the case that the demands imposed by justice on cooperators in their relations with noncooperators and disadvantaged are not onerous. (And this is where the considerations that I raised earlier concerning distributive justice are especially relevant.)[57] I shall suppose that our obligations of justice to noncooperators are minimal – for example, the duties of noninterference and fair treatment – and shall not dwell on this condition. (The question of the disadvantaged is more complex.)

What does justice, or morality generally, look like without internalism? In some respects, surprisingly like law and etiquette. Usually, but not always, we shall have reasons to act justly. But sometimes we may not. This should not be surprising, even if it is disappointing. But then, perhaps, as Foot suggests we need not

be frightened by the thought that there does not *have* to be an answer to be given, and that the rational cooperation of others in moral practices is not to be taken for granted. Things might get better, not worse, if we recognized that the reasons men have for acting justly and charitably depend on contingent human attitudes, and the identification of one man with another in society. For then we would see that it is up to us to cherish these things, and (above all) that it is no good treating people despitefully and divisively and then demanding morality of them with an alien "ought."[58]

Foot elaborates in another essay:

This conclusion may . . . appear dangerous and subversive of morality. We are apt to panic at the thought that we ourselves, or other people, might stop caring about the things we do care about, and we feel the categorical imperative gives us some control over the situation . . . Perhaps we should be less troubled than we are by the fear of defection from the moral cause; perhaps we should even have less reason to fear if people thought of themselves as volunteers banded together to fight for liberty and justice and against inhumanity and oppression.[59]

Abandoning internalism has an interesting implication for contractarian moral theory. Recall our consideration earlier of the distinctions between morally constrained and morally unconstrained contractarianism. Internalist contractarianism, I suggested, had to construe the relevant agreement as morally unconstrained, if reasons to be just are to be generated without begging the question. And, as I also mentioned, another problem that plagues internalist contractarian theory is that of indeterminacy. Prior to knowing what are the relevant coalitions of agents, one cannot determine the scope or the content of the requirements of justice.[60] Indeterminacy per se is not an objection to a moral theory. It may be that no plausible theory will have determinate implications, at least without detailed information about the relevant contexts and the like.

However, if the internalism condition leads to indeterminacy, then the first of the two possible aims of contractarian theory that I have mentioned – a discovery procedure for ethics – is threatened.

If we abandon internalism, the picture is different. Moralized contractarianism need no longer be unacceptable as question-begging, for the purpose of determining what individuals might agree to is no longer to generate reasons for action; contractarian agreement would be solely a heuristic device.[61] And – the interesting result – if we are able to moralize contractarianism, the indeterminacy resulting from the problem of coalitions may be overcome. We can morally constrain hypothetical agreement in a manner that restricts the possibilities for coalition formation. Of course, the relevant constraints have to be justified. But dropping internalism opens up the possibility of developing a much more determinate contractarian theory than is otherwise possible.[62] And the method may also serve to render our norms and ideals more consistent. However, developing these suggestions is something I cannot do here.

Notes

1. David Gauthier, *Morals by Agreement* (Oxford: Clarendon Press, 1986), p. 6.
2. Gregory S. Kavka, "The Problem of Group Egoism," in *Rationality, Rules, and Utility: New Essays on the Moral Philosophy of Richard B. Brandt,* ed. B. Hooker (Boulder, CO: Westview, 1993), pp. 149–50. See also Kavka's *Hobbesian Moral and Political Theory* (Princeton: Princeton University Press, 1986), pp. 437–46, and "The Reconciliation Project," in *Morality, Reason and Truth,* ed. D. Copp and D. Zimmerman (Totowa, NJ: Rowman & Allenheld), pp. 297–319.
3. Kavka, "The Problem of Group Egoism," p. 163.
4. See Philippa Foot, "Virtues and Vices," in her *Virtues and Vices* (Berkeley and Los Angeles: University of California Press, 1978), p. 3, and "Moral Beliefs," reprinted in *Virtues and Vices,* p. 125.
5. Foot, "Moral Beliefs," p. 125.
6. She says that she had sought "to show that there was a necessary connexion between virtues and self-interest. Where I came to grief was, predictably, over justice. It seems obvious that a man who acts justly must on occasion be ready to go against his interests; but so determined was I to think that every man must have a reason to act morally that I was prepared to doubt that justice is a virtue rather than give up that idea." Introduction to *Virtues and Vices,* p. xiii.
7. Moral contractarianism is much older than its modern political sibling, familiar to us in the writings of Hobbes and Locke and others. It appears to have been a view defended by many of the Greek Sophists (e.g., Antiphon), and it is best known to contemporary philosophers through Plato's Glaucon (*Republic,* bk. 2). The central idea of moral contractarianism may also be found in Epicurus, who asserts justice to be "a pledge of mutual advantage to restrain men from harming one another and save them from being harmed . . . a kind of compact." Epicurus, "Principal Doctrines," par. 31, trans. C. Bailey, in *The Stoic and Epicurean Philosophers,* ed. W. Oates (New York: Random House, 1940), p. 37.
8. I detail the different sorts of contractarian moral theory in "A Contractarian Account of Moral Justification," in *Moral Knowledge? New Essays in Moral Epistemology,*

ed. W. Sinnott-Armstrong and M. Timmons (New York: Oxford University Press, 1996), pp. 215–42.

9. John Rawls, *A Theory of Justice* (Cambridge, MA: Harvard University Press, 1971), p. 16. This famous remark offers a better characterization of Gauthier's theory than it does of Rawls's, and the latter now disowns it. The important idea expressed by this statement has to do not so much with the reference to the formal or mathematical theory of choice as with the idea that moral theory is part of the theory of rationality.

10. Ibid., p. 4.

11. For John Harsanyi's position see "Cardinal Utility in Welfare Economics and the Theory of Risk Taking," *Journal of Political Economy* 61 (1953), 434–5, and "Cardinal Welfare, Individualistic Ethics, and Interpersonal Comparisons of Utility," *Journal of Political Economy* 63 (1955), 309–21.

12. This free-rider problem should not be confused with another compliance problem, that of *assurance:* the temptation not to cooperate when one believes that others will not cooperate. The free-rider problem occurs when agents are disposed not to cooperate (even) when assured of the cooperation of others. For this approach to distinguishing the problems, see David Schmidtz, *The Limits of Government: An Essay on the Public Goods Argument* (Boulder, CO: Westview, 1991), p. 56.

13. See Gauthier, *Morals by Agreement,* and "Three against Justice: The Foole, the Sensible Knave, and the Lydian Shepherd" (1982), reprinted in his *Moral Dealing* (Ithaca: Cornell University Press, 1990), pp. 129–49.

14. "Theories of hypothetical consent discuss not consent but cognitive agreement." Joseph Raz, *The Morality of Freedom* (Oxford: Clarendon Press, 1986), p. 81n.

15. In her attack on the notion of "a good state of affairs," Foot suggests that "Perhaps no such *shared ends* appear in the foundations of ethics, where we may rather find individual ends and rational compromises between those who have them." "Utilitarianism and the Virtues," *Mind* 94 (1985), p. 209n. Hypothetical agreement may be nothing more than a device to determine the terms of such rational compromises.

16. Rawls, *A Theory of Justice,* p. 585.

17. As is James Buchanan's. See *The Limits of Liberty* (Chicago: University of Chicago Press, 1975). The qualification to be added is that Gauthier's theory is not morally unconstrained in the same manner that Buchanan's is. For in the later versions of his theory, that is, in *Morals by Agreement,* Gauthier adopts a two-stage account of agreement (inspired by Buchanan's similar account) but argues that the second stage is constrained by moral principles that emerge from rational interaction in the first. However, the constraints that Gauthier defends – a "Lockean proviso" and a set of rights regarding appropriation – are conventional, not natural.

18. Contrasting "Kantian contractarianism" (e.g., Rawls) with "Hobbesian" versions (e.g., Gauthier), Will Kymlicka claims that the former "is simply an expression of prior moral commitments . . . The ultimate evaluation of Kantian contractarianism depends, therefore, on one's commitments to the ideals of moral equality and natural duty that underlie it." Will Kymlicka, "The Social Contract Tradition," in *A Companion to Ethics,* ed. P. Singer (Oxford: Blackwell Publisher, 1991), p. 194. See also Jean Hampton, "Two Faces of Contractarian Thought," in *Contractarianism and Rational Choice,* ed. P. Vallentyne (Cambridge: Cambridge University Press, 1991), pp. 31–55.

19. There is much more to be said about this matter. Some who are tempted to understand contractarian agreement as a form of consent will infer (correctly) that the agreement must be morally constrained. But, as we shall see at the end of this es-

say, there is another way of understanding the imposition of moral constraints on such agreement.

20. See David Hume, *A Treatise of Human Nature*, III, ii, ii, and *An Enquiry Concerning the Principles of Morals*, iii, i; H. L. A. Hart, *The Concept of Law* (Oxford: Clarendon Press, 1961), pp. 189–95; Rawls, *A Theory of Justice*, pp. 126–8. The doctrine of the circumstances of justice is implicit in Hobbes' account in *Leviathan*, as well as in the thought of various proto-contractarians and moral conventionalists.

21. In order to avoid misunderstanding and to frame a certain objection, I wish to say that the contractarian project of trying to provide reasons to be just is not to show that one should act justly because it pays to do so (in a certain sense). The contractarian just person does not act as justice requires because it is advantageous; rather, he or she acts justly because he or she *is* just, and being that sort of person, as the story goes, advantageous. The account of justice offered is that of an indirect strategy; one better secures one's ends if one does not directly aim for them. Justice, of course, may require one to act against one's ends or desires, and to be just involves being disposed so to act. Being that sort of person, I am suggesting, may be advantageous.

22. For a more radical relativism, see Gilbert Harman, "Moral Relativism Defended," *Philosophical Review* 84 (1975), 3–22, and "Relativistic Ethics: Morality as Politics," in *Midwest Studies in Philosophy 3*, ed. P. French, T. Uehling, and H. Wettstein (Morris, MN: University of Minnesota Press, 1978), pp. 109–21. Russell Hardin's account of differences between dyadic and universalistic norms may be especially relevant here. See his *All for One: The Logic of Group Conflict* (Princeton: Princeton University Press, 1995).

23. Hardin, *Morals by Agreement*, pp. 16, 17, 268.

24. I develop some of these notions and relations elsewhere. See especially "Moral Standing and Rational-Choice Contractarianism," in Vallentyne, *Contractarianism and Rational Choice*, pp. 76–95.

25. Ibid. The argument depends on rejecting the assumption of self-interestedness, or "non-tuism," that Gauthier and other contractarians often make. For a criticism of these assumptions see my essay "The Relation between Self-Interest and Justice in Contractarian Ethics," *Social Philosophy and Policy* 5 (1988), 119–53, and P. Vallentyne, "Contractarianism and the Assumption of Mutual Unconcern," in *Contractarianism and Rational Choice*, pp. 71–5.

26. In "Moral Standing and Rational-Choice Contractarianism," I called this "secondary moral standing," a poor term if it is misunderstood to imply an inferior standing.

27. Kavka, "The Problem of Group Egoism," p. 157.

28. Ibid.

29. Coalition theory is, in the opinion of many, even less well developed or understood than bargaining theory. Contractarian theory of the sort we are examining depends on both, at least if it is to produce determinate results.

30. The full passage reads:
    This unfortunate difference of colour, and perhaps of faculty, is a powerful obstacle to the emancipation of these people [African slaves] . . . Among the Romans emancipation required but one effort. The slave, when made free, might mix with, without staining the blood of his master. But with us a second is necessary, unknown to history. When freed, he is to be removed beyond the reach of mixture.
    Notes on the State of Virginia, in *The Portable Jefferson*, ed. Merrill D. Peterson (1787; Harmondsworth, UK: Penguin, 1975), p. 193.

31. Hardin's *All for One* is very helpful here.

32. Bernard Boxill, "How Injustice Pays," *Philosophy and Public Affairs* 9 (1980), 359–71, p. 369.

33. "To this warre of every man against every man, this also is consequent: that nothing can be unjust." Thomas Hobbes, *Leviathan*, Head edition (1651) as reprinted in
C. B. Macpherson's Pelican edition (Harmondsworth, UK: Penguin, 1968), ch. xiii,
p. 188. The best interpretation of Hobbes, even of his mature work, may not have
him denying moral standing to people in a state of war or of nature.

34. The story is more complicated. Some of it is told in my essay "A Contractarian Account of Moral Justification."

35. He adds later that "when I deny justice to be a natural virtue, I make use of the word,
natural, only as oppos'd to *artificial*. In another sense of the word . . . no virtue is
more natural than justice . . . Tho' the rules of justice be *artificial*, they are not *arbitrary*." Hume, *Treatise*, III, ii, 2, 18–19, pp. 483, 484.

36. See Alan Donagan, "Consistency in Rationalist Moral Systems," *Journal of Philosophy* 81 (1984), 291–309.

37. James Griffin, "On the Winding Road from Good to Right," in *Value, Welfare, and
Morality*, ed. R. G. Frey and Christopher W. Morris (Cambridge: Cambridge University Press, 1993), pp. 171–2, 174.

38. Clearly, we can make certain moral judgments of contexts where justice does not
apply: although there is nothing unjust about a cat's torturing a mouse, it is cruel.

39. Hume, *An Enquiry Concerning the Principles of Morals*, iii, i, p. 191.

40. "[A] reason for action must relate the action directly or indirectly to something the
agent wants or which it is in his interests to have, but an agent may fail to be moved
by a reason, even when he is aware of it, and he may also be moved by something
that is not a reason at all, as e.g. by the consideration that something is contrary to
etiquette. Being moved is therefore neither a necessary nor a sufficient condition of
having a reason." Foot, "A Reply to Professor Frankena," in Foot, *Virtues and Vices*,
p. 179. This conclusion is even more plausible if reasons need not relate only to
wants or interests.
	We must assume that people characteristically or often are moved by reasons that
they recognize. If reasons rarely moved, things would be very different. On some influential contemporary views, we must ascribe to agents minimal rationality; accordingly, it would not be possible for people never or rarely to be influenced by reasons.

41. The latter view is termed "judgment internalism" or "appraiser internalism." See
Stephen Darwall, *Impartial Reason* (Ithaca: Cornell University Press, 1983),
pp. 54–5, and "Internalism and Agency," in *Philosophical Perspective 6: Ethics*, ed.
James E. Tomberlin (Atascadero, CA: Ridgeview, 1992), p. 155; David Brink, *Moral
Realism and the Foundations of Ethics* (Cambridge: Cambridge University Press,
1989), pp. 40–1, and "Objectivity, Motivation, and Authority in Ethics," typescript,
1995.

42. Some people may fail to be given reasons for action by certain moral facts or beliefs; they may nevertheless have reasons to approve enforcement of the value or
norm in question. The "noncooperators" I discuss presently also lack reasons of this
sort. But it is worth keeping in mind that many noncooperators may have reasons to
approve enforcement even when they lack reasons for action. Our distinctions regarding reason are very simple at this stage of the inquiry.

43. Gauthier, although an enthusiast of markets, stresses this point. See *Morals by
Agreement*, as well as "The Social Contract as Ideology" (1977), reprinted in *Moral
Dealing*, pp. 325–54, more pessimistic but still relevant.

44. If they are moved by considerations of gratitude or the like.

45. See my "Punishment and Loss of Moral Standing," *Canadian Journal of Philosophy* 21 (1991), 53–79.

46. It is worth remembering that "the circumstances of justice" are determined in part by people's ends. If these change, then whether or not people are in the circumstances of justice can change. Also, prospects are determined in part by social circumstance, as well as by norms and practices, and these can change and be changed.
47. I discussed this in "Reasons for Actions and the Scope of Justice," an address presented at a conference on distributive justice in New Orleans, 20–1 October, 1995.
48. My rejection of internalism is not based on the methodological advantages of leaving open the matter of the relation between justice and reasons. Rather, I take it to be true that for most of us, some of the time, and that for some of us, all of the time, there are no reasons to be just. (On leaving open the question, see Brink, *Moral Realism,* ch. 3.)
49. This is the sense in which I agree with my late friend Jean Hampton that the sort of contractarianism under consideration fails to capture our conception of morality.
50. The law also creates powers, assigns liabilities, and the like.
51. See, for instance, Raz, *The Morality of Freedom,* chs. 2–4. The law's claim to comprehensive and supreme authority is explained and related to his conception of practical reason in his *Practical Reason and Norms,* 2nd ed. (Princeton: Princeton University Press, 1990).
52. Or so would have the dominant position today on the obligation to obey the law. See, for instance, R. A. Wasserstrom, "The Obligation to Obey the Law," *UCLA Law Review* 10 (1963), 780–807; M. B. E. Smith, "Is There a *Prima Facie* Obligation to Obey the Law?", *Yale Law Journal* 82 (1973), 950–76; Joseph Raz, "The Obligation to Obey the Law," in *The Authority of Law* (Oxford: Clarendon Press, 1979), pp. 233–49; A. John Simmons, *Moral Principles and Political Obligations* (Princeton: Princeton University Press, 1979); and Leslie Green, *The Authority of the State* (Oxford: Clarendon Press, 1988).
53. See Foot, "A Reply to Professor Frankena," p. 176.
54. Philippa Foot, "Morality as a System of Hypothetical Imperatives," in her *Virtues and Vices,* p. 164.
55. These practices and institutions are also imperfect, in terms of both compliance and effects. The literature on "market failures" and "government failures" is huge. That on the failures of cultural practices is about to explode. One of the matters one should want to study is the interactive effects of all these practices and institutions operating together.
56. And be moved by them. As I mentioned in note 40, there has to be some characteristic connection between reasons and motivation.
57. I address some of the concerns about distribution in "Reasons for Actions and the Scope of Justice."
58. Foot, "Moral Beliefs," pp. 130–1, n. 6.
59. Foot, "Morality as a System of Hypothetical Imperatives," p. 167. (The extensive use I have made of Foot's early writings requires me to note that in her later work she rejects several key assumptions of her early thinking.)
60. Not every contractarian will agree. Gauthier, for instance, seeks through various idealizations and through an assumption of equal rationality to generate determinate conclusions. But I am skeptical that he succeeds in bypassing the problem of determining the relevant coalitions.
61. One could, of course, constrain such a heuristic by a requirement that the terms of agreement be such that a sufficient number of people would be moved to comply with a sufficient number most of the time, or by some similar requirement.
62. Or, of course, there already are several different moralized contractarian theories available (e.g., Rawls, *A Theory of Justice*).

Wrongful Life: Paradoxes in the Morality of Causing People to Exist

JEFF McMAHAN

I. Harm and Identity

The issue I will discuss can best be introduced by sketching a range of cases involving a character I will call the Negligent Physician.

The First Preconception Variant

A man and a woman are considering having a child but suspect that one of them may be the carrier of a genetic defect that causes moderately severe mental retardation or cognitive disability. They therefore seek to be screened for the defect. The physician who performs the screening is negligent, however, and assures the couple that there is no risk, although in fact the man is a carrier of the defect. As a result, the woman conceives a child with moderately severe cognitive impairments.

Had the screening been performed properly, a single sperm from the man would have been isolated and genetically altered to correct the defect. The altered sperm would then have been combined *in vitro* with an egg drawn from the woman, and the resulting zygote would have been implanted in the woman's womb, with the consequence that she would later have given birth to a normal child.

Notice, however, that the probability is vanishingly small that the sperm that would have been isolated and altered would have been the very same sperm that in fact fertilized the egg during natural conception. And let us suppose that the egg that would have been extracted for *in vitro* fertilization would also have been different from the one that was fertilized during natural conception. In that case the child who would have been conceived had the screening been done properly would have developed from a wholly different pair of gametes and

This essay is the second of two descendants of a common ancestor. Some of those from whose comments I have benefited are listed in an initial note to the sibling essay, "Cognitive Disability, Misfortune, and Justice," *Philosophy and Public Affairs* 25 (1996), 3–34. In the fall of 1996, I presented an intermediate version of the present essay at New York University and at Bar Ilan University in Israel. I am grateful to those two audiences and especially recall insightful comments from Richard Arneson, Frances Kamm, Arthur Kuflik, Liam Murphy, Peter Unger, and Noam Zohar. For written comments, I am indebted to Walter Glannon, Matthew Hanser, and David Wasserman.

would thus in fact (even if it is not a matter of metaphysical necessity) have been a *different* child from the retarded child who now exists.

This fact poses a serious problem, which Derek Parfit calls the *Non-Identity Problem*.[1] Let us assume that the life of the actual retarded child, though drastically limited in the goods it can contain, is not so bad as not to be worth living. But, if the child's life is worth living, then the Negligent Physician's action was not worse for the child. For if the Negligent Physician had not acted negligently, *that* child would never have existed; and to exist with a life that is worth living cannot be *worse* than never to exist at all.

Before exploring the implications of this problem, let us consider its scope. Parfit has shown that numerous types of act may affect the timing of a significant number of conceptions and thus, over time, greatly affect who will exist in the future. Because of this alone, the Non-Identity Problem is surprisingly wide in scope. But I want to consider a different dimension to the scope of the problem. Consider a second variant of the case of the Negligent Physician.

The Second Preconception Variant

A couple intend to conceive a child *in vitro*. A single sperm and a single egg have already been extracted. Before these genetic materials are joined, however, the couple request to be screened for the genetic defect that causes mental retardation. The physician performs the screening in a negligent manner, the genetic materials are combined without alteration, and in consequence the woman later gives birth to a child with moderately severe mental retardation.

In this variant, if the Negligent Physician had performed his task properly, the single sperm that had already been extracted would have been genetically altered before being combined with the egg. Thus the child who would have existed had the physician not been negligent would have developed from the same pair of gametes that the actual retarded child developed from. Would it have been the same child? Did the Negligent Physician cause the very same child who would have been cognitively normal to be retarded instead?

This is controversial. But it is not absurd to suppose that the cognitively normal child who would have existed had the sperm been altered would have been a different child from the actual retarded child – or, as I will say, that the genetic alteration would have been *identity-determining* with respect to the child. This is not simply because many of the properties or characteristics of the retarded child are very different from those that the cognitively normal child would have had. Whether or not an infant gets dropped on its head may make an equally profound difference to the properties the subsequent child will have, but no one doubts that the child who suffers brain damage from being dropped on its head would be the same child as the normal child who would have developed had the infant not been dropped. What makes the preconception case different is that the genetic alteration of the sperm significantly alters the conditions of the subsequent person's origin or coming-into-existence.[2] It is surely true that you would not have existed if a different man from your father had inseminated your mother at the time you were conceived. The substitution of a different sperm would have been identity-determining with respect to the child who would have existed. But if conception from a different sperm is identity-determining with respect to the subsequent child, then it is not absurd to suppose that conception from a radically altered sperm could be identity-determining as well.

This could be true for several reasons. The alteration might be sufficiently radical to result in the existence of a new and different sperm – that is, the original sperm would be destroyed, and a new one would exist in its stead. This, however, is most unlikely. It is somewhat more plausible to suppose that the alteration to the sperm would cause the conception to result in a different zygote, hence a different organism, and hence a different person. The most plausible supposition, however, is that the alteration of the sperm would be *identity-preserving* with respect to the sperm and the organism but would be identity-determining with respect to the self or person that would eventually emerge in association with the organism.

The view that alterations to genetic materials may be identity-determining with respect to the person who eventually develops from them seems compatible with the widely accepted doctrine of the necessity of origin. One can concede that a person could not have developed from any gametes other than those from which he in fact developed and yet hold that those gametes, had they been altered in certain ways, could have caused the existence of a different person.

If alterations to the physical materials from which a person will later develop can be identity-determining, then the scope of the Non-Identity Problem depends on when we begin to exist. Suppose we accept – as I believe we have reason to do – that each of us began to exist when the brain of his or her fetal organism developed the capacity for consciousness and mental activity.[3] Before that, all that existed was an unoccupied human organism that was not and never would be identical with the conscious subject to whose existence it would eventually give rise. With this assumption as background, consider

The Early Prenatal Variant

A woman is unaware that she is in the early stages of pregnancy. Her physician prescribes a powerful drug for her without ascertaining whether she is pregnant and without warning her that the drug causes serious birth defects if taken when one is pregnant. After taking a course of the drug, the woman moves to another area, where she discovers that she is pregnant. Unaware of the effects of the drug, she does not tell her new physician that she has taken it. Seven months later she gives birth to a child with moderately severe mental retardation.

Had this Negligent Physician not prescribed the drug, the woman would have had a cognitively normal child rather than a retarded child. Would it have been the same child? Most people believe that the woman's having taken the drug was identity-preserving with respect to the child – that is, that her retarded child would himself have existed and been normal had she not taken the drug. But this may be in part because they believe that the child already existed in the form of an embryo when his mother took the drug. On the assumption that we do not begin to exist until the fetal brain acquires the capacity to support consciousness, this belief is false. The damage that was done to the embryo preceded the coming-into-existence of the child and radically affected the nature of the organism that would eventually give rise to his existence. It is therefore not absurd to suppose that the damage was identity-determining with respect to the child – that is, that the cognitively normal child would have been a numerically different person from the retarded child.

The Early Prenatal Variant of the Negligent Physician case may thus contrast with

The Late Prenatal Variant

A physician negligently prescribes a powerful drug for a woman who is in the eighth month of pregnancy. The drug causes damage to the fetus's brain, and the child to whom she gives birth is, as a consequence, moderately to severely cognitively impaired.

In this case a conscious subject has already begun to exist in association with the fetal organism at the time the drug is taken. This case is, therefore, relevantly like that in which an infant suffers brain damage from being dropped on its head: the retarded child who develops as a result of the brain damage is numerically the same child as the child who would have existed had the damage not been done. The life of the retarded child and the hypothetical life of the cognitively normal child are two possible histories of one and the same person. The brain damage is, in short, identity-preserving rather than identity-determining with respect to the child.

The idea that damage to the developing fetal brain may be identity-determining when it occurs early in pregnancy but is identity-preserving late in pregnancy is challenged by a consideration of adjacent cases near the middle of the range – specifically, cases on either side of the time that the conscious subject begins to exist. Suppose that I began to exist at approximately time t. If, just prior to t, the fetal organism from which I developed had been damaged or genetically altered so as to cause moderately severe mental retardation, it is plausible to suppose, according to the view that I am defending, that this would have prevented my existence and caused the existence of a different, retarded individual instead. But if the same damage or genetic alteration had occurred shortly after *t*, it seems that this would have caused *me* to be retarded, since I would then have been on hand to suffer the damage. Yet it seems strange to suppose that the damage or alteration would have been identity-determining if it occurred just prior to *t* but identity-preserving if it occurred just after *t*, especially if the interval between the two times would not have been very great.

Perhaps this problem is not as embarrassing as it may seem. Most contemporary theorists are reductionists about personal identity over time. They hold that truths about personal identity over time are wholly analyzable into truths about physical or psychological continuity, or both. According to this view, there may be cases in which claims about personal identity are underdetermined by the facts of physical and psychological continuity. In these cases, identity may be indeterminate, so that claims about identity may be neither true nor false. If reductionism is correct in the case of personal identity over time, it is plausible to assume that it holds in the case of our problem as well – the problem, that is, of personal identity in different possible histories (or, to borrow the more technical term, across possible worlds). If reductionism is right, then it may be that the cases on either side of *t* are cases in which it is indeterminate whether the individual who would have been cognitively impaired would have been me. The problem is not epistemological: it is not that the truth is there but we do not have access to it. Rather, there is no truth of the matter whether I would have existed had the fetal organism from which I developed suffered serious brain damage either shortly before or shortly after *t*.

Here is another problem. Although very extensive alterations or damage to a human embryo may be identity-determining with respect to the child who will later develop from it, it seems intuitively clear that minor alterations are identity-preserving.[4] Imagine, for example, a genetic alteration to an embryo that has only one effect: to cause the resulting person to have blue eyes rather than brown. Surely the blue-eyed person would be numerically the same person as the brown-eyed person. I do not, however, have a criterion for distinguishing between those forms of damage or genetic alteration to a human embryo that are identity-determining with respect to the subsequent person and those that are not. I offer only a few vague suggestions. First, in order for damage or alteration to a developing human organism to be identity-determining with respect to the person whose life the organism supports, it generally must affect the conditions of the person's origin and thus must occur before the person begins to exist in association with the organism. Second, if it is true, as I believe, that we are essentially minds, then damage or alteration to a developing human organism is more likely to be identity-determining if it significantly affects the way that the brain develops and thus is profoundly determinative of the subsequent person's psychological properties and capacities. Third, and finally, if the damage or alteration does not significantly affect the development of the brain, it is more likely to be identity-determining the more radical or extensive the physical changes it causes would be. It seems, for example, that I would have existed had the embryo from which I developed been genetically altered in such a way that it failed to develop a left hand. But it is less plausible to suppose that I would have existed if the embryo had been altered in such a way as to change its sex.

The question whether the damage to the embryo is identity-determining in the Early Prenatal Variant of the Negligent Physician case is of some significance for arguments that are sometimes pressed by the disabilities movement. Spokespersons for the disabled often object to genetic screening programs. Programs that screen for genetic defects prior to conception are intended to allow people to avoid conceiving disabled children and hence are held to express the assumption that disabled people should not exist. Programs that screen for genetic defects in the fetus are intended to allow people to abort defective fetuses and subsequently conceive normal children. They are therefore held to express the assumption that the existence of a normal person is better than the existence of a disabled person. Both of these assumptions are held to be insulting to the dignity of the disabled. Neither of these assumptions seems to be implied, however, by the view that it can be better for a particular person not to have a certain disability than to have it. Thus it seems fully compatible with respect for the dignity of the disabled to object to *screening* programs while acknowledging that it would be desirable to find *cures* for certain disabilities. If, however, certain forms of gene therapy are identity-determining when applied to the human embryo, then these forms of intervention do not constitute cures for disability but rather have the same effect as screening programs: that is, they prevent the existence of a disabled person while causing the existence of a different, normal person instead. In short, certain forms of gene therapy that have been thought to be immune to the objection that they are implicitly demeaning to the disabled may not avoid that objection after all.

For most of my purposes in this essay, it is unnecessary to determine whether the Negligent Physician's action is identity-determining in the two controversial cases, the Second Preconception Variant and the Early Prenatal Variant. I mention these cases primarily in order to speculate about the scope of the problem I wish to consider. It is entirely clear that, on any view of the matter, the Non-Identity Problem does arise in the First Preconception Variant. And it is also intuitively clear as well as metaphysically defensible that it does not arise in the Late Prenatal Variant – that is, that damage or alteration to the late-term fetus does not cause one individual to cease to exist and another to appear in its place. Because I wish to focus on the contrast between these two cases, I will henceforth refer to the First Preconception Variant simply as the *Preconception Case* and the Second Prenatal Variant as the *Prenatal Case.*

Return now to the Preconception Case. It is clear that the Negligent Physician's action is morally objectionable, but *why* is it objectionable? It certainly seems that his negligence has harmed the couple, who have been denied many of the joys of parenthood and who instead have the often anguishing burden of caring for a relatively unresponsive and highly dependent child. In the law they would be warranted in bringing a "wrongful birth" suit against the physician, in which they as plaintiffs would claim damages for the harms his negligence has caused them.

Some, indeed, argue that the fact that the Negligent Physician's action was worse for the parents provides an exhaustive explanation of the wrongness of his conduct. Once it is noted that he has seriously harmed the parents, there is nothing more to be said.[5] This, however, seems wrong. To understand why, imagine a couple, both of whom are specialists in genetic engineering, who desire to have a child with moderately severe mental retardation (perhaps because they would prefer a child who would never desire or be able to live independently of them). Thus, rather than conceiving a child now in the normal way, they extract a single sperm from the male, genetically alter it, combine it *in vitro* with an egg extracted from the woman, and implant the zygote in the woman's womb, with the consequence that she later gives birth to a cognitively disabled child. Assume that both gametes from which this child developed are different from those that would have combined had they conceived a child in the normal way, and that the retarded child is therefore uncontroversially a different individual from the child they would otherwise have had. As in the Preconception Case, their action is not worse for the child that is born (assuming that its life is worth living). Nor have they been harmed, for they have achieved precisely the result they wanted. Most of us, however, strongly sense that what they have done is morally objectionable.

There is, indeed, some reason to question whether, even in the Preconception Case, the Negligent Physician's action is actually harmful to the parents. In many cases at least, the parents of cognitively disabled children come to love their child and thus find it difficult to wish that that child had never existed and that they had had a different, normal child instead. (In most cases, of course, the alternative that parents wistfully envisage is one in which their retarded child is born without disability. Being unaware of the Non-Identity Problem, they are unaware that this outcome was not among the possibilities.) If, however, the parents in the Preconception Case cannot sincerely wish that they had had a different child, then at the very least some argument is required to show that the physician's action has harmed them.[6]

I will not press this point but will grant that one reason why the physician's negligence is objectionable is that it harmed the parents. As I noted, however, there seems to be more to it than this. Most of us believe that, quite independently of the impact of the physician's action on the parents, the retarded child ought not to have been caused to exist and that, given that he *has* been wrongfully caused to exist, the physician should be required to pay damages, both to compensate the parents for the injury done to them and, insofar as possible, to enhance the life of the child. If pressed to defend these beliefs, our impulse is to claim that the physician's action was harmful to the child. But this response seems precluded by the recognition that, because of the Non-Identity Problem, the physician's action was not worse for the child.

Suppose that, in the Preconception Case, the retarded child's life would not be worth living. Changing this feature brings the case into conformity with the typical profile of "wrongful life" cases in the law.[7] These cases have created considerable confusion, in part because even when the child plaintiff's claim is that her life is not worth living, it seems impossible to sustain the charge that the act that caused her to exist was *worse* for her. This seems true as a matter of logic, since the claim that being caused to exist is worse for the child implies that the alternative would have been *better* for the child. But the alternative is for the child never to exist, in which case there is never any subject for whom anything could be good or bad, better or worse.

Some have thought that there is no more problem here than there is in claiming, contrary to Epicurus's argument, that continuing to exist can be better for a person than ceasing to exist. For that too may seem to require a comparison between existence and nonexistence. But this is a mistake; one can make the choice between continuing to exist and ceasing to exist by simply comparing two possible *lives* – a longer one and a shorter one – and asking which would be the better life. This kind of solution is not available when the choice is between life and total nonexistence rather than between continued life and posthumous nonexistence.

This problem is not insuperable, at least where morality is concerned. We can judge that it would be wrong to cause a person to exist on the ground that her life would be noncomparatively *bad,* even if it would not be *worse* than never to exist.[8] Such a life might be bad if, for example, its bad features outweighed the good. According to this view, one's reason not to cause a person to exist with a life that would not be worth living has the following peculiar character. It is a reason not to do what would be bad for an actual person (since the person would obviously be actual when she suffered the bad effect of one's act), though, if one acts on the reason, there is then no actual person whom one has spared from anything bad.

Although we can thus explain why it may be morally wrong to cause a person to exist whose life would not be worth living, there remain serious obstacles to recognizing wrongful life suits in the law. One concerns the measurement of damages due the plaintiff. The standard measure in tort law – make the plaintiff as well off as he or she would have been had the tortious act not been done – evidently cannot be applied, since, had the alleged tort not been committed, the plaintiff would never have existed. In many cases, moreover, the plaintiff's life is not worth living because of genetic defects that cannot be remedied. In these cases, the life *cannot* be made worth living, and an award of damages would be of no benefit to the plaintiff, whose suffering can be ended only by euthanasia. This would be awkward for the law to recognize, since it does not countenance euthanasia.

In this essay I will put these cases aside and focus instead on cases, such as the Preconception Case, in which a child is caused to exist with a handicap but nevertheless seems to have a life that is worth living. These too may be considered "wrongful life" cases, at least in an extended sense, because they are cases in which we think that, for one reason or another, the child ought not to have been caused to exist. Moreover, the same problem arises in these cases: How can it be wrong to cause the child to exist, if this is not worse for the child? The puzzle goes deeper in these cases, however, because the problem is not merely that the comparison required by the logic of the term "worse" cannot be made. As I noted, in the standard cases of wrongful life in which the child's life is not worth living, the logical problem can be circumvented by noting that even if it is not *worse* for the child to be caused to exist, it is *bad* for it. But in cases in which the child's life is worth living, it is not only not worse for the child to be caused to exist but it is not bad for it either, since the good aspects of its life seem to outweigh the bad. Indeed, if it is bad for a child to be caused to exist with a life that is not worth living, then it seems that, by parity of reasoning, it should be good for a child to be caused to exist with a life that is worth living. If that is right, then the challenge is to explain why it is objectionable in such cases as the Preconception Case to cause a child to exist when this is in fact *good* for the child. Are we reduced, after all, to appealing only to the effects on the parents?

II. Threats to Common Sense Beliefs

The Non-Identity Problem threatens a number of common sense moral beliefs. Certainly our initial response to the Preconception Case is that the Negligent Physician owes compensation not just to the parents but also to the child. And, as I noted earlier, we retain an obscure sense that the physician owes a debt to the child even when we understand that, because of the Non-Identity Problem, his action was not worse for the child and may even have been good for the child. Can this intuition be defended?

We will return to the question of the Negligent Physician's moral liability later. There is an even more serious problem – a problem with broad implications for moral theory – that should be introduced now. It can be seen, perhaps, in a comparison of the Preconception Case and the Prenatal Case. In both cases the Negligent Physician fails in his professional responsibilities, and in both cases his negligence results in the birth of a retarded child. The difference is that in the Prenatal Case this is the same child who would have existed had the physician not been negligent, whereas in the Preconception Case it is a different child. Does this difference make a *moral* difference? Many of us, when considering the two cases, fail to find that what happens in the Prenatal Case is worse.

The relevant point may be easier to appreciate in an example devised by Parfit. It differs from my Negligent Physician cases in three salient respects: it involves allowing disabilities to occur rather than causing them, it does not involve negligence or evident wrongdoing, and the stakes are higher, because the number of people involved is greater.

The Medical Programs

> There are two rare conditions, *J* and *K*, which cannot be detected without special tests. If a pregnant woman has Condition J, this will cause the child she is carrying to have a certain handicap. A simple treatment would prevent this effect. If a woman has Condition K when she conceives a child, this will cause the child to have the same particular handicap. Condition K cannot be treated, but always disappears within two months. Suppose next that we have planned two medical programmes, but there are funds for only one, so one must be cancelled. In the first programme, millions of women would be tested during pregnancy. Those found to have Condition J would be treated. In the second programme, millions of women would be tested when they intend to try to become pregnant. Those found to have Condition K would be warned to postpone conception for at least two months, after which this incurable condition will have disappeared. Suppose finally that we can predict that these two programmes would achieve results in as many cases. If there is Pregnancy Testing, 1,000 children a year would be born normal rather than handicapped. If there is Preconception Testing, there would each year be born 1,000 normal children rather than . . . 1,000 different, handicapped children.[9]

Is there a moral reason to cancel one program rather than the other? Both programs have equivalent effects on parents. So the difference is this. If Pregnancy Testing is canceled, 1,000 children will be born handicapped each year who would otherwise have been normal. Cancelation of Pregnancy Testing would be worse for those children. If Preconception Testing is canceled, 1,000 children will also be born handicapped each year. But these children would never have existed if there had been Preconception Testing; therefore the cancelation of Preconception Testing would not be worse for them.

Does this difference between the programs make it worse to cancel Pregnancy Testing? Parfit believes that both programs are equally worthwhile and that it makes no moral difference which is canceled. I will assume that this judgment, which he calls the *No-Difference View,* is correct. The relevant bad effect of canceling Pregnancy Testing – that there would be 1,000 handicapped children per year who would otherwise have been normal – is no worse than the corresponding bad effect of canceling Preconception Testing – that there would be 1,000 handicapped children per year rather than an equal number of different children who would have been normal. (Parfit notes, plausibly, that if Preconception Testing would detect more cases, it would be preferable to retain it rather than Pregnancy Testing.) Parfit claims, moreover, that we have the *same reason* not to cancel Pregnancy Testing that we have not to cancel Preconception Testing.[10] Since the reason not to cancel Preconception Testing cannot be that this would be worse for the children who would be born handicapped, he therefore concludes that the fact that the cancelation of Pregnancy Testing is worse for the children affected cannot be part of the explanation of why the cancelation would be bad. He then generalizes the No-Difference View, claiming, in effect, that the fact that an effect is *worse for people,* or bad *for them,* is never part of the fundamental explanation of why the effect is bad. The area of morality "concerned with beneficence and human well-being," he writes, "cannot be explained in person-affecting terms."[11] It must instead be explained in *impersonal* terms.

The latter inference has broad-ranging implications for moral theory. I will explore these in some detail in section IV; for the moment I will illustrate the significance of Parfit's claim by mentioning one implication that is of particular interest to me. I mentioned earlier my belief that each of us began to exist only when the brain of his or her physical organism developed the capacity to generate consciousness and mental activity. This understanding of personal identity, if correct, provides the basis for what seems to be a plausible argument for the permissibility of early abortion. For, according to this view, an early abortion does not kill one of us but instead merely prevents one of us from coming into existence. The organism that is killed is not numerically identical with the later person and thus is not deprived of the later life that is precluded. Early abortion, then, is morally comparable to contraception: there need be no one for whom it is worse. The power of this view is illustrated by its ability to explain a common but otherwise puzzling judgment: namely, that it is less objectionable to *kill* a perfectly healthy early fetus than it is to injure or damage it in a comparatively minor way, for example, a way that causes the subsequent person to have a minor physical disability. The explanation is that, provided that the abortion is desired by the parents, killing the fetus is not worse for anyone, while damaging the fetus harms the person to whose existence the fetus subsequently gives rise.[12] In short, the instance of prenatal injury has a victim whereas early abortion does not.

According to the No-Difference View, however, that an act is bad or worse *for someone* is no part of the explanation of why its effects are bad; accordingly, an act may have a bad effect, and thus be seriously morally objectionable, even if there is no one for whom it is worse or bad in any respect (for example, the cancelation of Preconception Testing would be bad even if it were not bad for the parents). Hence, if Parfit is right, the fact that prenatal injury is worse for the future child does not explain why it is bad to injure a fetus; nor can one infer, from the claim that an early abortion is worse for no one, that it is not bad, for it might be bad impersonally.[13] The No-Difference View thus appears to undermine this otherwise powerful argument for the permissibility of early abortion.

III. Approaches That Identify a Victim

Some writers have sought to address the threats that the Non-Identity Problem poses to common sense beliefs by arguing that even in such cases as the Preconception Case, a child born with a disability is adversely affected by the act that causes the disability, even if its life is worth living and it would never have existed had the act not been done. Imagine, for example, that yet another Negligent Physician gives a woman who is having trouble conceiving a child an inadequately tested fertility drug that both allows her to conceive a child and causes the child to suffer from some dreadful disease later in life. It seems reasonable to say that the physician's act was the cause of the child's contracting the disease and that, in causing the terrible disease, the act *harmed* the child – even though it was not, on balance, worse for the child that the act was done. And, according to one proponent of this approach, "that an agent is morally accountable for someone's suffering a harm, by virtue of having performed a certain action, seems a perfectly intelligible 'person-affecting' explanation [of] why his action is objectionable."[14]

This approach has to be extended somewhat if it is to be applied to cases such as the Preconception Case. For, although contracting a disease is a discrete event that involves the worsening of a prior condition, congenital mental retardation is an inherent, constitutive aspect of a person's nature, not a contingent addition to his life. It is less easy, therefore, to regard the fact that the child in the Preconception Case is retarded as a *harm*. Still, we may invoke Joel Feinberg's notion of a "harmed condition" in order to assimilate this case into the paradigm to which the vocabulary of harm is applicable. A harmed condition is "a condition that has adverse effects on [an individual's] whole network of interests" and is "the product of a prior act of harming."[15] Congenital retardation seems to doom many of the retarded individual's interests to frustration. And we may, if only for the sake of argument, grant that the Negligent Physician's action in the Preconception Case counts as an act of harming. The objection, then, to the physician's action is that it causes the child to exist in a harmed condition. The child is therefore appropriately seen as the victim of this action.

It is not clear whether this approach, which may be called the *harm-based approach,* presupposes that it can be a harm to be *caused to exist* in a harmed condition. Some proponents of the harm-based approach might wish to avoid being committed to the claim that to be caused to exist can be either good or bad for a person. They will therefore want to claim that the Negligent Physician harms the retarded child not by contributing to causing his existence but instead by causing him to be cognitively disabled. It is not obvious, however, that this distinction is tenable, since *this* child can exist only if he is disabled, and the actual effect of the Negligent Physician's action is simply to cause this child to exist rather than another child. But I will put this problem aside and assume for the sake of argument that the Negligent Physician's action causes the child's harmed condition – namely, its cognitive disability.

The harm-based approach raises many questions. What, for example, counts as a harmed condition? Is physical unattractiveness or low IQ a harmed condition? Presumably those who argue for this approach wish to avoid the implication that those whose genes make it likely that their offspring would be physically unattractive or have a low IQ would harm their children by causing them to exist (and therefore presumably ought not to have children). There are several options. One would be to equip the notion of a harmed condition with a threshold that would place ordinary ugliness or low intelligence below the threshold but would locate moderately severe mental retardation above it. But in restricting the harm-based approach to cases involving only relatively serious conditions, this revision leaves us without a response in a wide range of cases in which the Non-Identity Problem arises. Consider, for example, a further variant of the Preconception Case in which a couple seek screening for a genetic defect that causes one's child to have an IQ that is roughly 60 points lower than it would otherwise be. As a result of the physician's negligence, they have a child with an IQ of 90. If the defect had been detected, the man's sperm would have been altered to correct the defect, and they would have conceived a different child with an IQ of 150. Surely we want to condemn the physician's negligence in this variant on substantially the same ground on which we condemn it in the original Preconception Case. But, on the assumption that an IQ of 90 counts as only ordinary low intelligence, the Negligent Physician has not caused the child in this variant to exist in a harmed condition. So, when it incorporates the stipulated threshold, the harm-based approach lacks the resources to explain how the physician's action has had any bad effect other than the effect on the couple.

Another option is to try to distinguish among the various cases on the basis of differences in causal responsibility. It can be argued, for example, of parents who have a child that is predictably physically unattractive or of low intelligence that, although they are responsible for the child's existence, the fact that the child is unattractive or unintelligent is not attributable to the act that caused the child to exist. There is, in fact, *no* act that causes the child to be unattractive or unintelligent; this is just the way the child is. Thus parents who have an unattractive or unintelligent child do not thereby harm the child. By contrast, consider again the Negligent Physician who administers an untested fertility drug that enables a child to be conceived but also causes the child to develop a serious disease later in life. In this case one and the same act is both a causally necessary condition of the child's existence and the cause of the disease. This act harms the child, though it is not worse for him.

The problem with this response is that it does not seem to divide the cases in the desired manner. Reconsider the original Preconception Case. Here the Negligent Physician's action is a causally necessary condition of the retarded child's existence, but it does not seem to be the cause of the retardation, any more than the act of conceiving a predictably ugly child is the cause of the child's ugliness. In each case, that is just the way the child is. So any conception of causal responsibility that allows us to deny that the parents of an ugly child harm the child by causing him to exist seems also to imply that the Negligent Physician in the original Preconception Case does not harm the retarded child. Yet the desire to show that the physician *does* harm the child is precisely what motivates people to accept the harm-based approach.

Assume, then, that the harm-based approach accepts that to cause someone to exist with a congenital genetic defect is to harm that person if the defect constitutes or inevitably causes a harmed condition. In that case, it seems that we must revert to the option of distinguishing between congenital conditions that count as harmed conditions and those that are insufficiently serious, or perhaps sufficiently widespread or normal, not to count as harmed conditions. (Otherwise the same objection to causing the retarded child to exist in the Preconception Case will apply in *all* cases of causing people to exist, since *everyone* has congenital characteristics that adversely affect their interests – for example, I have a constellation of interests having to do with achieving great things in philosophy but am thwarted by deficiencies in native intelligence.)[16] As I noted earlier, this means that the harm-based approach is at most only a partial solution to the Non-Identity Problem, but even a partial solution may constitute progress.

There remains, however, a further problem. In the Preconception Case, and the other cases with which we are concerned, the child whose existence inevitably involves a harmed condition nevertheless has a life that is worth living. The life is worth living because the goods it contains together outweigh the badness of the harmed condition and its effects within the victim's life. Why cannot we say that the act that harmed the child by causing him to have a harmed condition was not bad because the harmed condition is compensated for by the goods of life that the child would not have had if the act had not been performed? There are many instances in which it is best to harm a person for the sake of the compensating benefits that the harmful act brings to that same person – for example, painful or disfiguring medical procedures that are necessary to save a life. If it is not bad, overall, to cause these harms, why is it bad for the Negligent Physician to cause the harm he causes, which is similarly outweighed? (It might be argued that what makes medical procedures that cause harm permissible is the patient's consent; thus the relevant difference between these cases and the Preconception Case is that in the latter the retarded child cannot consent to accept his retardation as the cost of having the compensating goods of life. But it is easy to imagine cases in which it is best to perform a disfiguring or otherwise harmful operation to save a person's life even when the person cannot consent – for example, because he is unconscious at the time that the decision to operate must be made.)

The problem here is more serious than it may initially seem. In any case in which a child is caused to exist there is a finite probability that the child will have a congenital defect that will constitute or inevitably cause a harmed condition. If, in cases of causing a person to exist, a harmed condition cannot be outweighed by the goods that the life will contain – in the sense that it remains worse, other things being equal, to cause the child to exist – then it is difficult to see how the *probability* of a congenital harmed condition can be outweighed by the probability that the life will also contain compensating goods.[17] But, if the probability that a child will have a congenital harmed condition cannot be outweighed by the probability of compensating goods, then it seems that, at least where *expected* effects are concerned and when other things are equal, it is worse to have a child than not to have a child.

One response to this objection is to claim that, in the Preconception Case, the Negligent Physician is responsible for the harmed condition (i.e., cognitive disability) but not for any of the goods that the retarded child's life contains. The goods are attributable to other causes. On this view, there are no benefits attributable to the Negligent Physician's action that are capable of compensating the child for the harm that the action has caused. This response, however, seems untenable. If the Negligent Physician is responsible for the retardation because it is an inherent aspect of the child's nature and is therefore attributable to those causal factors that produced *that* child with *that* nature, then he should be equally responsible for those inherent aspects of the child's nature that are good or beneficial for the child. If it makes sense (as it may not: see note 16) to say that the retardation adversely affects the child's interests, then it should also make sense to say that the good inherent aspects of the child's nature positively affect the child's interests. Finally, if to cause the retardation is to cause a harm (or a harmed condition), then to cause the good aspects of the child's nature should be to cause benefits (or beneficial conditions). If all this is right, then the Negligent Physician's action not only harms but also benefits the child – not necessarily by causing the child to exist but by causing the child's life to contain certain goods. And, since the child's life is worth living, it is reasonable to suppose that the benefits outweigh the harms.

A second response to the objection is to claim that, in the case of ordinary procreation, the risk of harming the child by causing him to have a congenital harmed condition is outweighed not by any probable compensating goods that the child's life might contain but instead by the expected benefits to the parents (and perhaps others in the society) of having the child. It might be thought that this response prevents us from objecting if a couple (such as the couple in my example in section I) deliberately conceive a child with a congenital harmed condition rather than a normal child. But this worry can be dispelled by noting that parental interests may be sufficiently important to outweigh a *slight* risk of causing a harmed condition without being important enough to outweigh a *high* risk of causing a harmed condition, which there would presumably be if the parents *intended* to cause such a condition. Still, the appeal to parental interests cannot rescue the harm-based approach. For this appeal in effect grants the objection that there is always a presumption against procreation based on the risk of causing a congenital harmed condition – a risk that cannot be offset by the probability of compensating benefits within the life. But it is hard to believe that procreation is, in ordinary conditions, an activity that requires the interests of the prospective parents or of other preexisting persons to tip the balance in favor of permissibility. In ordinary circumstances, there simply is no *prima facie* objection to or presumption against procreation – or, rather, if there is such a presumption, it derives from current conditions of overpopulation rather than from the risk of causing a congenital harmed condition.

The harm-based approach fails because it has no explanation of why an act that is assumed to cause a congenital harmed condition ought not to be done even when it also causes compensating benefits. There is, however, an alternative approach of the same sort – one that identifies a victim – that offers such an explanation. According to this approach, which we may call the *rights-based approach,* there are certain harmed conditions that are sufficiently serious that to cause them constitutes a violation of the victim's rights.[18] Assume that, according to this view, the Negligent Physician in the Preconception Case violates one of the retarded child's rights. (Again, this is problematic. It is not obvious exactly what right is supposed to be violated or that the requisite causal connections obtain between the Negligent Physician's action and the relevant aspect of the child's condition.[19] But waive these difficulties.) Although the Negligent Physician's action was not worse, or bad on balance, for the child, since the harm it caused is outweighed by compensating goods, that is not a sufficient justification for the action. For, even if an act is on balance beneficial to a person, or on balance promotes the person's well-being or good, that is in general not a justification for the act if the act also violates the person's rights. Our rights protect us even from certain well-meaning forms of action aimed at our own good. Thus the central objection to the harm-based approach – that it cannot explain why the Negligent Physician's action is wrong if the harm it causes is outweighed by compensating benefits – is met by the rights-based approach.

But the rights-based approach faces other objections. Imagine a disability – *condition X* – that is not so bad as to make life not worth living but is sufficiently serious that to cause someone to exist with condition X would be, according to the rights-based approach, to violate that person's rights. One objection to the rights-based approach is that, if it is wrong to cause someone to exist with condition X, then it should also be wrong to save someone's life if the only means of doing so would also cause the person to have condition X and it is not possible to obtain the person's consent to being saved in this manner. Suppose, for example, that a late-term fetus (which we may assume would be numerically identical with the person into whom it would develop) contracts a disease that requires a certain treatment in order to survive but that the treatment inevitably causes condition X. Whether or not there is a strong moral reason to save the fetus for its own sake, it seems intuitively clear that it would not be *wrong* to treat the fetus, thereby saving its life. But saving it involves causing it to have condition X and thus, apparently, violates its rights. If it is not permissible to violate a right on the ground that the act that violates the right on balance benefits the right-bearer, then it seems that the rights-based approach implies that it *would* be wrong to save the fetus.

The proponent of the rights-based view may reply that this is a case involving a conflict of rights. Although the fetus has a right not to be caused to have condition X, it also has a right to be saved.[20] And in this case the right to be saved, being more important, overrides the right not to be caused to have condition X. This reply assumes, however, that priority between the two rights is determined by the comparative strengths of the interests they protect. But the strength of a right does not vary proportionately with the strength of the interest it protects (assuming that it protects an interest at all). The importance of any interest it might protect is only one of a number of factors that contributes to determining the strength of a right. Among the more important determinants is whether the right is positive or negative. The right to life, or the right not to be killed, and the right to be saved both protect the same interest: namely, the interest in continuing to live or in avoiding death. But the right not to be killed is a negative right and is thus held, by theorists of rights, to be considerably stronger, other things being equal, than the right to be saved. But if negative rights are in general considerably stronger than corresponding positive rights, then it is at least arguable that the negative right not to be caused to be disabled is stronger, or more stringent, than the positive right to be saved.

Let us suppose, however, if only for the sake of argument, that it is true that the late-term fetus's right to be saved overrides its right not to be caused to have condition X, so that the rights-based approach does not imply that it would be wrong to save the fetus. Now consider a parallel case involving an *early-term* fetus. The fetus has a disease that will rapidly be fatal unless it is treated, but the treatment causes condition X.[21] Assume that the claim that I noted earlier is correct – namely, that individuals such as you and I do not begin to exist until our organisms acquire the capacity to support consciousness and mental activity. If that is right, then an early-term fetus does not support the existence of an individual of the sort that you and I essentially are. There is no one there to have a right to life or a right to be saved. Hence, according to the rights-based approach, there is a strong reason *not* to treat the fetus, since treating it would violate the right of the later person not to be caused to have condition X, but no countervailing rights-based reason to treat it. The rights-based approach therefore implies that it would be *wrong,* other things being equal, to treat the fetus.

This seems an implausible result. But what is even more implausible is that the rights-based approach distinguishes morally between the case of the late-term fetus and the case of the early-term fetus, claiming that one may treat the former but not the latter. As I indicated, the approach *may* imply that it is wrong to treat the late-term fetus as well. If so, the approach would avoid the embarrassment of treating the two cases asymmetrically. But the claim that it is wrong to treat the late-term fetus is itself quite implausible. There is, of course, a way around the dilemma, which is to reject the view that we do not begin to exist until the fetal organism develops the capacity to support consciousness. If we begin to exist when the human organism begins to exist, shortly after conception, then it may be defensible to claim that in both cases the fetus has a right to be saved and that this makes it permissible to treat the fetus, despite the fact that doing so infringes its right not to be caused to be disabled. But the supposition that even early fetuses have a right to be saved from death is quite a radical view, with implications for abortion and other issues that many will be reluctant to accept.

If I am right about the metaphysics, the case of the early-term fetus involves a choice between causing a child to exist with a disability and allowing it to be the case that the child fails to come into existence. It is *not* a feature of the case that, if the early-term fetus is untreated, a different, normal child (i.e., without either the disease or condition X) will be caused to exist instead. Cases of this sort are helpful in testing the plausibility of the harm-based and rights-based approaches. For these approaches hold that what is fundamentally objectionable about causing a person to exist with a congenital disability (i.e., one that constitutes a harmed condition or necessarily causes a right to remain unfulfilled) is found in the inherent condition of the person, not in anything extrinsic to the person's life. Thus their plausibility can best be tested by reference to cases in which the only conceivable objectionable features are intrinsic to the life of a person caused to exist with a disability. In other cases, such as the Preconception Case, in which a person is caused to exist with a disability *and* there was the alternative of causing a normal child to exist instead, these approaches may yield the intuitively correct judgment but for the wrong reason. For it may be that the comparative dimension to the case – namely, that the Negligent Physician causes a disabled child to exist *rather than* a normal child – is an essential part of the explanation of why it is objectionable to cause the disabled child to exist.

To test the approaches that identify a victim, we should therefore consider cases that lack this comparative dimension. Imagine, then, a situation in which *any* child one might cause to exist would have a congenital harmed condition, or a right that would necessarily remain unfulfilled. It is not possible, in the circumstances, to cause a normal child to exist instead. Would it be wrong for a couple who wish to have a child to conceive a child in these circumstances? Most people believe that, provided that the child's life would be worth living and that the motives of those who would cause the child to exist would not be discreditable, it would not be worse, or bad, or wrong (other things being equal) to cause the child to exist. This is not just an intuition. The reason that it is not bad to cause the child to exist is, as I suggested in discussing the harm-based approach, that the goods that the child's life contains compensate for the presence of the harmed condition, without which the child would not exist. Thus the fact that the harm-based and rights-based approaches imply that it *would* be wrong to cause the child to exist constitutes a serious objection to them.[22]

What we need is an account that explains why it is objectionable to cause a disabled child to exist when it would be possible to cause a normal child to exist instead (as in the Preconception Case) but accepts that it is not bad, and is thus permissible if other things are equal, to cause a child to exist with the same disability when any child one might cause to exist would necessarily have that disability. It is difficult to find an approach of the victim-based type that does both these things, since these approaches do not locate the objection to causing a disabled child to exist in factors that are comparative or in any way extrinsic to the condition of the child. There is, however, one approach of this sort that has a certain amount of promise. This account invokes the notion of a *restricted life* – a notion introduced by Kavka in his influential and important essay on the Non-Identity Problem.[23] Kavka defines a restricted life as "one that is significantly deficient in one or more of the major respects that generally make human lives valuable and worth living." He goes on to note, however, that "restricted lives typically will be worth living, on the whole, for those who live them."[24] I will use Kavka's suggestive term "restricted life" in a slightly different way to refer to a life that is objectively not worth living but is subjectively tolerable, and may indeed be overall enjoyable to the individual whose life it is. Such a life is, I will say, subjectively worth living but objectively not worth living. (I put aside the question whether there could be a life that was objectively worth living but subjectively not worth living.) As an example, consider the life of Adolf Hitler. There is reason to believe that Hitler was, during most of his adulthood, abundantly satisfied with his life. Judged by the usual standards, he was a reasonably happy man. His life was therefore subjectively worth living: *he* found it well worth living. But was his life *objectively* worth living? Was this in reality a good life for him to have – better, at least, than no life at all? It is plausible, I think, to claim that Hitler's adult life was a *dreadful* life – not just in its effects on others but dreadful *for him* (even though he himself failed to recognize this).[25] This is not the kind of life that it could be good for anyone to have. It would have been better *for Hitler* if he had died in his twenties.[26]

How does the notion of a restricted life help with the Non-Identity Problem? Assume that the retarded child in the Preconception Case has a restricted life. This explains why it was bad that the Negligent Physician's action resulted in the child's existence: the child's life is not worth living; it is objectively bad *for the child* to exist with that sort of life. If the child's life is genuinely restricted, then the goods that it contains do not, on balance, compensate for the child's harmed condition. This also supports the claim that the Negligent Physician owes the child compensation. For the physician's negligence was culpable and had a victim: the child, for whom the physician's action was bad.

This explanation is, however, essentially noncomparative: it does not mention the alternative possible outcome in which a normal child would have existed. It focuses entirely on the intrinsic features of the retarded child's life. How, then, can it explain the permissibility of causing a child with a life like this to exist when it would not be possible to cause a normal child to exist instead? This approach must, it seems, claim that there is a serious *prima facie* reason not to have such a child – namely, that it would be objectively bad for the child. Yet, although a life that is objectively not worth living is bad, it is not nearly so bad if it is subjectively worth living as it would be if it were also subjectively not worth living. For a life that is objectively not worth living but is nevertheless subjectively worth living is not experienced as a burden by the person whose life it is. Thus the moral presumption against causing a person to exist with a restricted life may be overridden by countervailing considerations that are considerably weaker than those that would be required to override the much stronger presumption against causing a person to exist with a life that would be both subjectively and objectively not worth living. Assuming, then, that the desire to have a child has a certain normative force (e.g., that it is supported by a right of procreation), it might be that the desire of a couple to have a child could be sufficient to outweigh the harm they would do to the child by causing it to exist with a restricted life. But this same desire would be insufficient to justify causing a child to exist with a restricted life when it would be possible to have a normal child instead. For the reasonable desire to have a child could be satisfied by having the normal child. There would have to be some *other* reason to justify doing what would cause a child with a restricted life to exist rather than a normal child. And in the ordinary circumstances of life it is doubtful that there could be a reason sufficiently strong to justify the harm to a child with a restricted life.

Even when it would be permissible for a couple to cause a child to exist with a restricted life, the child would have a claim to compensation comparable in force to that which the retarded child has against the Negligent Physician in the Preconception Case. In practice this means that a couple that chose to have a child with a restricted life would be morally required to make sacrifices for the child that would not be part of the normal burden of child-rearing. This, however, seems entirely plausible. Whether such parents would owe as much as the Negligent Physician depends on whether the fact that he is at fault compounds his liability.

The appeal to the notion of a restricted life thus has a certain promise. But it nevertheless faces serious objections. It may be objected, for example, that the killing of people judged to have restricted lives could be justified as euthanasia. This, however, is not a serious concern. For the morality of killing is not governed solely by considerations of harm and benefit. Even though there is a sense in which it would be better for a person with a restricted life to die rather than continue to live, it certainly does not follow that it would be permissible to kill that person against his or her will. It has to be conceded, however, that the notion of a restricted life is an exceedingly dangerous one, for it asserts the possibility that others could know that one's life was not worth living even if one were oneself convinced that it was worth living. As a matter of principle this in fact seems to be right: it is possible to believe that one's life is worth living when in fact it is not. But surely this occurs very rarely, and in most cases one's judgment about whether one's own life is worth living is, if not authoritative, then at least so nearly infallible that it would be the height of presumption for another person to dispute it.

This observation reveals the central weakness of the appeal to the notion of a restricted life – that there are scarcely any plausible instances of lives of this sort.[27] Perhaps the most plausible examples are of people whose lives, though enjoyable, are utterly morally debased. But these cases are largely irrelevant to the morality of causing people to exist because of the impossibility, at least at present, of predicting before a life begins that it will be morally degraded. Among predictable conditions, it is difficult to identify *any* that clearly make a life objectively not worth living without making it subjectively not worth living as well. Perhaps the most plausible candidate is severe congenital cognitive incapacity. Loren Lomasky contends that, "were one condemned . . . to remain a child throughout one's existence, or to grow in bulk without simultaneously growing in the capacity to conceptualize ends and to act for their sake, it would be a personal misfortune of the utmost gravity."[28] The idea that the severely retarded are appropriately viewed as permanently infantile suggests that a life in this condition may be objectively degraded or unworthy, even if it is subjectively tolerable. It is, however, difficult to reconcile this judgment with the commonly accepted assumption that the lives of nonhuman animals with comparable cognitive capacities may be worth living and are certainly not objectively degraded simply because they are not guided by the exercise of our higher cognitive capacities.[29]

The Non-Identity Problem arises in a large number of cases. Since it is difficult to think of a single case in which a predictable condition causes a person to have a restricted life, it is safe to conclude that the notion of a restricted life cannot help us solve this problem.[30]

IV. The Impersonal Comparative Approach

Other writers have discussed cases with the same structure as the Preconception Case under the heading of "wrongful life." Some have contended that the fundamental objection in these cases to causing a child to exist with a disability is that this gratuitously increases the amount of evil, or that which is bad, that the world contains. Joel Feinberg, for example, claims that the agent in a case such as the Preconception Case "must be blamed for wantonly introducing a certain evil into the world, not for harming, or for violating the rights of, a person." He then goes on to elucidate the nature of the evil when he observes that one could make the willful creation of a disabled child a criminal act, on the ground that "the prevention of unnecessary suffering is a legitimate reason for a criminal prohibition."[31] These remarks are echoed by John Harris, who writes: "What then is the wrong of wrongful life? It can be wrong to create an individual in a harmed condition even where the individual is benefited thereby. The wrong will be the wrong of bringing avoidable suffering into the world, of choosing deliberately to increase unnecessarily the amount of harm or suffering in the world."[32]

To say that some instance of suffering is "unnecessary" or "avoidable" is to imply that it is wrong to cause that suffering. But what exactly does it mean to say that suffering is unnecessary or avoidable? In one sense, it means simply that the suffering could have been avoided. But that is true of *all* human suffering, since it has always been possible for people simply to stop procreating. Thus those unguarded forms of Negative Utilitarianism that call simply for the minimization of suffering have notoriously been accused of implying that it is wrong ever to cause a sentient being to exist. But this is surely not the sense of "unnecessary" intended by Feinberg and Harris. The normal implication of the claim that some instance of suffering is unnecessary is that the suffering is not instrumental to or a necessary accompaniment of some greater good for the person who experiences the suffering. Thus suffering that is *not* unnecessary is suffering that has to occur if certain compensating goods are to be had by the sufferer. In this sense, the foreseeable suffering that any life that is worth living will inevitably contain is not unnecessary. But then this applies equally to the foreseeable suffering within the lives of the congenitally disabled, provided that their lives would be worth living. Their suffering is not unnecessary in this second sense.

Feinberg and Harris must therefore be invoking a third sense in which suffering may be unnecessary. Consider again the Preconception Case. Whatever suffering the child experiences as a result of the retardation is not unnecessary for the compensating goods of *that* life. But it is unnecessary for goods of the same type – indeed a greater quantity of those goods – within a *different* life that might have been caused to occur instead. The objection urged by Feinberg and Harris therefore takes an impersonal, comparative form. For it is not concerned with effects for better or worse on any particular individual but with the comparison between the possible effects on one possible individual with those on another. The objection to causing the retarded child to exist is that it was possible to cause a *different* child to exist whose life would have contained at least as much good but less of what is bad – in particular, less overall suffering. It is in this impersonal sense that the retarded child's suffering is unnecessary.

A more precise articulation of this sort of approach has been formulated by Parfit in the following principle: "If in either of two possible outcomes the same number of people would ever live, it would be worse if those who live are worse off, or have a lower quality of life, than those who would have lived."[33] Call this the *Impersonal Comparative Principle*. Notice that it is explicitly restricted to what Parfit calls "Same-Number Choices" – that is, cases in which the same number of people would exist in all the possible outcomes of a choice between acts. Note furthermore that, being impersonal, the Impersonal Comparative Principle is consistent with the No-Difference View, which asserts, in effect, that the correct principle of beneficence must take a fully impersonal form. Finally, notice that this principle presupposes that possible people count morally and must be taken into account in moral deliberation.

The Impersonal Comparative Principle has a distinct advantage. It does seem, intuitively, that the morality of causing a disabled child to exist is affected by whether or not it would be possible to cause a normal child to exist instead. The Impersonal Comparative Principle captures this. Thus it condemns the Negligent Physician's action in the Preconception Case because the normal child who might have existed would have been better off than the retarded child is. But it does not condemn a couple for having a child with the same disability, provided that the child's life is worth living and that any child they might have would also have that disability. It does not condemn such a couple because it has *no* implications for their choice. Their choice is between having a disabled child and having no child. It is therefore not a Same-Number Choice but what Parfit calls a "Different-Number Choice" – that is, a case in which different numbers of people would exist in some of the possible outcomes of a choice between acts.

Does the Impersonal Comparative Principle support the intuition that the Negligent Physician in the Preconception Case owes compensation to the retarded child? Here is an argument for the claim that it does. According to the Impersonal Comparative Principle, the physician has a moral reason *ex ante* to ensure that a normal child exists rather than a disabled child. Indeed, his general reason to bring about the better outcome is strengthened in this case by his professional commitment. Presumably he would even have been required, if necessary, to accept certain costs in order to ensure the conception of a normal child rather than a retarded child. (The extent of the cost he should accept in order to ensure the better outcome is, of course, limited. If, for example, the cost to him of ensuring the conception of a normal child rather than a disabled child would be as great as the cost to a couple of being unable to have a child, then it might be permissible for him to allow the conception of a disabled child. But it is hard to imagine circumstances in which personal costs this great would be required from a physician in order to ensure the conception of a normal rather than a disabled child.) Let us stipulate that the Negligent Physician in the Preconception Case would have been required to accept costs up to amount x in order to ensure that the couple would conceive a normal rather than a disabled child. If that is true, then it seems reasonable to suppose that, since his negligence has brought about the worse outcome, he should be required *ex post* to pay costs at least up to amount x in order to repair the result of his fault. In particular, he should be required to pay up to amount x, if necessary, to try to make the disabled child's life as good as the normal child's life would have been. If the compensation could succeed in benefiting the disabled child to that extent, this would cancel the bad effect of his previous action.

This argument is vulnerable to several objections. First, it is not plausible to suppose that there are grounds for liability whenever the Impersonal Comparative Principle implies that it was worse to cause some person to exist. For the Impersonal Comparative Principle implies that it is worse, other things being equal, to cause a person to exist whenever it would be possible to cause a different, better-off person to exist instead. Thus it implies that it would be worse to cause a normal person to exist if it would be possible to cause a person with an unusually high capacity for well-being to exist instead. But if, in these circumstances, one were to cause the normal person to exist, it is implausible to suppose that this would make one liable to compensate that person for being worse off than some extraordinary possible person might otherwise have been.

Second, the case for compensation depends on the availability of a better alternative. The Impersonal Comparative Principle does not imply that there is a reason not to cause a disabled child to exist when there is no possibility of causing a better-off child to exist instead. Hence there is no reason in these circumstances for an agent to accept costs *ex ante* to avoid causing a disabled child to exist and no basis for a claim to compensation *ex post*. But now imagine two equally disabled children, only one of whom was caused to exist in conditions in which a normal child could have been caused to exist instead. Although both have the same disability, only this child can claim compensation. But it may seem unfair to deny the other compensation just because there was no possibility of causing a normal child to exist in his place.

Finally, and most importantly, recall that the reason that the Impersonal Comparative Principle holds that the Negligent Physician's action was worse is not that it harmed or wronged the retarded child. His offense was instead *impersonal*. But, if the original action was objectionable for impersonal reasons, then the reason to redress the situation should be impersonal as well. There is, in other words, no reason why the remedy – that is, the action aimed at canceling the bad effect – should benefit the disabled child. After all, that child is not, according to the Impersonal Comparative Principle, a victim of the Negligent Physician's action.

Suppose that if the Negligent Physician were to pay costs up to amount x to the disabled child, this would be insufficient to raise the child's level of well-being anywhere near to the level that the normal child would have enjoyed had it existed instead. But suppose that there were some *other* child whose level of well-being was as low as that of the disabled child and who could be raised to the level that the normal child would have enjoyed if he or she were to receive amount x of the Negligent Physician's resources. Insofar as there is an impersonal reason for the Negligent Physician to repair the effects of his negligence, he should devote his resources to benefiting this other child rather than to "compensating" the disabled child. It is of course true that, in cases like the Preconception Case, the Negligent Physician *might* have a moral reason to pay damages to the disabled child, but only if, contingently, this were the most efficient means of repairing the impersonally bad effects of his previous negligence.

Despite initial appearances, therefore, the Impersonal Comparative Principle provides no basis for liability on the part of the Negligent Physician to compensate the disabled child. This may or may not constitute an objection to the principle. For it is unclear whether, in the Preconception Case, the child in fact deserves compensation. The child may deserve special compensation through relevant mechanisms of social redistribution simply for being badly off – either in absolute terms or relative to the norms of the society. In this respect the child is on a par with others who are badly off through no fault of their own. There is no reason why the Negligent Physician in particular should be required to do more than anyone else to help the child.

But, although it is not clear whether the disabled child in the Preconception Case deserves compensation, it *is* clear that the disabled child in the Prenatal Case deserves compensation and that it is the Negligent Physician who is morally (and legally) liable to pay it. Recall, however, that according to the No-Difference View, the objection in the Prenatal Case to the Negligent Physician's causing the child to be disabled rather than normal is the *same* as the objection in the Preconception Case to the Negligent Physician's causing a disabled child to exist rather than a normal child. The objection in the Preconception Case is impersonal in character; therefore the objection in the Prenatal Case must also be impersonal – which, of course, is exactly what the Impersonal Comparative Principle implies, since it treats the two cases in exactly the same way. Indeed, according to the generalized No-Difference View, the whole of the morality of beneficence is to be explained in impersonal terms. Person-affecting principles may often yield the right answers, but they *never* provide the correct explanation, which is always impersonal. If it is worse to perform some act, that is not because the act is bad or worse *for somebody;* there are never any victims in the relevant sense. Notice, however, what this implies. If the objection to the Negligent Physician's action in the Prenatal Case is impersonal, there can be no more basis for liability here than there is in the Preconception Case. Indeed, if the generalized No-Difference View is correct, then there can never be any basis for liability to compensate an individual for harm that one has done to that individual. Or at least this is true within the area of morality concerned with beneficence, or well-being. Parfit leaves it open that there may be areas of morality governed by respect for rights, or other considerations beyond the scope of beneficence. But if, as Parfit assumes, such cases as the Prenatal Case, in which one person's negligence causes another to suffer a serious disability, come within the morality of beneficence, then it seems that the areas governed by rights cannot be more than tiny provinces at the periphery.

Most of us firmly believe that, in the Prenatal Case, the Negligent Physician owes compensation to the child he has caused to be disabled rather than normal. That the Impersonal Comparative Principle seems incapable of supporting this belief is a serious objection to it, on the assumption that the No-Difference View is true. If the Prenatal Case were outside the proper scope of the Impersonal Comparative Principle, there would be no problem. But the No-Difference View holds that there is no relevant difference between the Prenatal Case and the Preconception Case, that the objection to the Negligent Physician's conduct is therefore the same in each, and that that objection is provided by the Impersonal Comparative Principle.

That the Impersonal Comparative Principle cannot account for the Negligent Physician's liability in the Prenatal Case is only one of many problems it faces. Here is another. As it is stated, the principle refers only to people. But there is no obvious reason why it should not apply to nonpersons as well. But, when extended in this fashion, it implies that it is worse, and therefore presumptively objectionable, to breed one's dog rather than to have a child, if one cannot do both. For to breed the dog would be to cause a worse-off rather than a better-off individual to exist.[34] And it would be worse to breed one's dog than to breed one's lizard, if one could not do both. And so on.

These implications are implausible. There are several ways that a defender of the Impersonal Comparative Principle might seek to avoid them. One would be to appeal to side effects – for example, by arguing that because of overpopulation, causing a person to exist has such bad side effects that on balance it would not be worse to breed one's dog instead. But this response is inadequate. It is not because of human overpopulation that it is permissible to breed one's dog. And in any case the principle still implies that it *was* worse, before overpopulation arose, to breed one's dog rather than to have a child.

A second possible response is to note that the Impersonal Comparative Principle, as stated by Parfit, refers only to what is *worse,* not to what is *wrong* – that is, it concerns only the evaluation of outcomes, not what one ought or ought not to do. Therefore, it is only if the principle is conjoined with something like Act Consequentialism that it has implausible implications about procreation and breeding. Again, however, this response is inadequate. For the Impersonal Comparative Principle must be conjoined with *some* principle that explains how considerations of consequences should guide our action; otherwise its utility will be extremely limited when applied to cases such as the Preconception Case. It is fairly obvious in that case that the Negligent Physician brings about the impersonally worse of two possible outcomes. What is important is the further claim that this is what explains why his action was morally objectionable or wrong, other things being equal. And it is reasonable to expect that any action-guiding principle that, when conjoined with the Impersonal Comparative Principle, implies that it is wrong to bring about the worse of the two outcomes in the Preconception Case will also imply that it is wrong to bring about the worse of the two outcomes when the choice is between having a child and breeding one's dog.

Perhaps the most plausible response to this challenge is to restrict the scope of the Impersonal Comparative Principle so that it applies only to cases involving lives of the same kind. Suitably restricted, it would imply that it is worse to cause the worse-off of two possible people to exist, and worse to cause the worse-off of two possible dogs to exist; but it would have nothing to say about whether it is worse to cause a dog to exist rather than a person. Although I am skeptical that a principled rationale for such a restriction could be found, I cannot exclude the possibility.

The deepest problems for the impersonal conception of beneficence that is required by the No-Difference View emerge when we try to extrapolate beyond the Impersonal Comparative Principle to a principle that covers not only Same-Number Choices but also Different-Number Choices. Among those choices in which different people exist in the different possible outcomes, Different-Number Choices are significantly more common than Same-Number Choices.

It is therefore essential to have a principle that covers those choices. There is, however, a formidable obstacle to extending the impersonal approach so that it applies in these cases. The extended principle must surely imply, as the Impersonal Comparative Principle does, that an outcome is worse if the people who exist in that outcome are worse off than the people who would exist in an alternative outcome. But when different numbers of people exist in the different outcomes, it becomes very difficult to determine which group is better off than the others. One has to weigh the number of lives, or perhaps the overall *quantity* of life, against the overall *quality* of life. And one has to determine how to measure the overall quality of life in a group in which individual lives may vary considerably in overall quality. Is the group with the best overall quality of life the one with the highest average quality of life, the highest maximum, or perhaps the lowest minimum? Should the measurement of overall quality of life take into account the relative levels of equality in the quality of life within the different groups? And if so, how is equality itself to be measured?[35]

These and other problems are explored with tremendous subtlety and ingenuity in Parfit's book, *Reasons and Persons*. He assigns the label "Theory X" to the theory that would plausibly extend the Impersonal Comparative Principle so that it would cover Different-Number Choices. Although he states a variety of requirements that Theory X would have to satisfy in order to be acceptable, he confesses his own inability to discover the content of the theory. He concludes, however, with an expression of optimism: "Though I failed to discover X, I believe that, if they tried, others could succeed."[36]

I believe that there is reason to doubt this. Theory X must take an impersonal form: it must presuppose that the fact that an act is bad or worse *for someone* cannot be part of the fundamental explanation of why its effects are bad or why the act itself is wrong. Because of this, I suspect that any candidate for Theory X will have implications that undermine its credibility. In order to try to substantiate this suspicion, I will indicate what I think some of these implications are. I must acknowledge, however, that I cannot demonstrate that Theory X will have these implications. As yet there is no Theory X; therefore neither I nor anyone else can say what its implications might be. My claim can only be that it is difficult to see how any candidate for Theory X can avoid the implications to which I will call attention.

Let us revert to a problem mentioned earlier, in section II: the problem of abortion. On the assumption that a new individual of our kind does not begin to exist until some time during the second half of pregnancy, the choice between having and not having an early-term abortion is a Different-Number Choice: the number of people who will ever exist if one has the abortion will be different from the number who will exist if one does not. This is, however, a very simple Different-Number Choice. Consider

The Early-Term Abortion

A woman is in the very early stages of pregnancy. If she continues the pregnancy, the child she has will have a life that is well worth living. It would be better for her and her partner, however, if she has an abortion. But, because the society in which they live is underpopulated, the abortion would also have certain bad effects on other preexisting people. Assume that these various good and bad effects counterbalance one another – that is, they cancel each other out. The couple decide to have the abortion. Overall, this is not worse for the people who ever exist.

Suppose we want to know which of the two possible outcomes is better *impersonally*. The complications mentioned earlier that typically make it so difficult to determine which of two different-sized groups is better off simply do not arise in this case. In the actual outcome, a certain number of people exist. If the abortion had not been performed, exactly those same people would have existed, and overall their collective level of well-being would have been the same. The only difference is that in the second outcome there would have been one additional person whose life would, we may assume, have been worth living. (There are instances in which, when one thing that is good when taken by itself is added to a second thing that is also good by itself, the result is a decrease in the degree of goodness of the second thing. Nothing like this would occur if, in the Early-Term Abortion, the abortion were not performed.) But if, from an impersonal point of view, the two outcomes differ only in that one contains an additional life in which the good elements outweigh the bad, then it seems that the outcome with the additional good must be better impersonally.

One might arrive at the same conclusion by a slightly more circuitous route. Let us define three outcomes: having a Happy Child, having a Less Happy Child, and having No Child. According to the Impersonal Comparative Principle, having a Less Happy Child is worse than having a Happy Child, other things being equal. This is not because having the Less Happy Child would be bad in itself; it is just that having a Happy Child contributes more to making the world better. But if having a Happy Child is better than having a Less Happy Child because it adds more good to the world, then it seems that having a Happy Child must also be better than having No Child, other things being equal, and for the same impersonal reason.

In the Preconception Case, the Negligent Physician causes the couple to have a Less Happy Child rather than a Happy Child. In the Early-Term Abortion, the couple have No Child rather than a Happy Child. From an impersonal point of view, the latter should be as objectionable as the former. If we conclude that the Negligent Physician *ought not* to have caused the less good outcome rather than the better one, and for reasons that are impersonal, then it may be difficult to avoid the conclusion that the woman in the Early-Term Abortion *ought not* to have had the abortion. It seems that Theory X, which will extend the claim of the Impersonal Comparative Principle so that it covers Different-Number Choices, may imply that abortion is wrong. The impersonal approach to the Non-Identity Problem thus not only threatens a powerful argument in favor of the permissibility of abortion (as I suggested in section II) but also supports a strong argument against the permissibility of abortion.

Indeed, the problem runs deeper than this. The objection to abortion that seems to be implied by the impersonal approach cannot, of course, be that abortion is murder, that it harms the fetus, or that it is against the fetus's interests. It is simply that abortion prevents the existence of a person whose existence would make the outcome better in impersonal terms. But this is equally true of the use of contraception and indeed of any choice that results in abstention from procreation. To the extent that abortion is objectionable from an impersonal point of view, these other forms of behavior must be objectionable as well, other things being equal, and for the same reason.

I have suggested that it is natural to infer from the claim that it is impersonally worse to have a Less Happy Child rather than a Happy Child that it is also worse to have No Child rather than a Happy Child. One might challenge this by pointing out that, according to the Impersonal Comparative Principle, the objection in the one case is essentially comparative: the Happy Child would be *better off than the Less Happy Child.* One is comparing the conditions of two possible people. In the second case, however, this sort of comparison is not possible. If the alternatives are having a Happy Child and having No Child, there is no one whom the Happy Child would be better off than. The problem with this response, however, is that it seems irrelevant from the *impersonal* point of view. The claim that "the Happy Child is better off than the Less Happy Child" is reducible to "the outcome with the Happy Child contains a greater amount of good than that with the Less Happy Child." From the impersonal point of view, the references to individuals are eliminable without loss. If the outcome with No Child contains less good than the outcome with a Happy Child, then having No Child is worse than having a Happy Child for the same reason that having a Less Happy Child is worse than having a Happy Child.

The common sense view is of course entirely different. Most of us believe that there is no moral reason to cause a person to exist just because the person's life would be worth living – that there is no reason, other things being equal, to have a Happy Child rather than No Child. But we also believe that, *if* one is going to have a child, one has reason, other things being equal, to have a Happy Child rather than a Less Happy Child. The moral reason for having a Happy Child is conditional on a prior determination to have a child. Thus we believe that it is permissible to have No Child rather than a Happy Child, even though it is wrong to have a Less Happy Child rather than a Happy Child, other things being equal. I have suggested, however, that it is difficult to see how this set of beliefs could be defensible within an impersonal conception of beneficence.

Parfit has suggested an analogy that might be thought to show how these beliefs could be consistent.[37] "Suppose," Parfit writes, "that I have three alternatives:

A: at some great cost to myself, saving a stranger's right arm;
B: doing nothing;
C: at the same cost to myself, saving both the arms of this stranger."[38]

Most of us believe that, if these are the alternatives, it is permissible to do B – that is, to save neither arm. But, if one has decided to help the stranger, it would be wrong to do A – that is, to save one arm rather than two. If one has decided to accept a certain cost to help the stranger, and the cost will be the same whether one saves one arm or both, it would be perverse not to do what would achieve the greater good. In short, although there is no duty to do C rather than B, there is a duty to do C rather than A.

Now alter the values of the variables so that one's alternatives are

A: having a Less Happy Child;
B: having No Child;
C: having a Happy Child.

Again the common view is that, if these are the alternatives, it is permissible to do B – that is, it is permissible not to have a child. But, if one has decided to have a child, it would be wrong to do A – that is to have a Less Happy Child rather than a Happy Child. As in the first set of alternatives, there is no duty to do C rather than B, though there is a duty to do C rather than A. This is the common sense conception of the morality of procreation. The parallel with the first set of alternatives suggests that this conception is defensible and hence that I was mistaken to claim that if C is better than A, it must also be better than B.

This counterargument fails, for the two sets of alternatives are not in fact parallel. Once parallelism is established, the comparison between them supports rather than refutes my claim. In the first set of alternatives, C is the best outcome, impersonally considered. There is also a strong moral reason to do C rather than B. It is only because there is a great cost to the agent attached to C that it is permissible to do B rather than C.[39] If we subtract the stipulations about costs from the first set of alternatives, so that this set becomes analogous to the second, then one would be required to do C rather than B (which is the conclusion that I assume is implied by the impersonal approach in the second set of alternatives). Alternatively, if one adds parallel stipulations about cost to the second set of alternatives, common sense intuitions may be upheld, but the explanation of why it is permissible to have No Child is no longer that this outcome is not worse than having a Happy Child. The explanation instead appeals to considerations of cost, which are extraneous to the impersonal evaluation of the outcomes.[40] Indeed, to maintain parallelism with the first set of alternatives, it must be granted that there is a strong moral reason to have a Happy Child rather than No Child. This reason is overridden only by considerations of cost to the agent.

Is there any other way, within an impersonal conception of beneficence, to defend the common sense view that, although it would be worse to have a Less Happy Child rather than a Happy Child, it would not be worse to have No Child rather than a Happy Child? Jonathan Glover has suggested a different analogy. He contends that "a principle that did not tell us to create extra happy people" could nevertheless imply that "when we are going to add to the population, where the choice arises we must always prefer to add a happier rather than a less happy person . . . A policy of always choosing the best ones when picking apples does not commit us to picking as many as possible" – or, he might have added, to picking any at all.[41] This further analogy, though suggestive, is still inadequate. If creating new people were like picking apples, then, although there would be a reason to have a Happy Child rather than a Less Happy Child, the reason would be entirely instrumental, having to do with the interests of the parents. Thus, if the interests of preexisting people were not engaged, there would be no reason to have the Happy Child rather than the Less Happy Child – just as there would be no reason to pick better apples if there were no important reason to pick apples in the first place.

So the point still stands: it seems that Theory X will imply that it is better for a Happy Child to exist than for No Child to exist and consequently that there is a moral reason to have a Happy Child rather than No Child. Although common sense resists this claim, it is not obviously wrong. But there is worse to come. For, from an impersonal point of view, there seems to be no fundamental difference between starting a life and extending a life. Provided that each would be worth living, one's reason to create a new life is the same as one's reason to extend an existing life: namely, that doing either makes the outcome better by causing there to be more of what is good, or that which makes life worth living. This suggests that, other things being equal, Theory X will imply that there is as much reason to cause a new person to exist as there is to save a person's life. Indeed, since the outcome of saving a life contains only a *part* of that life, whereas the outcome of causing a person to exist contains the *whole* of a life, it will normally be *better,* other things being equal and from an impersonal point of view, to cause a person to exist than to save a person's life.

This is very hard to believe. But there is more. Accounts of the morality of beneficence that are impersonal in character tend to treat as irrelevant certain aspects of an agent's mode of agency. They tend, for example, to deny that there is any moral significance to the distinction between doing and allowing, or to the distinction between effects that are intended and those that are foreseen but

unintended. Although there is no necessary incompatibility between an impersonal theory of beneficence and claims about the significance of agency that are
essentially deontological in character, it is nevertheless natural that a theory
that evaluates outcomes impersonally should also take an impersonal view of
agency. If the identity of the beneficiary or victim of an act makes no difference
to the morality of the act, then it should not be surprising if neither the identity
of the agent nor his or her mode of agency matters either. Thus many writers
who accept an impersonal theory of beneficence deny that there is any fundamental or intrinsic difference between failing to save a person and killing a person (i.e., between killing and letting die). But, if this is right, and if there is also
no fundamental difference between saving a person and causing a person to exist (or between not saving a person and not causing a person to exist), then it
follows that there is no difference, other things being equal, between killing a
person and failing to cause a person to exist. From an impersonal point of view,
both are bad for the same reason: the outcome is worse because it contains less
good – less good than it would have contained had a person with a life worth
living continued to exist or been caused to exist. Indeed, failing to cause a person to exist will, other things being equal, be *worse,* for the same reason that it
is normally impersonally worse than failing to save a person.

It might be argued that, even if Theory X has these implications, this does
not show that it is unacceptable. For Theory X is an account of beneficence
only, and there is more to the morality of killing than considerations of beneficence. Killing may be especially objectionable, for example, because it involves a violation of rights. But, if this defense works at all, it applies only to
the comparison between killing and failing to cause a person to exist. For it is
implausible to suppose that the morality of saving lives lies outside the scope
of beneficence.

A second response might be to argue that it is compatible with a wholly impersonal conception of beneficence to suppose that there is a moral asymmetry
between harms and benefits, or between suffering losses and forgoing gains, or
something of the sort. If there is such an asymmetry, then, even within the
morality of beneficence, killing a person is worse than failing to cause a person
to exist, since killing involves harm or loss whereas the failure to cause a person to exist involves only the absence of benefit or gain. This, however, is a mistake. The harm of death consists primarily, if not exclusively, in the loss of the
benefits of continued life. Death and the failure of a person to come into existence involve the same sorts of loss, from the impersonal point of view.

Finally, even if there are dimensions to the morality of killing beyond the
evaluation of outcomes (and I believe that there are), Theory X seems to get
even the evaluation of outcomes wrong. If we compare an act of killing with a
failure to cause a person to exist, it seems obvious that the *outcome* of the killing
is worse. It is a worse state of affairs when someone dies (whether from being

killed or from natural causes) than it is when a person fails to come into existence, assuming that in both cases the lives would have been worth living.

In sum, it is difficult to see how Theory X can avoid implying that, other things being equal, (1) it is better to have a Happy Child rather than No Child; hence (2) there are moral objections to abortion, contraception, and celibacy; (3) the failure of a person to come into existence is at least as bad an outcome as the death of a person; hence (4) the failure to cause a person to exist is at least as bad as the failure to save a person's life and (5) the failure to cause a person to exist is at least as bad as killing a person. These claims, or at any rate the last three, are plainly unacceptable. The only hope for Theory X is that it can avoid having them as implications. Despite my earlier remarks, those who are attracted to the impersonal approach may remain optimistic. They may point out that there are, after all, some familiar candidates for Theory X that do not necessarily have these implications. If, for example, a Happy Child would have a level of well-being at or below the average, then Average Consequentialism would not imply that it is better to have the Happy Child than to have No Child; yet it would imply that, *if* it were inevitable that *some* child were going to exist, then it would be better to have the Happy Child than to have a Less Happy Child. But this is just an accident of the arithmetic. If the Happy Child would be above the average, then it would be better, other things being equal, to have the Happy Child. And if the existing population was quite large and the Happy Child would be well above the average and would live long, then it would be better, according to Average Consequentialism, to have the Happy Child than to save a person whose life was well below the average. It is important to note these facts, since Average Consequentialism is, in effect, concerned exclusively with the quality of life (which it measures in terms of the average) and gives no weight to increasing the number of lives, except insofar as this affects the overall quality of life. Among the known impersonal theories of beneficence, therefore, this is the one least likely to have the claims just cited among its implications.[42]

V. Conclusion

To be acceptable, Theory X must imply that failing to save a person whose life would be worth living is, other things being equal, not just worse but significantly worse than failing to cause a person to exist. And this implication must not just be a contingent feature of the way the mathematics works out. It must instead flow from the theory in a way that plausibly explains why the death of a person is a worse outcome than failure of a person to come into existence.

I cannot prove that no impersonal theory can satisfy this condition, yet there is good reason to believe that no impersonal theory can. For it seems essential to the explanation of why the death of a person is worse than the failure of a person to come into existence that the former is worse *for someone* whereas the latter is not. Person-affecting considerations seem indispensable.

In many cases involving the Non-Identity Problem, a choice seems to have a bad effect but is nevertheless not worse for anyone. Parfit asks whether, in these cases, the fact that the choice is not worse for anyone makes a moral difference. "There are," he writes, "three views. It might make all the difference, or some difference, or no difference. There might be no objection to our choice, or some objection, or the objection may be just as strong."[43] Parfit accepts the third view, the No-Difference View. According to this view, whether or not the choice is worse for anyone is morally irrelevant; impersonal considerations alone matter. I have tried to show why I think this view will prove to be unacceptable. According to the first view, impersonal considerations have no weight; person-affecting considerations alone matter. As Parfit has shown, this first view is untenable. This leaves the second view.

As I understand it, the second view holds that an effect may be bad even if it is not worse for anyone, but not as bad as it would be if it *were* worse for someone. In short, impersonal considerations matter, but person-affecting considerations matter more. Recall the Medical Programs Case. (And put aside consideration of the effects on the couples, which, though they occur in different lives, are much the same whichever program is canceled.) What the second view seems to imply here is that, although the cancelation of Preconception Testing would be bad (because it would be impersonally bad), the cancelation of Pregnancy Testing would be worse. There are two possible explanations of why the cancelation of Pregnancy Testing would be worse. One is that impersonal considerations and person-affecting considerations are additive. According to this understanding, the cancelation of Pregnancy Testing would be worse because it would be bad for the same impersonal reasons that the cancelation of Preconception Testing would be bad but would be additionally bad for person-affecting reasons – that is, it would be bad impersonally *and* bad because it would be worse for the children who would be born disabled. The second possible explanation is that, although impersonal considerations and person-affecting considerations are distinct and nonadditive, person-affecting considerations matter more. According to this understanding, the cancelation of Preconception Testing would be bad for impersonal reasons, whereas the cancelation of Pregnancy Testing would be bad for entirely different, person-affecting reasons. And these latter reasons would be stronger. Even though the cancelation of each program would result in the same number of disabled children, this effect is worse if it is worse *for people*. More generally, an effect E (e.g., a child is born with a disability) may be bad impersonally (e.g., because a better effect might have been caused instead), even if it is not bad for anyone. But, in other conditions, E may be bad for someone. In those instances in which it is bad for someone, E is worse than it is when it is bad only in impersonal terms.

The three options cited by Parfit are not exhaustive. There is another view, which I will call the *Encompassing Account,* that I believe is more plausible than any of the three views Parfit mentions. It is similar to, but more complex than, the second view cited by Parfit, as interpreted in the second of the two ways sketched above. According to the Encompassing Account, person-affecting considerations and impersonal considerations are distinct and nonadditive. Neither type of consideration is reducible to the other. Both matter; both provide reasons for action. An effect E, for example, may be worse impersonally, or it may be worse in person-affecting terms (that is, worse for someone). If E is worse in person-affecting terms, *that* fact provides whatever reasons there are to prevent it, mitigate it, or suppress it. That E is also worse in impersonal terms is, in the circumstances, irrelevant. If, however, E is not worse in person-affecting terms, then whatever reasons there are to prevent, mitigate, or suppress it are impersonal in character.

When E is worse in person-affecting terms, the reason one has to prevent it is always at least as strong as the reason one has to prevent it when it is worse only impersonally. When E is worse only in impersonal terms, the reason one has to prevent it is either as strong as or weaker than the reason one would have to prevent it if it were worse in person-affecting terms. Suppose, for example, that we agree with Parfit that the cancelation of Preconception Testing would be just as bad as the cancelation of Pregnancy Testing. If so, we believe that, in this case, the relevant impersonal considerations are as strong as the corresponding person-affecting considerations. But one might not accept this. One might think that, even here, the relevant person-affecting considerations are stronger. One might reason as follows:

If Pregnancy Testing is canceled, each disabled child could reasonably have this thought: "It could have been better for me." That is a bitter reflection. If Preconception Testing is canceled, the only thought to which each disabled child would be entitled is: "A better-off person might have existed instead of me." This is not a disturbing thought; virtually all of us could reasonably believe this of ourselves. Thus, if we take up the points of view of the various disabled children rather than surveying the possible outcomes from a distance, we have reason to think that the effects of canceling Pregnancy Testing would be worse. This is not because the children born disabled if Pregnancy Testing were canceled would actually have this thought and be made miserable by it. It is, rather, that the accessibility of this thought to them is supposed to reveal something important about the nature of the outcome.

If one were to reason in this manner, one would conclude that there is an asymmetry in the strengths of the impersonal and person-affecting considerations even in the Medical Programs Case. It is hard to believe, however, that such an asymmetry could be more than very slight.

Here is another pair of cases in which an asymmetry may be manifest. Suppose that a woman knows that she has a condition such that, if she conceives a child now, it will have a slight cognitive deficit but will still be exceptionally bright. If she waits a few months for the condition to clear, she will then have a different child, who will lack the cognitive deficit. The difference is that, if she has a child now, it will have an IQ of 160, whereas if she waits she will have a child with an IQ of 170. Next imagine a case in which a pregnant woman takes a certain drug that damages her fetus, causing the subsequent child to have an IQ of 160 rather than 170. Viewed impersonally, the bad effect in these two cases is the same. But in the second case this effect is also bad in person-affecting terms. It is not absurd to suppose that the effect in the second case is worse.

Again, the difference can only be very slight. We have seen, however, that there may be pairs of cases in which there is a vast asymmetry between impersonal and person-affecting considerations. It seems, for example, that it is bad in impersonal terms if a person whose life would have been well worth living fails to come into existence. Goods that might have existed never in fact occur. But it is clearly significantly worse if there is a corresponding loss that is bad in person-affecting terms – for example, when goods of comparable quality and quantity are lost because a person dies. In this comparison, if E is the nonoccurrence of these goods, then, although E may be bad impersonally, it is far worse when it is bad in person-affecting terms. Hence the impersonal reason one has to cause a person to exist is not nearly so strong as the person-affecting reason one has to save a person's life.

According to the Encompassing Account, the morality of beneficence is governed by both impersonal and person-affecting considerations. In some instances, the two types of consideration may be of comparable strength; in others, person-affecting considerations may be far stronger than corresponding impersonal considerations. This raises large questions. Why is the comparative strength of person-affecting considerations greater in some instances than in others? And how are the two types of consideration to be integrated into a unified account of our moral reasons? I cannot answer these questions. My aim here must be the more modest aim of suggesting how one can accept that the Impersonal Comparative Principle provides the correct account of the Preconception Case without committing oneself to the generalized No-Difference View – that is, the view that the whole of the morality of beneficence must be explained in impersonal terms. One can accept that there is a dimension to the Negligent Physician's conduct in the Preconception Case that can be criticized only in impersonal terms, that the Negligent Physician's conduct in this case is no less bad than his conduct in the Prenatal Case, but that his conduct in the Prenatal Case is objectionable for entirely different reasons. Thus it may be true that in the Prenatal Case the Negligent Physician owes compensation to the disabled child, whereas this is not true in the Preconception Case.

Notes

1. Derek Parfit, *Reasons and Persons* (Oxford: Oxford University Press, 1984), ch. 16. Parfit's is the seminal discussion of this problem and remains the best discussion in the literature.
2. The failure to distinguish between events that occur after a subject has begun to exist and those that affect the conditions of the subject's origin casts doubt on Ingmar Persson's argument for the claim that all forms of gene therapy on human conceptuses are identity-preserving, even if we begin to exist after the human organism ceases to be a conceptus. See his "Genetic Therapy, Identity, and the Person-regarding Reasons," *Bioethics* 9 (1995), 21–3. Persson does not consider genetic interventions carried out prior to conception.
3. This view presupposes that we are not identical with our physical organisms. I defend it in "The Metaphysics of Brain Death," *Bioethics* 9 (1995), 91–126, and more thoroughly in *Killing at the Margins of Life* (New York: Oxford University Press, in press).
4. Thus Kripke, with whom the doctrine of the necessity of origin is most closely associated, writes: "I might have been deformed if the fertilized egg from which I originated had been damaged in certain ways, even though I presumably did not yet exist at that time." Saul Kripke, *Naming and Necessity* (Cambridge, MA: Harvard University Press, 1980), p. 115, n. 57.
5. This view was urged, in discussion, by Raziel Abelson and Gertrude Ezorsky.
6. For further discussion of these issues, see Robert Merrihew Adams, "Existence, Self-Interest, and the Problem of Evil," *Noûs* 13 (1979), 53–65.
7. For a clear instance in which a child's life is not worth living, see the description of the child born with dystrophic epidermolysis bullosa in Jonathan Glover's "Future People, Disability, and Screening," in *Justice between Age Groups and Generations,* ed. Peter Laslett and James S. Fishkin (New Haven: Yale University Press, 1992), pp. 129–30.
8. I discuss this further in "Problems of Population Theory," *Ethics* 92 (1981), 104–7.
9. Parfit, *Reasons and Persons,* p. 367.
10. Discussing another pair of acts, both of which have the same bad effect (in impersonal terms) but only one of which is worse for anyone, Parfit writes that "on the view presented in my book, [the] objections [to the two acts] are equally strong. This suggests that there is the same objection to each act." See Derek Parfit, "Comments," *Ethics* 96 (1986), 832–72, at p. 858.
11. *Reasons and Persons,* pp. 370–1.
12. The stipulation that the damage causes only a minor physical disability is intended to preclude the Non-Identity Problem.
13. The cases that Parfit cites to illustrate the Non-Identity Problem are all cases in which an act that affects who will exist has an intuitively bad effect, even though the act is worse for no one. An early abortion is also an act that affects who will exist and may be worse for no one.
14. Matthew Hanser, "Harming Future People," *Philosophy and Public Affairs* 19 (1990), 47–70, at p. 59.
15. Joel Feinberg, "Wrongful Life and the Counterfactual Element in Harming," in his *Freedom and Fulfillment* (Princeton: Princeton University Press, 1992), pp. 3–36, at p. 6.
16. There is a question here about the relation of one's interests to one's innate capacities. The application of Feinberg's notion of a harmed condition to the case of the

congenitally retarded child appears to assume that the retarded child has interests comparable to those of a cognitively normal child. This, however, is controversial. Consider a nonhuman animal with cognitive and emotional capacities and potentials comparable to those of the retarded child. Are its interests adversely affected by the fact that its cognitive capacities are significantly lower than ours? If not, it is not obvious why one should suppose that the interests of the retarded child are adversely affected by his or her cognitive capacities. One's interests are shaped by one's cognitive capacities. See Jeff McMahan, "Cognitive Disability, Misfortune, and Justice," *Philosophy and Public Affairs* 25 (1996), 3–34.

17. There is a possible ambiguity here. The relevant countervailing probability might be (1) the probability, *if* there is a congenital harmed condition, that the life will also contain compensating goods and thus be worth living. Or it might be (2) the probability that the life will not contain a congenital harmed condition. I am assuming that it is 1 that is relevant. It is hard to see how 2 could weigh against the probability of a harmed condition unless the goods the life would contain in the absence of the harmed condition are taken to offset the risk.

18. For a careful exposition of an approach of this sort, see James Woodward, "The Non-Identity Problem," *Ethics* 96 (1986), 804–31.

19. One way of dealing with this difficulty is to claim, not that the Negligent Physician violates the child's rights but that his action causes the child to exist with rights that cannot be fulfilled. Respect for the potential child's rights therefore required that the physician refrain from doing what would cause the child (and therefore the rights) to exist. Compare my "Problems of Population Theory," p. 125.

20. I owe this response to Frances Kamm.

21. For the purposes of this example, it does not matter whether the treatment would be identity-determining or identity-preserving with respect to the subsequent person.

22. For an intricate and detailed critique of the harm-based and rights-based approaches, see Parfit, "Comments," pp. 854–62.

23. Gregory S. Kavka, "The Paradox of Future Individuals," *Philosophy and Public Affairs* 11 (1982), 93–112.

24. Ibid., p. 105.

25. Compare Aristotle's claim, in *Ethica eudemia,* tr. J. Solomon, 1215b.25–26, that "many incidents involving . . . pleasure but not of a noble kind are such that, as far as they are concerned, non-existence is preferable."

26. A colleague tells me that when, in one of the *Godfather* movies, a character who is the wife of a Mafia leader obtains a clandestine abortion, there is reason to believe that she does this because she fears that the child she might have would also become a Mafia leader. Her concern need not have been for anyone but her child. She might have wanted to prevent the child's coming into existence on the ground that the life the child would be likely to have would not be one that she would want a child she would love to have. This is perfectly intelligible, if she suspects that the child would have had a restricted life.

27. The limited applicability of Kavka's notion of a restricted life to the Non-Identity Problem is noted by Derek Parfit in his reply to Kavka, "Future Generations: Further Problems," *Philosophy and Public Affairs* 11 (1982), 120–1.

28. Loren Lomasky, *Persons, Rights, and the Moral Community* (New York: Oxford University Press, 1987), pp. 113–72, at p. 202.

29. Cp. my "Cognitive Disability, Misfortune, and Justice."

30. It may be easier to find examples in which a part of a life is restricted. Imagine that a person whose life has hitherto been devoted to intellectual pursuits suffers brain

damage and becomes a contented idiot. Her subsequent life may be subjectively tolerable from her present point of view but objectively not worth living in the light of values that she autonomously embraced prior to the loss of her cognitive competence. There is a penetrating discussion of cases of this sort in Ronald Dworkin, *Life's Dominion* (New York: Knopf, 1993), ch. 8.

31. Feinberg, "Wrongful Life and the Counterfactual Element in Harming," pp. 27–8.
32. John Harris, *Wonderwoman and Superman: The Ethics of Human Biotechnology* (Oxford: Oxford University Press, 1992), p. 90.
33. Parfit, *Reasons and Persons,* p. 360. Kavka proposed a similar principle but rejected it in "The Paradox of Future Individuals," pp. 99–100.
34. Here I follow Robert Merrihew Adams, "Must God Create the Best?", *Philosophical Review* 81 (1972), 317–32, at p. 329.
35. Some of these problems arise even in Same-Number Choices. In these choices, the outcome with the highest total good will also have the highest average good per person. But, among outcomes with the same total good, the one with the highest individual quality of life may also have greater inequality in the distribution of good. Therefore it is not always obvious in which outcome people are better off overall.
36. Parfit, *Reasons and Persons,* p. 443.
37. Parfit is discussing his own revised version of a principle suggested but ultimately rejected by Kavka. This revised principle is not actually impersonal in character, though it is closely related to an impersonal maximizing principle in that it requires that, other things being equal, one do what would benefit people most on the assumption that people can be benefited by being caused to exist. Thus Parfit does not himself employ his analogy as I do here, and my critique of the analogy is not directed against his discussion. See his "Future Generations: Further Problems," pp. 127–32.
38. Ibid., p. 131.
39. Suppose that cost x is sufficient to release the agent from what would otherwise be a duty to do C rather than B. If the cost to the agent of doing C rather than A were also x, then presumably it would also be permissible for the agent to do A rather than C.
40. Parfit's own discussion of the parallels between the first and second sets of alternatives explicitly appeals to considerations of cost to the agent in order to explain why "most of us . . . have no duty to have unwanted children." Ibid., p. 128.
41. Jonathan Glover, *Causing Death and Saving Lives* (Harmondsworth, UK: Penguin, 1977), p. 69.
42. Average Consequentialism has been extensively criticized. See, e.g., my "Problems of Population Theory," pp. 111–15.
43. Parfit, *Reasons and Persons,* p. 363.

Gregory S. Kavka's Writings

Compiled by Eddie Yeghiayan

1974

"Moral Ideals." Ph.D. diss., University of Michigan, Ann Arbor, 1973. Abstract in *Dissertation Abstracts International* (August 1974), 35(2A):1161-A.

"Wittgensteinian Political Theory." Review of Hanna Fenichel Pitkin's *Wittgenstein and Justice: On the Significance of Ludwig Wittgenstein for Social and Political Thought. Stanford Law Review* 26 (1974), 1455–80.

"Wrongdoing and Guilt." *Journal of Philosophy* 71 (1974), 663–4.

1975

"Extensional Equivalence and Utilitarian Generalization." *Theoria* 41 (1975), 125–47.

"Rawls on Average and Total Utility." *Philosophical Studies* 27 (1975), 237–53.

1976

"Equality in Education." In *Indeterminacy in Education: Social Science, Educational Policy and the Search for Standards,* ed. John E. McDermott. Berkeley: McCuthchan, 1976. Pp. 211–52.

"Eschatological Falsificationism." *Religious Studies* 12 (1976), 201–5.

1978

"The Futurity Problem." In *Obligations to Future Generations,* ed. Richard Sikora and Brian Barry. Philosophical Monographs, no. 2. Philadelphia: Temple University Press, 1978. Pp. 186–203.

"Some Paradoxes of Deterrence." *Journal of Philosophy* 75 (1978), 285–302. See *Moral Paradoxes of Nuclear Deterrence* (1987), ch. 1, pp. 15–32.

1979

"The Numbers Should Count." *Philosophical Studies* 36 (1979), 285–94.

1980

"Deterrence, Utility, and Rational Choice." *Theory and Decision* 12 (1980), 41–60. See *Moral Paradoxes of Nuclear Deterrence* (1987), ch. 3, pp. 57–77.

"What Is Newcomb's Problem About?" *American Philosophical Quarterly* 17 (1980), 271–80.

1981

Review of Renford Bambrough's *Moral Scepticism and Moral Knowledge. Philosophical Review* 90 (1981), 630–3.

1982

"Deterrence and Utility Again: A Response to Bernard." *Theory and Decision* 14 (1982), 99–102. A response to George Bernard's "Deterrence, Utility, and Rational Choice: A Comment," in the same issue, pp. 89–97.

"An Internal Critique of Nozick's Entitlement Theory." *Pacific Philosophical Quarterly* 63 (1982), 371–80.

"The Paradox of Future Individuals." *Philosophy and Public Affairs* 11 (1982), 93–112.

"Two Solutions to the Paradox of Revolution." In *Social and Political Philosophy,* ed. Peter A. French, Theodore E. Uehling, Jr., and Howard Wettstein. Midwest Studies in Philosophy, no. 7. Minneapolis: University of Minnesota Press, 1982. Pp. 455–72.

1983

"Doubts about Unilateral Nuclear Disarmament." *Philosophy and Public Affairs* 12 (1983), 255–60. See "Unilateral Nuclear Disarmament," ch. 6 in *Moral Paradoxes of Nuclear Deterrence* (1987), pp. 119–25.

"Hobbes's War of All against All." *Ethics* 93 (1983), 291–310.

(With Virginia L. Warren.) "Political Representation for Future Generations." In *Environmental Philosophy: A Collection of Readings,* ed. Robert Elliot and Arran Gare. St. Lucia: University of Queensland Press/University Park: Pennsylvania State University Press, 1983. Pp. 21–39.

Review of A. John Simmons' *Moral Principles and Political Obligations. Topoi* 2 (1983), 227–30.

"Right Reason and Natural Law in Hobbes's Ethics." *Monist* 66 (1983), 120–33.

"Rule by Fear." *Noûs* 17 (1983), 601–20.

"The Toxin Puzzle." *Analysis* 43 (1983), 33–6.

"When Two 'Wrongs' Make a Right: An Essay on Business Ethics." *Journal of Business Ethics* 2 (1983), 61–6.

1984

"Deterrent Intentions and Retaliatory Actions." In *The Security Gamble: Deterrence Dilemmas in the Nuclear Age,* ed. Douglas MacLean. Maryland Studies in Public Philosophy. Totowa, NJ: Rowman & Allanheld, 1984. Pp. 155–9. A few paragraphs reprinted in *Moral Paradoxes of Nuclear Deterrence* (1987), ch. 2, pp. 33–56.

"Nuclear Deterrence: Some Moral Perplexities." In *The Security Gamble: Deterrence Dilemmas in the Nuclear Age,* ed. Douglas MacLean. Maryland Studies in Public Philosophy. Totowa, NJ: Rowman & Allanheld, 1984. Pp. 123–40. See *Moral Paradoxes of Nuclear Deterrence* (1987), ch. 4, pp. 79–99.

"The Reconciliation Project." In *Morality, Reason and Truth: New Essays on the Foundations of Ethics,* ed. David Copp and David Zimmermann. Totowa, NJ: Rowman & Allanheld, 1984. Pp. 297–319.

Review of Antony Flew's *The Politics of Procrustes: Contradictions of Enforced Equality. Philosophical Review* 93 (1984), 107–9.

1985

"Space War Ethics." *Ethics* 95 (1985), 673–91. See "Strategic Defense," ch. 8 in *Moral Paradoxes of Nuclear Deterrence* (1987), pp. 147–64.

1986

"A Critique of Pure Defense." *Journal of Philosophy* 83 (1986), 625–33. See *Moral Paradoxes of Nuclear Deterrence* (1987), ch. 8, pp. 157–64.

Hobbesian Moral and Political Theory. Princeton: Princeton University Press, 1986.

"Morality and Nuclear Politics: Lessons of the Missile Crisis." In *Nuclear Weapons and the Future of Humanity: The Fundamental Questions,* ed. Avner Cohen and Steven Lee. Totowa, NJ: Rowman & Allanheld, 1986. Pp. 233–54. See "Nuclear Coercion," ch. 9 in *Moral Paradoxes of Nuclear Deterrence* (1987), pp. 165–91.

1987

Moral Paradoxes of Nuclear Deterrence. Cambridge: Cambridge University Press, 1987.

Chapter 1. "Some Paradoxes of Deterrence," pp. 15–32.

Chapter 2. "A Paradox of Deterrence Revisited," pp. 33–56.

Chapter 3. "Deterrence, Utility, and Rational Choices," pp. 57–77.

Chapter 4. "Nuclear Deterrence: Some Moral Perplexities," pp. 79–99.

Chapter 5. "Dilemmas of Nuclear Protest," pp. 101–16.

Chapter 6. "Unilateral Nuclear Disarmament," pp. 119–25.

Chapter 7. "World Government," pp. 127–45.

Chapter 8. "Strategic Defense," pp. 147–64.

Chapter 9. "Nuclear Coercion," pp. 165–91.

Chapter 10. "Mutual Nuclear Disarmament," pp. 193–207.

"Nuclear Weapons and World Government." *Monist* 70 (1987), 298–315. See "World Government," ch. 7 in *Moral Paradoxes of Nuclear Deterrence* (1987), pp. 127–45.

Review of Arnold A. Rogow's *Thomas Hobbes: Radical in the Service of Reaction. Ethics* 97 (1987), 898.

Review of David Gauthier's *Morals by Agreement. Mind* 96 (1987), 117–21.

1988

"Some Neglected Liberal Aspects of Hobbes's Philosophy." *Hobbes Studies* 1 (1988), 89–108.

1989

"Sweethearts of SDI: A Response to Woodward." *Ethics* 99 (1989), 572–3.

1990

"Some Social Benefits of Uncertainty." In *The Philosophy of the Human Sciences,* ed. Peter A. French, Theodore E. Uehling, Jr., and Howard K. Wettstein. *Midwest Studies in Philosophy,* 15. Notre Dame, Ind.: University of Notre Dame Press, 1990. Pp. 311–26.

1991

"Is Individual Choice Less Problematic than Collective Choice?" *Economics and Philosophy* 7 (1991), 143–65.

"Nuclear Hostages." In *Violence, Terrorism, and Justice,* ed. R. G. Frey and Christopher W. Morris. Cambridge: Cambridge University Press, 1991. Pp. 276–95.

"Rational Maximizing in Economic Theories of Politics." In *The Economic Approach to Politics: A Critical Reassessment of the Theory of Rational Action,* ed. Kristen Monroe. New York: HarperCollins, 1991. Pp. 371–85.

Review of Jules L. Coleman's *Markets, Morals and the Law. Economics and Philosophy* 7 (1991), 105–12.

Review of Richard A. Fumerton's *Reason and Morality: A Defense of the Egocentric Perspective. Ethics* 101 (1991), 644–5.

"Was the Gulf War a Just War?" *Journal of Social Philosophy* 22 (1991), 20–9.

1992

"Richard B. Brandt." In *The Encyclopedia of Ethics,* ed. Lawrence Becker and Charlotte B. Becker. New York: Garland, 1992.

"Deterrence, Threats and Retaliation." In *The Encyclopedia of Ethics,* ed. Lawrence C. Becker and Charlotte B. Becker. New York: Garland, 1992.

"Disability and the Right to Work." *Social Philosophy and Policy* 9 (1992), 262–90.

"Nuclear Ethics." In *The Encyclopedia of Ethics,* ed. Lawrence Becker and Charlotte B. Becker. New York: Garland, 1992.

Review of David Schmidtz's *The Limits of Government: An Essay on the Public Goods Argument. Ethics* 102 (1992), 399–401.

1993

"Internal Prisoner's Dilemma Vindicated." *Economics and Philosophy* 9 (1993), 171–4.

"The Problem of Group Egoism." In *Rationality, Rules, and Utility: New Essays on the Moral Philosophy of Richard B. Brandt,* ed. Brad Hooker. Boulder, CO: Westview, 1993. Pp. 149–63.

"Rationality Triumphant: Gauthier's Moral Theory." *Dialogue* 32 (1993), 347–57.

Review of Peter Laslett and James S. Fishkin, eds., *Justice between Age Groups and Generations. Ethics* 104 (1993), 184–6.

1994

"The Costs of Crimes: Coleman Amended." Review of Jules L. Coleman's *Risks and Wrongs. Ethics* 104 (1994), 582–92.

Review of George Ainslie's *Picoeconomics: The Strategic Interaction of Successive Motivational States within the Person. Economics and Philosophy* 10 (1994), 333–8.

"Upside Risks: Social Consequences of Beneficial Biotechnology." In *Are Genes Us? The Social Consequences of the New Genetics,* ed. Carl F. Cranor. New Brunswick, NJ: Rutgers University Press, 1994. Pp. 155–79.

1995

"The Rationality of Rule-Following: Hobbes's Dispute with the Foole." *Law and Philosophy* 14 (1995), 5–34.

"When Morally Perfect People Would Need Government." *Social Philosophy and Policy* 12 (1995), 1–18. (This issue was dedicated to Kavka's memory.)